Google® Workspace

Google® Workspace

by Paul McFedries

Google® Workspace For Dummies®

Published by: **John Wiley & Sons, Inc.,** 111 River Street, Hoboken, NJ 07030-5774, www.wiley.com

Published simultaneously in Canada

For general information on our other products and services, please contact our Customer Care Department within the U.S. at 877-762-2974, outside the U.S. at 317-572-3993, or fax 317-572-4002. For technical support, please visit https://hub.wiley.com/community/support/dummies.

Wiley publishes in a variety of print and electronic formats and by print-on-demand. Some material included with standard print versions of this book may not be included in e-books or in print-on-demand. If this book refers to media such as a CD or DVD that is not included in the version you purchased, you may download this material at http://booksupport.wiley.com. For more information about Wiley products, visit www.wiley.com.

Library of Congress Control Number: 2024936888

ISBN 978-1-394-25322-7 (pbk); ISBN 978-1-394-25324-1 (ebk); ISBN 978-1-394-25323-4 (ebk)

SKY10078186_062424

Contents at a Glance

Table of Contents

PART 2: MAKING STUFF: DOCUMENTS, SPREADSHEETS, AND MORE 89

Introduction

Knowledge is of two kinds. We know a subject ourselves, or we know where we can find information upon it.

— SAMUEL JOHNSON

The sheer size and scope of Google Workspace is enough to give even the best thesaurus a run for its money. Choose just about any large or complex adjective — massive, sprawling, gargantuan, labyrinthine, brain-bending — and it's bound to seem just right to describe the Google Workspace gestalt.

With so many apps in the Google Workspace package, and so many features and settings in each of those apps, you need some sort of guide that not only tells you what these tools and technologies are but also shows you how to get the most out of them so that you can get the most out of your (or your company's) Google Workspace investment.

And that's precisely where *Google Workspace For Dummies* comes in. I've scoured Google Workspace from head to toe, rung its bells and blown its whistles, and generally just pushed the entire package to its limits to see what would happen. The result is the book you're holding (physically or virtually).

About This Book

Google Workspace For Dummies takes you on a tour of all the main (and a few of the minor) Google Workspace apps. This book contains 19 chapters, but that doesn't mean that you have to, as the King of Hearts says gravely in *Alice's Adventures in Wonderland*, "Begin at the beginning and go on till you come to the end: then stop." If you've already done a bit of work with any of Google's apps or in a rival suite such as Microsoft Office, please feel free to dip into this book wherever it strikes your fancy. The chapters all present their info and techniques in readily digestible, bite-size chunks, so you can certainly graze your way through this book.

However, if you're brand-spanking-new to Google Workspace — particularly if you're not sure what Google Workspace even *is* — no problem: I'm here to help. To get your Google Workspace education off to a solid start, I highly recommend reading Chapter 1 to get some of the basics down cold. From there, you can travel to more advanced territory, safe in the knowledge that you have some survival skills to fall back on.

Foolish Assumptions

Google Workspace For Dummies is for people who are new (or relatively new) to Google Workspace. That doesn't mean, however, that the book is suitable for people who have never used a computer or a web browser. So, first I assume that you have not only a computer — either a Microsoft Windows PC or a Mac — and a web browser installed on that computer (all computers do, these days) but also some experience with both. That means I assume that you know at least how to perform the following basic tasks:

- Starting your computer
- Launching your computer's web browser
- Navigating to a particular website given that site's address
- Working with basic app doohickeys such as pull-down menus, buttons, text boxes, check boxes, and radio buttons

This book also assumes you have a Google Workspace account and that your Google Workspace administrator has given you your sign-in info (that is, your Google Workspace account's email address and password).

What's that? You don't have a Google Workspace account? Surprisingly, I'm okay with that! You still have access to the Google apps through your personal Google account, so 96.5 percent of what you read in this book will apply to you. Why not 100 percent? Because a few features and settings are unique to Google Workspace or work differently for Google Workspace users.

Icons Used in This Book

Like other books in the *Dummies* series, this book uses icons, or little margin pictures, to flag info that doesn't quite fit into the flow of the chapter discussion.

This icon marks text that contains info that's useful or important enough that you'd do well to store the text somewhere safe in your memory for later recall.

This icon marks text that contains some for-nerds-only technical details or explanations that you're free to skip.

This icon marks text that contains a shortcut or an easier way to do things, which I hope will make your life — or, at least, the data analysis portion of your life — more efficient.

This icon marks text that contains a friendly but unusually insistent reminder to avoid doing something. You have been warned.

Beyond the Book

To locate this book's cheat sheet, go to `https://www.dummies.com/` and search for *Google Workspace For Dummies*. See the cheat sheet for an absurdly long list of keyboard shortcuts that you can use with Google Workspace.

Where to Go from Here

This book consists of several hundred pages. Do I expect you to read every word on every page? Yes, I do. Just kidding! No, of course I don't. Entire sections — heck, maybe even entire *chapters* — might contain information that's not relevant to what you do. That's fine, and my feelings won't be hurt if you skim (or — who's kidding whom? — skip over) those parts of the book. However, if you're just getting your feet wet with Google Workspace, flip the page and start perusing the first chapter.

If you have some experience with Google Workspace or you have a special problem or question, see the table of contents or the index to find out where I cover that topic, and then turn to that page.

Either way, happy Google Workspace-ing!

1

Keeping Your Affairs in Order

IN THIS PART . . .

Get acquainted with what Google Workspace is and what you can do with it.

Learn the ins and outs, the ups and downs, the receives and sends of Gmail.

Turn Calendar into your own private assistant and never be late again.

Keep your friends close and your enemies closer with Contacts.

IN THIS CHAPTER

- **Getting to know Google Workspace**
- **Peering inside the Google Workspace box**
- **Answering your urgent Google Workspace questions**
- **Introducing online collaboration**
- **Getting a glimpse of Google Workspace mobile apps**

Chapter 1

Google Workspace: The 50¢ Tour

Way, way back in 2006 (an era so far in the past that people somehow had to manage without iPhones or Android devices), the wonderful eggheads at Google came up with an idea: What if, they mused amongst themselves, businesses could avoid dealing with the headache-inducing and sanity-destroying complexity of managing high-tech services such as email, messaging, scheduling, and file storage? What if, they continued, *Google* managed those services and all businesses had to worry about was, well, *business*? "Wouldn't that be *great*?" they asked themselves.

The answer to that last question must have been a resounding "Yes!" because in that year Google Apps was born. This collection of online apps for email, messaging, calendars, and, a year or so later, documents and spreadsheets was an instant hit and has been sprouting new apps ever since. Formerly named G Suite but now known to the world as Google Workspace, Google's business-focused collection of online apps just keeps getting better and more popular. In this chapter, you discover what Google Workspace is all about, explore what Google Workspace offers, and have your most pressing Google Workspace questions answered. Won't that be *great*?

What Is Google Workspace?

In the world of business jargon, a *silo* is a person or department that can't or won't share information with other people or departments in the company. Not all that long ago, *all* employees were silos in a way. Why? Because they beavered away at their computers using installed software such as Microsoft Word and Microsoft Excel, with all of their documents stored safely on their hard drives. Sure, every now and then they shared a document on the network or by email, but for the most part they worked in not-so-splendid isolation from their peers.

But as management gurus and overpaid consultants have been telling anyone who'll listen for at least a couple of decades now, silos are bad. On an individual level, silos make everyone less efficient and less productive; on a departmental level, silos create duplication of effort and endless turf wars; on a company level, silos inhibit growth and innovation.

Yes, silos are nasty things, but how do you get rid of them? An alarmingly large number of management reports and business books have been written to answer that question. It's a complex and difficult topic, but here are three solutions that are almost certainly common to all those reports and books:

- Make it easy for individuals to access their software and documents no matter where they are or what type of device they're using.
- Make it easy for people on the same team or in the same department to collaborate with each other.
- Make it easy for people on different teams or in different departments to share information with each other.

And that, at long last, is where Google Workspace comes in. Google Workspace is a set of applications that's designed to tear down silos. How? By implementing the preceding list of solutions in the following ways:

- **Google Workspace apps aren't installed on your computer.** Instead, they live online — in the *cloud*, as the nerds say — so you can access them from any location that has internet access, using any type of device — desktop PC, notebook PC, tablet, smartphone, you name it — that you have handy.
- **Google Workspace apps are built with collaboration in mind.** For example, two or more people can work on the same document at the same time. No, I'm not just making that up — it's a real feature. Google Workspace also enables you to easily email, meet, and chat with members of your team or department, so everyone stays in the loop.

» **Google Workspace documents aren't stored on your computer.** Instead, all Google Workspace data and documents reside online — yep, in the cloud — so it's a snap to share them with anyone in your company.

Silos, schmi-los!

What You Get with Google Workspace

My dictionary defines a *suite* as "a connected series of rooms to be used together." You're probably thinking *hotel suite,* but that definition is actually a succinct and useful definition of Google Workspace, which is a kind of software suite (remember that it used to be called G Suite). You can, in fact, define Google Workspace as "a connected series of Google apps to be used together." That is, the Google Workspace apps are all awesome when used by themselves, but when they're connected, they make your work life easier, more efficient, and more productive.

Okay, so what are these apps that I've been going on and on about? Table 1-1 provides the list, with pointers to where you can find more info later in this book.

TIP

I assume you have a Google Workspace account through your organization. If that's not true and you're the person in your business who takes care of such things, you can set up a Google Workspace account by surfing to `https://workspace.google.com/` and clicking Get Started.

TABLE 1-1 The Google Workspace Apps

App	What You Can Do with It	Where to Find More Info
Gmail	Send and receive email messages. (See Figure 1-1.) You can also share files as attachments, organize messages, control email conversations, and more.	Chapter 2 Chapter 18
Calendar	Maintain an online schedule of appointments and other events. (Check out Figure 1-2.) You can also see reminders of upcoming events, schedule repeating events, share calendars, and more.	Chapter 3 Chapter 12
Contacts	Create and maintain an online address book. (See Figure 1-3.) For each contact, you can store info such as the person's name, email address, and phone number. You can also import contacts, group related contacts, and more.	Chapter 4

(continued)

TABLE 1-1 ***(continued)***

App	What You Can Do with It	Where to Find More Info
Docs	Create, edit, and collaborate on word processing documents. You can change the layout, add bulleted and numbered lists, work with headers and footers, format text, paragraphs, and pages, and more.	Chapter 5 Chapter 6 Chapter 7 Chapter 11
Sheets	Create, edit, and collaborate on spreadsheets. You can build formulas, sort and filter data, analyze data, and more.	Chapter 8 Chapter 9 Chapter 11
Slides	Create, edit, and collaborate on presentations. You can change the theme, show your presentation, create slides that include text, images, shapes, and more.	Chapter 10 Chapter 11
Meet	Set up and join online meetings. You can invite people to a meeting, share resources, record and live-stream a meeting, and more.	Chapter 13
Chat	Exchange real-time messages with members of your team, department, or organization.	Chapter 14
Groups	Join and create groups for posting messages, sharing files, and more.	Chapter 15
Forms	Create forms, quizzes, and surveys to gather information and opinions from members of your team, department, or organization.	Chapter 16
Keep	Create, edit, and share notes.	Chapter 16
Drive	Store, manage, and share files online.	Chapter 11

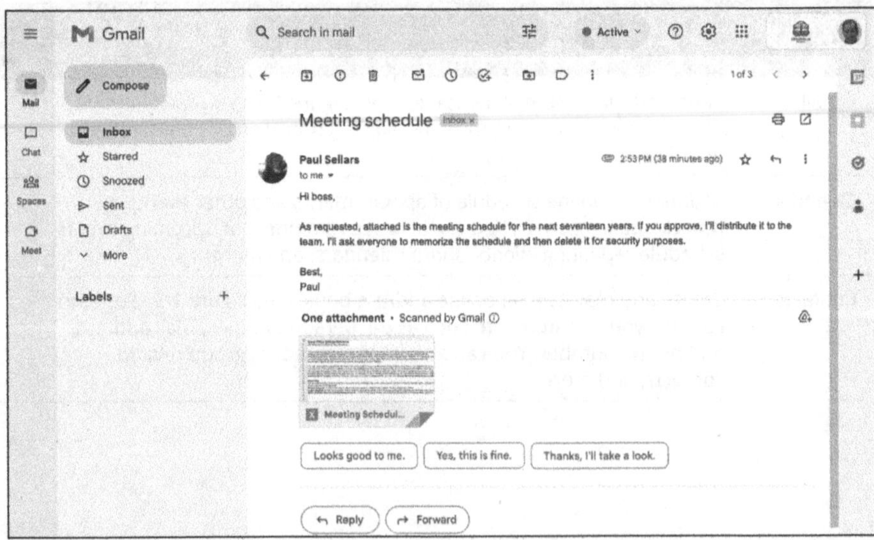
Gmail
Search in mail
Active
Compose
Mail
Chat
Spaces
Meet
Inbox
Starred
Snoozed
Sent
Drafts
More
Labels
1 of 3
Meeting schedule
Inbox
Paul Sellars
to me
2:53 PM (38 minutes ago)
Hi boss,
As requested, attached is the meeting schedule for the next seventeen years. If you approve, I'll distribute it to the team. I'll ask everyone to memorize the schedule and then delete it for security purposes.
Best,
Paul
One attachment • Scanned by Gmail
Meeting Schedul...
Looks good to me.
Yes, this is fine.
Thanks, I'll take a look.
Reply
Forward

FIGURE 1-1: Gmail: Google Workspace's email app.

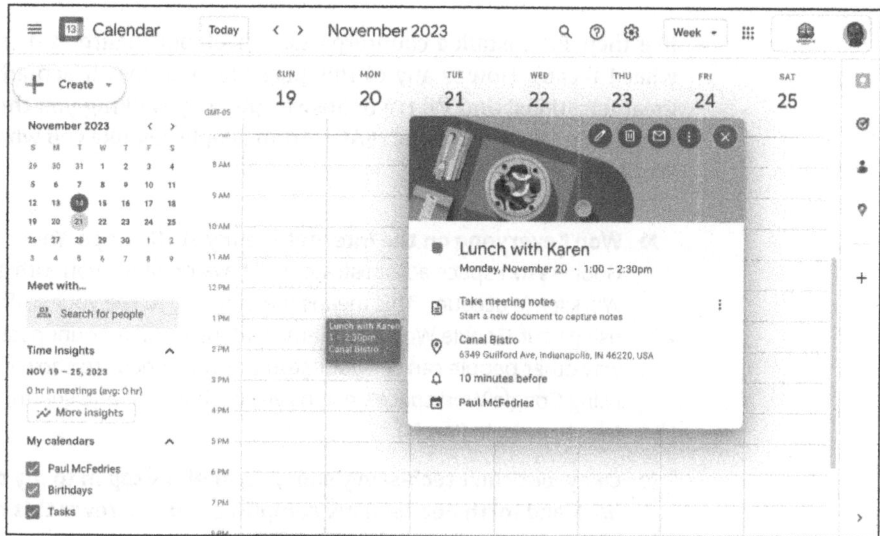

FIGURE 1-2: Calendar: Google Workspace's scheduling app.

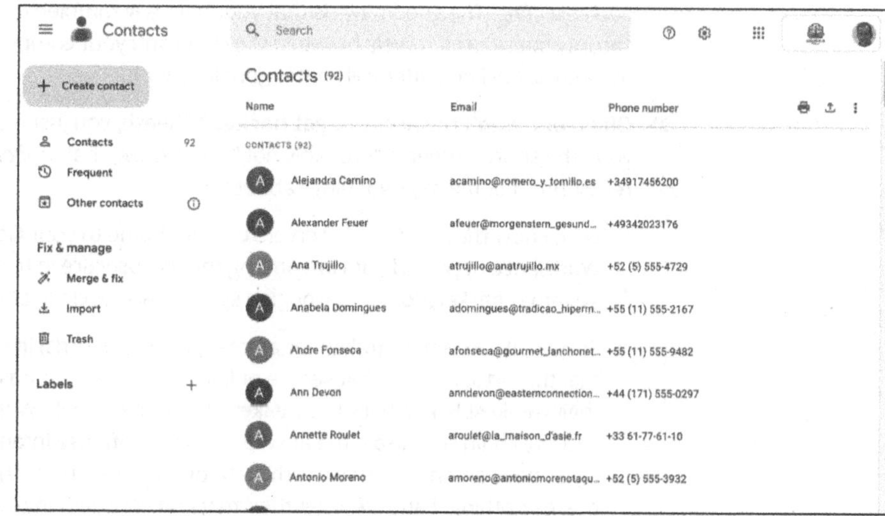

FIGURE 1-3: Contacts: Google Workspace's contact management app.

Using Apps Online — Really? Here Are the FAQs

When folks who switch to Google Workspace are used to working with programs installed on their PCs, the idea of using apps that somehow work online is the stuff of science fiction. It doesn't help that the Google Workspace apps *look* just like their PC-installed counterparts. (Check out Figures 1-1, 1-2, and 1-3 to see what I mean). How is any of this possible, and does it actually work? Those are great questions, and I'll try to answer them by walking you through a long list of frequently asked questions (FAQs) from people just like you who are new to Google Workspace:

- **Won't everyone on the internet see my stuff?** Nope. Your company's Google Workspace administrator will have provided you with a Google Workspace account. This means the only way to see your stuff is to sign in using your Google Workspace email address and account password. The only way other people can see your stuff is if you choose to show it to them by using Google Workspace's extensive collaboration and sharing features. (See the chapters in Part 3.)
- **Okay, but can't tech-savvy snoops somehow tap in to my data as it goes back and forth between my computer and wherever this cloud is located?** Dang, but that's a good question! The bad news is that, yes, it's technically possible for someone to eavesdrop on your data, a practice called *packet-sniffing.* The good news is that your data is scrambled (*encrypted,* in security-speak) as it travels between the cloud and your computer, so all that theoretical packet-sniffer will sniff is gobbledygook.
- **Okay, but won't my account get hacked?** Sheesh, you just won't let up, will you? The short answer is "Probably not." Yes, I know, that *probably* isn't very reassuring. Let me say two things about this:
  - First, know that the Google servers that are home to your Google Workspace apps and data are among the most secure in the world. No system is hackerproof, but Google's systems are as close as you can get.
  - Second, it's axiomatic (taken for granted, in other words) in security circles that the virtual chains that secure online systems are only as strong as their weakest link. What's the weakest link in the Google Workspace security chain? I'm afraid the answer is *you.* No offense intended, but even if you have an online service with state-of-the-art security, that protection means nothing if attackers get their mitts on your sign-in data. So, keep your password to yourself and be sure to carefully read all the good security stuff in Chapter 19.
- **Is my data safe?** Definitely. Google Workspace keeps multiple copies of your data in different locations in the cloud, and it also regularly backs up your data.
- **But won't there be big problems if the power goes out?** Nope. The Google Workspace apps save your documents and data as you work, so even if your power goes down for the count, your data remains safe and sound on the Google Workspace servers, waiting patiently for you to return.

» **Can I work when I'm offline?** I'm afraid not. Google Workspace's apps are online-only, so you need an internet connection to access and work with any Google Workspace app. The one exception here is that you can usually read messages in Gmail when you're offline.

» **Google Workspace has *so many* apps! Do I need to keep them all updated whenever new versions come out?** No, and this is one of the key benefits of using online apps. You'll never — I repeat, *never* — have to install or update any Google Workspace apps! All that malarkey is handled behind the scenes by Google, so every time you access, say, Gmail, you can rest assured that you're using the very latest version of the app.

» **A nerd I know described Google Workspace as "SaaS," which is too weird for me. Do I need to know what SaaS is?** Not even a little bit. (But if your curiosity gets the better of you, have a read of the nearby sidebar "Another FAQ: What's all this about a cloud?" for the answer.)

ANOTHER FAQ: WHAT'S ALL THIS ABOUT A CLOUD?

TECHNICAL STUFF

I mentioned the term *cloud* a couple of times now, so let me take a few minutes of your precious time to explain what I'm talking about. In many network diagrams (schematics that show the overall layout of a network's infrastructure), the designer is most interested in the devices that connect to the network, not in the network itself. After all, the details of what happens inside the network to shunt signals from source to destination are often extremely complex and convoluted, so all that minutiae would serve only to detract from the network diagram's larger message of showing which devices can connect to the network, how they connect, and their network entry and exit points.

When the designers of a network diagram want to show the network but not any of its details, they almost always abstract the network by displaying it as a cloud symbol. (It is, if you will, the yadda-yadda-yadda of network diagrams.) At first, the cloud symbol represented the workings of a single network, but in recent years it has come to represent the internet (the network of networks).

So far, so good. Earlier in this millennium, some folks had the bright idea that, rather than store files on local computers, you could store them on a server connected to the internet, which meant that anyone with the proper credentials could access the files from anywhere in the world. Eventually, folks started storing programs on internet servers, too, and started telling anyone who'd listen that these files and applications resided

(continued)

(continued)

"in the cloud" (meaning on a server — or, more typically, a large collection of servers that reside in a special building called a *data center* — accessible via the internet).

All the Google Workspace components (Gmail, Calendar, Docs, and so on) are examples of such apps — in the rarefied world of cloud computing geeks, these apps are described as *software as a service*, or *SaaS* — and they all reside inside Google's cloud service called, boringly, Google Cloud. So that's why I say that Google Workspace apps and your data live "in the cloud." That's also why you need an internet connection to use Google Workspace: It requires that connection to access all its cloud stuff.

Introducing Online Collaboration

When I talk to people about Google Workspace, the feature that invariably raises eyebrows is online collaboration. Just the notion that two or more people can work on a document at the same time seems, well, *magical.* Yep, there's some mind-bogglingly sophisticated technology behind Google Workspace's collaboration features, but you don't require a PhD in computer science to use them.

As an example, take a look at Figure 1-4, which shows a file open in Docs. The figure shows a fistful of collaboration features, but I want to bring your attention to just these four:

» In most cases, inviting fellow collaborators is a simple matter of clicking the Share button, pointed out near the top-right corner of Figure 1-4. You choose whom you want to share the document with, add a brief note (optional), and then send the invite. The invitees receive a link that they can click to be taken directly to the file to start their editing duties.

» The Google Workspace app lets you know who's editing the document alongside you by displaying an icon for each collaborator. You can hover the mouse pointer over an icon to see that person's name and email address, plus options to contact that person via email, set up a meeting, send a message, or start a video call.

» The Google Workspace app also displays the show chat icon (labeled in Figure 1-4), which enables everyone to send messages back and forth. The potential for fun here is unlimited!

» The Google Workspace app even shows you, in real-time, a tiny pop-up with the name of each collaborator so that you can see at a glance where each person is performing their editing chores.

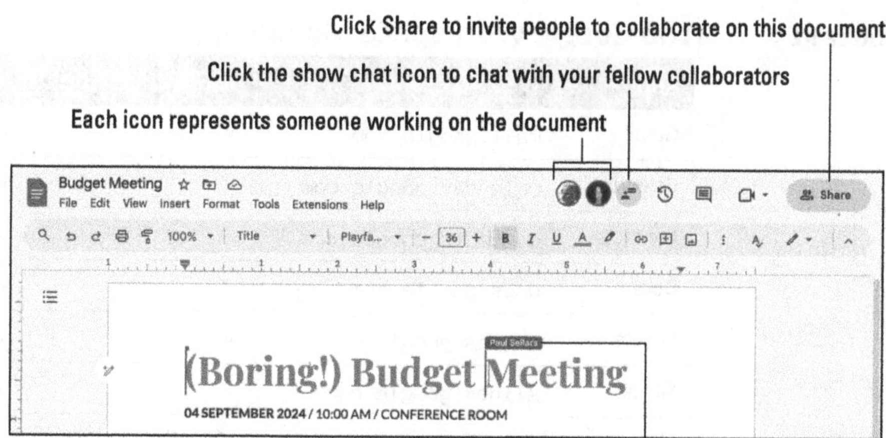
Click Share to invite people to collaborate on this document
Click the show chat icon to chat with your fellow collaborators
Each icon represents someone working on the document
Budget Meeting
File Edit View Insert Format Tools Extensions Help
Share
(Boring!) Budget Meeting
04 SEPTEMBER 2024 / 10:00 AM / CONFERENCE ROOM
The name of the person editing this part of the document

FIGURE 1-4: A Docs file, with several people editing.

REMEMBER

I wrote this section to give you just a taste of Google Workspace collaboration prowess using the Docs app. For the full scoop on Docs collaboration, head for Chapter 11.

Going Mobile

Although I don't talk about them in this book (otherwise, the book would be twice as long as it is), most of the Google Workspace apps come with mobile versions that run on Android, iOS, and iPadOS devices. See either Google Play on your Android device or the App Store on your iOS or iPadOS device to install any of the Google Workspace apps.

To give you an idea of what's available, Table 1-2 runs through the Google Workspace apps, shows you how to access each one on the web, and lets you know whether an Android or iOS version is available.

REMEMBER

If a Google Workspace app lacks a version for your mobile device, you can still access the service on your phone or tablet by using your mobile web browser to surf to the app's web address.

TABLE 1-2 The Google Workspace Mobile Apps

App	Web Access	iOS/iPadOS App	Android App
Gmail	mail.google.com	✓	✓
Calendar	calendar.google.com	✓	✓
Contacts	contacts.google.com		✓
Docs	docs.google.com	✓	✓
Sheets	sheets.google.com	✓	✓
Slides	slides.google.com	✓	✓
Meet	meet.google.com	✓	✓
Chat	chat.google.com	✓	✓
Groups	groups.google.com		
Forms	forms.google.com		
Keep	keep.google.com	✓	✓
Drive	drive.google.com	✓	✓

IN THIS CHAPTER

» Taking a tour of Gmail

» Shipping and receiving: Sending and getting messages

» Replying to and forwarding messages

» Handling file attachments (carefully!)

» Helpful tips and techniques for managing all that email

Chapter 2
Taming the Email Beast

To the world's technology nerds, a *killer app* is a software application that is so useful, so popular, or so essential to its underlying technology that the app is seen as indispensable to that technology. Email has been called the killer app of the internet, and it certainly deserves that title. Yes, text messaging is ubiquitous these days; social networks such as Facebook, X/Twitter, and Instagram get a lot of press; and for-kids-only programs such as TikTok come and go. However, while not everyone uses these services, it's safe to say that almost everyone uses email. You probably use email all day, particularly during those few hours each day you describe as "work," so learning a few useful and efficient email techniques can make your day a bit easier and save you time for more important pursuits.

The Google Workspace email app is called Gmail, and in this chapter you learn the basics of sending and receiving messages with Gmail, and then you delve a bit deeper to discover some Gmail gems that will kick your email know-how into a higher gear.

Rhymes with Email: Getting to Know Gmail

The good news about Gmail is that when it comes to the basic email operations — I'm talking sending and receiving messages, replying to messages, dealing with attached files, keeping your messages organized — the program is a beacon of simplicity in a world burdened by overly complex software. This is music to the ears for those of us (and that would be all of us) who wrestle with email all day long.

The bad news about Gmail is, well, I can't think of any! Put simply, Gmail does the job it was designed to do, which goes a long way toward explaining why Gmail boasts about 1.8 billion (yep, that's right: *billion*) active users.

I'm assuming you're new to Gmail, so I start by taking you on a guided tour of the app so that you know where all the major (and a few minor) landmarks are. If you've used Gmail for a while, you might want to take the tour anyway, because you never know what useful features you might have missed.

Touring the Gmail app

To get things started with the Gmail app, point your favorite web browser to `http://mail.google.com/` and then sign in with your Google Workspace credentials, if asked. If you see a box with the title Get Started with Gmail, click the X in the upper-right corner to close the box.

The Gmail app that shows up looks fairly plain, but quite a few knickknacks are scattered around the screen. Let's run through the main features (which are pointed out in Figure 2-1):

- **Navigation bar:** This is the pane on the far left, and it enables you to quickly navigate to four key Google Workspace features: Mail (that is, Gmail), Chat, Spaces, and Meet.
- **Main menu:** This is the pane to the right of the navigation bar, and it consists of a giant Compose button (to start a new email) and the Labels list. When you work in Gmail, your messages aren't stored in folders the way they are in most other email apps. Instead, Gmail uses labels to organize your messages, and all your labels appear on the Main menu's Labels list. When you click a label in this list, you see all your messages that have that label applied. For example, when a new message arrives, Gmail automatically applies the Inbox label to it, so to see all your new messages, you click the Inbox label.

REMEMBER

Why use labels instead of good old-fashioned folders? Because folders are storage areas, which means a message can reside in only one place at a time. However, you can slap as many labels on a message as you like. If a new message comes in and you give it the Starred label, that message is available to you in both the Inbox label and the Starred label. If the benefit of this strategy isn't clear right now, don't worry: I talk much more about labels later in this chapter.

- **Main menu toggle:** Click this icon to hide the main menu. This gives you a bit more horizontal space to display messages. Click the icon again to display the main menu.
- **Select:** Click the empty box icon to select all the messages in the current label. Alternatively, you can select the check boxes that appear beside individual messages.
- **Refresh:** Click the curved arrow icon to check for new messages.
- **Search mail:** Enter text here to locate messages.
- **Settings:** Click the gear icon to work with Gmail's most common settings. In the pane that appears, click See All Settings to work with the full complement of Gmail options (there are a lot of them!).
- **Google apps:** Click this icon to display icons for all the Google Workspace apps. You then click an app icon to open that app.
- **Google account:** Click this icon to manage your Google account.
- **Side panel:** This sidebar, which is on the right, gives you access to the following Google Workspace elements:
  - *Calendar:* Opens a pane for quick access to Google Calendar.
  - *Keep:* Enables you to write a quick note to store in the Keep app.
  - *Tasks:* Enables you to create a quick task to store in the Tasks app.
  - *Contacts:* Opens a pane for quick access to Google Contacts.
- **Hide side panel:** Click this arrow to collapse the side panel and gain a little extra horizontal legroom. Click the arrow again (it points to the left now) to redisplay the side panel.

Touring the Gmail inbox

Now I want to zoom in a bit and focus on just the inbox portion of the Gmail screen. I talk about many of the inbox features later in this chapter, so I'll just hit a few highlights here (check out Figure 2-2, which offers handy pointers to the features in the following list):

- **Message actions:** These icons represent actions you can take on the selected message, such as moving the message to another label or deleting the message. I talk about each of these icons later in this chapter.
- **More:** Click this icon to see even more message actions.

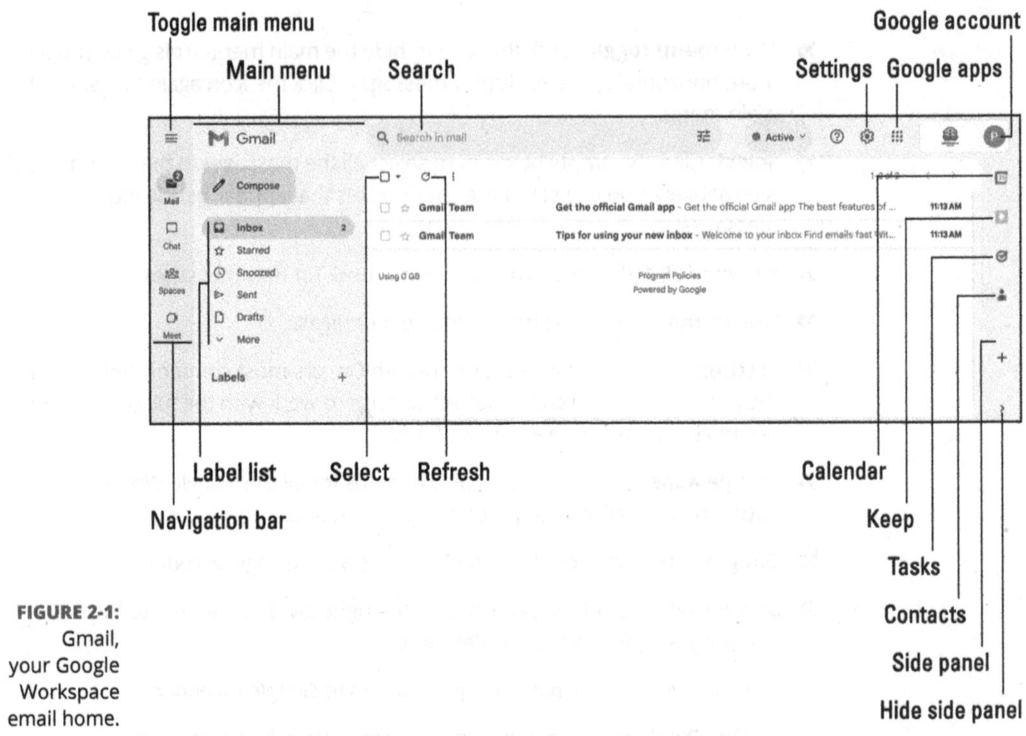

FIGURE 2-1: Gmail, your Google Workspace email home.

» **Message navigation:** If you have more than one screenful of messages in the current label, you can click these arrows to navigate the messages one screenful at a time.

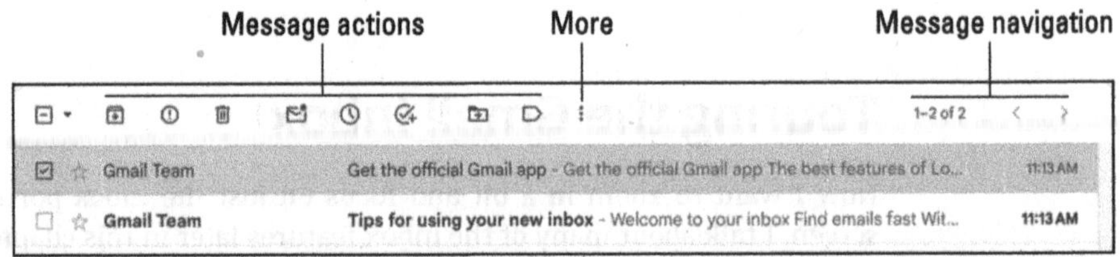

FIGURE 2-2: The Gmail inbox.

Showing your good side: Adding a profile picture

When you send an email to another Gmail user, participate in a chat or a meeting, collaborate on a document or spreadsheet, or do any number of other Google Workspace activities, your presence in those activities is indicated by your Google Workspace profile picture. For a new Google Workspace account, that picture is a circle containing the first letter of your first name. (Refer to the "Google account" callout in Figure 2-1.) It's bland, in other words. Believe me, you do *not* want a mere letter to represent you to your colleagues, friends, and family.

REMEMBER

You can change your profile picture only if your Google Workspace admin has enabled that feature on your account.

Fortunately, the road to a flattering profile picture consists of just the following steps:

1. **In the Gmail window, click the Google Account icon (that is, your default profile picture, pointed out earlier, in Figure 2-1).**

   The Google Account dialog appears.

2. **Click your existing profile picture.**

   The Profile Picture page appears.

3. **Click Add Profile Picture.**

   If the Add Profile Picture icon is disabled, it means your Google Workspace admin hasn't enabled this feature on your account. Sorry about that.

   The Add Profile Picture page appears.

4. **Click a tab:**

   - *Illustrations:* Click to use a prefab illustration as your profile picture. Scroll down to explore different illustration categories and collections, and then click the image you want to use.
   - *From Computer:* Click to select a picture by using your computer. You can use File Explorer (Windows) or Finder (macOS) to drag an image file and drop it on the *avatar* (the generic image of a person's head and upper body). If you prefer to use a dialog, click Upload from Computer, locate and select the image file, and then click Open. If you want to take a new photo instead, click Take a Picture, click Allow when your web browser asks for permission to use your camera, and then take the photo.

5. **Adjust the picture to your liking:**

   - *Illustration:* Use the tools in the lower-left corner to choose a preset effect or a predefined crop, change the colors, and zoom, crop, and rotate the illustration. When you're done, click Next.
   - *Image file:* Crop, move, and rotate the image, and then click Next.

6. **Click Save as Profile Picture.**

   Gmail uploads the image and uses it as your profile pic across all Google Workspace apps. Looking good!

The Outbox: Sending an Email Message

Okay, enough lollygagging. It's time to get to work and learn how to foist your e-prose on unsuspecting (or even suspecting, for that matter) colleagues, friends, family, and former *Brady Bunch* cast members. This section shows you the basic technique to use and then gets a bit fancier in discussing the contacts list, attachments, using AI, and other snippets of Gmail sending lore.

The basics: Composing and sending a message

Without further ado (not that there's been much ado to this point, mind you), here are the basic steps to follow to fire off an email message to some lucky recipient:

1. **On Gmail's main menu, click Compose.**

   You end up with the New Message window onscreen, as shown in Figure 2-3.

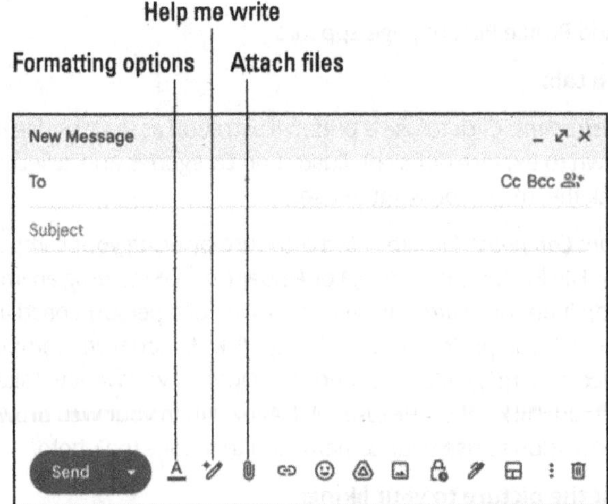

FIGURE 2-3: You cobble together an email message in the New Message window.

2. **In the To text box, type the email address of the recipient.**

   It's perfectly acceptable to enter multiple addresses in this text box. After each address, press Enter or Tab.

   What if you make a mistake in the address? Don't sweat it: Click the address, and then press Shift+F to open it for editing. (Alternatively, double-click the address and then click Change Email Address in the menu that appears.) Fix the error, and then press Enter.

What if you want to remove an address? Again, easy money: Click the X that appears to the right of the address.

3. **To shoot off a copy of the message to a secondary recipient, click Cc (short for courtesy copy) and then enter the email address in the Cc text box that shows up.**

   Note that the address you put in the To box is the main recipient of the message. And again, you can enter multiple addresses, if you're so inclined.

   You might also want to send the message to someone as a blind courtesy copy (Bcc), which does in fact send a copy of the message to that person but also ensures that none of the other recipients sees that person's address anywhere. Click Bcc and type the address in the Bcc text box.

REMEMBER

   It seems awfully stealthy to send a Bcc to someone, so when would you ever do such a thing? The most common reason is that you want that person to see the contents of your message, but you don't want to burden that person with the subsequent conversation. That is, if one of your To or Cc recipients clicks Reply All (which I talk about later in this chapter), that reply doesn't go to anyone in the Bcc field.

TIP

   Another good reason to use the Bcc field is when you want to send a message to a large group, but you don't want each person to see everyone else's email address. This is useful, for example, if you're sending a change of address message.

4. **In the Subject line, enter a subject for the message.**

   Now, don't rush things here. The subject acts as a title for your message. It's the first thing the recipient sees, so it should accurately reflect the content of your message, but it shouldn't be too long. Think pithy.

5. **In the large, empty area below the Subject line, type the message text (also known in Nerdsville as the *message body*).**

6. **Click the formatting options icon (shown in the margin) to display the impressive collection of commands shown in Figure 2-4.**

   Use these icons and commands to change the font, type size, and type style. You can also click more formatting options icon (pointed out in Figure 2-4) to format paragraphs, add a bulleted list, and more.

TIP

   Check your spelling before sending your message to the recipient. It just takes a sec, and if the spell checker finds an error or two, you'll save yourself a bit of embarrassment. To run the spell checker, click the more options icon (shown in the margin) and then click Check Spelling.

7. **When your message is fit for human consumption, click Send.**

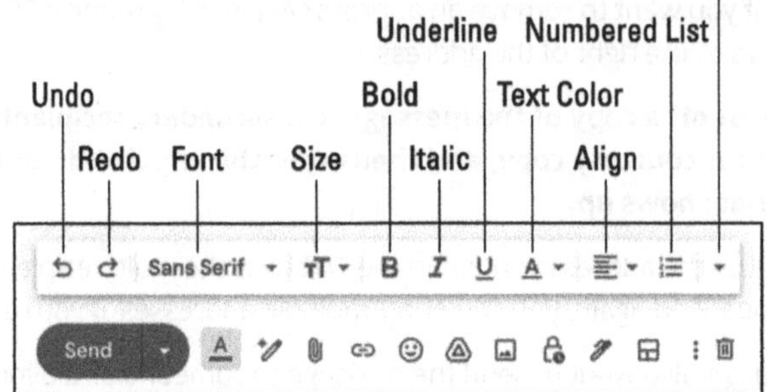

FIGURE 2-4: When you click the formatting options icon, you get these commands for sprucing up your message text.

REMEMBER

After your message is outward bound, Gmail is kind enough to save a copy of it under the Sent label. This label is handy because it gives you a record of all the missives you launch into cyberspace.

Easier addressing: Using the Contacts app

If you find yourself with a bunch of recipients to whom you send stuff regularly (and it's a rare emailer who doesn't), you'll soon grow tired of entering their addresses by hand. The solution is to toss those regulars into the Contacts app. That way, you can fire them into the To or Cc (or even Bcc) lines with just a few mouse clicks.

I cover how to add folks to your Contacts app in just the right amount of detail in Chapter 4. So, assuming that you have your email regulars safely stowed in Contacts, follow these steps to send one or more of them a message:

1. **On Gmail's main menu, click Compose.**
2. **In the New Message window, click To.**

   Gmail displays the Select Contacts window.
3. **Select the check box to the left of the contact's name.**

   Note that you see this check box only when you hover the mouse pointer over the contact.
4. **Repeat Step 3 as required.**
5. **Click Insert.**
6. **Adding contacts to the Cc and Bcc fields is similar:**
   - *Cc field:* Click Cc to display the field, and then click Cc to the left of the field to display the Select Contacts window. Select the check box beside each contact you want to add to the Cc field, and then click Insert.

- *Bcc field:* Click Bcc to display the field, and then click Bcc to the left of the field to display the Select Contacts window. Select the check box beside each contact you want to add to the Bcc field, and then click Insert.

7. **Fill in the rest of the message and then click Send.**

Easier writing: Getting AI to help with a message

The problem with email is that it can seem as though you spend most of your day crafting messages, whether it's asking a colleague for a favor, pleading with your boss for more resources, or trying to find out why your kid was sent to the principal's office. Each of these notes requires a particular mix of style, language, and tone, and coming up with just the right combo each time can be exhausting.

So, what's a harried emailer to do? In the modern age, when the going gets tough, the tough get artificial intelligence (AI) to help. Specifically, you can enlist the assistance of *generative AI,* which is AI that can generate writing based on a simple request (or *prompt*, in AI-speak). ChatGPT is a famous example of generative AI, but you don't need to bother with that because there's a good chance you have generative AI built right in to your Google Workspace account.

How can you tell whether your have AI at your beck and call? In Gmail's New Message window, look for the help me write icon, shown in the margin. If you see that icon, you have AI on your side.

Using AI help to a draft message

Here's how to use the AI built into Gmail to create a draft of a message:

1. **In the New Message window, click the help me write icon (shown in the margin).**

   The Help Me Write pop-up toolbar appears.

2. **Click the help me write icon.**

   Gmail displays a prompt box.

3. **Type a prompt that describes the message you want the AI to draft for you.**

   You don't need anything too elaborate here: just the content of the message (such as "a thank-you letter for a birthday present" or "an invitation to a conference") and to whom the message is for (such as "an old friend" or "a busy colleague").

4. **Click Create.**

   The AI sets to work and displays a draft message in a few seconds. Figure 2-5 shows an AI-generated email based on the prompt "A thank-you letter for some homemade cookies given to me by an old friend for my birthday."

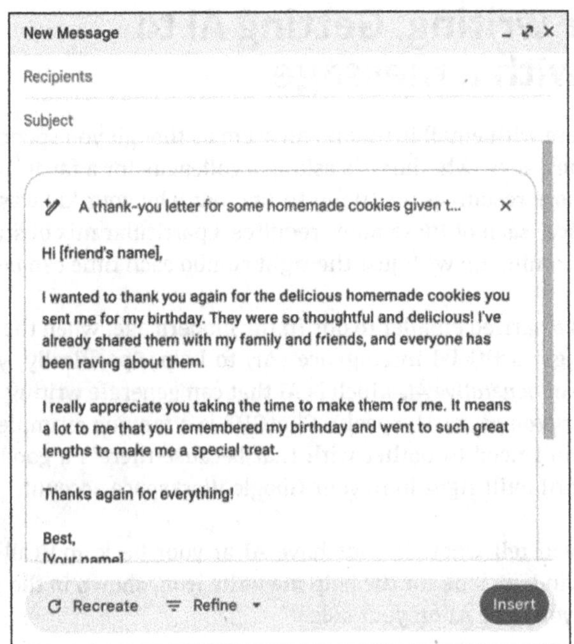

FIGURE 2-5: A draft email generated by AI.

5. **If you're happy with the draft, skip to Step 6. Otherwise, you have two choices:**

   - *Generate a new message:* Click Recreate to ask the AI to generate a new version of the message.
   - *Refine the existing message:* Click Refine and then click how you want the AI to rewrite the message: Formalize, Elaborate, or Shorten.

6. **Once you're okay with the text, click Insert to add it to your message.**
7. **Adjust the text as needed.**

   For example, if the AI included placeholders (such as a placeholder for your name), fill those in. Also, you should consider this text a draft and rewrite it so that there's at least a little "you" in there (especially for personal messages).

8. **Address and send your message.**

Using AI help to improve a message

If you already have a message written, you can ask AI to help you improve the message in the following ways:

- **Formalize:** Make the overall tone and word choices more formal.
- **Elaborate:** Make the message more detailed.
- **Shorten:** Make the message more concise.

Follow these steps to use the AI built into Gmail to improve an existing message:

1. **In the New Message window, write a draft of your message.**
2. **Click the help me write icon (shown in the margin).**

   The Help Me Write pop-up toolbar appears.
3. **Click the refinement icon you want to use, as pointed out in Figure 2-6.**

   The AI rewrites the message based on the refinement you chose.

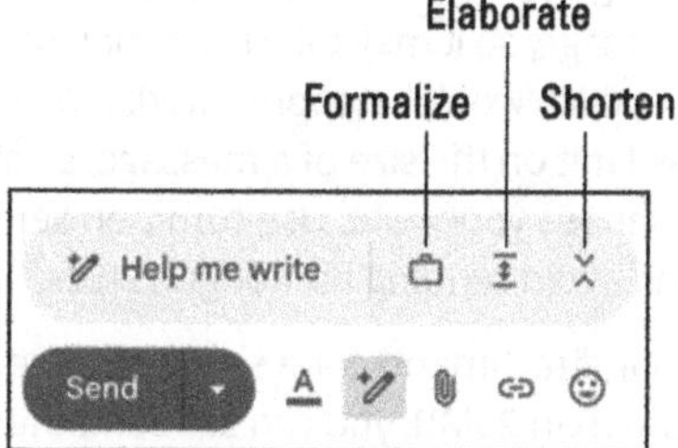

FIGURE 2-6: Click a refinement icon to rewrite your draft.

4. **If you're happy with the new message, skip to Step 5. Otherwise, you have two choices:**
   - *Generate a new message:* Click Recreate to ask the AI to generate a new version of the message.
   - *Refine the existing message:* Click the refinement icon and then click how you want the AI to rewrite the message: Formalize, Elaborate, or Shorten.
5. **Once you're okay with the text, click Insert to add it below your existing message.**
6. **Adjust the text as needed.**

   That is, you likely want to delete your original message and edit the AI's refined message to make it your own.
7. **Address and send your message.**

Inserting attachments and other hangers-on

Most of your messages will be text-only creations (perhaps with a bit of formatting tossed in to keep things interesting). However, it's also possible to send entire files along for the ride. Such files are called, naturally enough, *attachments*. They're common in the business world, and it's useful to know how they work. Here goes:

1. **On Gmail's main menu, click Compose.**
2. **Click the attach files icon (shown in the margin).**

   The Open dialog rears its head.
3. **Find the file you want to attach and then select it.**
4. **Click Open.**

   Gmail returns you to the New Message window, where you see a new box near the bottom that includes the name and size of the file.

   Why does Gmail show you the file size? It's a reminder not to bolt an attachment or six onto every message you send. Adding attachments can greatly increase the size of your message, so it may take the recipient quite a while to download your message — which won't be appreciated, I can tell you. Some email services put an upper limit on the size of a message, so it's also possible that your recipient may never see your note. Use common sense: Attach files only when it's necessary and avoid sending humongous files.

   REMEMBER

   The maximum size of all your attachments for a single email is 25MB. If your attachments add up to more than 25MB, you can still send the message, but instead of attachments your recipient sees a Google Drive link that they can use to download the files. For the record, the maximum message size you can receive with Gmail is 50MB.
5. **Fill in the rest of the message and then click Send.**

Creating a signature

In email lingo, a *signature* is a chunk of text that appears at the bottom of all your messages. Most people use their signature to give contact information, and you often see *sigs* (that's the hip short form) adorned with witty quotations or sayings.

Here are the steps you need to plow through to create a signature:

1. **Click the gear icon (Settings) and then click See All Settings.**

   Gmail opens the Settings page with the General tab displayed.

2. **Scroll way down until you come to the Signature setting.**
3. **Click Create New.**

   The Name New Signature dialog appears.

4. **Enter the name to identify your signature and then click Create.**
5. **In the large text box, compose the signature.**

   Figure 2-7 shows an example.

   Feel free to enhance your signature with any of the formatting options that appear just below the text box.

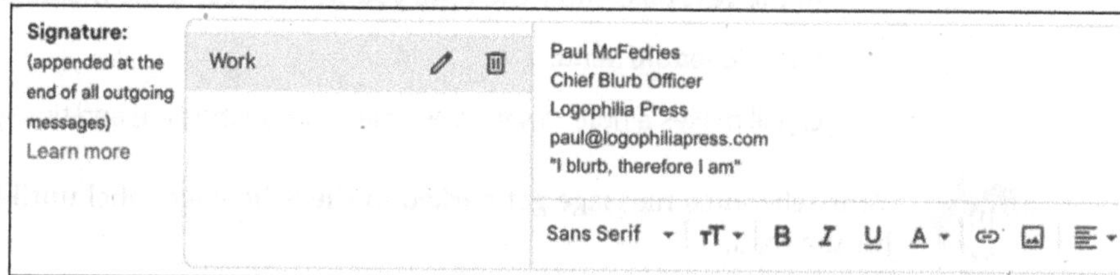

FIGURE 2-7: Use the Signature setting to create a signature that says "you."

6. **If you want Gmail to add a signature whenever you create an email message, select the signature in the For New Emails Use list.**
7. **If you want Gmail to tack on the signature whenever you reply to a message or forward a message to someone, select the signature in the On Reply/Forward Use list.**
8. **When you're done, scroll down to the very bottom of the Settings page and click Save Changes.**

Scheduling a send

When you compose an email and click Send, Gmail dutifully ships out your message right away. However, you might want your email delayed until a certain time or even a certain day. For example, you might want a newsletter email to go out at midnight tonight. Similarly, you might prefer that a message to your team be delivered first thing Monday morning.

Whatever the reason for the delay, you can set up a message to be sent later, by following these steps:

1. **Create, address, and write your email in the usual way.**
2. **Click the more send options icon.**

   The more send options icon is the downward-pointing arrow to the right of the Send button.

3. **Click Schedule Send.**

   Gmail offers up the Schedule Send dialog.

4. **If one of the three offered dates and times works for you, go ahead and click it and then ignore the rest of these steps. Otherwise, click Pick Date & Time.**

   Gmail opens the Pick Date & Time dialog, which offers a calendar and a time text box.

5. **In the calendar, select the date on which you want your message fired off.**

6. **In the text box, enter the time you want to send the message.**

7. **Click Schedule Send.**

   Gmail makes a note to send your message on the date and time you specified.

REMEMBER

Your scheduled message get parked in the Scheduled label until it's time for it to hit the road.

TIP

What happens if you have a message scheduled to be sent later, but you realize you'd rather send it now? No problem: Gmail is happy to cancel the schedule and send your message right away. To make this happen, choose Scheduled on Gmail's main menu, click the message, and then click Cancel Send. Gmail opens the message in a separate window, and you can then click Send to fire the message into the ether right away.

Undoing a send

It's a rare emailer who hasn't experienced "post-Send" regret, which is the sinking feeling in the pit of your stomach that comes when you realize you've just posted a long lament about the sad state of your love life to the entire company.

The Gmail programmers must have experienced that regret a time or two themselves because they did something about it: They created the Undo command. After you click Send, Gmail displays the Message Sent pop-up, shown in Figure 2-8, for a few seconds. Crucially for those of us with overly sensitive Send trigger fingers, that pop-up includes an Undo command. Click Undo and Gmail plucks your message out of the outbox and opens it again so that you can make whatever changes you need (or toss the message in the trash). Whew!

FIGURE 2-8: Right after you send a message, you can change your mind by clicking Undo.

By default, Gmail displays the Message Sent pop-up (and therefore the Undo command) for only 5 seconds. If you'd like a bit more time, follow these steps:

1. **Click the gear icon (Settings) and then click See All Settings.**

   Gmail opens the Settings page with the General tab displayed.

2. **For the Undo Send setting, set the number of seconds you want in the Send Cancellation Period: *X* Seconds drop-down list.**

   You can choose 5, 10, 20, or 30 seconds.

3. **Scroll down to the bottom of the Settings page and click Save Changes.**

The Inbox: Handling Incoming Messages

Some people like to think of email as a return to the days of *belles lettres* and *billets-doux*. (These people tend to be a bit pretentious.) Yes, it's true that email has people writing again, but this isn't like the letter-writing of old. The major difference is that the turnaround time for email is usually much quicker. Rather than wait weeks or even months to receive a return letter, a return email might take as little as a few minutes or a few hours. So, if you send a message with a question or comment, chances are you'll receive a reply before too long. This section shows you what to do with those messages after they arrive.

Refreshing your messages

One of Gmail's handiest features is that whenever it receives a message, it automatically adds it to your inbox. Nice! However, Gmail sometimes doesn't add a new message to the inbox immediately. It will get there soon enough, but if you're waiting impatiently for a particular message to arrive, you can often speed things up a bit by clicking the refresh icon (shown in the margin).

Reading your messages

Figure 2-9 shows the Inbox label with a few messages. The first thing to notice is that Gmail uses a bold font for all messages you haven't read yet. For each message, you also see the name of the sender, the Subject line and the first few words of the body (separated by a hyphen), and the delivery time (if it was delivered today) or date (if it was delivered before today).

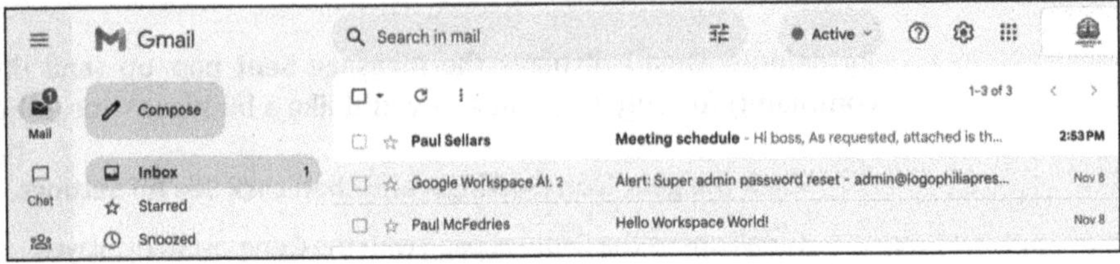

FIGURE 2-9: The inbox with a few messages received.

To read a message, click it. Gmail opens the message and displays its text, as shown in Figure 2-10. To navigate your messages, use the following techniques (all shown in Figure 2-10):

- To display the next older message, click Older.
- To display the next newer message, click Newer.
- To return to the inbox, click Back to Inbox.

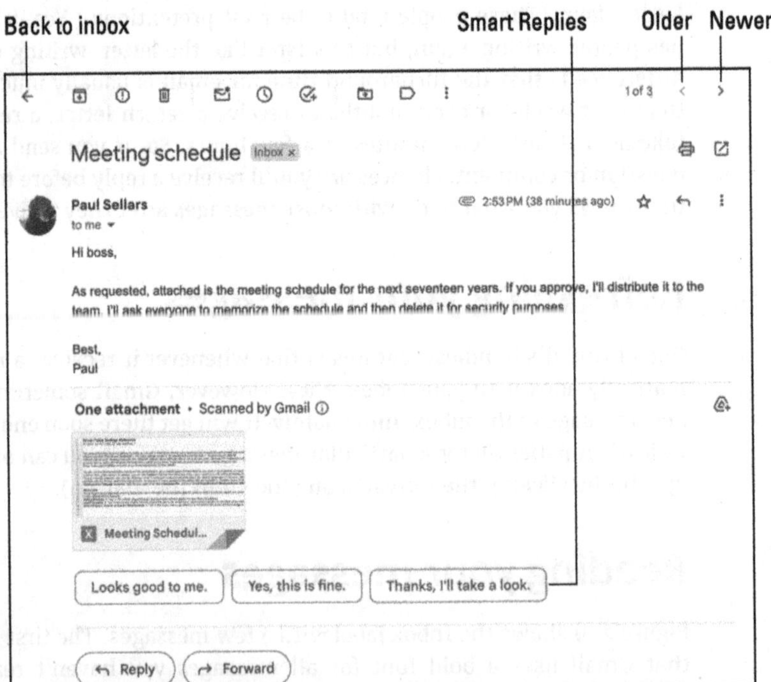

FIGURE 2-10: Click a message to open it and see what it says.

Easier reading with the reading pane

Reading messages isn't hard, but it does involve a few more clicks than you might like. To fix that, you can sit Gmail down and ask it to display the reading pane, which is a separate area displayed alongside the inbox. When you select a message, Gmail displays the message text in the reading pane. One-click reading!

You have two choices when it comes to the position of the reading pane:

- **To the right of the inbox:** This option splits the inbox area vertically so that you end up with the inbox on the left and the reading pane on the right. This gives you the most vertical reading space, so it's best if you tend to get long messages.
- **Below the inbox:** This option splits the inbox area horizontally so that you end up with the inbox on the top and the reading pane on the bottom. This gives you the most horizontal inbox space, which makes it easier to navigate your messages.

Follow these steps to start using the reading pane:

1. **Click the gear icon (Settings) and then click See All Settings.**

   Gmail opens the Settings page with the General tab displayed.

2. **Click the Inbox tab.**
3. **In the Reading Pane section, select the Enable Reading Pane check box.**
4. **For the Reading Pane Position setting, select the radio button you prefer: Right of Inbox or Below Inbox.**

   You also see a third option here: No Split. This tells Gmail to go ahead and activate the reading pane, but not to show it right away. You can then display the reading pane whenever you need it by using the Toggle Split Pane Mode list, pointed out in Figure 2-11.

5. **Scroll to the bottom of the Settings page and click Save Changes.**

Figure 2-11 shows the inbox with the reading pane lurking below the message list, dutifully displaying the text of the selected message. Note, too, the new Toggle Split Pane Mode list, which you can use to adjust the reading pane position to the right of the inbox (Vertical Split), below the inbox (Horizontal Split), or hidden (No Split). To change the size of the reading pane, drag the split bar up or down (if the reading pane is below the message list, as pointed out in Figure 2-11), or left or right (if the reading pane is to the right of the inbox).

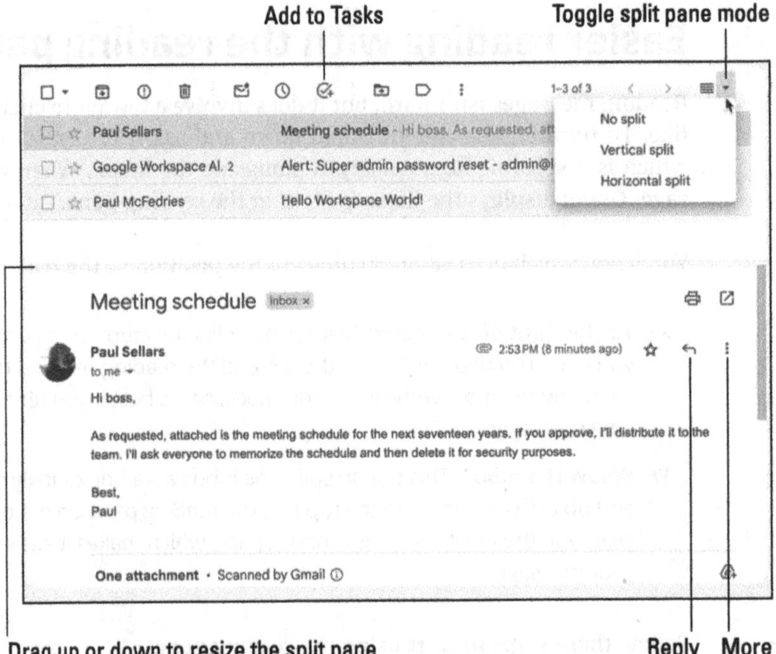

FIGURE 2-11: The reading pane, positioned below the inbox message list.

Attending to attachments

If you receive a message that has one or more files tied to it, you see a thumbnail version of each attached file when you open that message (either directly or in the reading pane). Gmail gives you quite a few ways to handle any attachments in the current message:

» **View the file.** If you just want to see what's in the file, you can open the file for viewing by clicking the file thumbnail. Gmail opens the file and displays a toolbar similar to the one shown in Figure 2-12. With this toolbar, you can open the file in a compatible Google Workspace app (such as Sheets), add the file to My Drive, print the file, or download the file.

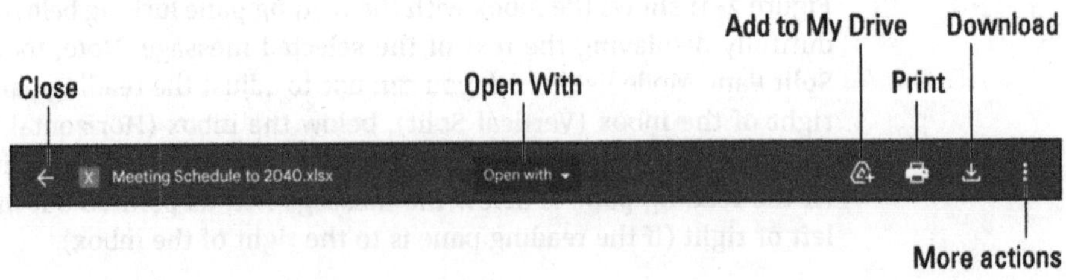

FIGURE 2-12: You see a toolbar similar to this one when you view an attached file.

» **Download the file.** Hover the mouse pointer over the file thumbnail and then click Download. (Refer to Figure 2-13.) Alternatively, click the thumbnail to open the file for viewing and then click the download icon (refer to Figure 2-12).

WARNING

Each file attachment you receive is scanned by Gmail for viruses and other types of nasty bugs. That's great news, but you should never just blithely open a downloaded attachment, particularly if the email comes from someone you don't know. There's a small but non-zero possibility that a virus or other type of malware might sneak through Gmail's defenses. My advice? If the sender is a stranger, delete the message; if the sender is known to you but you weren't expecting the file attachment, write the person back and confirm they sent the file; or if you know the sender and were expecting the file, go ahead and open it.

FIGURE 2-13: Hover the mouse pointer over the thumbnail to see the icons shown here.

» **Save the file to your Google Drive.** Hover the mouse pointer over the file thumbnail and then click Add to Drive (refer to Figure 2-13). Alternatively, click the thumbnail to open the file for viewing and then click Add to My Drive (refer to Figure 2-12).

» **Open the file for editing.** Hover the mouse pointer over the file thumbnail and then click the edit icon (shown in the margin). Alternatively, click the thumbnail to open the file for viewing, click Open With, and then click the app you want to use. (Refer to Figure 2-12.)

Responding to a message

If you receive a message that asks a question, solicits an opinion, or otherwise requires feedback from you, you can send a response. Open the message and then run one of the following commands:

» **Reply:** Click this button at the bottom of the message (or click the reply arrow pointed out in Figure 2-11) to send a response to the sender of the message.

Mail automatically addresses the message to the sender, includes the original subject line preceded by *Re:* (regarding), and adds the original message's text.

REMEMBER

Gmail also usually displays several so-called Smart Replies below the message (some are pointed out in Figure 2-10). For example, if you receive an attached file, you might see a Smart Reply such as "Looks good to me" or "Yes, this is fine." Click a Smart Reply button to create a reply that includes the Smart Reply text. To turn off Smart Replies, click the gear icon (Settings), select the Smart Reply Off radio button (in the Smart Reply section of the General tab), and then click Save Changes.

- **Reply All:** Click this button at the bottom of the message (or click the more icon pointed out in Figure 2-11 and then click Reply to All) if the note was foisted on several people and you want to send your response to everyone who received the original (except anyone who was included in the Bcc field). Mail automatically addresses the message to the sender and all recipients of the original message, includes the original subject line preceded by *Re:*, and adds the original message's text.

WARNING

When I say "all recipients," I mean all recipients, so be extra careful when running the Reply All command. Why? Because the "all" you're dealing with could be your team, your department, or even your entire organization, so a complaint about the "jerks over in Marketing" that gets sent accidentally to all recipients might result in tears later on.

- **Forward:** Click this button at the bottom of the message (or click the more icon pointed out in Figure 2-11 and then click Forward) to have someone else take a gander at the message you received. Mail automatically includes the original subject line preceded by *Fwd:* and adds the original message's text. Note that you need to supply the recipient's address.

Add your own text to the message and then click Send to fire off the response.

Creating a task from a message

Many email messages (and, on bad days, *way* too many email messages) require you to perform some action. It could be making a phone call, completing a report, sending a file, or donating to yet another co-worker's walkathon for *Insert Name of Obscure Disease Here*. You could leave such messages in your inbox and hope you get around to them one day, or you can be more proactive and create a task from each message. That way, you can use the Tasks app to keep track of what you need to get done.

Here are the steps to tackle to create a task from a Gmail message:

1. **Open or select the message you want to work with.**

2. **Click the add to Tasks icon (shown in the margin).**

   Gmail opens the Tasks pane and adds a new task that includes a link to the email message.

Setting up a vacation responder

Remember the days when you'd go on vacation for a couple of weeks and leave your work behind? No, I don't either! These days, we live in a cruel world where people send you a message and expect an instant reply. And it's a sure sign of pending cultural collapse that you're expected to reply even when you're on vacation. Boo!

Okay, fine. Maybe you do have to reply while you're out of the office, but there's no rule (yet) that says you have to reply immediately. Unfortunately, your correspondents might not know you're away, so to forestall an angry "Why didn't you answer my message in less than ten seconds?" follow-up, set up a vacation responder. A *vacation responder* is an automatic reply that gets fired off to everyone who has the temerity to send you a message while you're trying to have a relaxing vacation with your family.

REMEMBER

"Wait a minute," I hear you say. "What if someone doesn't get the hint and keeps sending me messages? Will they end up with dozens of these automatic replies?" Nope. Gmail is smart enough to recognize when someone sends multiple messages your way and only ships out an autoreply every four days.

Here are the steps to plow through to create a vacation responder:

1. **Click the gear icon (Settings) and then click See All Settings.**

   Gmail opens the Settings page with the General tab displayed.

2. **Scroll down until you come to the Vacation Responder section, which is near the bottom of the page.**
3. **Select the Vacation Responder On radio button.**
4. **In the First Day date picker, select the day you want to start sending the automatic replies.**

5. **(Optional) Select the Last Day check box and then use the date picker to select the day you want to stop sending the automatic replies.**

   If you don't choose the Last Day option, you'll need to remember to turn off the automatic replies manually by selecting the Vacation Responder Off radio button.

6. **In the Subject text box, enter a Subject line for your automatic replies.**
7. **In the large text box, compose the reply.**

   Feel free to spruce up your reply text with any of the formatting options that loom just above the text box.

8. **If you want Gmail to respond only to messages from folks in your contacts list, select the Only Send a Response to People in My Contacts check box.**
9. **If you want Gmail to respond only to messages from folks in your company, select the Only Send a Response to People in *Company* check box (where *Company* is the name of the place where you work).**
10. **Click Save Changes.**

Selecting messages

When you want to work with one or more messages in Gmail, you begin by selecting the message or messages you want to work with. Here are the techniques to use:

- » To select a single message, select the check box that appears to the left of the message.
- » To select multiple messages, select the check box beside each message.
- » To select all messages, select the select icon (a box, pointed out way back in Figure 2-1) or pull down the Select list and click All.
- » To select none of the messages, clear the select icon or pull down the Select list and click None.
- » To select those messages that you have read, pull down the Select list and click Read.
- » To select those messages that you haven't read yet, pull down the Select list and click Unread.

- To select those messages that have a star, pull down the Select list and click Starred.
- To select those messages that have no star, pull down the Select list and click Unstarred.

Starring a message acts as a visual reminder that the message is special in some way. To star a message, click the star icon that appears to the right of the message check box.

Dealing with the Onslaught

Do you receive a lot of email? No, really, I mean do you receive a *lot* of email? I thought so. Welcome to life in the 21st century! Email is a massive part of everyone's life these days, but the in-your-faceness of email doesn't mean that you have to let email run your life. Gmail offers quite a few tools for making email manageable. No, Gmail can't reduce the sheer volume of messages you receive every day, but you can use some techniques and tricks to put email in its place.

Cleaning out your inbox

You probably don't want your messages gumming up your inbox forever, so Gmail gives you a fistful of ways to deal with the clutter. Select the message or messages you want to work with, and then click one of the following icons (see Figure 2-14):

- **Archive:** Moves the message to the All Mail label. (To see this label, click More on Gmail's main menu and then click All Mail.)
- **Report spam:** Moves the message to the Spam label. (To see this label, click More on Gmail's main menu and then click Spam.)
- **Delete:** Moves the message to the Trash label. (To see this label, click More on Gmail's main menu and then click Trash.)
- **Move to:** Moves the message to a label you specify. If the label doesn't exist yet, click Create New in the dialog that appears. You can also drag the message from the inbox and drop it on a label on the main menu.

For more ways to get your inbox squeaky clean, see "Muting a conversation" and "Snoozing a conversation" later in this chapter.

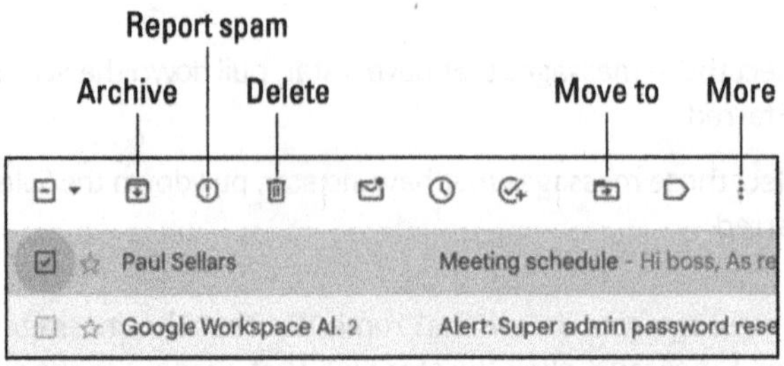

Report spam

Archive Delete Move to More

FIGURE 2-14: Commands you can run to move the selected message out of the inbox.

Labeling your messages

Earlier in this chapter, I talk about how Gmail eschews the usual email folders in favor of labels, which look and act very much like folders. However, labels are much more flexible than folders because you're free to apply multiple custom labels (but not system-generated labels such as Inbox, Sent, and Drafts) to a message. Whatever label you apply to a message, you can see that message and all the other messages that have the same label by clicking the label name on Gmail's main menu.

Gmail, bless its do-it-myself heart, often labels messages for you. For example, newly received messages automatically get the Inbox label; messages you're working on get the Drafts label; messages you've dispatched get the Sent label; and messages you've deleted get the Trash label. Gmail can also apply a label to an incoming message based on the sender, subject, or body. For example, a message from your boss or your Google Workspace administrator might get the Important label.

How do labels help you deal with your daily deluge? Essentially, labels enable you to categorize your emails in a way that makes it easy to find the ones you want to work with. If your inbox is overstuffed with a few hundred or a few thousand messages, scrolling through such a seemingly endless list to find a message from your boss can be both time-consuming and frustrating. But if you know that either you or Gmail have slapped the Important label on that message, you can head for the Important label on the main menu and the message will be there — and no doubt much easier to find because that label will have comparatively fewer messages.

Putting a label on a message

To apply a label to a message, first select the message and then use any of the following techniques:

» To remove the Important label, click the more icon (three vertical dots; see Figure 2-15) and then click Mark as Not Important.

- To apply the Important label, click the more icon and then click Mark as Important.
- To apply the Starred label, click the star icon that appears to the right of the message check box.
- To apply the Snoozed label (which I discuss in more detail a bit later in this chapter), click the snooze icon (labeled in Figure 2-15.)
- To apply the Mute label (which I discuss any minute now), click the more icon (three vertical dots) and then click Mute.
- To apply the Trash label, click the delete icon (labeled in Figure 2-15).
- To apply the Spam label, click the report spam icon (again, labeled in Figure 2-15).
- To apply any other label (including labels you make up yourself, as I discuss next), click the labels icon, select the check box of each label you want to use (refer to Figure 2-15), and then click Apply.

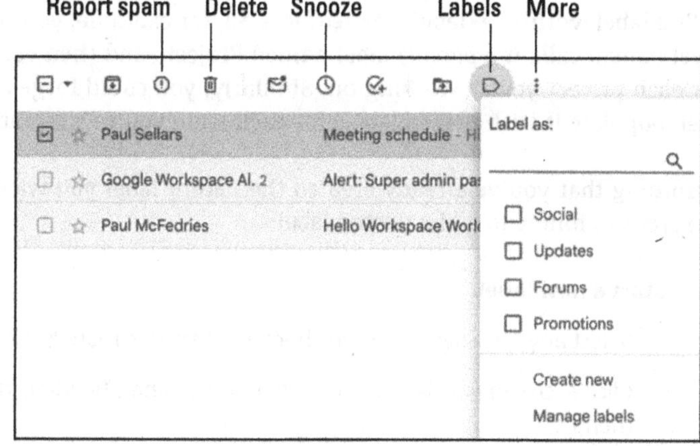

FIGURE 2-15: Click the labels icon and then select the label (or labels) you want to apply to the message.

Creating a label

Labels become truly useful when you make up your own. What labels do you need? That depends on the types of email you get, the people you correspond with, and so on. You can make up labels for people, projects, teams, departments, your current mood — whatever makes sense to you and whatever fits with your email workload.

Here are the steps to follow for creating a custom label:

1. **Start a new label.**

   Gmail gives you two main ways to get the label-making process off the ground:

   - Select any message and then choose Labels ➪ Create New.
   - Click + (create new label) to the right of the Labels heading on Gmail's main menu.

   Gmail displays the New Label dialog.

2. **In the Please Enter a New Label Name text box, type the label name.**
3. **Click Create.**

   Gmail creates your label and adds it to the Labels list.

Creating a nested label

In the same way that you can have subfolders within a folder, you can have sublabels with a label. However, rather than use the awkward term *sublabel*, Gmail calls a label-within-a-label a *nested label.* So, for example, you could create a top-level (Gmail calls it a *parent*) label named Projects and then create a nested label for each project you're working on. Similarly, you could forge a Teams label and then populate it with nested labels for each team you're a member of.

Assuming that you've already created the parent label you want to use, here are the steps to follow to add a nested label:

1. **Start a new label.**

   - Select any message and then choose Labels ➪ Create New.
   - Click + (create new label) to the right of the Labels heading in Gmail's main menu.

   Gmail conjures up the New Label dialog.

2. **Enter a name for the nested label.**
3. **Select the Nest Label Under check box.**
4. **In the Nest Label Under drop-down list, select the parent label you want to use.**

   Figure 2-16 shows an example.

5. **Click Create.**

   Gmail creates the label and nests it under the parent label.

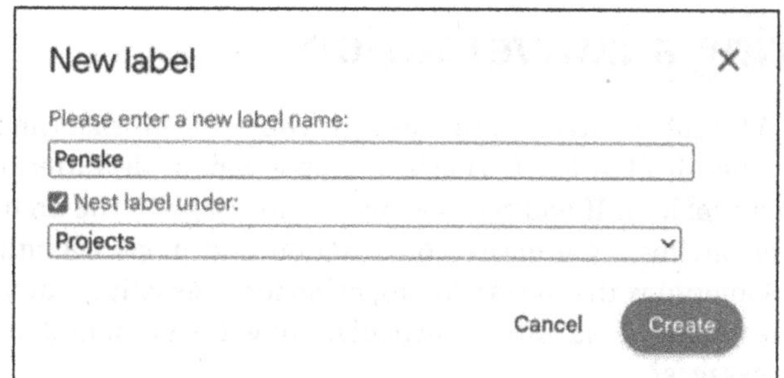

FIGURE 2-16: Select Nest Label Under and then select the parent label.

Customizing the Labels list

The main menu's Labels list contains five labels by default: Inbox, Starred, Snoozed, Sent, and Drafts. To see more labels, click More to expand the list and see all your labels. To contract the label list, click Less.

If you have a few important labels that you use frequently, it's a pain if those labels appear only in the expanded Labels list because you have to click the more icon to get at them. Forget that. Here's how to cajole Gmail into always displaying a label above the more icon:

1. **Click the gear icon (Settings), click See All Settings, and then click the Labels tab.**

   Gmail gives you two other ways to get to the Labels tab:

   - Select any message and then choose Label ⇨ Manage Labels.
   - Click More in the main menu's Labels list and then click Manage Labels near the bottom of the expanded list.

   The Labels tab displays a complete list of the predefined Gmail labels (these are in the System Labels section) and your custom labels (which you'll find in the Labels section).

2. **If you want a label to appear above the More command in the Labels list, click that label's Show link.**

   Alternatively, if you want the label to appear above the More command only if the label has one or more unread messages, click the label's Show If Unread link. (Note that the Show If Unread link is available for only some labels, including all your custom labels.)

   If a label already appears above the More link, you can remove it by clicking its Hide link.

Muting a conversation

Earlier, I talk about archiving a message, which means that Gmail moves the message to the All Mail label. That's a simple way of decluttering your inbox, but there's a problem: If you receive another message in the archived conversation, Gmail de-archives the entire conversation and plops everything back into the inbox. Sometimes that de-archiving behavior is exactly what you want, but what if you really are done with a particular conversation and don't want to see any more messages?

When an email conversation has lost its luster (assuming it had any luster to begin with), rather than archive the conversation, you need to *mute* it. When you mute a conversation, Gmail moves the original message out of your inbox and into the All Mail label, but it keeps the conversation there, no matter how many new messages pour in. Ah, silence!

If that sounds like bliss, mute the conversation by selecting it, clicking the more icon (three vertical dots), and then clicking Mute.

REMEMBER

If needed, you can always restore a silenced conversation to your inbox by opening the All Mail label, selecting the muted conversation, clicking the more icon (three vertical dots), and then clicking Unmute.

Snoozing a conversation

If an email conversation has gone off on a tangent that no longer interests you or is no longer useful to you, muting (as I describe in the preceding section) is the right strategy for keeping that conversation from clogging your inbox. However, sometimes you might want to remove a conversation from your inbox only temporarily. For example, if you're busy, you might not want a conversation's frequent notifications interrupting your train of thought.

You can remove a conversation temporarily from your inbox by using Gmail's handy snooze feature, which sends the conversation to bed until a date and time you specify. The conversation is still available in the Snoozed label, should you need to check in.

To snooze a conversation, follow these steps:

1. **Select the conversation's check box.**
2. **Click the snooze icon (shown in the margin).**

   Gmail displays the Snooze Until menu, which looks an awful lot like the one shown in Figure 2-17.

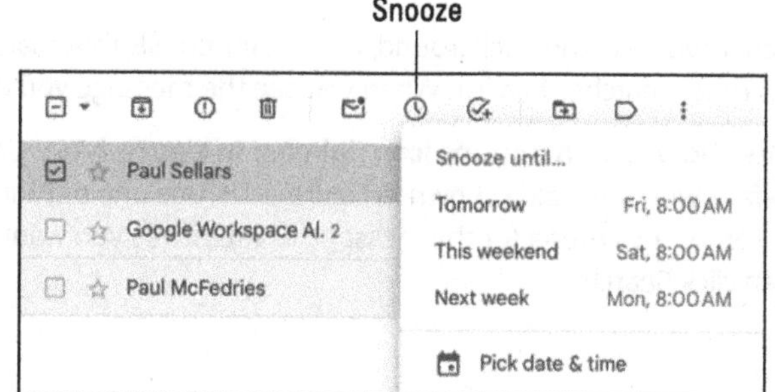

FIGURE 2-17: Use the Snooze Until options to set an end time for the conversation's nap.

3. **If you see a date and time that works for you, click it and skip the rest of this procedure.**
4. **Click Pick Date & Time.**

   Gmail opens the Pick Date & Time dialog, which offers a calendar and a time text box.
5. **In the calendar, select the date on which you want the snooze period to end.**
6. **In the text box, enter the time you want the snooze to end.**
7. **Click Save.**

   Gmail makes a note to restore your conversation on the date and time you specified.

REMEMBER

To wake up a snoozed conversation, open the Snoozed label, select the snoozed conversation, click Snooze, and then click Unsnooze.

Searching for messages

There's a good chance you have a scarily large number of email messages squirreled away in Gmail's nooks and crannies. Even if you've moved messages out of your inbox and into one or more labels, deleted messages you don't want, and reported all that spam, finding a particular message is often a real needle-in-a-haystack exercise. Fortunately, Gmail comes with a power Search tool that can help you quickly and easily find any message anywhere in Gmail.

You search Gmail using the big Search Mail text box at the top of the page. You can use one of these two methods:

- **Enter some text in the text box.** You can enter a word, part of a word, or a phrase that matches the content of the message you want to find. As you type, Gmail works in the background, looking for emails that match, and then displays those matches in a list. When you see the message you want, click it.

» **Click the show search options icon (labeled in Figure 2-18).** Gets you face-to-face with the dialog shown in Figure 2-18. Use one or more of the fields to enter the criteria for the message or messages you want to locate, and then click Search.

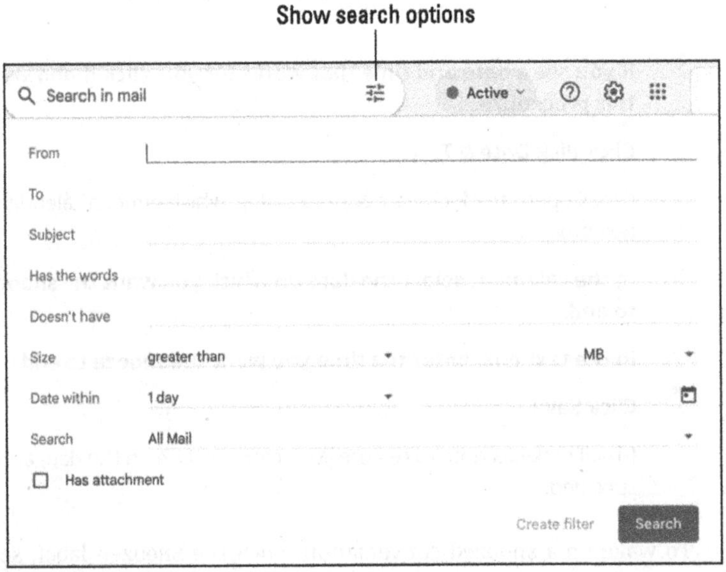

FIGURE 2-18: Click the show search options icon to use this dialog for more targeted searches.

Filtering your messages

One reason that email dominates everyone's lives is that it requires so much maintenance: moving, archiving, labeling, starring, forwarding, deleting, and on and on. Take applying labels, for example. In theory, labeling messages is a great way to keep your email organized, but it soon becomes a chore to apply labels to the majority of your messages.

You might have noticed that labeling and other email chores feel burdensome partly because you repeat the same task over and over. That repetitiveness is good news because it means you can foist some of the work on Gmail. Specifically, you can create a filter that looks for messages that meet certain criteria and then runs one or more actions on any messages that match, such as applying a label, starring, or deleting.

It's a sweet technique, and once you start using it, you'll wonder how you ever lived without it. The good news is that if you already know how to search your email, as I describe in the preceding section, you're halfway home because that's how you begin a filter. Here are the steps:

1. **Click the show search options icon, shown in the margin.**
2. **Use one or more of the fields to enter the criteria for your filter.**

   Remember that Gmail applies your filter to any incoming message that matches your criteria.

TIP

   If you're creating a rule based on the address of an existing message, you can save yourself a bit of time by opening the message, clicking the message's more icon, and then clicking Filter Messages Like This. Gmail opens the criteria dialog with the From line filled in automatically with the address of the sender.

3. **Click Create Filter.**

   Gmail opens the dialog shown in Figure 2-19.

← When a message is an exact match for your search criteria:

- [ ] Skip the Inbox (Archive it)
- [ ] Mark as read
- [x] Star it
- [x] Apply the label: Projects/Penske
- [ ] Forward it Add forwarding address
- [ ] Delete it
- [ ] Never send it to Spam
- [ ] Always mark it as important
- [ ] Never mark it as important
- [ ] Categorize as: Choose category...
- [ ] Also apply filter to 0 matching conversations.

Learn more | Create filter

FIGURE 2-19: Use this dialog to tell Gmail which actions to perform on incoming messages that match your criteria.

4. **Select the check box beside an action you want Gmail to perform on any incoming message that matches your criteria.**
5. **If the action requires more info, enter that info.**

   For example, if you select the Apply the Label check box, use the Choose Label list to select the label you want Gmail to apply to the matching message.

6. **Repeat Steps 4 and 5 until you've defined all the actions you want to run on the matching message.**
7. **Click Create Filter.**

   Gmail creates the filter and starts looking for incoming messages that match.

TIP

If you want to create a filter that automatically deletes messages from a certain person, an easier method is to open a message from that person, click the message's more icon, and then click Block *Name*, where *Name* is the name of the person bothering you.

REMEMBER

To manage your filters, click the gear icon (Settings), click See All Settings, and then click the Filters and Blocked Address tab. From there, you can edit a filter, delete a filter, and create new filters.

IN THIS CHAPTER

» Touring the Calendar app

» Navigating dates in Calendar

» Scheduling appointments, get-togethers, and other events

» Creating all-day and repeating events

» Designing tasks in Calendar

Chapter 3

Places to Go, People to See: Managing Your Calendar

It seems almost redundant to describe modern life as busy. Everyone is working harder, cramming more appointments and meetings into already packed schedules, and somehow finding the time to get their regular work done between crises. As many a management consultant has advised over the years (charging exorbitant fees to do so), the key to surviving this helter-skelter, pell-mell pace is time management. And although there are as many theories about time management as there are consultants, one key is that you should always try to make the best use of the time available. Although that often comes down to self-discipline and prioritizing your tasks, an efficient scheduling system can certainly help.

That's where Google Workspace's Calendar app comes in because it offers a great way to manage your bee-busy schedule. You can use Calendar to create items called *events*, which represent your appointments, vacations, trips, meetings, and anything else that can be scheduled. Calendar is the place where you can safely and handily store all your events, which is great news because getting all those dates, times, and places out of your head leaves your brain free to concentrate on more important duties. In this chapter, you explore the most useful features and settings of the Calendar app.

Navigating the Calendar Window

Calendar is a sort of electronic personal assistant that, while it won't get coffee for you, will at least help you keep your schedule on track. You can use this simple electronic day planner to keep track of appointments, meetings, tasks, and other commitments. So, whether you have a date and you can't be late or you have a rendezvous you need to remember, Calendar can handle it.

Assuming you have no pressing appointments (although even if you do, you're still in the right place!), get started now by doing one of the following:

- Point the nearest web browser to `https://calendar.google.com`.
- In any Google Workspace app, click the grid-like Google apps icon (pointed out in Figure 3-1) and then click Calendar.

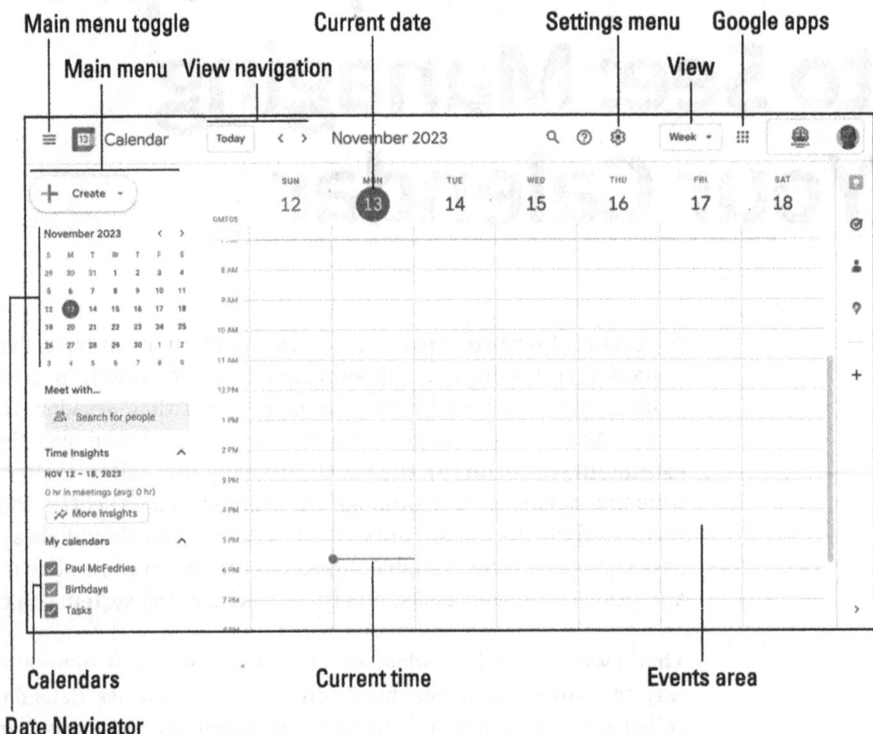

FIGURE 3-1: Calendar: Your Google Workspace scheduling assistant.

Sign in to your Google account, if asked. You end up face-to-face with the Calendar app, which will appear quite a bit like the one shown in Figure 3-1.

Calendar is laid out more or less like a day planner or desk calendar (assuming you're old enough to remember those relics of a bygone era). There's quite a lot to examine here, so this is a good time to step back and check out the main features of the Calendar screen. (Handily, Figure 3-1 points out the features in the list that follows.)

- **Main menu:** Displays the following elements:
  - *Date Navigator:* Shows one month at a time (usually, the current month). You use Date Navigator to change the date displayed in the events area. Note that today's date always has a blue circle around it.
  - *Meet with:* Enables you to search for people in the Contacts app so that you can set up a meeting with them (refer to Chapter 13).
  - *My Calendars:* Lists the calendars that the app is using to display events. Most people use just a single calendar (the one with your name), but you might want separate calendars for, say, business use and personal use. Your Google Workspace account also comes with a Birthdays calendar (based on the birthdays you enter in the Contacts app) and a Holidays calendar for your country (Holidays appears in the Other Calendars section, not shown in Figure 3-1; you need to scroll the main menu down to display that section).
- **Main menu toggle:** Hides the main menu, which gives you a bit more horizontal space for Calendar. Click the icon again to display the main menu.
- **View navigation:** Enables you to change the date or dates shown in the main Calendar window based on the current view (refer to the "View" item, later in this list).
- **Settings menu:** Gives you access to all the Calendar settings.
- **View:** Displays a list of the different ways you can view dates in the main Calendar window. For example, you can view dates by day, week, month, or year.
- **Google apps:** Displays icons for all Google apps.
- **Current date:** Marks today's date on the calendar.
- **Current time:** Indicates the current time and moves down as the day progresses.
- **Events area:** Shows the appointments and meetings you schedule.

Changing the Calendar View

By default, Calendar uses week view in the events area, which shows a week's worth of appointments and meetings. However, Calendar is flexible and has several other views you can use. Here's the complete list:

- **Day:** Displays a single day's worth of events. In the View list, click Day (or press D).

  TIP

  You can switch to day view and simultaneously navigate to a specific date by clicking that date's day number in week view or month view. You can also do this in Year view, but that requires two separate clicks (not a double-click, though!) on the day number.

- **Week:** Displays Sunday through Saturday for the current week. In the view list, click Week (or press W).

  TIP

  By default, Calendar uses Sunday as the first day of the week. If Monday feels to you like the true start of the week, you can configure Calendar to oblige. Click the gear icon (Settings menu), click Settings, and then click View Options. In the Start Week On list, select Monday. (Note that you can alternatively choose Saturday as the starting day, if that floats your boat.)

- **Month:** Displays the current month. In the View list, click Month (or press M).
- **Year:** Displays the current year. In the View list, click Year (or press Y).

  TIP

  In most multiday views, Calendar includes weekends. If you use Calendar exclusively for work, you might never schedule anything on a Saturday or Sunday, so you can get a bit more room in the Events area by excluding weekends for the view. On the View menu, deselect the Show Weekends command.

- **Schedule:** Displays a list of your upcoming events. In the View list, click Schedule (or press A).
- **4 days:** Displays four days' worth of events. In the View list, click 4 Days (or press X).

TIP

The 4 days view is a custom view you can modify to display whatever number of days suits your style. To change this view, click the gear icon (Settings menu), click Settings, and then click View Options. In the Set Custom View list, select the number of days or weeks you want Calendar to display in the view.

Time Traveling: Changing the Date

Calendar usually opens with the current week displayed and today's date selected. However, if you want to work with a different day, Date Navigator makes it easy: Just click a date and Calendar immediately adjusts the events area to display that date in whatever view you're currently using.

Date Navigator starts off displaying the current month, but if you need to navigate to a date in a different month, use either of the following techniques to pick a different month:

- **Click the previous month arrow** (pointed out in Figure 3-2) to move backward one month at a time.
- **Click the next month arrow** (again, check out Figure 3-2) to move forward one month at a time.

FIGURE 3-2: In Date Navigator, use the previous month and next month arrows to display the month you want.

You can also navigate the current view by using the following techniques:

- **To move forward to the next period of the current view:** Click the next *period* arrow (refer to Figure 3-3), where *period* is the current view setting: Day, Week, Month, Year, or 4 Days. (For this last view, the arrow title is Next Period.)
- **To move backward to the previous period of the current view:** Click the previous *period* arrow (check out Figure 3-3), where *period* is the current view setting: Day, Week, Month, Year, or 4 Days. (For this last view, the arrow title is Previous Period.)
- **To navigate the current view so that it includes today's date:** Click Today.

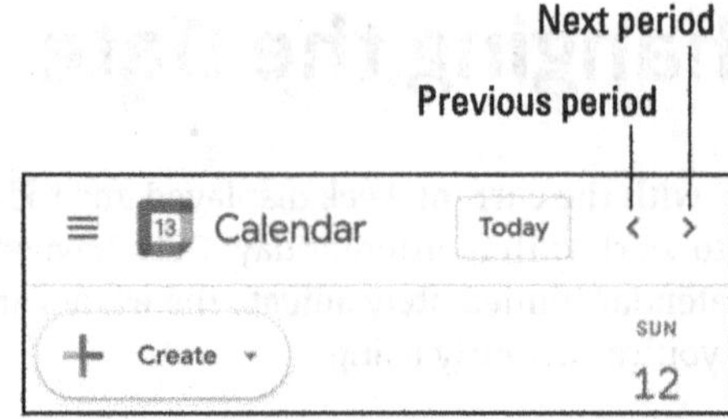

FIGURE 3-3: Use the view navigation controls to navigate the current view.

Setting Your Social Schedule: Entering Events

Got a party to plan, a meeting to make, or a lunch to linger over? The gadabouts, hobnobbers, and other social butterflies in the crowd will like how easy Calendar makes it to schedule these and other get-togethers.

Before getting down to scheduling details, you should know that Calendar lets you create two kinds of events:

- **Event:** An event is the most general Calendar item. It refers to any activity for which you set aside a block of time. Typical events include a lunch date, a trip to the dentist or doctor, or a back waxing appointment. You can also create recurring appointments that are scheduled at regular intervals (such as weekly or monthly).
- **All-day event:** An all-day event is any activity that consumes one or more entire days. Examples include conferences, trade shows, vacations, and mental-health days. In Calendar, all-day events don't occupy blocks of time. Instead, they appear as banners above the affected days. You can also schedule recurring all-day events.

The next few sections show you how to create events and all-day events.

Adding an event

Here are the steps you need to trudge through to set up an event:

1. **Navigate to the date on which the event occurs.**
2. **Switch to either day view or week view.**

3. **Select the time you want to set aside for the event.**

   If the event is an hour long, click the time in the events area when the event begins. (If you're in week view, be sure to click the time under the date the event occurs.) For example, if the event starts at noon, click the 12 P.M. line; if the event starts at 3:30 P.M., click halfway between the 3 P.M. and 4 P.M. lines.

   When you click a time in the events area, Calendar creates an hourlong event. If that hourlong default works for you, then feel free to skip over the next couple of sentences. Otherwise, you can set up a different default duration. Click the Settings menu icon (shown in the margin), and then click Event Settings. In the Default Duration list, select the number of minutes you prefer Calendar to use as the default whenever you create an event.

   For all other event durations, move the mouse pointer to the start time of the event (again, in week view, make sure you're under the correct date), and then drag the mouse pointer down until you reach the end time for the event. As you drag, Calendar helpfully displays the starting and ending times, as shown in Figure 3-4.

   REMEMBER

   Don't worry too much if you don't get the time exactly right; you'll get a chance to fix both the start time and the end time in a sec.

   After all that work, Calendar displays the dialog shown in Figure 3-5, which is already filled in with the event's start and end information. This information consists of three fields, which are, from left to right, the event date, the start time, and the end time.

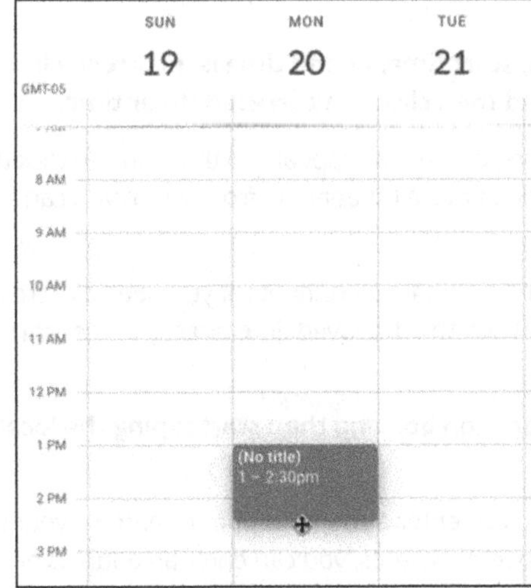

FIGURE 3-4: Drag down in the Events area to specify the event's start and end times.

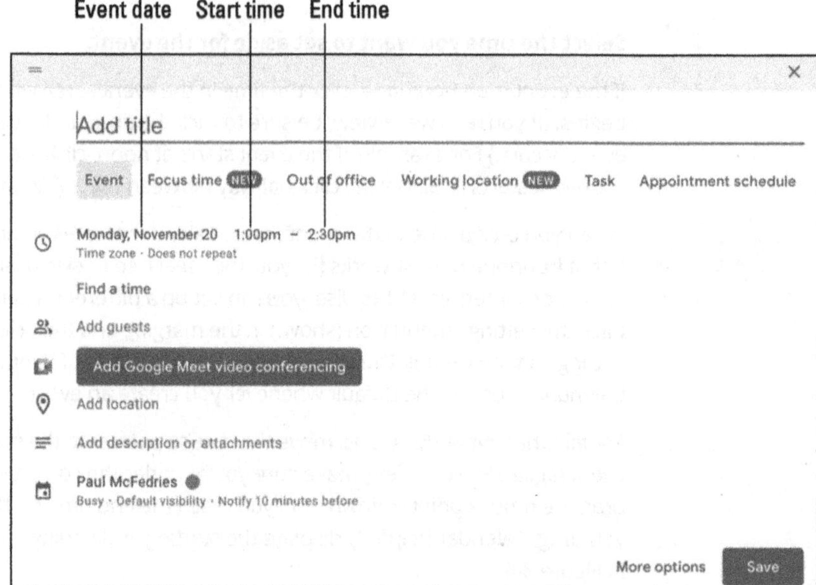

FIGURE 3-5: The dialog for a basic event, with the starting and ending dates and times filled in.

4. **In the Add Title text box, type a title that describes your event.**

   For many events, you don't need to add anything else, so if that's the case for you, go ahead and jump down to Step 8 to finish.

   Otherwise, continue with Step 5 to fill in more event details.

   If you're seeking info on how to invite guests to your event, mosey on over to Chapter 12.

5. **If the event's date, start time, or end time is incorrect, click the info you want to change and then click the correct date or time.**

   When you click a date, a calendar appears so that you can click the correct date. When you click a time, a list appears from which you can select the correct time.

   TIP

   The list of times is in 15-minute increments. If you need a more exact start time or end time, you can edit the displayed time directly in the Start Time and End Time fields.

6. **Click in the Add Location box and then start typing the location for the event.**

   For the location, you can enter a room number or name if your event takes place at work. For external events, you can enter an address or a business name (such as a restaurant). As you type the name, Calendar displays a list of locations that match (refer to Figure 3-6), so if your location shows up, you can stop typing and click the location to add it.

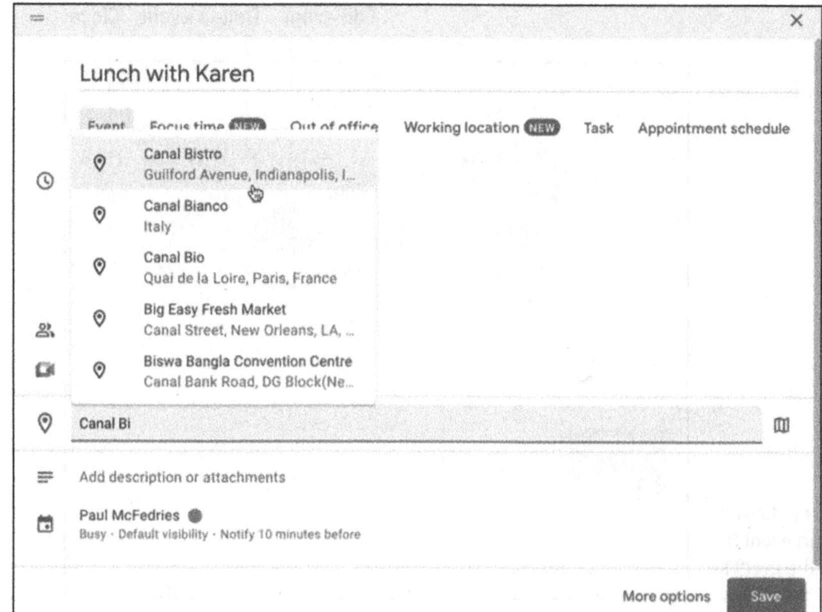

FIGURE 3-6: As you type a name in the Location text box, Calendar displays a list of matching locations.

7. **In the Add Description text box, type a summary of what the event is about.**

   Feel free to use the Add Description text box to also enter anything else you think might be pertinent to the event: details to note, things to remember, tales to tell, and so on.

8. **Click Save.**

   Calendar adds the event to the events area.

Editing an event

If anything changes about your event — the start or end time, the location, whatever — you can follow these steps to make some adjustments:

1. **Navigate to the date of the event.**
2. **In the events area, click the event.**

   Calendar displays the event summary dialog box, which will have a family resemblance to the one shown in Figure 3-7.

3. **Click the pencil icon (edit event), pointed out in Figure 3-7.**
4. **Make whatever changes you need for the event.**
5. **Click Save.**

   Calendar updates the event with your changes.

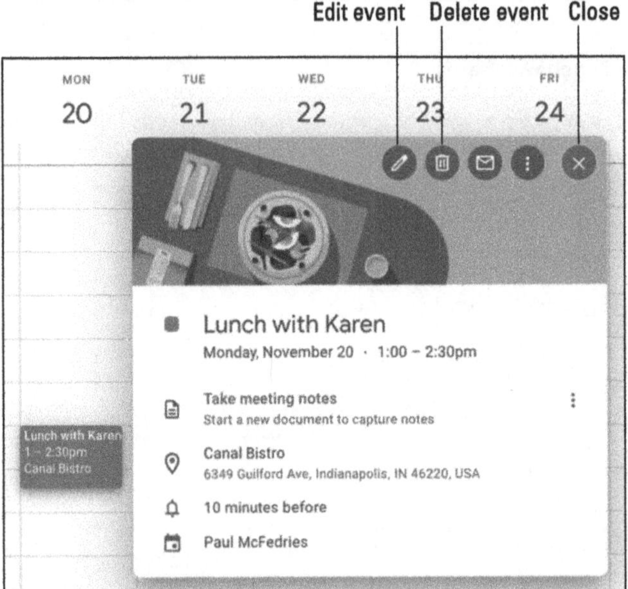

FIGURE 3-7: Click an event to read the event's summary.

You can also use the event's summary dialog box to remove the event from your calendar by clicking the trash can icon (delete event), labeled in Figure 3-7.

Lather, rinse, repeat: Creating a repeating event

One of the truly great timesavers in Calendar is the repeat feature. It enables you to set up a single event and then get Calendar to automatically repeat it at a regular interval. For example, if your team dance party occurs every Friday at 5:00, you can set up that event for the next Friday and then tell Calendar to automatically repeat it every Friday at the same time. You can continue repeating events indefinitely or end them on a specific date. Repeat after me: The repeat feature is both handy and dandy!

Here are the steps to follow to set up a repeating event:

1. **Navigate to the date on which the event occurs.**
2. **Switch to either day view or week view.**
3. **Select the time you want to set aside for the event:**
   - *If the event is an hour long:* In the Events area, click the time when the event begins.

- *For all other event durations:* In the Events area, move the mouse pointer to the start time of the event, and then drag the mouse pointer down until you reach the end time for the event.

4. **In the Add Title text box, type a title that describes your event.**
5. **If the event's start date, start time, or end time is incorrect, click the info you want to change and then click the correct date or time.**
6. **In the Add Location box, specify the location for the event.**
7. **In the Add Description text box, type a summary of the event.**
8. **Click More Options — the button to the left of the Save button.**

   Calendar displays all the event details.
9. **Click the Does Not Repeat value to open the list of repeat intervals.**

   The items in the list vary, depending on the date of your event. Figure 3-8 shows an example.

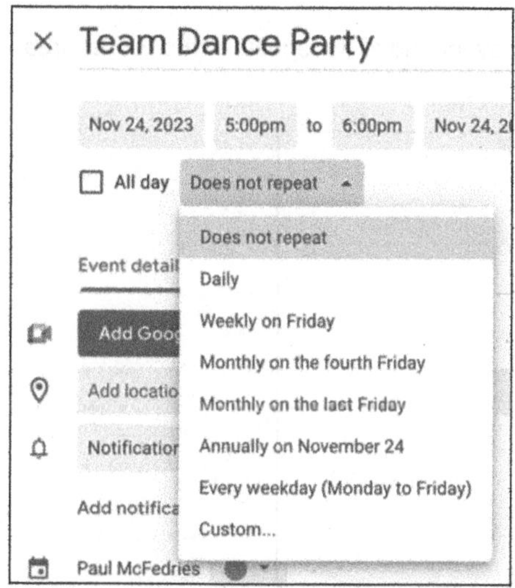

FIGURE 3-8: Calendar offers several default repeat intervals.

10. **Click the item that corresponds to the repeat interval you want to use.**

    If none of the default intervals is quite right or you want to specify when the recurrence ends, click Custom to open the Custom Recurrence dialog box, shown in Figure 3-9. Begin by specifying the Repeat Every *X Units* options, where *X* is how often you want the event to repeat and *Units* is one of the following:

- *Day or Days:* The number of days between each occurrence of the event.
- *Week or Weeks:* The number of weeks between each occurrence of the event. Use the Repeat On control to click the day of the week on which you want the event to recur.
- *Month or Months:* The number of months between each occurrence of the event. In the Monthly On Day list (which appears only after you select Months in the list), select the day of the month on which you want the event to recur.
- *Year or Years:* The number of years between each occurrence of the event.

Use the controls in the Ends section to specify when you want the repeating to stop. Select the Never radio button to keep repeating the event until the end of time; select the On radio button to specify the last date of the recurrence; or select the After radio button to specify the total number of repeats you want. Click Done when you're, you know, done.

11. **Click Save.**

Calendar adds the event and all its repeats to the Events area.

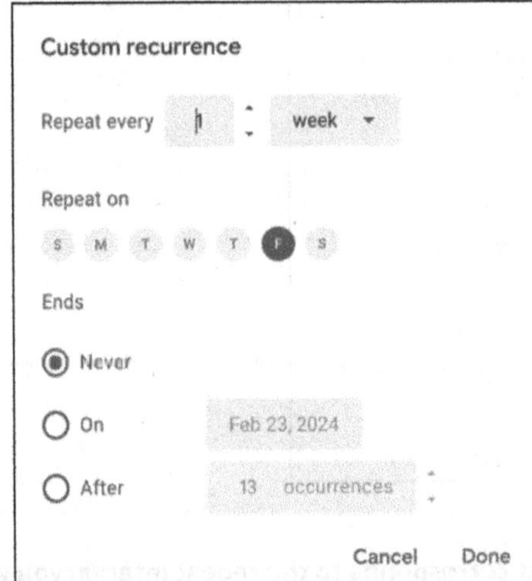

FIGURE 3-9: In the Custom Recurrence dialog box, set up a repeat interval that works for you.

Scheduling an all-day event

As I mention earlier in this chapter, an *all-day* event is an activity that consumes one or more days. (Or, at least, the working part of those days; you do have a life outside of work, right?) Some activities are obvious all-day events: trade shows, sales meetings, corporate retreats, and so on. But what about, say, a training session that lasts from 9 A.M. to 4 P.M.? Is that an all-day event or just a really long event?

From Calendar's point of view, the main difference between an event and an all-day event is that an event is entered as a time block in the Events area, but an all-day event is displayed as a banner in the time zone area at the top of the Events area. (See Figure 3-10.) This means that you can also schedule events on days that you have all-day events.

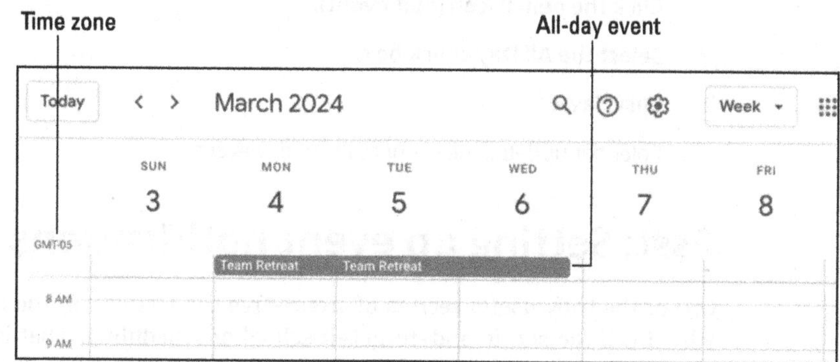

FIGURE 3-10: All-day events appear at the top of the Events area.

A good example that illustrates these differences is a trade show. Suppose that the show lasts an entire day, and you're a sales rep who will attend the show. Sure, you *could* schedule the show as a day-long event. However, what if you also want to visit with customers who are attending the show? It's possible to schedule conflicting events, but having that daylong event in there just clutters the Events area. In this case, it makes more sense to schedule the show as an all-day event. This leaves the Events area open for you to schedule events with your customers.

Calendar offers a couple of ways to schedule an all-day event:

- *For a single-day event:* Navigate to the date, switch to day view, and then click inside the time zone area. (The time zone area is the narrow strip under the date, as pointed out in Figure 3-10, and is labeled either GMT-*X* or GMT+*X*, where *X* is the number of hours earlier or later, respectively, your time zone is from Greenwich Mean Time, or GMT.) Alternatively, switch to month view, navigate to the month of the event, and then click the date of the event.
- *For a multiday event:* Navigate to the dates, switch to week view, and then click-and-drag across the time zone area for each day of the event. Alternatively, switch to month view and then click-and-drag across each day of the event.

Either way, Calendar automatically creates an all-day event, and all you need to do is fill in a title and any other event options you need.

What if you've already set up a regular event and you want to turn it into an all-day event? Calendar has you covered:

1. **Navigate to the date of the event.**
2. **In the Events area, click the event to open the event's summary dialog box.**
3. **Click the pencil icon (edit event).**
4. **Select the All Day check box.**
5. **Click Save.**

   Calendar updates the event to an all-day event.

Psst: Setting up event notifications

One of the truly useful secrets of stress-free productivity in the modern world is what I call the set-it-and-forget-it school of scheduling. That is, you set up an event electronically and then get the same technology to remind you when the event occurs. That way, your mind doesn't have to waste energy fretting about missing the event, because you know your technology has your back.

With Google Workspace, the technology of choice for doing this is Calendar and its notifications feature. When you add a notification to an event, Calendar automatically displays a reminder of the event in the form of a pop-up window, similar to the one shown in Figure 3-11.

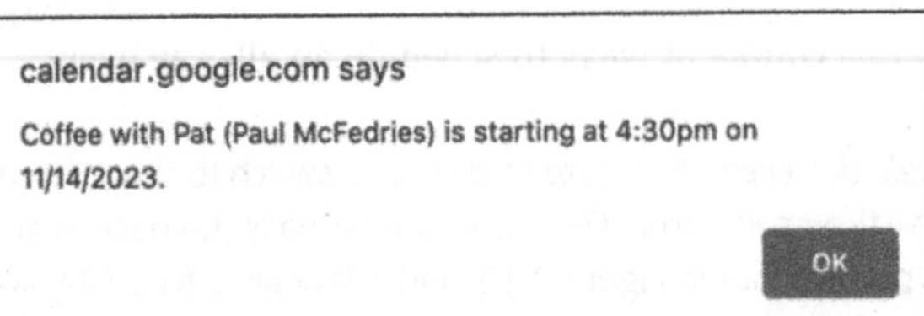

calendar.google.com says
Coffee with Pat (Paul McFedries) is starting at 4:30pm on 11/14/2023.
OK

FIGURE 3-11: An example of a Calendar notification.

By default, Calendar sets up all regular events with a notification that appears 10 minutes before the event. Here are the steps to march through to set up a custom event notification.

1. **Create the event as I describe earlier in this chapter, in the section "Adding an event."**

   If you want to modify an existing event, navigate to the date of the event, click the event to open the event's summary dialog box, and then click the pencil icon (edit event). Skip to Step 3.

2. **Click More Options to open the event details.**

   The Event Details tab includes a notification area, the particulars of which are pointed out in Figure 3-12.

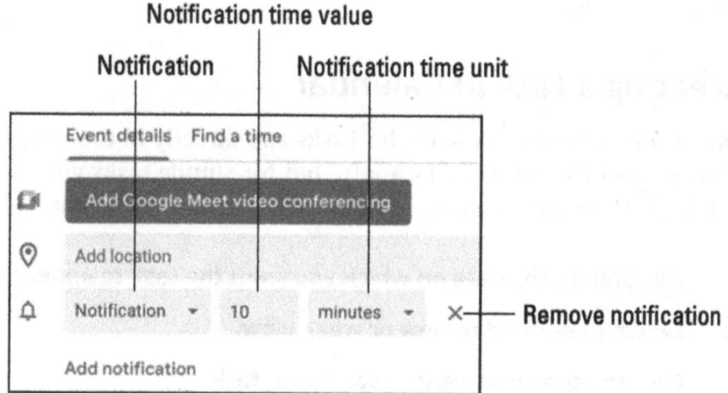

FIGURE 3-12: In the notification area, set up your custom notification.

3. **Select a time unit: Minutes, Hours, Days, or Weeks.**

   Minutes is selected in Figure 3-12.

4. **Use the spin box to set the time value.**

   To display the spin box, move your pointer over the time (which is 10 in Figure 3-12).

5. **To add another notification (hey, you can't be too careful these days), click Add Notification and then repeat Steps 3 and 4 for the new notification that shows up.**

6. **Click Save.**

   Calendar updates the event with your custom notification.

TIP

The default notification is a web browser pop-up window, but you can choose to have your notification emailed to your Gmail address. To switch to the Email Notification type, follow Steps 1 and 2 in the preceding list, and then select Email in the Notification list (refer to Figure 3-12).

Things to do: Creating a task

One of the secrets of modern-day productivity (and sanity) is a simple maxim: Get all the tasks you need to do out of your head and into some kind of recorded form. That way, you can stop endlessly ruminating on everything you need to do because now you know those tasks are safely recorded and can't be forgotten.

In days of yore, the medium of choice for recording tasks was the venerable paper to-do list. You can still go that classic route, if you choose, but your Google Workspace account comes with a Tasks app that you can use to maintain an electronic to-do list for all those seemingly endless chores and responsibilities that litter your days.

Creating a task in Calendar

I show you how to work with the Tasks app directly in the next section (check out "Creating a task in the Tasks app"), but for simple tasks you can work directly in Calendar. Here are the steps to follow to create a new task in Calendar:

1. **Navigate to the date on which you want the task to appear.**
2. **Switch to either day view or week view.**
3. **Click the time you want to start your task.**
4. **In the Add Title box, enter a title for the task.**
5. **Click the Task tab.**

   Calendar switches to the interface shown in Figure 3-13.

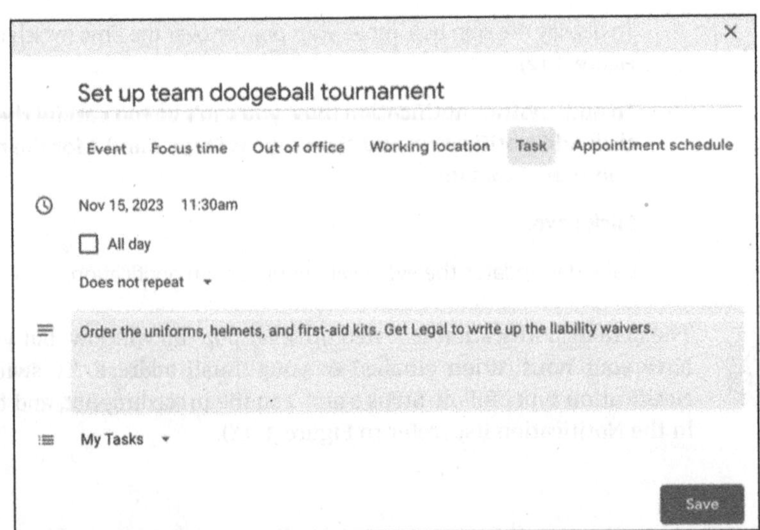

FIGURE 3-13: Use the Task tab to set up a task in Calendar.

6. **If the task's time is incorrect, click the time and then either edit it to the correct time or choose the time you want from the list.**
7. **If you want the tasks to appear on your calendar (and in your schedule view) but not at a particular time, select the All Day check box.**
8. **In the Add Description text box, enter a summary of what the task is about.**
9. **Click Save.**

   Calendar adds the task to the Events area and to the Tasks app.

TIP

If you don't want tasks littering Calendar's Events area, you can hide your tasks by deselecting the Tasks check box in the My Calendars section of the main menu.

Creating a task in the Tasks app

You can also use the Tasks app directly to add a task. One benefit you get with the Tasks app is the ability to create one or more *subtasks*, which are tasks performed within another task. For example, a task titled Organize Trip to Vanuatu might include subtasks such as Purchase Plane Tickets, Book Hotel Room, and Find Out Where Vanuatu Is.

Here are the steps to follow to create a new task using the Tasks app:

1. **In Calendar's side panel, click Tasks.**

   Calendar opens the Tasks pane, which appears uncannily similar to the one shown in Figure 3-14.

REMEMBER

As I mention in Chapter 2, in the section about taming the email beast, Gmail's side panel also has a Tasks icon, so you can also follow these same steps to create a task when you're working in Gmail.

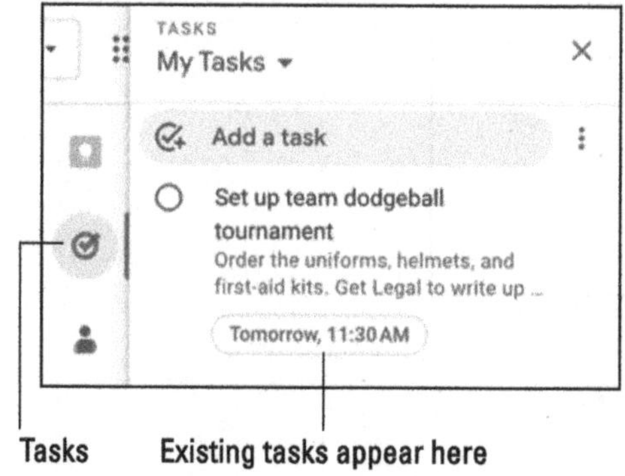

FIGURE 3-14: Clicking the Tasks icon opens the Tasks pane.

2. **Click Add a Task.**

   Tasks creates a new task with a text box ready for editing.

3. **Enter a title for the task.**
4. **If you don't need to specify anything else about the task (such as the time you want to start the task), press Enter or Return and skip the rest of these steps.**
5. **Click Details.**

   Tasks opens the Details text box for editing.

6. **In the Details text box, enter a summary of what the task is about.**
7. **To add a date or time or both for the task, click Date/Time, click a date, enter a time, and then click OK.**
8. **To create a subtask, click the task options icon (three vertical dots, labeled in Figure 3-15), click Add a Subtask, and then type the subtask title.**
9. **Repeat Step 8 for each subtask you want to add.**

   Figure 3-15 shows a task with a few subtasks added.

10. **Click X (close tasks) in the top-right corner of the task details pane.**

    Calendar closes the Tasks pane.

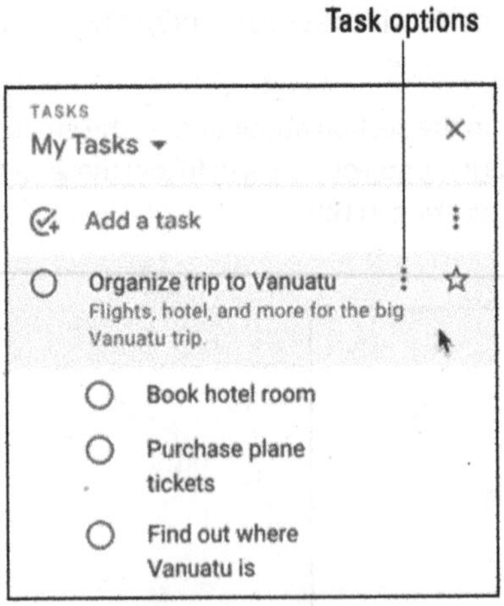

FIGURE 3-15: A task with several subtasks.

Going Calendar Crazy: Adding Even More Calendars

The Calendar app comes with four calendars right out of the box: one each for your events and tasks; a Birthdays calendar for birthdays listed in Contacts; and a Holidays calendar for your country. That's a lot of calendars, but it's not every calendar you can display, not by a long shot. You can add all kinds of calendars.

Most of the calendars you can add belong to other people, so I talk about that topic in detail in Chapter 12. For now, though, you can create one or more other calendars for your own use. For example, you might want to use the original calendar for business events only and create a second calendar for personal stuff.

Here's how to create a calendar:

1. **On Calendar's main menu, click the add other calendars icon (shown in the margin), which appears to the right of the Other Calendars heading.**

   Calendar displays a menu of commands.

2. **Click Create New Calendar.**

   Calendar opens Settings and displays the Create New Calendar section, as shown in Figure 3-16.

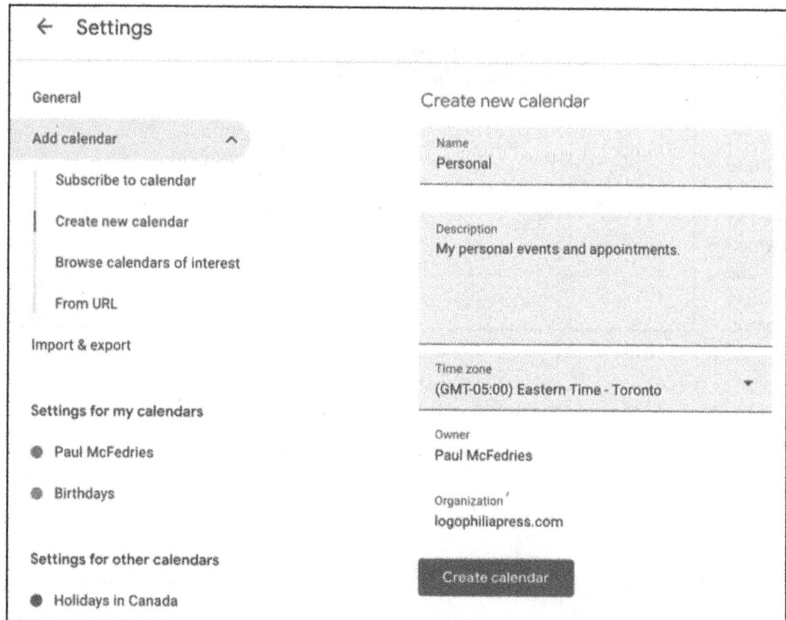

FIGURE 3-16: In the Create New Calendar section, set up your calendar.

3. **In the Name text box, type a name for your new calendar.**

4. **(Optional) In the Description box, type a description of your calendar.**

5. **In the Time Zone list, select the time zone you want to use with this calendar.**

6. **Click Create Calendar.**

Calendar creates the calendar. Click the back icon (shown in the margin) to return to the Calendar page and see the new calendar in the My Calendars list.

With your new calendar up and running, you now have an extra step to negotiate when you create an event. As shown in Figure 3-17, the Event tab now includes a list of your event calendars, and you need to select the calendar in which you want the event to appear.

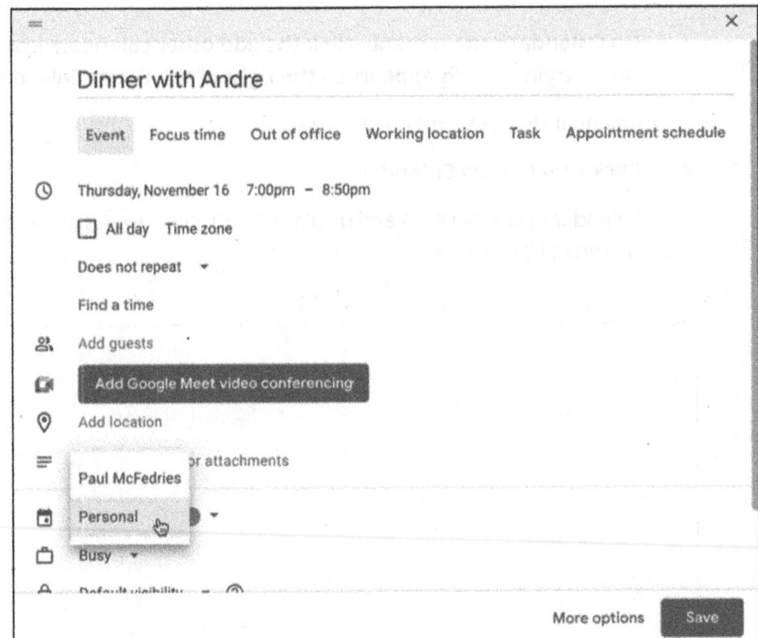

FIGURE 3-17: With multiple calendars on the go, you need to select which calendar to use for each new event.

IN THIS CHAPTER

» Taking a tour of the Contacts app

» Putting people on your contacts list

» Editing, grouping, merging, and other necessary contact tasks

» Emailing and calling contacts

Chapter 4

Friends, Romans, Countrymen: Managing Your Contacts

The Contacts app is your Google Workspace address book, where you can store all kinds of useful (and even useless) information about your ever-growing network of colleagues, clients, friends, family, acquaintances, high school classmates, and anyone else who falls within the borders of your social circle. You can use Contacts to store mundane information such as phone numbers and email addresses, but with its over 30 predefined fields available, you can also preserve the minutiae of other people's lives: their birthdays and anniversaries, the names of their spouses and children, their nicknames, and even their web page addresses.

This chapter takes you inside the Contacts app and shows you how to add and edit contacts, import contact data from other programs, and customize the app.

Eyeballing the Contacts App

Let's get right down to business. You have a couple of ways to get started:

- » Point the nearest web browser to `https://contacts.google.com`.
- » In any Google Workspace app, click Google Apps (pointed out in Figure 4-1) and then click Contacts.

Then sign in to your Google account, if asked, and you end up with the Contacts app staring back at you, as shown in Figure 4-1.

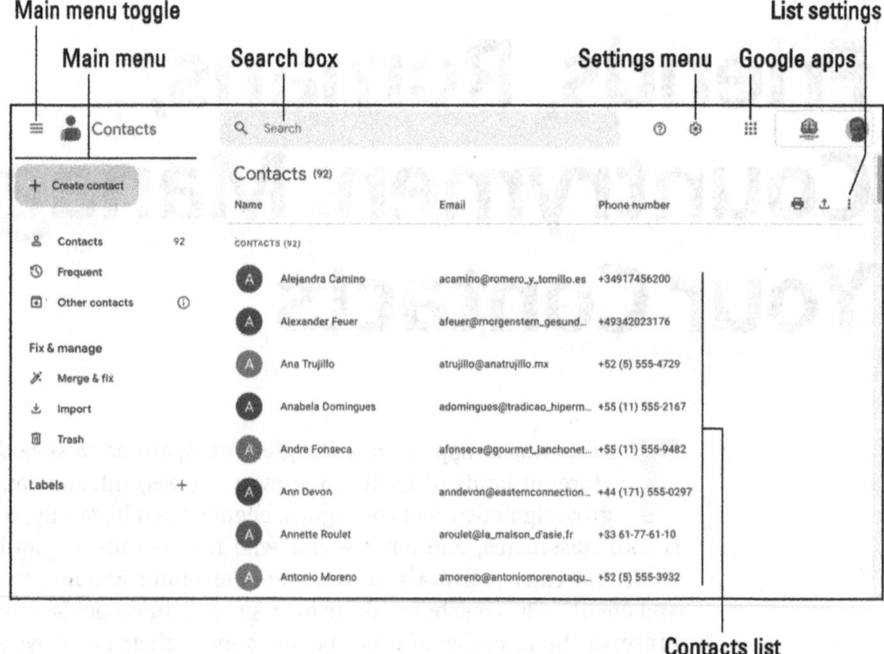

FIGURE 4-1: Contacts: Your Google Workspace address book.

Contacts is laid out as a simple list of people's names and email addresses, making it a kind of digital Rolodex. There's quite a lot on the Contacts screen, so let's step back and check out its main features (handily, Figure 4-1 points out the features in the list that follows):

- » **Main menu:** Displays a few important Contacts elements. For now I'll point out just the following landmarks:
  - *Contacts:* Returns you to your main Contacts list
  - *Frequent:* Displays a list of the people you correspond with most often

- *Other Contacts:* Displays people you've contacted who aren't in your Contacts list
- **Main menu toggle:** Hides the main menu, which gives you a bit more horizontal space for Contacts. Click the icon again to display the main menu.
- **Search box:** Enables you to search for a particular contact.
- **Settings menu:** Gives you access to all the Contacts settings.
- **Google apps:** Displays icons for all Google apps.
- **Contacts list:** Displays your contacts.

What's with those "other" contacts?

The Contacts main menu includes an item named Other Contacts. Who are these people, and why does Contacts separate them from the herd? The addresses (and sometimes names) that appear in this section are tossed here by Gmail when you send an original message, reply to a message, or forward a message to someone who isn't in Contacts.

Why would Gmail perform this apparently senseless behavior? Because Gmail wants to do everything in its power to make your life easier, and one of those things is the auto-complete feature. When you start typing an email address or a person's name in the To, CC, or BCC field, auto-complete monitors your typing and displays matching people from the Contacts app. If the person you want appears in the list, stop typing, select the name, and press Tab (or Enter or Return).

Auto-complete is a sweet, can't-live-without-it feature. Here's the good news: When Gmail is auto-completing an address, it checks not only your main contacts list but *also* the Other Contacts list. That way, even if you've emailed someone only once and a long time ago, that person's email address shows up during the auto-complete and your life is just a tad easier.

So that's why Gmail adds the addresses of one-off correspondents to the Other Contacts section. Here's how to configure this setting:

1. **In Gmail, choose Settings ⇨ See All Settings.**

   Gmail opens the Settings page with the General tab displayed.

2. **Scroll down to the Create Contacts for Auto-Complete setting and then select one of the following radio buttons:**

   - *When I Send a Message to a New Person, Add Them to Other Contacts So That I Can Auto-Complete to Them Next Time:* Gives the thumbs-up to add non-Contacts folks to Other Contacts.

- *I'll Add Contacts Myself:* Prevents Gmail from automatically adding non-Contacts correspondents to the Other Contacts section.

3. **Click Save Changes at the bottom of the Settings page.**

Configuring the Contacts columns

The Contacts list in Figure 4-1 shows only three columns — Name, Email, and Phone Number — but there can be up to two more columns — Job Title & Company and Labels — on wider screens. You also have the option to swap out the Email, Phone Number, Job Title & Company, or Labels column for an Address or Birthday column. (That's right: The Name column is permanent and can't be moved or changed to something else.)

If you want to customize the columns of your contacts list, follow these steps to make it so:

1. **Click the list settings icon (labeled in Figure 4-1).**

   Note that any customization you make in the following steps applies to *all* your contacts lists: Contacts, Frequently Contacted, Other Contacts, and any groups you create.

2. **Click Change Column Order.**

   Contacts opens the Change Column Order dialog, shown in Figure 4-2.

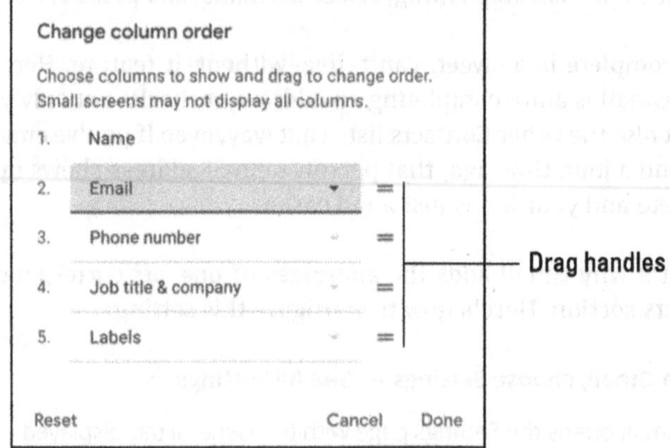

FIGURE 4-2: In the Change Column Order dialog, customize your contacts list columns.

3. **To change what a column displays, click the column and then click an item in the drop-down list that appears (such as Address or Birthday).**
4. **To change where a column appears in the list, move the mouse pointer over the column's drag handle (pointed out in Figure 4-2), drag the handle up or down until the column is in the position you want, and then drop the handle.**

REMEMBER

If you make a mess of the columns, Contacts has your back: Click Reset to return the column list back to its default configuration.

5. **Click Done.**

   Contacts redisplays the list according to the settings you selected.

TIP

If you want more contacts on each screen, you can cajole Contacts into displaying the list in a more compact style. Click the list settings icon (pointed out in Figure 4-1) and then click Display Density to open the Display Density dialog. Click Compact and then click Done. You're welcome.

Changing the sort order

By default, Contacts organizes its entries in alphabetical order by first name. If that seems silly to you (and many people would agree), follow these steps to sort your contacts by last name:

1. **Click Settings Menu ⇨ More Settings.**

   The Settings dialog appears.

2. **Select the Last Name radio button.**
3. **Click Save.**

   Contacts now sorts your peeps by last name. Ah, isn't that better?

Populating Your Contacts List

When you first open the Contacts app, there might not be a single contact. That empty contacts list is a bit depressing, so let's get right down to adding some new entries. This section shows you various methods of setting up new contacts. You also learn how to import contact data from other programs.

Adding a contact from scratch

The most straightforward way to get a contact from out there to in here (where *here* is the Contacts app) is to create a fresh contact right from the Contacts app itself. Here are the steps:

1. **On the Contacts app's main menu, choose Create Contact ➪ Create a Contact.**

   Contacts displays the fields for a new contact, as shown in Figure 4-3.

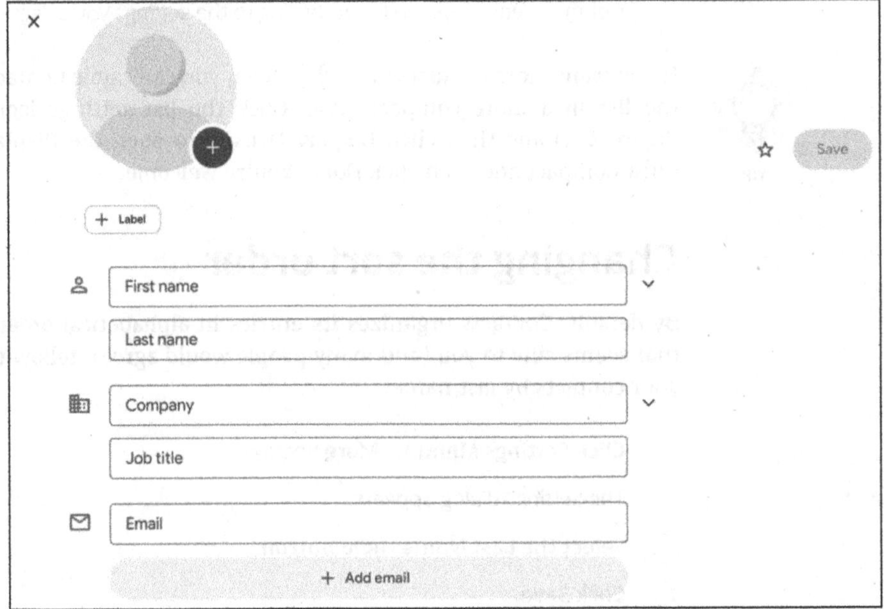

FIGURE 4-3: A new contact, ready to be filled in.

2. **Enter the person's first name and surname.**

   To add other info such as the contact's middle name, click the show more icon (shown in the margin) to the right of the First Name field and then use the extra fields that appear.

3. **Enter the person's company name and job title.**

   To add the contact's department name, click the show more icon to the right of the Company field and then type in the Department field that appears.

4. **Enter the contact's email address.**

   Contacts adds a Label field to the right of the email address.

5. **Click the Label field, and then click a label that describes the type of email address you entered.**

   Your choices are Home, Work, and Other.

6. **To add another email address, click Add Email to create new email fields, and then repeat Steps 4 and 5 for that address.**
7. **Enter the contact's phone number.**

   Contacts adds a Label field to the right of the phone number.

8. **Click the Label field, and then click a label that describes the type of phone numbers you entered.**

   Your choices are Home, Work, Other, Mobile, Main, Home Fax, Work Fax, Google Voice, and Pager. (Note to kids: Ask your parents what a fax is and what a pager is.)

9. **To add another phone number, click Add Phone, and then repeat Steps 7 and 8 for that number.**
10. **Use the Notes field to enter extra info about the contact, such as their dog's name or cat's breed.**
11. **If you have all kinds of time on your hands, you can add much more info about your contact by clicking Show More and then filling in the contact's minutiae as needed.**

    Actually, not all the extra info is obscure or trivial. For example, when you click Show More, you can click the buttons that appear to display fields for the contact's street address, birthday, relationship to you, website, and more.

12. **Click Save.**

    Contacts creates the new contact and then displays a summary of the contact data.

13. **When you're finished, click X (close).**

Adding a contact from Gmail

If someone sends you an email message or if someone is included in a message's CC field, you might decide that this someone ought to be in your contacts list. Sure, you can add that person from scratch, but Gmail offers a slightly easier route:

1. **In Gmail, click the message that contains the person you want to add as a contact.**

2. **In the email message to you, hover the mouse pointer over the name or photo of the person you want to add.**

   Gmail displays the options shown in Figure 4-4.

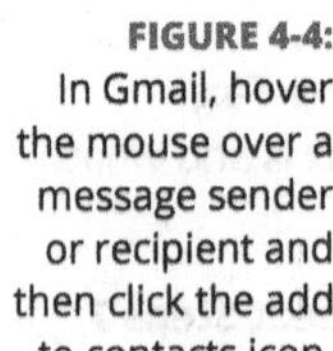

3. **Click the add to contacts icon (shown in the margin).**

   Gmail throws the contact's name and email address over to the Contacts app.

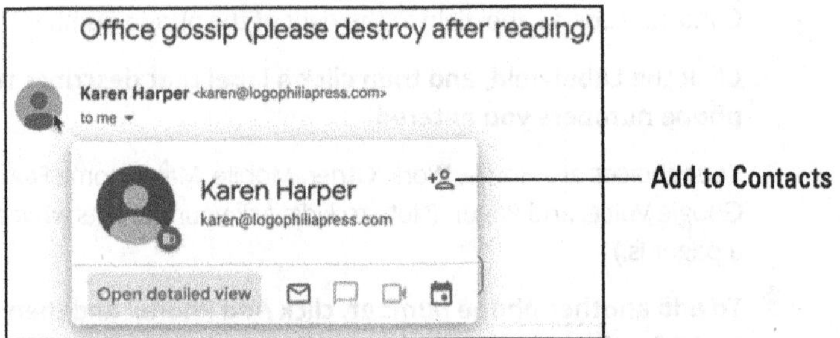

FIGURE 4-4: In Gmail, hover the mouse over a message sender or recipient and then click the add to contacts icon.

Going legit: Turning an "other" contact into a real contact

Earlier in this chapter, I talk about the Contacts app's ostracization of some of your Gmail correspondents into the dreaded Other Contacts section. (Refer to "What's with those 'other' contacts?"). If you have someone in that Other Contacts section that you want to turn into an honest-to-goodness "real" contact, Contacts gives you a way to do it that's slightly easier than adding that person from scratch:

1. **On the Contacts app's main menu, click Other Contacts.**
2. **Hover the mouse pointer over the contact you want to add.**

3. **Click the save contact icon (shown in the margin) and in Figure 4-5.**

   Contacts tosses the person into the main contacts list and removes them from Other Contacts purgatory.

It's great that your new, legitimate-at-last contact is in the contacts list, but that person's contact data consists of just an email address and, possibly, a name. If that's good enough for you, please feel free to move on to more interesting pursuits. However, if you want to beef up the new contact with a phone number, company name, and whatever other info you know about this person, head down to the "Editing a contact" section.

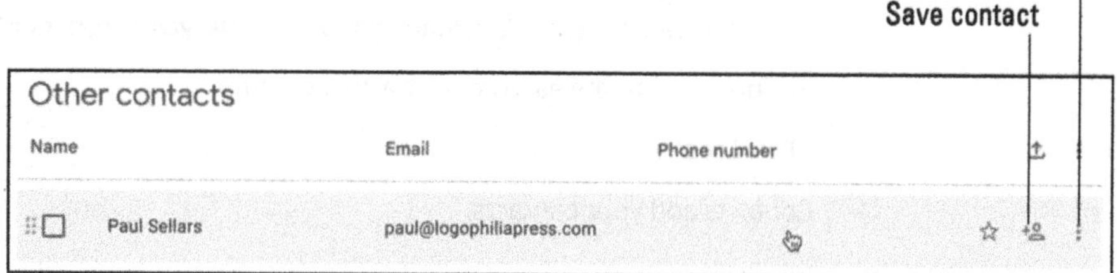

FIGURE 4-5: Click the save contact icon to transform an "other" contact into a "real" contact.

TIP

If you have entries in Other Contacts that you're certain you'll never deal with again, you should delete those entries to avoid cluttering Other Contacts (and your auto-complete results) with useless items. To delete an entry from Other Contacts, move the mouse pointer over the entry, click the more actions icon (shown in the margin), and then click Delete. When Contacts asks you to confirm, click Delete.

REMEMBER

Though it's not hard to transfer an "other" contact to your main contacts list, it's not trivial, either, especially if you want to bulk up the entry with extra info. Here's my advice: Don't let your Other Contacts list grow so large that you can't even face the task of cleaning it up. Once a week or so, get in there and do two things: Move important or useful entries to your main Contacts list, and delete entries that you know you'll never use.

Adding multiple contacts all at once

If you have a few contacts to add — especially if for all or most of those contacts you want to enter just each person's name or email address or both — Contacts has an alternative method that enables you to add all those contacts at one time. Here's what you do:

1. **On the Contacts app's main menu, choose Create Contact ⇨ Create Multiple Contacts.**

   The Create Multiple Contacts dialog appears.

2. **Use the text box to enter your contacts.**

   Use any of the following formats when entering each contact:

   - *Name only:* Enter just the name (Eliza Doolittle, for example).
   - *Email address only:* Enter just the address (such as `edoolittle@pygmalion.com`).

- *Name and email address:* Enter the name and then the email address in angle brackets (Eliza Doolittle <edoolittle@pygmalion.com>).

   Be sure to separate each contact with a comma.

3. **Click Create.**

   Contacts add your contacts.

Importing contacts

If you have your contact data in some other application, chances are that you'll be able to import that data into Contacts and save yourself the hassle of retyping all that information.

I hedged that last sentence with the words *chances are* because your ability to import contact data depends on whether the application that has your current contact info can save that data to a CSV file. A *what* file? CSV. It stands for comma separated values, and it's a standard format for exchanging data in a row-and-column format. In this case, each row represents a contact, and each column represents a particular type of contact data, such as a name, an email address, or a phone number. In each row, these different bits of data are separated by commas — hence the name of the file format.

Before you get to the importing part, you need to return to your existing Contacts app and find the command that exports or saves the data. Then, when you run that command, be sure to choose the option for exporting or saving the data to a CSV file.

For example, if you've been using Microsoft Outlook, here are the steps you'd follow to export your contacts to a CSV file:

1. **In Outlook, choose File ⇨ Open & Export.**

   TIP

   If your version of Outlook doesn't have a File option, ignore these steps and do the following instead: Click People to display your contacts, choose Manage Contacts ⇨ Export Contacts, and then click Export.

2. **Click Import/Export.**
3. **Click Export to a File and then click Next.**
4. **Click Comma Separated Values and then click Next.**
5. **Click Contacts and then click Next.**

6. **Click Browse, select the folder in which you want the file stored, type a name for the file (such as contacts.csv), and then click OK.**
7. **Click Next.**
8. **Click Finish.**

With your contacts CSV file safely stowed on your PC, you can now run through these steps to import that file into Google Contacts:

1. **On the Contacts app's main menu, click Import.**

   The Import Contacts dialog appears, as shown in Figure 4-6.

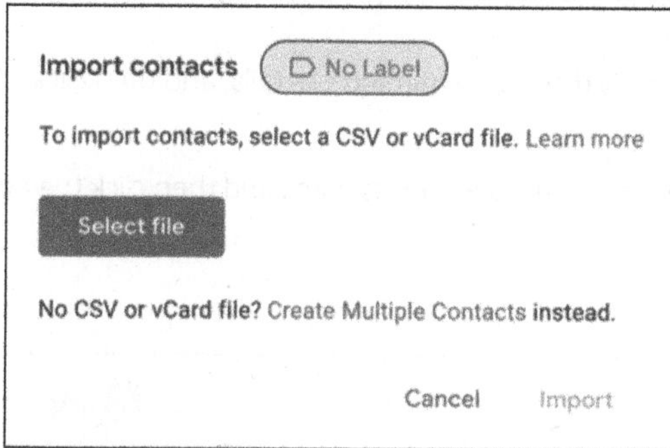
Import contacts
No Label
To import contacts, select a CSV or vCard file. Learn more
Select file
No CSV or vCard file? Create Multiple Contacts instead.
Cancel
Import

FIGURE 4-6: In the Import Contacts dialog, choose the CSV file you want to import.

2. **Click Select File.**

   The Open dialog appears.

3. **Open the folder that contains your CSV file, click the file, and then click Open.**
4. **Click Import.**

   Contacts imports the CSV file and displays a dialog to let you know.

5. **Click X (close) in the completion dialog.**

REMEMBER

An alternative import strategy is to grab data from a *vCard* file, which is a special file format that contains the data from one or more contacts. In iOS, for example, you can share a vCard from the iOS Contacts app by opening the contact, tapping Share Contact, and then selecting the share method you want to use. You can then follow the same steps in this section to import the resulting vCard file into Google Contacts.

Managing Your Contacts

Now that your contacts list is a bit more crowded with friends and family, and with co-workers you barely know, it's time to learn a few useful techniques for working with these contacts. The next few sections cover editing contacts, organizing contacts into groups, checking for duplicate contacts, and more. Give your knuckles a quick crack and we'll begin.

Editing a contact

If you want to make changes to a contact or add more data, you need to open that contact for editing. The Contacts app gives you two methods to get started:

- Click the contact to display the person's details, and then click Edit, as shown in Figure 4-7.
- Hover the mouse pointer over the contact, and then click the edit contact icon (pencil).

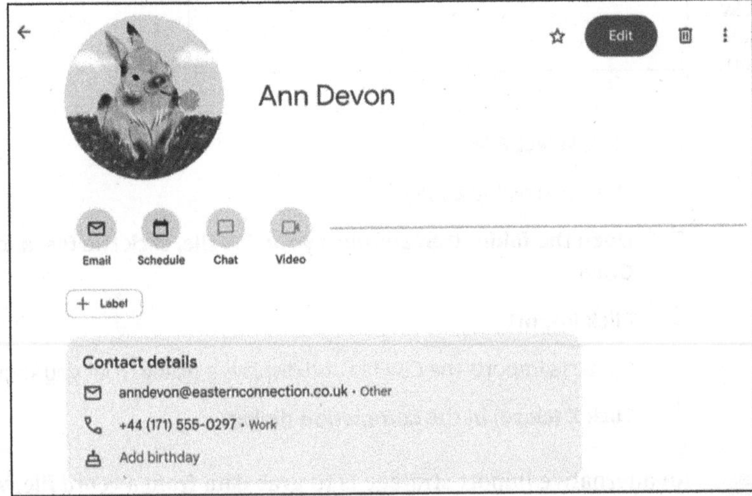

FIGURE 4-7: From the contact's details page, click Edit.

Either way, you end up nose-to-nose with the edit contact page, an example of which is shown in Figure 4-8. This dialog bears more than a passing resemblance to the page for creating a new contact dialog (shown earlier, in Figure 4-3). Make your changes and additions, as needed, and then click Save to preserve your work.

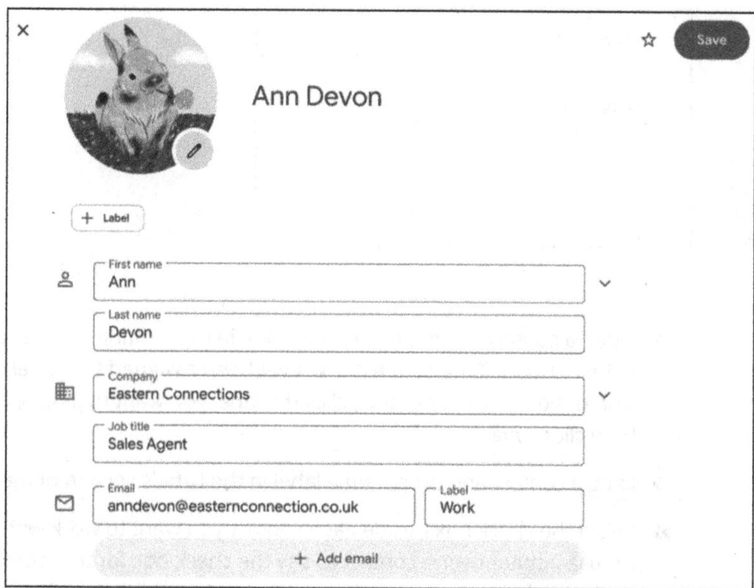

FIGURE 4-8: Make your changes in the edit contact page.

Grouping contacts with labels

One of the Contacts app's handiest features is called *labels*, which enables you to create groups of related contacts. For example, you might have a Work label for all your business colleagues, a Family label for all your kinfolk, and a What Happens in Vegas label for your road-trip buddies. After you create a label for some contacts, you can easily view those contacts by clicking the label in the Contacts app's Labels section.

Here are the steps you need to follow to create a label:

1. **On the Contacts app's main menu, click the + icon (create label) to the right of the Labels header.**

   Contacts opens the Create Label dialog.

2. **Type a name for the label, as shown in Figure 4-9.**
3. **Click Save.**

With your label saved, you can now add the label to one or more contacts. The Contacts app gives you a bunch of ways to go about this:

- » Move the mouse pointer over a contact, click the more actions icon (three vertical dots, labeled in Figure 4-5), and then click a label.

Create label

Book Nerds

Cancel Save

FIGURE 4-9: In the Create Label dialog, make your label.

- » Open a contact for editing (as I describe in the "Editing a contact" section), click either + Label (if the contact hasn't yet been assigned to a label) or the pencil icon beside an existing label, click the label you want to assign, click Apply, and then click Save.
- » Drag a contact and drop it on a label in the Labels section of the main menu.
- » Select the check box beside each contact you want to work with (hover the mouse pointer over a contact to see the check box for that contact), click the manage labels icon (pointed out in Figure 4-10), click the label (or labels) you want to assign to the selected contacts, and then click Apply.

REMEMBER

To get rid of a label you no longer want to use, hover the mouse pointer over the label in the Labels section and then click the trash can icon (delete). In the Delete This Label dialog, select the Keep All Contacts and Delete This Label radio button, and then click Delete.

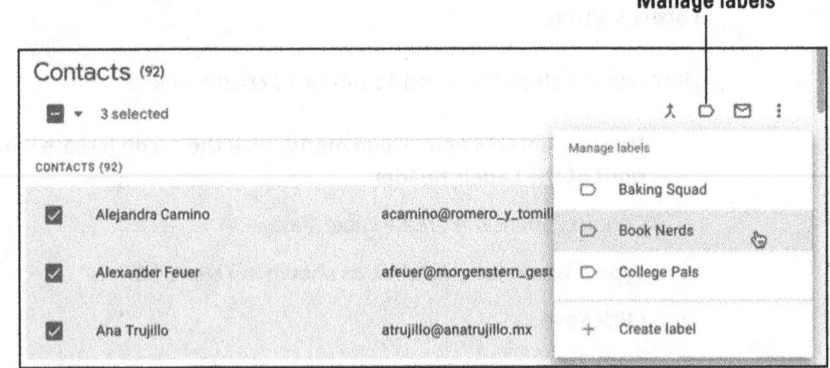

FIGURE 4-10: You can apply a label to multiple contacts all at once.

Merging duplicate contacts

You probably don't need me to tell you that the scourge of every online contact management app ever created is the duplicate entry. For some reason, despite recruiting some of the smartest people in tech, no company has been able to create a contacts app that doesn't spontaneously produce duplicates. It's maddening, but at least the Google programmers have created a tool that makes it relatively painless to find and fix double (or even triple) entries.

The tool in question is called Merge & Fix. You might first come across this tool when you add a new contact and a few seconds after you click Save, the Merge & Fix dialog appears, an example of which is shown in Figure 4-11. Contacts displays this dialog when it detects that your new contact duplicates an existing entry. Click Merge to combine the two entries or click Dismiss to keep them separate.

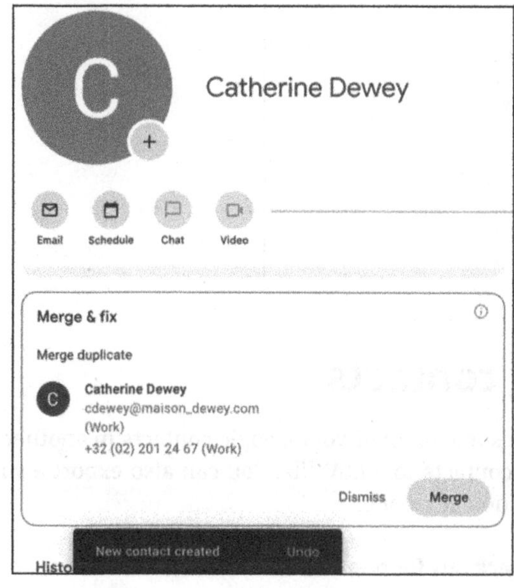

FIGURE 4-11: If your new contact duplicates an existing entry, the Merge & Fix dialog shows up.

In the Contacts main menu, if you see a number to the right of the Merge & Fix command, it means that Contacts has detected at least one duplicate entry. Click Merge and Fix on the main menu. Contacts opens the Merge Duplicates pane, shown in Figure 4-12.

Examine the suggested duplicates to make sure they really do refer to the same person. Then you have three ways to proceed:

- **If you want to go ahead and merge every displayed duplicate,** click Merge All.
- **If you want to merge a specific duplicate into a single entry,** click that duplicate's Merge button.
- **If you want to skip a specific duplicate** (say, because you know the two entries are separate people), click that duplicate's Dismiss button.

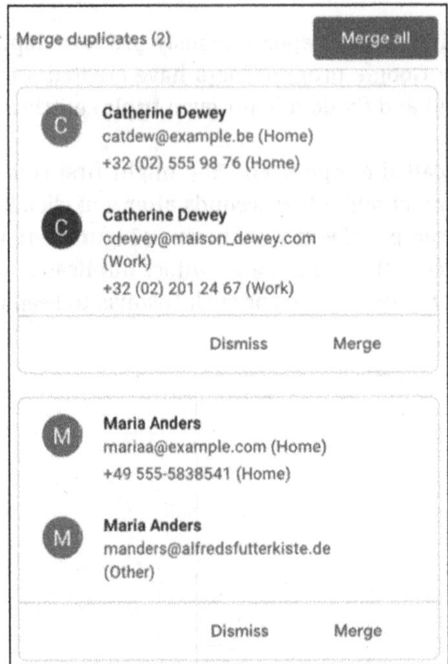

FIGURE 4-12: If you have duplicate contacts, they appear in the Merge Duplicates pane.

Exporting contacts

If you want to use some or all of your Google contacts in another application, you can export those contacts to a CSV file. You can also export a single contact to a vCard file. Here's how it's done:

1. **Select the check box for one or more contacts as follows:**
   - *To export just some of your contacts:* Select the check box for each contact you want to export.
   - *To export all your contacts:* Select the check box for any contact.

   Note that you can select the check boxes in the main contacts list, in your Frequently Contacted list, or in a label.
2. **Click the more options icon (three vertical dots, labeled in Figure 4-5) and then click Export.**

   The Export Contacts dialog appears, as shown in Figure 4-13.
3. **Choose what you want to export:**
   - *Selected Contacts:* Click this radio button if you want to export only the contacts you selected in Step 1.

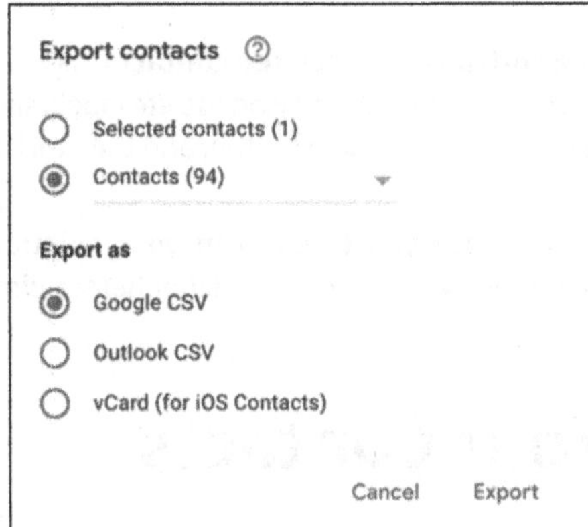

FIGURE 4-13: In the Export Contacts dialog, choose what to export and the file format to use.

- *Contacts:* Select this radio button to export all your contacts. Alternatively, drop down the menu to select either your Frequently Contacted list or one of your labeled lists.

4. **Select how you want the contacts exported:**
   - *Google CSV:* Exports the contacts as a CSV file compatible with other Google apps.
   - *Outlook CSV:* Exports the contacts as a CSV file compatible with Outlook (and most other contact management apps).
   - *vCard (for iOS contacts):* Exports the contact (or, if you have multiple contacts selected, the contacts) to a vCard.

5. **Click Export.**

   The Contacts app exports your contact or contacts.

Deleting contacts

To keep your contacts list neat and relatively tidy, you should delete any entries that you never use. The Contacts app gives you a bunch of ways to get rid of unwanted contacts:

- **Delete a single contact.** Hover the mouse pointer over the contact, click the more actions icon (three vertical dots), and then click Delete. When Contacts asks you to confirm, say "Yep" and click Move to Trash. Alternatively, click the contact, click the trash can icon (delete), and then click Move to Trash.
- **Delete two or more contacts.** Select the check box for each contact, click the more actions icon, and then click Delete. When Contacts asks you to confirm, say "But of course" (to yourself) and then click Move to Trash.

» **Delete a label along with all its associated contacts.** Move the mouse pointer over the label, click the trash can icon (delete label), select the Delete All Contacts and Delete This Label radio button, and then click Delete.

WARNING

Note that Contacts does *not* ask you to confirm your deletion, so double, nay, *triple*-check that you really want to remove the label before clicking Delete!

Doing Stuff with Your Contacts

You didn't go to all the trouble of entering or importing contact data just to look up someone's birthday or the name of their spouse. No, with all that information at your fingertips, you'll want to do things that are a bit more substantial. Like what? Well, Contacts gives you lots of choices. You can send an email message to one or more contacts, you can call a contact, and you can surf to a contact's web page. The following sections give you a quick run-through of the methods you use to accomplish all these tasks from the Contacts app.

Emailing a contact

To send an email to a contact, follow these steps:

1. **Click to open the contact you want to email, and then click the Email button.**

   Or select the check box for the contact you want to email, and then click the send email icon (pointed out a bit later in Figure 4-15).

   Gmail opens a New Message window, addressed to the contact's email address.

2. **Fill in the subject, message body, and any other email stuff you need to specify, and then click Send.**

   Gmail sends the message to the contact.

Emailing a contact who has multiple addresses

If you have a contact with two or more email addresses, selecting that contact and then clicking Send Email, as I describe in the previous section, sends the message to that person's first email address. That might not be the address you want to use, so follow these steps instead:

1. **Click to open the contact you want to email.**
2. **Click the Email button.**

   If the contact has multiple email addresses, Contacts displays them in a pop-up list, as shown in Figure 4-14.

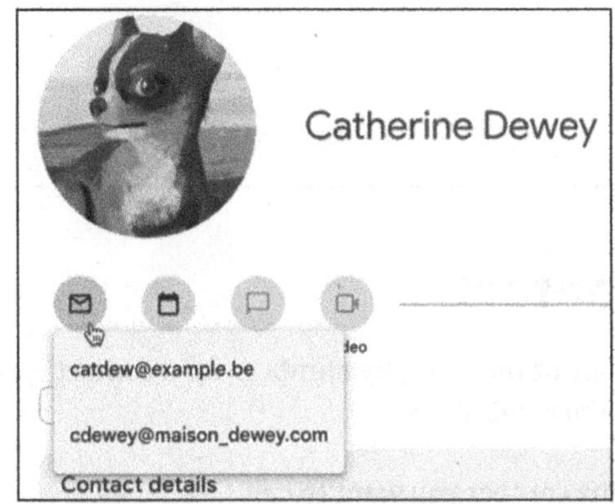

FIGURE 4-14: A contact with multiple email addresses.

3. **Click the email address you want to use to send your message.**

   Gmail opens a New Message window and inserts into the To field the address you clicked.

4. **Write a subject and message body, add your other email knickknacks as necessary, and then click Send.**

   Gmail sends the message to the contact.

Emailing multiple contacts

To send an email to two or more contacts, try this:

1. **Select the check box for each contact you want to email.**
2. **Click the send email icon, pointed out in Figure 4-15.**

   Gmail opens a New Message window with the contacts' email addresses added to the To field.

3. **Specify a subject, write the message body, set whatever other options you need, and then click Send.**

   Gmail sends the message to every contact you selected.

Send Email

Contacts (93)	
3 selected	
CONTACTS (93)	
Alejandra Camino	acamino@romero_y_tomillo.es
Alexander Feuer	afeuer@morgenstern_gesundkost.de
Ana Trujillo	atrujillo@anatrujillo.mx

FIGURE 4-15: Select the check box for each contact, then click Send Email.

Calling a contact

If you've specified one or more phone numbers for a contact, you can follow these steps to call one of those numbers:

1. **Click to open the contact you want to call.**

   Contacts opens the contact's details page.

2. **Click the phone number you want to call.**

   Google places the call.

Surfing to a contact's website

If a contact has a website and you've noted the address in the contact's Website field, you can follow these steps to surf to that address:

1. **Click to open the contact whose website you want to visit.**

   Contacts opens the contact's details page.

2. **Click the website address.**

   Your web browser opens a new tab and uses it to display the contact's website.

2

Making Stuff: Documents, Spreadsheets, and More

IN THIS PART . . .

Learn how to create, format, and lay out documents.

Make spreadsheets that make numbers make sense.

Craft eye-catching and persuasive presentations.

IN THIS CHAPTER

» Taking a tour of the Docs landscape

» Creating, saving, opening, and other document chores

» Navigating, selecting, deleting, and other editing basics

» Getting AI help to write, revise, and proofread text

» Making sure your spelling and grammar pass muster

Chapter 5

Getting Started with Docs

Google Docs is the Google Workspace app for word processing. Wait a minute: *word processing*. Ugh. I've never liked the term. It sounds so cold and so, well, computer-like. I mean, processing words? What the heck does that mean? The bank processes checks, the Internal Revenue Service processes tax returns. Who processes words? We write them, play with them, misuse them, misspell them, forget them — but process them? No.

However, the computer geeks of the world decided long ago that that's what digital writing should be called, so it appears that we're stuck with it. Okay, but what is *it*, exactly? Well, in watch-their-eyes-glaze-over terms, *word processing* is using a computer to write, edit, format, and print documents. Yeah, I know, it doesn't sound glamorous, but it's not supposed to be. I mean, think about it: Most of the writing we do is grunt work anyway: memos, letters, essays, diatribes, and harangues of one sort or another. All we need is to get the words down, dot the *i*'s and cross the *t*'s, and make our writing presentable. Everything else — whether it's putting together a newsletter or writing a report — is just an extension of this basic stuff.

In this chapter, you learn how to process words with Google Docs. This chapter offers a few Docs basics, and then you get into ever-so-slightly more advanced topics in Chapters 6 and 7.

Opening Docs

Perform a few jumping jacks, head rolls, or other warm-up activities. Then, when you're good to go, use either of the following techniques to get Docs on the stage:

- Take your web browser by the hand and gently point it toward `https://docs.google.com`.
- If you're in a Google Workspace app that has the Google apps icon (shown in the margin), choose Google Apps ➪ Docs.

Touring the Google Docs Home Page

When you first land on Docs, the home page shows up, which looks pleasingly similar to the page shown in Figure 5-1.

Let's take a quick trip around the screen so that you know what's what here:

- **Main menu:** Displays the main menu, which gives you access to other Google Workspace apps (such as Sheets and Slides), Settings, and Drive. To close the menu, click any empty space outside the menu.
- **Search:** Enables you to search Docs for the document you want.
- **Google apps:** Displays icons for all the Google apps.
- **Start a new document:** Displays a few templates you can use to start a new document. (A *template* is a document that comes with predefined text, formatting, and even an image or three to get you off to a good start.)
- **Template gallery:** Displays the complete list of templates.
- **Recent documents:** Lists the documents you've worked on most recently.
- **Open file picker:** Displays the Open a File dialog so that you can open a file from Drive or your computer.

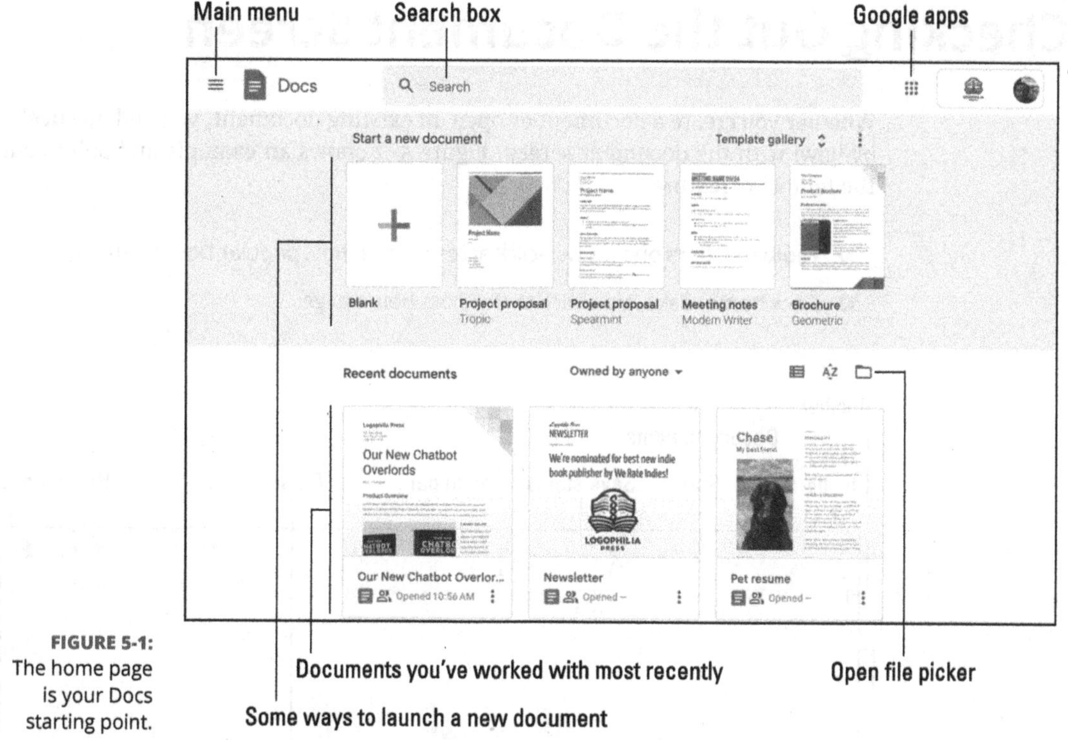

FIGURE 5-1: The home page is your Docs starting point.

Creating a Shiny, New Document

After you land on the Docs home page, you can open a file you worked on previously (more on that later, in the section "Opening an existing document"), but most of the time you'll want to create a document. You can ask Docs nicely in one of two ways to fire up a new document for you:

- **To open an empty document (that is, a document with no predefined text or formatting):** In the Start a New Document section, click the Blank template tile.
- **To open a document that has some ready-to-edit text and formatting:** Either click a template tile other than Blank Document shown in the Start a New Document section or click Template Gallery and then select a template from the long list of possibilities that Docs displays.

Either way, the home screen disappears and the new document takes its place.

Checking Out the Document Screen

Whether you create a document or open an existing document, you end up cheek-by-jowl with the document screen. Figure 5-2 shows an example and points out the following features:

- **Toolbar:** Offers one- or two-click access to the most popular Docs features.
- **Docs home:** Takes you back to the Docs home page.

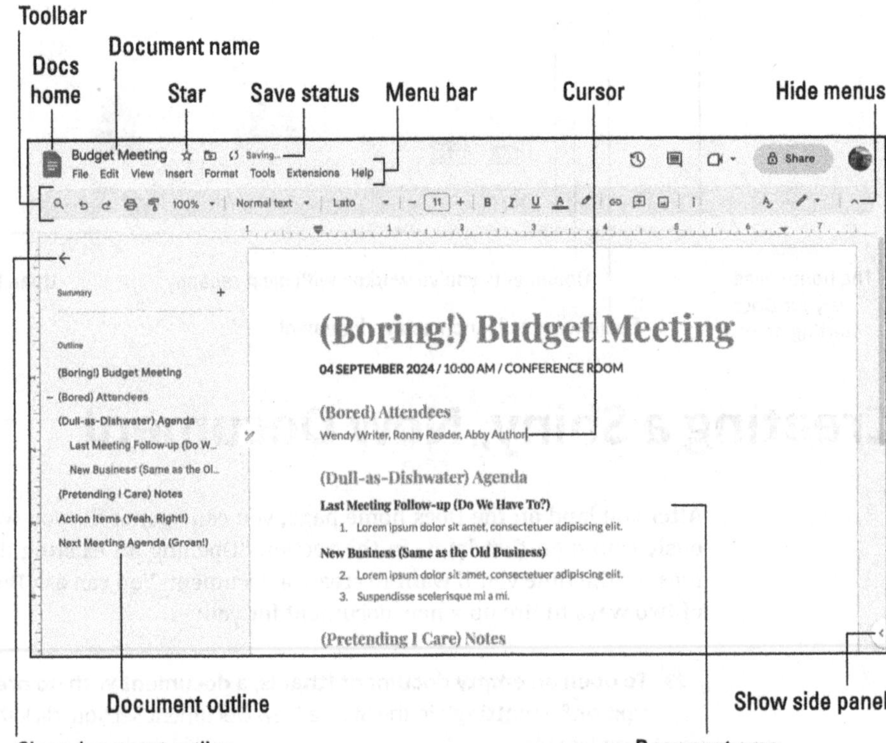

FIGURE 5-2: A typical document and the Docs features that surround it.

- **Document name:** Displays the name you've given your document. When you start a new document, the area is labeled either Untitled Document (if you chose the Blank template) or the template name (if you chose any other template).
- **Star:** Marks the document as one of your favorites or as special in some way.

- **Menu bar:** Gives you access to the full arsenal of Docs commands, features, and tools.
- **Save status:** Lets you know when Docs is saving your work (among other things).
- **Hide menus:** Hides the Docs home icon, the menu bar, and the document name to gain a bit more vertical headroom for your document. Click the icon again (it's now a downward-pointing arrow) to display the menus. You can also press Ctrl+Shift+F to toggle the menus.
- **Show side panel:** Displays the side panel, which gives you access to quick actions associated with Calendar, Keep, Tasks, Contacts, and Maps.
- **Document area:** Contains the document content. This is where you add, edit, and format your document text.
- **Cursor:** Marks the spot where the next character you type will appear.
- **Document outline:** Displays the main headings of your document, which gives you a bird's-eye view of the structure of your document. You can also navigate your document by clicking the headings.
- **Close document outline:** Hides the outline if you don't need it. To get it back, click the show document outline icon that replaces the outline.

Dealing with Documents

As you might expect from its name, Docs is all about documents. So, before you learn how to add, edit, and format text, it pays to take a few short moments (I promise) to learn some basic document chores.

Saving your work — just kidding!

One of the unexpected benefits you get with Docs is a better night's sleep. Why? Because you'll no longer wake up at 3 A.M. wondering whether you forgot to save the last document you were working on. Why not? Because Docs saves all your work automatically. Add some text and Docs saves it. Change the formatting and Docs saves that, too. Docs even saves changes to brand-new documents that you haven't even named yet.

With each change you make as you work in Docs, the document's Save Status text (pointed out earlier, in Figure 5-2) changes to *Saving...* as shown in the top image of Figure 5-3. When the save is complete, the status becomes *Saved to Drive*, as shown in the bottom image of Figure 5-3. There's your good night's sleep right there.

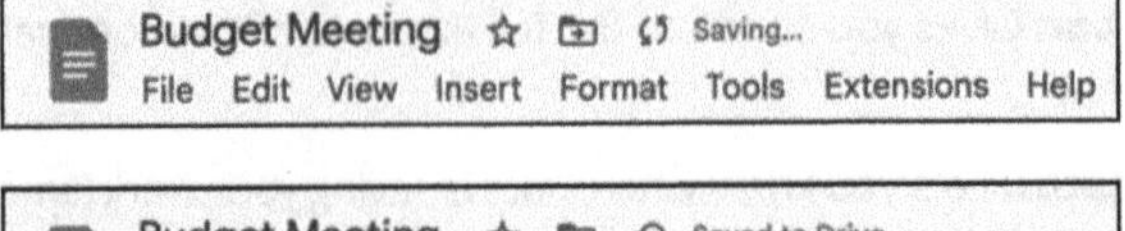

FIGURE 5-3: Docs lets you know when it's saving your changes (top) and when the save is complete (bottom).

Every time you make a change to the document, the saving status changes briefly to *Saving*, followed a second or two later by the calm-inducing message *Saved to Drive.*

Naming a new document

If you've just started a new document, one of your earliest tasks should be to give the document a descriptive name. Docs launches new, blank documents with the accurate but decidedly unhelpful name Untitled Document. Similarly, if you used a nonblank template to launch your document, it will have the same name as the template, such as Meeting Notes or Brochure. Boring!

No self-respecting document should walk around with an unhelpful or dull moniker, so follow these steps to give your document a proper name:

1. **Click the current document name (such as Untitled Document), which appears near the top-left corner of the page.**

   Alternatively, you can choose File ➪ Rename. Either way, Docs opens the filename for editing.

2. **Delete the existing name.**
3. **Type the name you want to use for the new document.**
4. **Press Enter or Return.**

   Docs saves the document using the new name.

REMEMBER

If you're not happy with the name you gave your document, feel free to follow these same steps to rename the document as often as it takes to get it right.

Opening an existing document

Some documents are one-shot deals. That is, you create the document, name it, add text and formatting, and then you're done with the document and it never sees the light of day again. A much more common scenario is that you create the document, name it, add text and formatting, work on something else for a while, and then return to the original document and work on it some more.

To return to a document so that you can take another crack at it, you need to open it by following these steps:

1. **Open the Docs home page.**
2. **If the document you want to open appears in the Recent Documents area, click it and then skip the rest of this procedure. Otherwise, click the open file picker icon (pointed out earlier, in Figure 5-1).**

   Docs displays the Open a File dialog, shown in Figure 5-4.

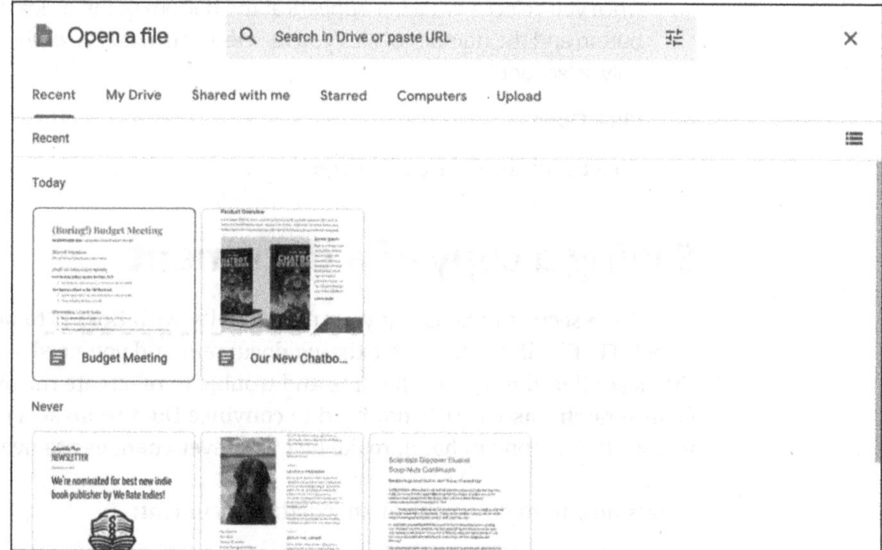

FIGURE 5-4: In the Open a File dialog, choose which document you want to work on.

3. **Choose the document you want to mess with.**

   Note that Docs gives you several tabs to play with in the Open a File dialog. Here's what they mean:

   - *My Drive:* Select a document that's stored in your online Drive.
   - *Shared with Me:* Select a document that someone else has shared with you. To learn how this sharing thing works, see Chapter 11.
   - *Starred:* Select from a list of Drive documents that you've starred (meaning the documents are your favorites or are special in some way). To star a document, open the document and then click the star icon (labeled in Figure 5-2).

- *Recent:* Select from a list of Drive documents that you've worked on in the last month.
- *Computers:* Double-click a computer or device that's synced to your Google Workspace account, double-click the folder that contains the file (you might need to drill down through multiple subfolders), and then select a document.
- *Upload:* Select a document by copying it from your computer to Drive. You can either drag a document into the tab or click the Browse button and then select a file.

Once you select a file, a bar appears at the bottom of the dialog with an Open button and the number of files you've selected (I'm not sure why since you can only select one!).

4. **Click Open.**

   Docs opens the file, free of charge.

Saving a copy of a document

One of the secrets of boosting your productivity with Docs is to never reinvent the wheel. That is, if you have an existing document and you need a second document that's similar, don't go to the time and trouble to re-create the original document from scratch. Instead, it's not hard to convince Docs to make a copy of the original. With that copy in hand, make just whatever changes are needed.

Here's how to make a copy of an existing document:

1. **Open the document you want to copy.**
2. **Choose File ⇨ Make a Copy.**

   Docs opens the Copy Document dialog. The Name text box shows *Copy of,* followed by the name of the original document. (Check out Figure 5-5 for an example.)
3. **In the Name text box, give the copy a descriptive name.**
4. **If you want to store the copy in a specific folder, click My Drive in the Folder section, select the folder you want to use, and then click Select.**
5. **Click OK.**

   Docs opens a new browser tab and displays the copy you just created.

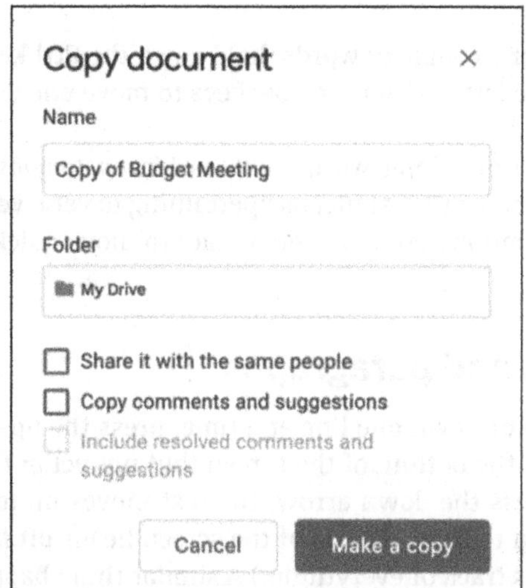

FIGURE 5-5: In the Copy Document dialog, clone an existing document.

Learning Some Editing Basics

You almost certainly have better things to do than hang around all day in Docs. To get your Docs duties out of the way so you can move on to more interesting or fun things, you need to learn a few editing basics, which will stand you in good stead throughout your Docs career. The next few sections take you through a few pretty much painless keyboard-and-mouse editing techniques.

Navigating with the keyboard

Docs has a fistful of ways to navigate your documents from the keyboard. In this section, you work your way up from short hops between characters and words to great leaps between screens and pages.

Navigating characters and words

The simplest move you can make in a document is to use the left- and right-arrow keys to move left or right one character at a time. If you have a bit of ground to cover, try holding down the arrow key. After a slight delay, the cursor starts racing through each line. (Notice that when it hits the end of one line, it starts over at the beginning of the next.)

If you need to jump over a couple of words, hold down the Ctrl key (Option key on a Mac) and then use the left- or right-arrow keys to move one word at a time.

TIP

If you're in the middle of a long word, such as *hippopotomonstrosesquipedalian* (which is a very, very long word that means "pertaining to very, very long words"), press Ctrl+left arrow (Option+left arrow on a Mac) to move quickly to the beginning of the word.

Navigating lines and paragraphs

If you need to move up or down one line at a time, press the up- or down-arrow key. If your cursor is at the bottom of the screen (but not yet at the bottom of the document) and you press the down arrow, the text moves up to reveal the next line. (The line that used to be at the top of the screen heads off into oblivion, but don't worry: Docs keeps track of everything.) A similar thing happens if your cursor is at the top of the screen (unless you're at the top of the document): If you press the up arrow, the text moves down to make room for the next line. Moving text up or down like this is called *scrolling* the document.

To move to the beginning of the current line, press Home (⌘+left arrow on a Mac); to move to the end of the current line, press End (⌘+right arrow on a Mac).

REMEMBER

Some keyboards sneakily hide the Home and End keys inside other keys (usually the left and right arrow keys). To "press" these hidden keys, you need to hold down the Fn key. That is, to select Home, press Fn+Home, and to select End, press Fn+End.

If you need to jump around a paragraph at a time, press Ctrl+up arrow (to move up one paragraph; press Option+up arrow on a Mac) or Ctrl+down arrow (to move down one paragraph; press Option+down arrow on a Mac).

Navigating headings, screens, and documents

For really big documents, you need to know how to cover a lot of ground in a hurry. Docs, of course, is up to the task.

With the cursor within a heading, to move to the next heading, hold down Ctrl+Alt (Control+⌘ on a Mac), press n (for next), and then press h (for heading). To move to the previous heading, hold down Ctrl+Alt (Control+⌘ on a Mac), press p (for previous), and then press h (for heading).

TIP

As you learn in Chapter 6, Docs has six levels of headings, from Heading 1 through Heading 6. To navigate to the next heading level *x*, make sure the cursor is within a heading, hold down Ctrl+Alt (Control+⌘ on a Mac), press n, and then press *x* (where *x* is a number from 1 to 6). To navigate to the previous heading level *x*, hold down Ctrl+Alt (Control+⌘ on a Mac), press p, and then press *x* (where *x* is a number from 1 to 6).

To move down one screenful, press Page Down. To move up one screenful, press Page Up.

REMEMBER

Some smaller keyboards bury the Page Up and Page Down keys inside other keys (usually the up and down arrow keys). To "press" these hidden keys, you need to hold down the Fn key. That is, to select Page Up, press Fn+Page Up (Fn+up arrow on a Mac), and to select Page Down, press Fn+Page Down (Fn+down arrow on a Mac.).

For truly large leaps, press Ctrl+Home to move to the beginning of the document (Fn+⌘+left arrow on a Mac), or Ctrl+End to move to the end of the document (Fn+⌘+right arrow on a Mac).

Selecting text

Before you can do anything with text, you need to select it. Docs gives you these main techniques:

- **Select a word:** Double-click the word.
- **Select a line:** Click at the beginning of the line, hold down Shift, and then click at the end of the line.
- **Select a sentence:** Click at the beginning of the sentence, hold down Shift, and then click at the end of the sentence.
- **Select any text:** Move the mouse pointer to the beginning of the text, and then click-and-drag the mouse over the entire text (including down if you need to select text on multiple lines).
- **Select a paragraph:** Triple-click inside the paragraph.
- **Select text to the end of the paragraph:** Press Shift+Ctrl+down arrow.
- **Select text to the beginning of the paragraph:** Press Shift+Ctrl+up arrow.
- **Select everything:** Press Ctrl+A.

Deleting stuff

Everyone has trouble deleting things they've written. I think we just get too attached. However, Docs isn't at fault, because it gives you all kinds of ways to nix troublesome text. This section shows you how.

TIP

Before going on any kind of deletion rampage, you should know that there's a section, later in this chapter, called "To err is human, to undo divine." If you wipe out anything you shouldn't have, read ahead to that section to learn how to make everything okay again.

Deleting characters

Did you spell potato with an *e* again? Or perhaps you've just watched *The Crown* on TV and have typed words like *colour* and *cheque*. Well, not to worry: Docs makes it easy to expunge individual characters. You have two options:

- **To delete the character to the right of the cursor:** Press the Delete key.
- **To delete the character to the left of the cursor:** Press the Backspace key (Forward Delete on a Mac, or Fn+Delete if your Mac keyboard doesn't have a Forward Delete key).

If you'd like to delete several characters in a row, hold down Delete or Backspace until all the riffraff is eliminated. (Be careful, though: The cursor really picks up speed if you hold it down for more than a second or two.)

Deleting words

To handle any stray words that creep into your documents, Docs lets you delete entire words with a single stroke. Again, you have two methods you can use:

- Place the cursor just in front of the word and then press Ctrl+Delete (Option+Forward Delete on a Mac, or Fn+Option+Delete if your Mac keyboard doesn't have a Forward Delete key).
- Place the cursor just after the word and then press Ctrl+Backspace (Option+Delete on a Mac).

For fine-tuned deleting, you can even delete portions of a word. Here's how:

- **To delete from the cursor to the end of a word:** Press Ctrl+Delete (Option+Forward Delete on a Mac, or Fn+Option+Delete if your Mac keyboard doesn't have a Forward Delete key).
- **To delete from the cursor to the beginning of a word:** Press Ctrl+Backspace (Option+Delete on a Mac).

REMEMBER

Here's how I remember whether to use Ctrl+Backspace or Ctrl+Delete: The word *end* ends with *d*, so you use Ctrl+Delete to delete to the end of a word; the word *beginning* begins with *b*, so you use Ctrl+Backspace to delete to the beginning of a word. Clearer? No? Well, I tried.

To err is human, to undo divine

Let's face facts: *Everybody* deletes stuff accidentally, and one day you'll do it, too. It's one of those things that you just can't avoid (like nose hair and income taxes). Fortunately, there's a way to ease the pain: Use the Undo command. As its name implies, this command miraculously reverses your most recent action, such as an errant deletion. (Which, believe me, has saved my bacon on more than one occasion.)

To undo your most recent action in Docs, use either of the following techniques:

- Click the undo icon (shown in the margin) on the toolbar.
- Press Ctrl+Z (⌘+Z on a Mac).

If you want to undo your last two or more actions, keep either clicking the undo icon or pressing Ctrl+Z (or ⌘+Z) until you've reversed all the actions you no longer need.

TIP

If you undo an action accidentally, you can reverse the reversal, so to speak, by clicking the toolbar's redo icon (shown in the margin) or by pressing Ctrl+Y (⌘+Y on a Mac).

Fooling around with special characters

Were you stumped the last time you wanted to write *Dag Hammarskjöld* because you didn't know how to produce one of those ö thingamajigs? I thought so. Well, you'll be happy to know that your documents aren't restricted to just the letters, numbers, and punctuation marks you can poke on your keyboard. In fact, Docs comes with all kinds of built-in characters that will supply you with not only an *ö* but also a whole universe of oddball symbols.

Here's how it works:

1. **Position the cursor where you want to insert the symbol.**
2. **Choose Insert ➪ Special Characters.**

   Docs opens the Insert Special Characters dialog, shown in Figure 5-6. You get an impressive array of arrow symbols by default. I show you how to find what you need (assuming it's not an arrow) next.

3. **Locate the character you want to add. Docs gives you several ways to do this:**
   - *Scroll through the displayed symbols until you locate the one you want.*
   - *Click the list on the right (it's labeled Arrows, by default) and select the category for your character.*

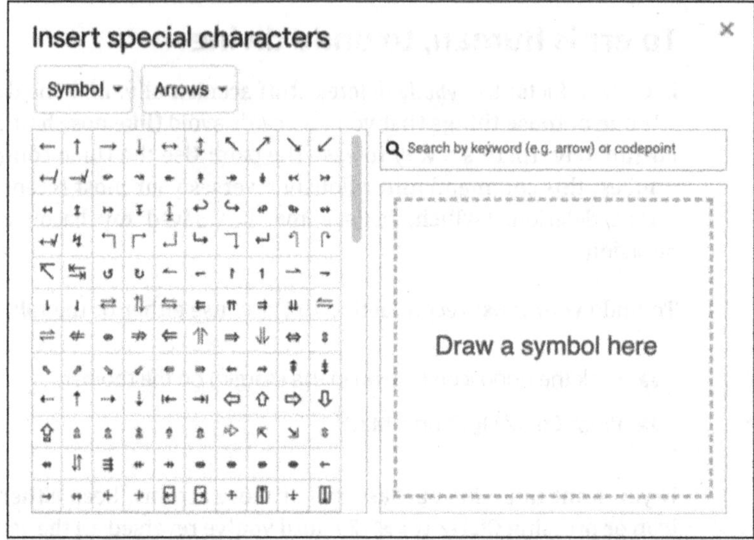

FIGURE 5-6: In the Insert Special Characters dialog, add silly symbols to your document.

- *In the search box, enter a word or phrase that describes the character (such as diaeresis or cedilla).*
- *In the Draw a Symbol Here box, draw a reasonable facsimile of your character, as shown in Figure 5-7.* You can use the mouse or trackpad, but it's easier if you have a digital pen or touchscreen. Either way, this *is* a fun feature.

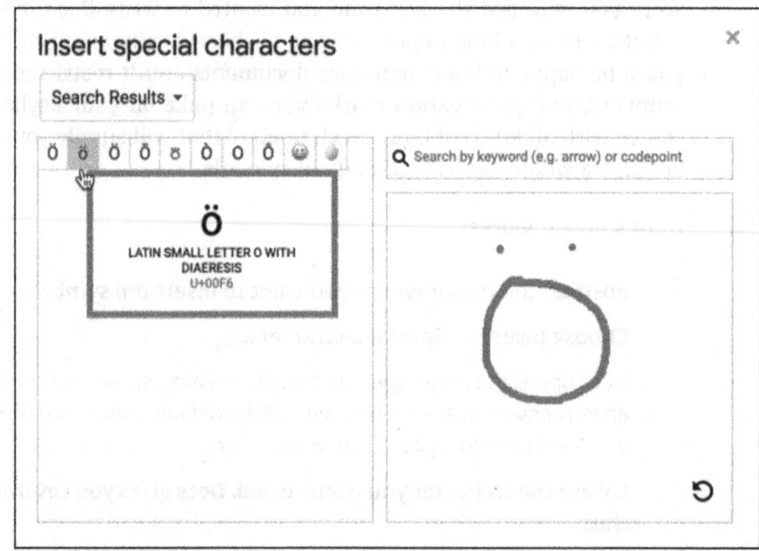

FIGURE 5-7: Yep, you can draw the character you want and Docs locates it based on your rendition.

4. **Click the character.**

   If you're not sure whether a particular symbol is the one you want, hover the mouse pointer over the character to display a larger version of the character and its description. (Refer to Figure 5-7.)

   Docs inserts the character into the document at the cursor position.

5. **Click X (close).**

Stating your case: Uppercase versus lowercase

On most keyboards, the Caps Lock key is just above the Shift key. In the heat of battle, you might end up hitting Caps Lock by mistake a few times a day. The result: ANYTHING FROM A FEW WORDS TO A FEW LINES APPEARS IN UPPERCASE! Fortunately, Docs can get you off the hook easily with its case-conversion feature, which you can invoke to change your letters back to all-lowercase. If needed, you can also change your letters to all-uppercase versions, and you can convert your text to *title case*, which converts only the initial letter in each word to uppercase (to change, say, *the curious case of benjamin button* to *The Curious Case Of Benjamin Button*).

To convert the case of some text, follow these steps:

1. **Select the text you want to convert.**
2. **Choose Format ➪ Text ➪ Capitalization.**
3. **Click the command you want: lowercase, UPPERCASE, or Title Case.**

   Docs converts the text to the case you chose.

Adding links

Your documents live on the web, so it makes sense that they should contain a link or two. These can be links to websites or links to other Docs files. Whatever you need, here are the steps to follow to insert a link:

1. **(Optional) Copy the address of website or Docs file.**

   You can copy the address now or type the address later, in Step 5.

2. **(Optional) Select the text you want to change into a link.**

   You can select text now or type text later, in Step 4.

3. **Choose Insert ⇨ Link.**

   Alternatively, press Ctrl+K (⌘+K on a Mac) or click the insert link icon on the toolbar (shown in the margin).

   Docs displays a dialog for entering the link specifics.

4. **If you didn't select text in advance, type the link text in the Text box.**
5. **Type (or paste) the link address in the Link text box.**

   Docs displays a website related to your selected text as well as one or two recent documents, so you can click the website or a document if that's what you want to link to.

6. **Click Apply.**

   Docs inserts the link.

Setting tab stops

Documents look much better if they're properly indented and if their various parts line up nicely. The best way to do this is to use tabs instead of spaces whenever you need to create some room in a line. Why? Well, a single space can take up different amounts of room, depending on the font and size of the characters you're using. So, your document can end up looking pretty ragged if you try to use spaces to indent your text. Tabs, on the other hand, are fastidiously precise: Whenever you press the Tab key, the insertion point moves ahead exactly to the next tab stop — no more, no less.

Docs lets you set three kinds of tab stop:

- **Left:** Text lines up with the tab on the left. This tab type is represented by a right-facing triangle on the ruler at the top of your document.
- **Right:** Text lines up with the tab on the right. The ruler shows this tab type as a left-facing triangle.
- **Center:** Text is centered on the tab. This tab type is represented by a diamond shape on the ruler.

To set tab stops, first make sure Docs is displaying the ruler by pulling down the View menu and seeing whether the Show Ruler command has a check mark beside it. If it doesn't, click the command. With that done, set a tab stop by clicking the ruler at the spot where you want the stop to appear and then choosing from the menu that appears:

» Add Left Tab Stop
» Add Center Tab Stop
» Add Right Tab Stop

With your tab stop set, position the cursor at the beginning of the text you want to align with the tab stop, and then press Tab.

Figure 5-8 shows a document with each type of tab stop set and some text tabbed to each stop.

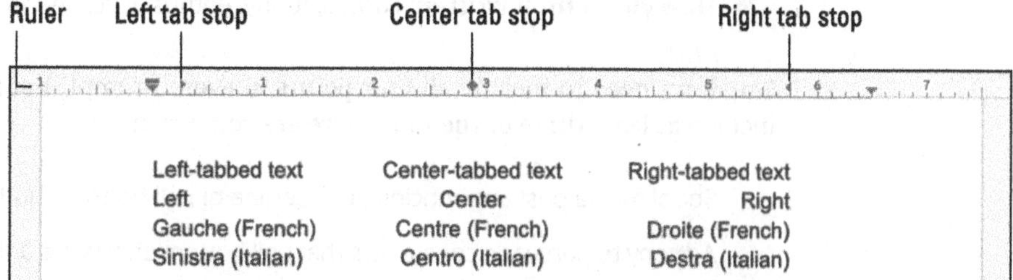

FIGURE 5-8: Some examples of tab stops.

Writing and Refining Text with AI

Writer's block is a common affliction in which an author finds it impossible to start or continue a piece of writing. Many a writer has owned up to a crippling *blank page fear*, where the white expanse of the not-yet-written-on page is seen as a cold and forbidding place that evokes terror instead of creativity.

These and similar authorial maladies might soon become things of the past in this new age of artificial intelligence, where every writer has access to multiple language models that specialize in *generative AI*, which from a simple text prompt can produce everything from essays to emails, brochures to blog posts.

Even better, if your Google Workspace includes Google's Duet AI service, you have direct access to a powerful AI model in any Docs document. In Docs, you can use AI to both write new text from a prompt and refine existing text. This section takes you through the details.

Prompting AI to write new text

The key to most generative AI is the *prompt*, which is a sentence or two that describes the writing you want the AI language model to generate. Most prompts are short, to-the-point descriptions of what you want. However, to help ensure that you get text you can work with, it helps to craft your prompts with the following points in mind:

- **What you want to write:** A letter, a social media post, a memo, an ad, an email, or perhaps just a document title or image caption. If you want the output to include specific elements, be sure to specify them in your prompt.
- **Who you're writing to:** A customer, a recruiter, a friend, your team, your company, and so on.
- **Why you're writing this text:** To persuade, to thank, to motivate, and so on.
- **How you want it written:** Formal, funny, enthusiastic, heartfelt, and so on.

You don't need to include all four points in every prompt, but most prompts will include at least three of the four. Here are some examples:

Social media post announcing our new line of bell bottom shorts.

Ad copy to persuade consumers that bell bottom shorts are a thing.

Testy cease-and-desist letter to an overly persistent job recruiter.

Motivational speech to the team, especially to those who insist on taking weekends off.

TIP

If you've already completed some writing, you can use the prompt *Add another paragraph* to ask AI to continue your writing.

Google Docs has three basic methods for displaying a box to prompt AI:

- **Start a new, blank document:** On the Docs Home page, click the Blank template. Then, on the blank document that shows up, click the Help Me Write button, shown in Figure 5-9. (In case you're wondering, the other buttons you see in Figure 5-9 represent *building blocks,* which are prefabricated document parts. You can see more such parts by choosing Insert ➪ Building Blocks.)

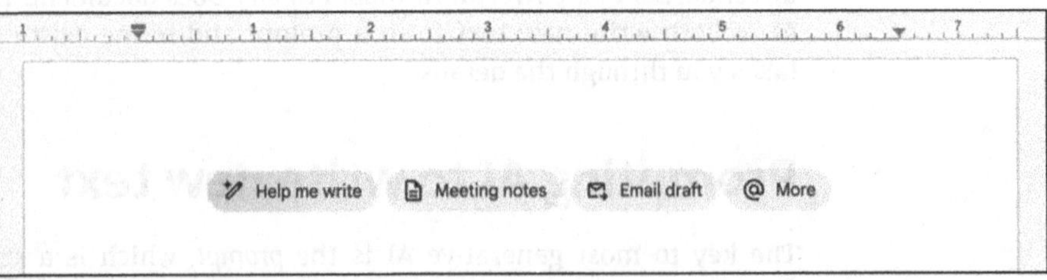

FIGURE 5-9: New blank documents come with a Help Me Write button for generating AI text.

» **Click the Help Me Write icon:** If your document already has some writing, position the cursor where you want the generated text to appear. The help me write icon (shown in the margin) appears to the left of the line that contains the cursor, as shown in Figure 5-10. Click that icon.

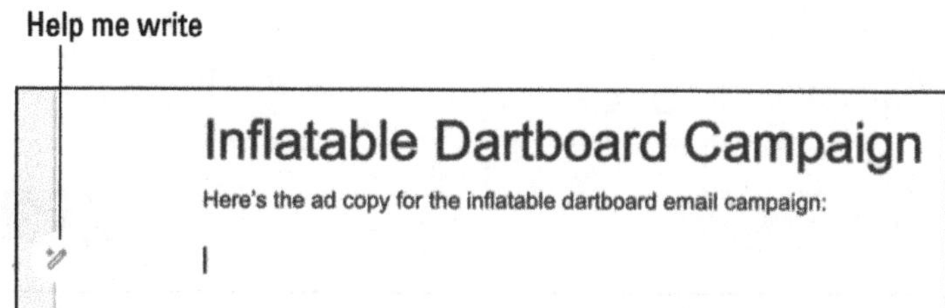
Help me write
Inflatable Dartboard Campaign
Here's the ad copy for the inflatable dartboard email campaign:

FIGURE 5-10: The help me write icon appears to the left of the line that contains the cursor.

» **Right-click the document:** If your document already has some writing, right-click the document where you want the generated text to appear. In the context menu that appears, click Help Me Write.

Whichever method you choose, Docs displays the Help Me Write dialog, where you enter your prompt as shown in Figure 5-11.

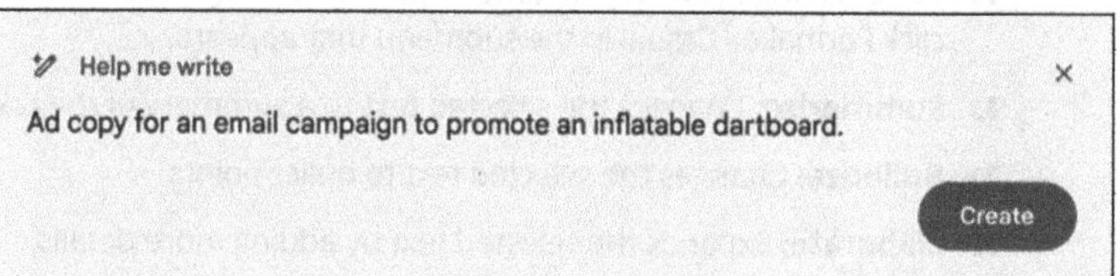
Help me write
Ad copy for an email campaign to promote an inflatable dartboard.
Create

FIGURE 5-11: In the Help Me Write dialog, write the prompt that tells the AI what you want.

When your prompt is ready, click Create and the AI goes to work converting your prompt to the requested text. Figure 5-12 shows an example result. If you're happy with the text, click Insert to add the text to your document. Otherwise, click Refine and then choose one of the options in the pop-up menu that appears (refer to the next section to learn more about these refinements). When you're done, click Insert.

TIP

If you want to modify the prompt and then regenerate the text, click the prompt at the top of the results to open the text for editing, make your changes, and then click Update.

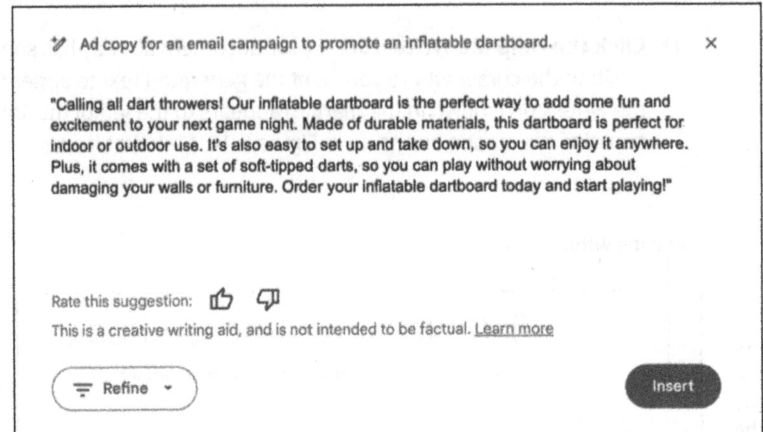

Ad copy for an email campaign to promote an inflatable dartboard.
"Calling all dart throwers! Our inflatable dartboard is the perfect way to add some fun and excitement to your next game night. Made of durable materials, this dartboard is perfect for indoor or outdoor use. It's also easy to set up and take down, so you can enjoy it anywhere. Plus, it comes with a set of soft-tipped darts, so you can play without worrying about damaging your walls or furniture. Order your inflatable dartboard today and start playing!"
Rate this suggestion:
This is a creative writing aid, and is not intended to be factual. Learn more
Refine
Insert

FIGURE 5-12: Some AI-generated text based on the prompt shown in Figure 5-11.

Asking AI to refine existing text

If you've written something that you're not happy with, perhaps the Docs AI model can help. Select the text, and then either click the help me write icon (labeled in Figure 5-10) to the left of the text or right-click the text and then click Refine the Selected Text. Either way, you see a pop-up menu with the following refinement options:

- **Tone:** Changes the overall tone of the selected text based on whether you click Formal or Casual in the submenu that appears.
- **Summarize:** Changes the selected text to a summary of the text
- **Bulletize:** Changes the selected text to bullet points
- **Elaborate:** Expands the selected text by adding more details
- **Shorten:** Contracts the selected text by removing details
- **Custom:** Modifies the selected text based on a prompt that you enter

Search and Ye Shall Replace

If you've ever found yourself lamenting a long-lost word adrift in some humongous megadocument, the Google Docs folks can sympathize (because it has probably happened to them a time or two). In fact, they were even kind enough to build a special find feature into Docs to help you locate missing text. And that's not all: You can use this feature also to seek out and replace every instance of one word with another. Sound like fun? Well, okay, maybe not, but it *is* handy, so you might want to read this section anyway.

Finding stuff

If you need to find a certain word or phrase in a short document, it's usually easiest just to scroll through the text. But if you're dealing with more than a couple of pages, don't waste your time rummaging through the whole file. Bring the find feature onboard and let it do the searching for you:

1. **Choose Edit ⇨ Find and Replace.**

   Docs unearths the Find and Replace dialog.

   If you feel like it, you can also display Find and Replace by pressing Ctrl+H (Windows) or ⌘+Shift+H (macOS).

2. **In the Find text box, enter the text you want to locate.**

   Docs helpfully highlights all instances of the text. Docs also adds *X* of *Y* to the right side of the text box, where *X* is the number of the instance of your search text that's selected in the document and *Y* is the total number of instances of the search text in the document.

3. **If the selected instance of the search text isn't the one you want, click either Next (to move forward) or Previous (to move backward) to select other instances until you reach the one you want.**
4. **When you're done, click X (close).**

Some notes on searching

Searching for text is a relatively straightforward affair, but it wouldn't be Docs if there weren't 5,000 other ways to confuse the heck out of us. To makes things easier, here are a few plain-English notes that'll help you get the most out of the search feature:

- **For best results, keep your search text as short as possible.** A word or two is all you usually need. Trying to match long phrases or even entire sentences can be a problem because you increase your chances of misspelling a word or accidentally leaving a word out of the search text. (For example, if you want to search for *It's a wonderful day in the neighborhood* and you enter *It is a wonderful day in the neighborhood*, Docs scoffs at your efforts because the beginning of the two sentences don't match.) And besides, it just takes longer to type a lengthy phrase or sentence.
- **If you're not sure how to spell a word, just use a piece of it.** Docs still finds *egregious* if you search for *egre* (although, efficient beast that it is, it also finds words like *regret* and *degree*).

» **To find only words that begin with the search text, add a space before the text.** Bear in mind, however, that this technique fails for words that appear at the beginning of a paragraph.

» **You can match not only the letters but also whatever uppercase and lowercase format you use.** If you need to differentiate between, say, *Bobby* (some guy) and *bobby* (as in a bobby pin or an English bobby), select the Match Case check box in the Find and Replace dialog.

Finding-and-replacing stuff

If you do a lot of writing, one of the features you'll come to rely on the most is *find-and-replace*, where Docs seeks out a particular bit of text and replaces it with something else. This may not seem like a big deal for a word or two, but if you need to change a couple of dozen instances of *irregardless* to *regardless*, it can be a real timesaver.

Searching and replacing is, as you might imagine, not all that different from plain old searching. Here's how it works:

1. **Choose Edit ⇨ Find and Replace (or press Ctrl+H).**

   Docs digs up the Find and Replace dialog.

2. **In the Find text box, enter the text you want to locate.**
3. **In the Replace With text box, enter the text you want to use in place of what's in the Find box.**

   Docs selects the first instance of the Find text in the document.

4. **If the selected instance of the Find text isn't the one you seek, click Next (to move forward) or Previous (to move backward) to select other instances until you get to the one you want.**
5. **Click Replace.**

   Docs replaces the selected instance with the Replace With text and then selects the next instance.

6. **Repeat Steps 4 and 5 until you've replaced all the instances you want.**

   As an alternative to Steps 4–6, you can just click Replace All, which performs the replacement for every instance in the document.

WARNING

Clicking Replace All sure seems like the easy way to get this chore finished faster, but some caution is required. Double-check (and maybe even triple-check) your Find and Replace With text and try to think of any ways a Replace All operation can go wrong. For example, you might want to replace the word *egret* with the word *heron*. That's your business, but know that if you run Replace All willy-nilly, you might also change *regret* to *rheron* and *allegretto* to *allheronto*.

7. **When you're done, click X (close).**

Checking Spelling and Grammar

Words. Whether you're a *logophile* (a lover of words) or a *logophobe* (one who has an aversion to words), you can't leave home without 'em. Whether you suffer from *logomania* (the excessive use of words) or *logagraphia* (the inability to express ideas in writing), you can't escape 'em. So far, I've offered ways to edit words and ways to find words, but when it comes down to using words, well, you've been on your own. That changes now because in this section you learn about Spelling and Grammar Check, an off-the-scale useful tool that'll help you become word-wise. Who knows? You might become a full-fledged *logolept* (a word maniac).

Handling spelling slip-ups

Nothing can ruin the image of your finely crafted documents more than a few spelling mistakes. In the old days, you could just shrug your shoulders and mumble something about never being good at spelling. With Docs, though, you have no excuses because the program comes with a tool that checks your spelling attempts automatically. If Docs finds something that isn't right, it lets you know and gives you a chance to correct it. You can make the spell checker smarter by adding your own words to its dictionary.

When Docs finds a spelling snafu, it points out the rogue word by underlining it with a red squiggle. Click the underlined word and Docs displays a banner like the one shown in Figure 5-13.

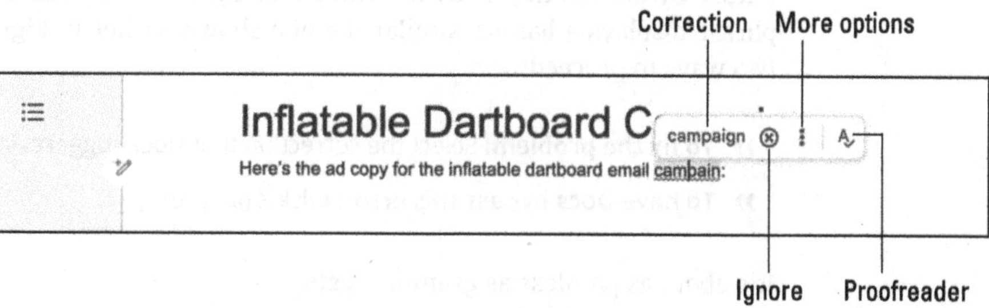

FIGURE 5-13: Docs underlines in red those words it thinks are spelling lapses.

You have a bunch of possible moves you can make from here:

- **To change the word:** Select the correction that Docs suggests in the banner.
- **To have Docs skip this error:** Click X (ignore).
- **To have Docs always make this correction automatically in the future:** Click the more options icon (three vertical dots) and then select Always Correct to *"correction"* (where *correction* is the suggested correction).
- **To tell Docs that your word is correct and to have Docs add the word to its dictionary (and therefore never bug you about it again):** Click the more options icon (three vertical dots) and then select Add to Personal Dictionary.
- **To start the Docs proofreader, click Proofreader:** The proofreader runs through the entire document, flagging each spelling and grammar error as it goes. You can also crank up the proofreader by choosing Tools ⇨ Proofread ⇨ Proofread This Document.

Handling grammar gaffes

Grammar ranks right up there with a root canal and a tax audit on most people's Top Ten Most Unpleasant Things list. And it's no wonder: all those dangling participles, passive voices, and split infinitives. One exposure to that stuff and the usual reaction is, "Yeah, well, split *this!*"

If, like me, you couldn't tell a copulative verb from a correlative conjunction if your life depended on it, help is just around the corner. Docs comes with a tool that checks your grammar for you. That's right: This utility analyzes your document, phrase by phrase, sentence by sentence, and tells you when things aren't right. It even tells you how to fix the problem — and often can do it for you at the click of a mouse.

When Docs trips over a grammatical gotcha, it shames the offending word or phrase by underlining it with a wavy blue line. Clicking the underlined word or phrase displays a banner similar the one shown earlier in Figure 5-13. You have two ways to proceed:

- **To fix the problem:** Select the correction that Docs suggests in the banner.
- **To have Docs bypass this error:** Click X (ignore).

It's about as painless as grammar gets.

IN THIS CHAPTER

» Playing with fonts, type sizes, and other typographical niceties

» Messing with alignment, line spacing, indentation, and more

» Taking advantage of styles

» Learning what numbered and bulleted lists are all about

» Inserting photos and other images into your documents

Chapter 6 Looking Good: Formatting Documents

"The least you can do is look respectable." That's what my mother always used to tell me when I was a kid. This advice holds up especially well in these image-conscious times. If you don't look good up front (or if your work doesn't look good), you'll often be written off without a second thought.

When it comes to looking good — whether you're pecking out a memo, putting together a report, or polishing up your résumé — Docs gives you a massive tool chest stuffed to the brim with formatting implements. This chapter gives you the skinny on these tools, including lots of hints about how best to use them.

Making Your Characters Look Good

The first step on your road to looking good is the lowly character. I know, I know — you want to try out some really big stuff, but don't forget all that blather about the longest journey beginning with a single step yadda-yadda.

Besides, working with even little characters can make a big difference. Why, just a little bit of bolding here, a couple of italics there, throw in a font or two, and suddenly that humdrum, boring memo is turned into a dynamic, exciting thing of beauty. People from all over will be clamoring to read your stuff. You will be, in short, a star.

Getting familiar with fonts

Until now, you may not have given much thought to the individual characters that make up your writings. After all, an *a* is an *a*, am I right? Well, Docs will change all that. When you start working with different fonts, you learn that not all *a*'s are the same (or *b*'s or *c*'s, for that matter).

Fonts are to characters what architecture is to buildings. Architectural styles are characterized by certain features and patterns; if you can tell a geodesic dome from a flying buttress, you can tell whether the building is Gothic or art deco or whatever. Fonts, too, are distinguished by a set of unique design characteristics. Specifically, there are four things to check for: the typeface, the type style, the type size, and the type position.

Typeface

Any related set of letters, numbers, and other symbols has its own distinctive design, called the *typeface*. Typefaces, as shown in Figure 6-1, can be wildly different, depending on the shape and thickness of characters, the spacing, and whatever the designer had for breakfast that day.

This is a font called Arial and it's the Docs default. Arial is an example of a "sans serif" font. It has a clean look that makes it ideal for online reading or for document headings.

This is a font called Georgia. Type types call it a "serif" font. It's very readable, so it's a good choice for long text passages.

This weird thing is called Corsiva. It's known in Typeface Land as a "decorative" font. It's useful for special occasions such as fancy-schmancy invitations.

This decidedly unattractive font is called Courier New. Every letter is the same width, so it's called a "monospace" font.

FIGURE 6-1: Some typeface examples.

Type nerds differentiate between a typeface and a font in a way that's analogous to the difference between an architectural style and an example of that style. For instance, French Gothic is an architectural style, and the Notre-Dame Cathedral in Paris is an example of that style. Similarly, Arial is a typeface, and 12-point, bold Arial is a font. Happily, despite all this type geekery, in this chapter (and indeed throughout this book), I use the terms *typeface* and *font* interchangeably.

Typefaces come in three flavors (refer to the first three examples in Figure 6-1):

- **Serif:** These typefaces contain fine cross strokes — typographic nerds call them *feet* — at the extremities of each character. These subtle appendages give the typeface a traditional, classy look. Georgia is a common example of a serif typeface.
- **Sans serif:** These typefaces lack these cross strokes. As a result, sans serif typefaces usually have a cleaner, more modern look.
- **Decorative:** These typefaces are usually special designs used to convey a particular effect. For example, if your document needs a sophisticated look for a wine-and-cheese invitation or some similarly swanky event, Corsiva is ideal.

You can classify typefaces also according to the space they allot for each character. This is called the *character spacing* of a font, and it can take one of two forms:

- **Monospaced:** These fonts reserve the same amount of space for each character. For example, examine the Courier New font shown earlier in Figure 6-1. Note that skinny letters, such as *i* and *l*, take up as much space as wider letters, such as *y* and *w*. Though this strategy is admirably egalitarian, these fonts tend to look like they were produced with a typewriter. (In other words, they're ugly.) However, if your writing includes programming code for some reason, monospace is ideal for that.
- **Proportional:** These fonts, such as Arial and Georgia in Figure 6-1, allot space to each letter according to its width. So, the scrawny *i* and *l* take up only a small amount of horizontal space, and wider loads such as *y* and *w* take up a larger amount of space.

Type style and size

The *type style* of a font usually refers to whether the characters are **bold** or *italic*, but Docs also lets you set character attributes, such as underlining. These styles are normally used to highlight or add emphasis to words or phrases.

The *type size* measures the font's height. The standard unit of measurement is the *point*, where an inch is 72 points. For example, the individual letters in a 24-point font are twice as tall as those in a 12-point font. (In case you're wondering, this book is printed in a 10-point font.)

TECHNICAL STUFF

To be nerdily precise about it, type size is measured from the highest point of a tall letter, such as *f* or *h*, to the lowest point of an underhanging letter, such as *g* or *y*.

Using different character sizes and styles is an easy way to fool people into thinking you're a competent professional. For example, you can make titles and section headings stand out by using bold characters that are larger than regular text. Italics are good for emphasizing important words or phrases, but you can use them also for, say, company names and book titles.

Type position

Characters normally follow each other along each line. However, you can also format the *type position* of a character, which moves the character vertically relative to the regular characters. You can set two positions: a *superscript*, which raises the character slightly higher than normal, for example, $e = mc^2$, or a *subscript*, which drops the characters slightly lower than normal, for example, H_2O.

Formatting with fonts

Okay, enough theory. Let's get down to business and learn how to go about applying different fonts to characters. To begin, select the block of text you want to format. You then apply the formatting using any one of the following three methods (depending on your mood):

- On the menu bar, choose Format ⇨ Text, and then select the formatting you want to apply from the menu that appears.
- Press a shortcut key.
- Click a toolbar icon.

Table 6-1 shows the Text menu commands and their corresponding shortcut keys that you can select.

If you do a lot of work with fonts, you'll appreciate the convenience of the font-related icons on the Docs toolbar. Table 6-2 shows you the available icons for font-related chores.

TABLE 6-1 Font Formatting via Menu and Keyboard

Text Menu Command	Windows Shortcut Key	Mac Shortcut Key
Bold	Ctrl+B	⌘+B
Italic	Ctrl+I	⌘+I
Underline	Ctrl+U	⌘+U
Strikethrough	Alt+Shift+5	⌘+Shift+X
Superscript	Ctrl+. (period)	⌘+. (period)
Subscript	Ctrl+, (comma)	⌘+, (comma)
Size, Increase Font Size	Ctrl+Shift+. (period)	⌘+Shift+. (period)
Size, Decrease Font Size	Ctrl+Shift+, (comma)	⌘+Shift+, (comma)

TABLE 6-2 Font Formatting from the Toolbar

Toolbar Icon	Icon Name	What It Does
Arial ▾	Font	Displays a list of typefaces and then applies the typeface you select to the text
− 11 +	Font size	Applies a font size to the text; either type the font size or click the – or + icon
B	Bold	Toggles bold for the text
I	Italic	Toggles italics for the text
U	Underline	Toggles underline for the text
A	Text color	Displays a color palette and then applies the color you select to the text
	Highlight color	Displays a color palette and then applies the color you select to the background of the text

TIP

By default, Docs offers 30 or so typefaces for your text formatting pleasure. However, Google (via its famous Google Fonts service — check out `https://fonts.google.com`) is home to hundreds of typefaces. If none of the default Docs typefaces speaks to your inner designer, pull down the toolbar's Font menu and select More Fonts. This scores you an immediate appointment with the Fonts dialog, which displays typefaces from Google Fonts, as shown in Figure 6-2. If you come across a font you like, click it to add it to the My Fonts list. (Feel free to add as many fonts as you like.) When you're done, select OK, and Docs adds the font (or fonts) to the Font list.

FIGURE 6-2: In the Fonts dialog, you have hundreds of choices from Google Fonts.

Avoiding the ransom note look

The downside to the easy-to-use font features in Docs is that they can sometimes be *too* easy to use. Flush with your newfound knowledge, you start throwing every font formatting option in sight at your documents. This can turn even the most profound and well-written documents into a real dog's breakfast (known in the trade as the *ransom note look*). Here are some tips to avoid overdoing the formatting:

- Never use more than a few fonts in a single document. Anything more looks amateurish and will only confuse the reader.
- If you need to emphasize something, bold or italicize it in the same font as the surrounding text. Avoid using underlining for emphasis.

- Use larger sizes only for titles and headings.
- Avoid bizarre decorative fonts for large sections of text. Most of those suckers are hard on the eyes after a half dozen words or so. Serif fonts are usually very readable, so they're a good choice for long passages. The clean look of sans serif fonts makes them a good choice for headlines and titles.

Copy text formatting by "painting" it

If you have gone to a lot of trouble to format some text and want to use the same formatting elsewhere, you don't have to start from scratch. Docs has a marvelously useful tool called paint format that can transfer formatting from one bit of text to another. Here's how it works:

1. **Select the text that has the formatting you want to use elsewhere.**

2. **Click the paint format icon on the toolbar.**

   The mouse pointer sprouts an icon that looks like a paint roller.

3. **Select the text you want to format.**

   If you're working with a single word, just click the word. Otherwise, drag the pointer over the text you want to format.

   Without splattering or dripping, Docs applies the formatting from the text in Step 1 to the new text.

Making Your Lines and Paragraphs Look Good

The preceding section shows you how to format characters, but now I bump things up a notch and look at formatting lines and paragraphs. How will this help your writing look good onscreen? Well, all the character formatting in the world doesn't do you much good if your lines are scrunched together and the various pieces of text aren't lined up like boot camp recruits. Documents like these appear cramped and uninviting, and often get tossed in the trash without a second look. This section can help your documents avoid this sorry fate.

Getting your text ducks in a row: Aligning paragraphs

Aligning stuff is about getting your paragraphs dressed up so that they look all prim and proper. Specifically, I'm talking about lining up the left and right ends of your paragraph lines with respect to the left or right margin — or both. (I talk about margins in detail in the next chapter, but for now all you need to know is that the *left margin* is the blank space to the left of your document text and the *right margin* is the blank space to the right of your document text.)

Docs offers three ways to apply alignment:

- On the menu bar, choose Format ➪ Align & Indent, and then click an alignment option in the menu that appears.
- Press a shortcut key.
- Click an option on the toolbar's Align menu. Depending on the width of your browser window, you might need to click the more icon (three vertical dots) to display the Align menu.

Table 6-3 shows the Align & Indent menu commands, their corresponding shortcut keys, and the equivalent toolbar icons for the four Docs alignment options.

TABLE 6-3 Paragraph Alignment in Docs

Align & Indent Menu Command	Windows Shortcut Key	Mac Shortcut Key	Toolbar Icon	What It Does
Left	Ctrl+Shift+L	⌘+Shift+L		Aligns each line on the left margin
Center	Ctrl+Shift+E	⌘+Shift+E		Centers each line between the left and right margins
Right	Ctrl+Shift+R	⌘+Shift+R		Aligns each line on the right margin
Justified	Ctrl+Shift+J	⌘+Shift+J		Aligns each line on both the left and right margins, and left-aligns the last line in a paragraph if it's too short to justify

Before you select an alignment option, first tell Docs what you want to format:

- » To format a single paragraph, click anywhere inside that paragraph.
- » To format multiple, consecutive paragraphs, select those paragraphs.
- » To format the entire document, pull down the Edit menu and choose Select All, or press Ctrl+A (⌘+A on a Mac).

With your selection made, choose the menu command, toolbar icon, or shortcut key to apply the alignment. Figure 6-3 puts these alignment commands through their paces.

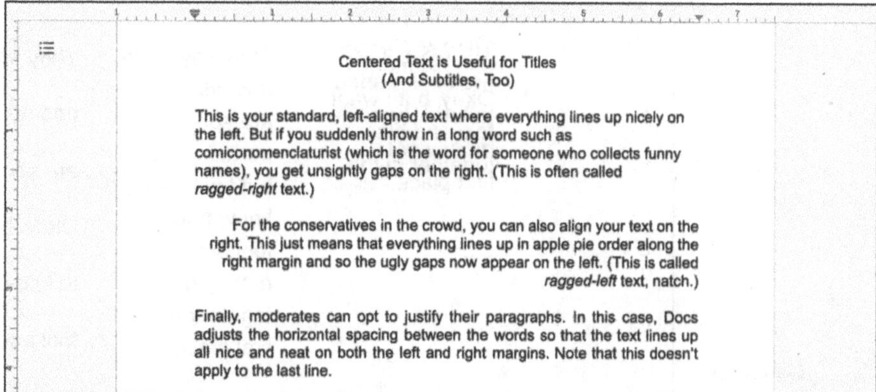

FIGURE 6-3: Some paragraph alignment examples.

REMEMBER

Left-justified text is said to be *ragged right* because the right ends of each line in the paragraph usually don't line up. Similarly, right-justified text is called *ragged left* because the left ends of each line in the paragraph don't line up.

Breathing room: Changing the line spacing

You can improve the look of your document's paragraphs by adjusting the *line spacing* — the formatting tweak that determines the amount of space between each line in the paragraph. For example, double spacing leaves twice as much space between the lines as standard single spacing. Increasing the spacing creates more white space in the document, which can make the document easier to read. However, don't go overboard, because if you increase the line spacing too much, your text can become harder to read because the lines are too far apart.

For example, Figure 6-4 shows the same text with three different line spacing values:

- The text on the left uses a line spacing of 0.6. Note that the lines are far too close to be read easily.
- The text on the right uses a line spacing value of 2 (double spacing). In this case, the lines are too far apart for comfortable reading.
- The text in the middle uses a line spacing value of 1.15. Now the distance between each line is just right for reading.

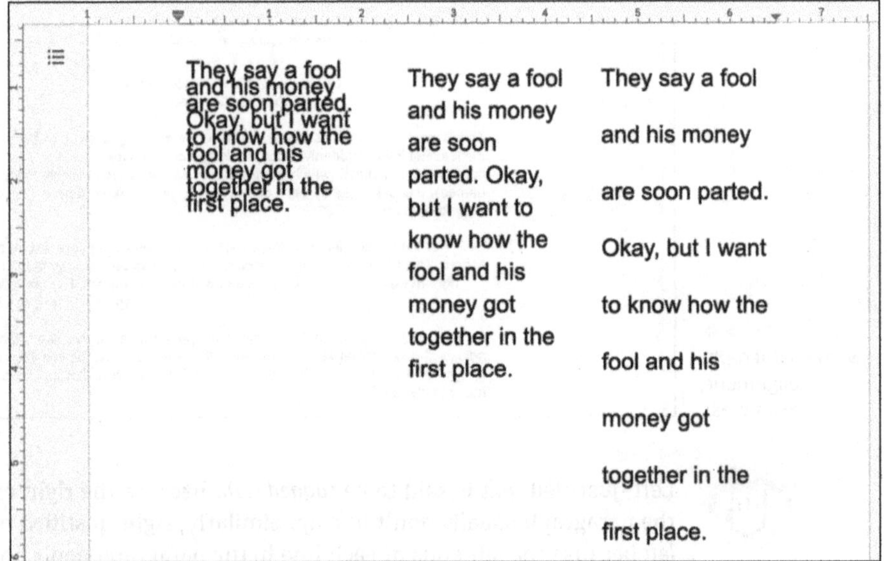

FIGURE 6-4: Line spacing values that are too small (left), too large (right), and just right (middle).

To set the line spacing, first specify what you want to format:

- To format one paragraph, click anywhere within that paragraph.
- To format multiple, consecutive paragraphs, select those paragraphs.
- To format the entire document, pull down the Edit menu and choose Select All, or press Ctrl+A (⌘+A on a Mac).

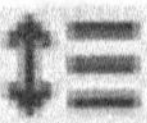

Now choose Format ➪ Line & Paragraph Spacing, or click the line & paragraph spacing toolbar icon. (If the icon doesn't appear on your toolbar, select it by first clicking the toolbar's more icon — three vertical dots.) You now have two choices:

- Select a preset line spacing value: Single, 1.15, 1.5, or Double.
- Select Custom Spacing to open the Custom Spacing dialog, shown in Figure 6-5. Enter a value in the Line Spacing text box and then click Apply. (If you're wondering about the Before and After settings, hold on a sec; I cover them in the next section.)

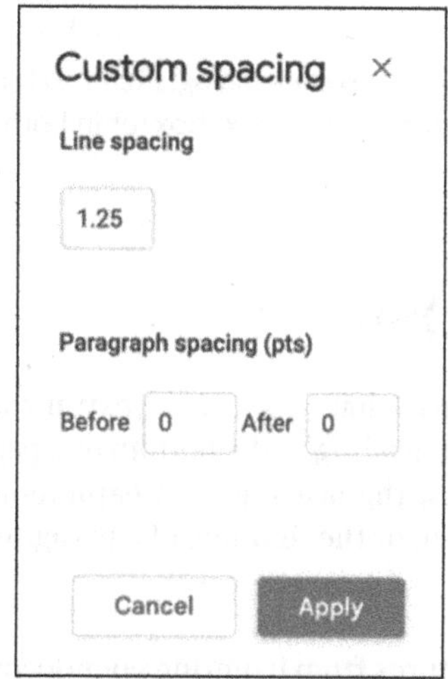

FIGURE 6-5: In the Custom Spacing dialog, set your own line spacing value.

Giving paragraphs some elbow room

There's a long-running debate in typographical circles about whether to add space between paragraphs. Fortunately for you, the specifics of that debate aren't important here. Instead, I offer the following advice:

- If you indent the first line of your paragraphs (as I describe in the later section "Indenting paragraphs"), you don't need space between them.
- If you don't indent, you need to add some space between paragraphs so that it's always clear to the reader when one paragraph ends and the next one begins.

To set the spacing between paragraphs, first specify what you want to format:

- To format one paragraph, click anywhere within that paragraph.
- To format multiple, consecutive paragraphs, select those paragraphs.
- To format the entire document, pull down the Edit menu and choose Select All, or press Ctrl+A (⌘+A on a Mac).

Choose Format ➪ Line & Paragraph Spacing, or click the line & paragraph spacing toolbar icon. (If the icon doesn't appear on your toolbar, select it by first clicking the toolbar's more icon — three vertical dots.) You now have three spacing options:

- **Add Space Before Paragraph:** Adds a 10-point space before each selected paragraph.
- **Add Space After Paragraph:** Adds a 10-point space following each selected paragraph.
- **Custom Spacing:** Opens the Custom Spacing dialog. (Refer to Figure 6-5.) Enter a value, in points, in the Before or After text box (or in both — why not?), and then select Apply.

Keeping stuff together

One way to jar your readers is to have what appear to be extraneous lines just sitting there on the page. It might be a heading at the bottom of a page, an important paragraph broken across two pages, the last line of a paragraph at the top of a page (known in the trade as a *widow*), or the first line of a paragraph at the bottom of a page (known as an *orphan*).

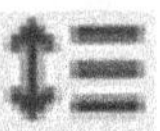

You can prevent these pathetic creatures from haunting your documents by selecting the paragraph you want to format, choosing Format ➪ Line & Paragraph Spacing or clicking the line & paragraph spacing toolbar icon. You can work with these four commands:

- **Keep with Next:** Ensures that the selected paragraph (such as a heading) always appears on the same page as the paragraph that follows it
- **Keep Lines Together:** Ensures that all lines in the selected paragraph appear on the same page
- **Prevent Single Lines:** Ensures that the selected paragraph has no widows or orphans
- **Add Page Break Before:** Ensures that the selected paragraph always appears at the top of whatever page it's on

Indenting paragraphs

Indenting a paragraph means shifting some or all paragraph text relative to the margins. Docs offers four paragraph indentation possibilities:

- **Left:** Shifts the entire paragraph relative to the left margin by a specified amount
- **Right:** Shifts the entire paragraph relative to the right margin by a specified amount
- **First line:** Shifts just the first line of the paragraph away from the left margin by a specified amount
- **Hanging:** Shifts all but the first line of the paragraph away from the left margin by a specified amount

REMEMBER

The term *hanging indent* sounds weird, but it can be useful. For example, a hanging indent is often used for the items in a bibliography and for dictionary entries.

To set the indentation, first specify what you want to work with:

- To indent one paragraph, click anywhere within that paragraph.
- To indent two or more consecutive paragraphs, select those paragraphs.
- To indent the entire document, pull down the Edit menu and choose Select All, or press Ctrl+A (⌘+A on a Mac)

Docs offers three left indentation methods:

- On the menu bar, choose Format ➪ Align & Indent, and then select an alignment option from the menu that appears.
- Press a shortcut key.
- Click a toolbar icon.

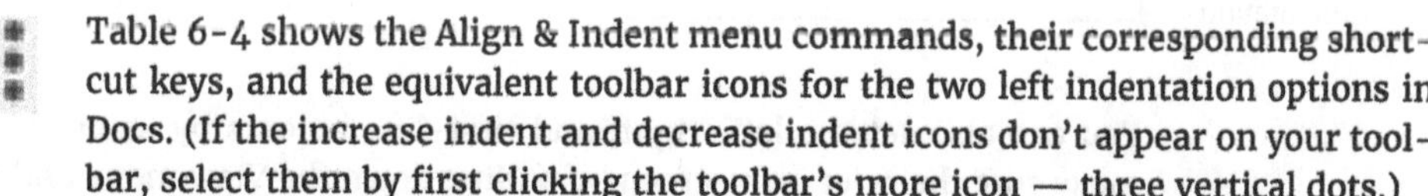

Table 6-4 shows the Align & Indent menu commands, their corresponding shortcut keys, and the equivalent toolbar icons for the two left indentation options in Docs. (If the increase indent and decrease indent icons don't appear on your toolbar, select them by first clicking the toolbar's more icon — three vertical dots.)

TABLE 6-4 **Left-Indent Paragraphs in Docs**

Align & Indent Menu Command	Windows Shortcut Key	Mac Shortcut Key	Toolbar Icon	What It Does
Increase indent	Ctrl+]	⌘+]		Increases the left indentation of the paragraph by half an inch
Decrease indent	Ctrl+[	⌘+[		Decreases the left indentation of the paragraph by half an inch

To set a custom indentation, follow these steps:

1. **Choose Format ⇨ Align & Indent ⇨ Indentation Options.**

   Docs opens the Indentation Options dialog, shown in Figure 6-6.

2. **To set the left indentation, enter a value (in inches) in the Left text box.**
3. **To set the right indentation, enter a value (in inches) in the Right text box.**
4. **Use the Special Indent list to select either First Line or Hanging, and then enter an indentation value (in inches) in the text box.**
5. **Click Apply.**

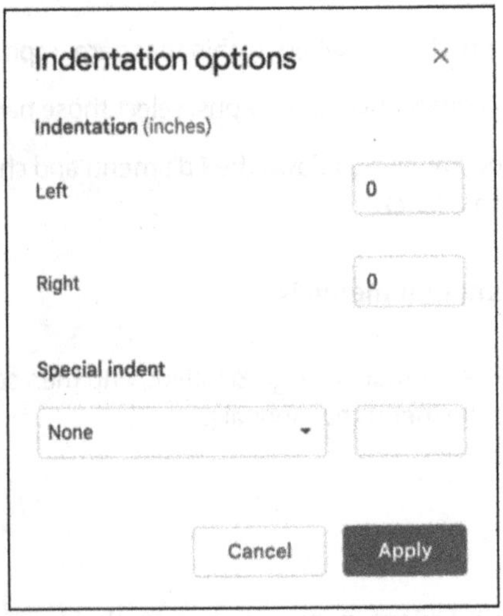

FIGURE 6-6: In the Indentation Options dialog, set up a custom indentation.

You can also set the left, right, and first-line indents by using the ruler. First, make sure the ruler is onscreen by pulling down the View menu and selecting the Show Ruler command. Then, using the ruler features pointed out in Figure 6-7, you can make the following indent adjustments for the selected paragraph or paragraphs:

- Click-and-drag the left indent marker to set the left indent.
- Click-and-drag the right indent marker to set the right indent.
- Click-and-drag the first line indent marker to set the first-line indent.

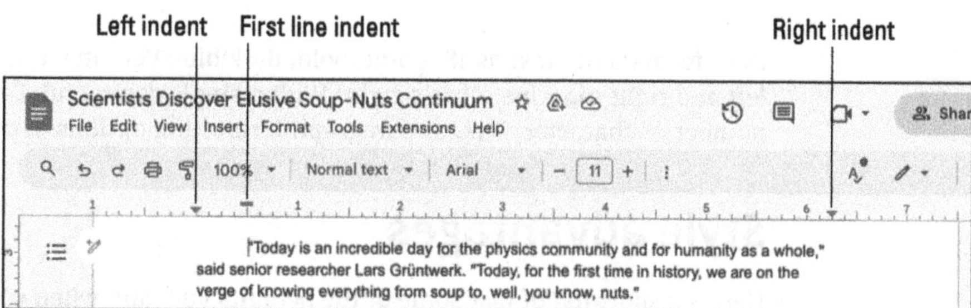

FIGURE 6-7: You can set the left, right, and first-line indents by using the ruler.

Making Looking Good Look Easy with Styles

As I hope I've shown so far in this chapter, formatting is essential if you want to produce good-looking documents that get noticed. The problem is that formatting always seems to take up *so much* time.

Suppose that you want to add a title to a document. Titles usually appear in a larger, sans serif font, so you type the text, select it, and then use the Font and Font Size commands to set up the appropriate formatting. For good measure, you also center the title. It looks not bad, but you decide that the text needs to be bold. So, you select the text again and apply the bolding. Things are looking good, but then you decide to apply a larger type size. Once again, you select the text and make the size adjustment. After fiddling with a few more options (maybe underlining or dark blue text would look good), you finally get the title exactly right. You've just wasted ten minutes of your busy day, but, hey, that's the reality of working with Docs, right?

Wrong. You don't have to stand for this! By learning how to use styles, you can accomplish the same chore in ten seconds instead of ten minutes. How is that possible? Well, a *style* is nothing more than a predefined collection of formatting and layout settings. Docs comes with a few built-in styles, including a style named Title. This means that rather than fuss around with formatting options, you can just select the text you want to use as the title and then apply the Title style. Docs immediately applies all the Title style's predefined formatting options — just like that.

What if you don't like the default formatting of the Title style? That's not a problem because it's also easy to define your own version of each built-in style. For example, you can format some text with an 18-point, bold, dark blue, Verdana font that's centered between the left and right margins and then tell Docs to use that formatting instead of its default formatting for the Title style. You'd then enter the document title, select it, and apply the Title style. In the blink of an eye,

Docs formats the text as 18-point, bold, dark blue Verdana, centered between the left and right margins. That's right: With a single command, Docs can throw any number of character, line, or paragraph formatting options at the selected text.

Style advantages

Here's a short list of just some of the benefits you gain when you use styles:

- The most obvious, of course, is the time you save. After you've invested the initial few minutes to define your version of a style, applying any style takes only a few mouse clicks.
- You eliminate the trial-and-error that goes into many formatting chores. After you've decided on a look that you like, you can capture it in a style for all time.
- If you change your mind, however, a style can be easily edited. Does this mean that you have to go back and reapply the style throughout the document? No way. Any text that's formatted with that style is automatically reformatted with the revised style. This feature alone is worth the price of admission.
- Styles make it easy to create documents that have a consistent look and feel because you can access your styles from any document.
- Styles reduce the number of keystrokes and mouse clicks you need to get the job done. In this age where repetitive strain injuries such as carpal tunnel syndrome are reaching almost epidemic proportions, anything that reduces the wear-and-tear on our sensitive anatomy is a welcome relief.

If it all sounds too good to be true, well, there's a downside: Styles can save you so much time that you may run out of things to do during the day. (Pause while the laughter dies down.)

Applying default Docs styles to avoid reinventing the style wheel

Before you go off in some kind of style-defining frenzy, check out the default, or built-in, styles. Docs has nine default styles, listed here with their keyboard shortcuts when they have one:

- **Normal text (Ctrl+Alt+0; ⌘ +Option+0 on a Mac):** This 11-point, black Arial font is used for regular document text.
- **Title:** This 26-point, black Arial font is ideal for document titles.

- **Subtitle:** This 15-point, dark gray 3, Arial font is normally used for document subtitles.
- **Heading 1 (Ctrl+Alt+1; ⌘+Option+1 on a Mac):** This 20-point, black Arial font is used for first-level document headings.
- **Heading 2 (Ctrl+Alt+2; ⌘+Option+2 on a Mac):** This 16-point, black Arial font is used for second-level document headings.
- **Heading 3 (Ctrl+Alt+3; ⌘+Option+3 on a Mac):** This 14-point, dark gray 4 Arial font is used for third-level document headings.
- **Heading 4 (Ctrl+Alt+4; ⌘+Option+4 on a Mac):** This 12-point, dark gray 3 Arial font is used for fourth-level document headings.
- **Heading 5 (Ctrl+Alt+5; ⌘+Option+5 on a Mac):** This 11-point, dark gray 3 Arial font is used for fifth-level document headings.
- **Heading 6 (Ctrl+Alt+6; ⌘+Option+6 on a Mac):** This 11-point, italic, dark gray 3 Arial font is used for sixth-level document headings.

To apply these styles, first select the text you want to format. Docs then gives you three choices:

- Choose Format ➪ Paragraph Styles, select the style you want to apply, and then choose Apply *Style*, where *Style* is the name of the style.
- Select the Styles list on the toolbar (see Figure 6-8) and then select the style you want to apply. (Note that not all default styles appear in this list. If you want to apply Heading 4 through Heading 6, you need to use either of the other methods in this list.)
- Press the style's shortcut-key combo, which I've included in the preceding list.

Updating a default style to taste

Well, since fine words butter no parsnips, as they say (no, they really do), let's get down to business and learn how to define your own versions of the default styles. The simplest way to go about this is to first format a section of text exactly the way you want it. You can then update a default style so that it uses your formatting instead of the predefined Docs formatting. Here are the steps you need to follow:

1. **Using some existing text, apply the formatting options you want to include in the updated style.**

   You can use any of the formatting features I discuss in this chapter.

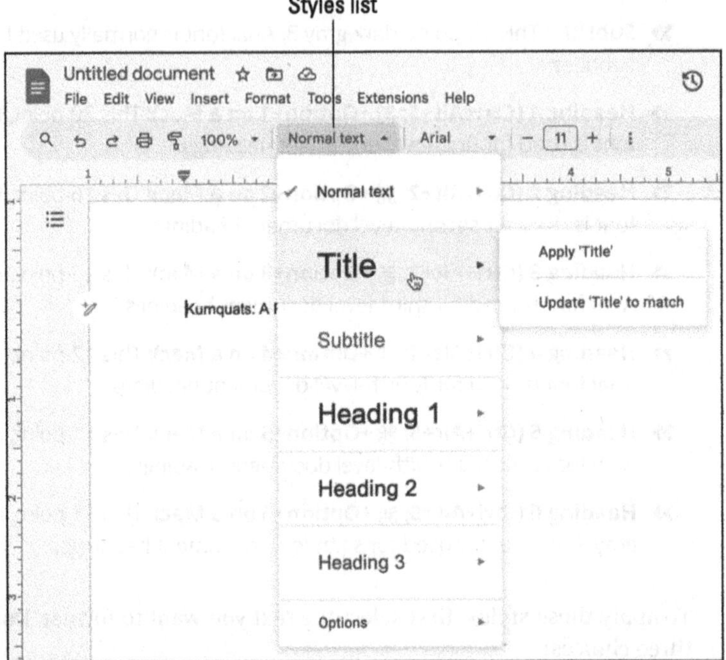

FIGURE 6-8: The easiest way to apply most default styles is via the Styles list on the toolbar.

2. **When you're done, make sure the cursor is inside the formatted text.**
3. **Choose Format ⇨ Paragraph Styles, select the style you want to update, and then choose Update *Style* to Match, where *Style* is the name of the style.**

   Alternatively, select the Styles list on the toolbar, hover the mouse pointer over the style you want to update, and then select Update *Style* to Match, where *Style* is the name of the style.

   Docs updates the style to match your formatting and applies that formatting to any other text in your document that currently uses the same style.

REMEMBER

The new style applies only to the current document. If you want to use the new style in other documents, you need to save the style; I talk about that in the next section.

Saving your updated styles

If you want to use an updated style only in the current document, that's perfectly fine. However, you might find that you want to reuse one or more of your updated styles in other documents. For example, if you've updated some styles to match corporate formatting guidelines, you'll want those updates available in every work document you create.

Docs is happy to comply, as long as you follow these instructions:

1. **Follow the steps in the preceding section to update the default Docs styles as needed.**
2. **Choose Format ➪ Paragraph Styles ➪ Options ➪ Save as My Default Styles.**

   Alternatively, select the Styles list on the toolbar and then choose Options ➪ Save as My Default Styles.

   Docs saves your updated styles.

Telling Docs to use your updated styles

If you find that a particular document isn't using your saved default styles, you can give Docs a nudge in the ribs and tell it to use your styles, by using either of these techniques:

- » Choose Format ➪ Paragraph Styles ➪ Options, and then select Use My Default Styles.
- » Pull down the toolbar's Styles list and then choose Options ➪ Use My Default Styles.

Resetting the default styles

If you make a mess of your style updates or if your style updates have served their purpose and you no longer need them, you can reset all the styles to their original Docs default formatting by using either of the following techniques:

- » Choose Format ➪ Paragraph Styles ➪ Options ➪ Reset Styles.
- » Pull down the toolbar's Styles list and then choose Options ➪ Reset Styles.

Making Lists, Optionally Checking Them Twice

Lists are one of the most common document structures. Whether it's a to-do list, a list of action items, a grocery list, or a list of steps to follow, breaking items out so that they appear individually instead of running them all together in a paragraph can make those items easier to read.

If you do want to include a list in your document, what's the best way to go about it? You can use separate paragraphs or headings and number them yourself or add, say, asterisks (*) at the beginning of each. I suppose that would work, but hold your list horses — there's a better way. Docs has a couple of commands designed to give you much more control over your list-building chores.

Putting your affairs in order with numbered lists

To include a numbered list of items — a top-ten list, bowling league standings, or any kind of ranking — don't bother adding the numbers yourself. Instead, you can use the Numbered List command in Docs to generate the numbers for you.

Before I get to the specifics, you should know that Docs is happy to create multi-level numbered lists, where each level has its own numbering format. Here's the default numbering format (see Figure 6-9 for an example):

- The top level of the list uses regular numbers followed by periods (1., 2., 3., and so on).
- The second level of the list uses lowercase letters followed by periods (a., b., c., and so on).
- The third level of the list uses lowercase Roman numerals followed by periods (i., ii., iii., and so on).

1. What is the point of this list?
a. To provide an example.
i. Okay, but is it a *good* example?
ii. It's certainly not a real-world example.
iii. True, but does that matter?
iv. You'll have to ask the reader.
b. To give the author something to do.
c. To give the reader something to do.
2. Anything else we should know?
a. Yes, you get to this second level by pressing Tab.
i. And you get to this third level by pressing Tab again.
3. When, exactly, will this list end?
a. Right
b. About
i. Wait for it...
c. Now.

FIGURE 6-9: An example of a default, multilevel numbered list.

To forge a numbered list of your own, follow these steps:

1. **If you have some existing text that you want to convert to a numbered list, select that text.**

   Make sure that each item in your existing text is in its own paragraph.

2. **Choose Format ➪ Bullets & Numbering ➪ Numbered List Menu.**

   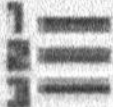

   Alternatively, click the numbered list icon on the toolbar. (If the numbered list icon doesn't appear on your toolbar, select it by first clicking the toolbar's more icon — three vertical dots.)

   Docs displays a menu of numbered-list formats, as shown in Figure 6-10.

   For each format, Docs shows the numbering scheme that it uses for the first, second, and third levels of the list.

3. **Select the numbering scheme you want to use.**

   If you selected some text in advance, Docs converts the text to a numbered list. To add an item to that list, place the cursor at the end of the last item and then press Enter or Return.

4. **For a second-level item, press Tab; for a third-level item, press Tab again.**
5. **Enter your item text and then press Enter or Return to create a new item in the list.**
6. **Repeat Steps 4 and 5 until your list is complete.**
7. **To tell Docs you've finished entering list items, press Enter or Return a second time.**

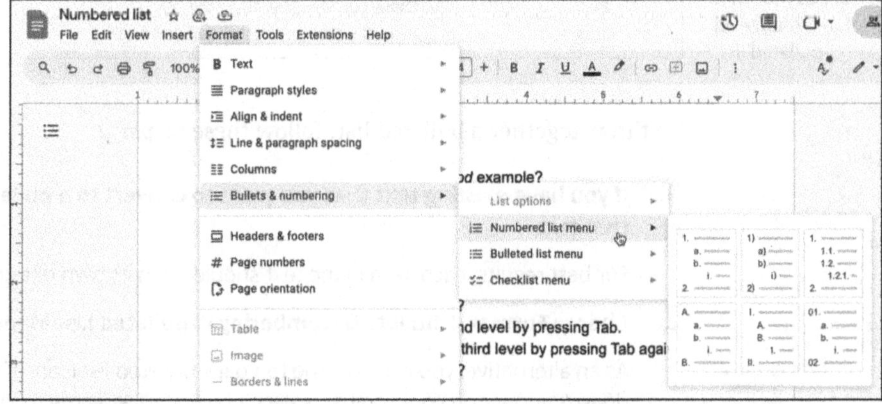

FIGURE 6-10: Select Numbered List to display the available numbering schemes.

Scoring points with bulleted lists

The numbered lists that I discuss in the preceding section aren't suitable for every type of list. If you just want to enumerate a few points, a bulleted list might be more your style. They're called *bulleted* lists because Docs displays a cute little dot, called a *bullet*, to the left of each item.

Most bulleted lists are one level, but Docs doesn't mind creating lists that have two or even three levels. Here's the default bullet format (see Figure 6-11 for an example):

- The top level of the list uses filled-in discs.
- The second level of the list uses circles (discs that aren't filled in).
- The third level of the list uses filled-in squares.

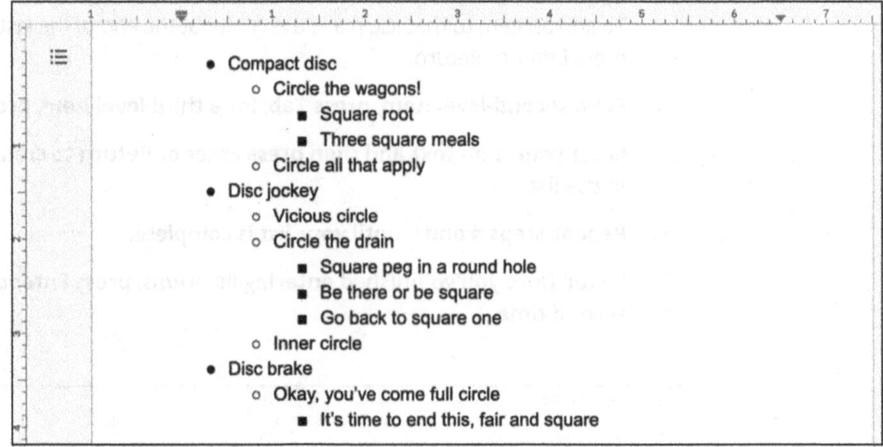

FIGURE 6-11: An example of a default, multilevel bulleted list.

To throw together a bulleted list, follow these steps:

1. **If you have existing text that you want to convert to a bulleted list, select that text.**

   For best results, each item in the text should be in its own paragraph.

2. **Choose Format ⇨ Bullets & Numbering ⇨ Bulleted List Menu.**

   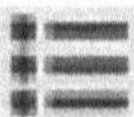

   As an alternative, you can click the toolbar's bulleted list icon. (If the icon doesn't appear on your toolbar, select it by first clicking the toolbar's more icon — three vertical dots.)

Docs offers you a menu of bulleted list formats, as shown in Figure 6-12. For each format, Docs shows the numbering scheme that it uses for the first, second, and third levels of the list.

3. **Choose the bullet scheme you want to use.**

   If you selected text in advance, Docs converts the text to a bulleted list. To add an item to the list, place the cursor at the end of the last item and then press Enter or Return.

4. **For a second-level item, press Tab; for a third-level item, press Tab again.**
5. **Enter your item text and then press Enter or Return to create a new item in the list.**
6. **Repeat Steps 4 and 5 until your list is complete.**
7. **To tell Docs you've finished entering list items, press Enter or Return a second time.**

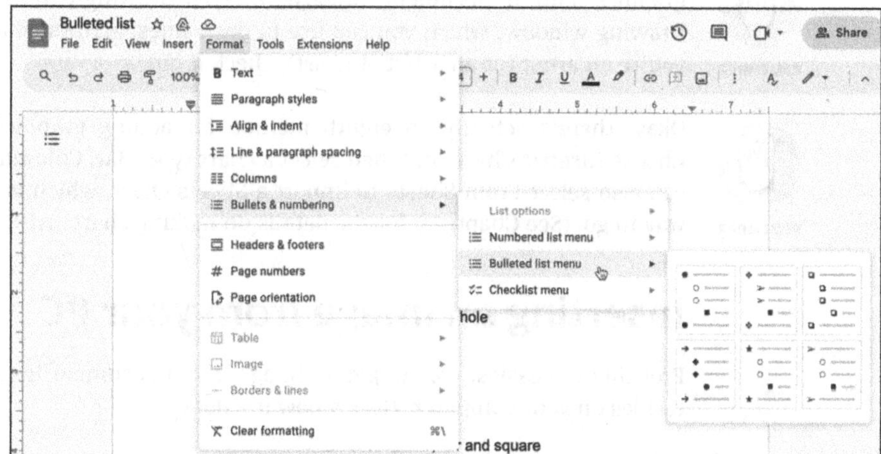

FIGURE 6-12: Click Bulleted List to display the available bullet schemes.

Making a Splash: Adding Graphics

I've shown so far in this chapter how a few fonts and other formatting options can do wonders for drab, lifeless text. But anybody can do that kind of stuff. To make your documents stand out from the crowd, you need to go graphical with images, photos, or other types of eye candy. Happily, Docs has the tools that not only get the job done but also make the whole thing a snap.

In fact, the image-related tools in Docs border on overkill because they give you no fewer than a half dozen ways to insert an image into a document:

- **Upload from computer:** Inserts an image file that resides on your PC
- **Search the web:** Enables you to search for and then insert an image from the web
- **Drive:** Inserts an image file stored on your Google Drive
- **Photos:** Inserts an image file you've uploaded to Google Photos
- **By URL:** Inserts an image file that resides at a specific web address
- **Camera:** Inserts a photo taken via your computer's camera

In the next few sections, I walk you through the details of each method.

Although I don't cover it in this book, Docs gives you a seventh method to get graphics into a document: Choose Insert⇨Drawing⇨New. This opens the Drawing window, which you can use to draw lines, arrows, shapes, and more. If you're an artist (or an artist at heart), check it out.

Okay, there's actually an eighth method for adding graphics to a document. Choose Insert⇨Chart, and then select a chart type: Bar, Column, Line, or Pie. You can also select From Sheets to import a Sheets chart, which is probably the best way to go. (See Chapter 9 for the details on making charts with Sheets.)

Inserting an image from your PC

Probably the easiest way to get an image into a document is to insert a file that resides on your computer. Here's how it's done:

1. **Position the cursor at the spot where you want the image to appear.**
2. **Choose Insert ⇨ Image ⇨ Upload from Computer.**

   Alternatively, click the insert image toolbar icon and then choose Upload from Computer.

   Docs displays the Open dialog.
3. **Select the image file you want to insert into your document.**
4. **Select Open.**

   Docs inserts the image.

Inserting an image from the web

If the image you want to use is on the web somewhere — and you have permission to use that image — follow these steps to search for and insert that image:

1. **Place the cursor at the position where you want the image to appear.**
2. **Choose Insert ➪ Image ➪ Search the Web.**

   Alternatively, click the insert image toolbar icon and then choose Search the Web.

   Docs displays the Search in Google Images pane.
3. **In the Search in Google Images text box, enter some text that describes the image you want and then press Enter or Return.**

   Google Images goes to work looking for images that match your search text.
4. **Select the image you want to use.**

   If you want to use multiple images, go for it: Select each image.
5. **Click Insert.**

   Docs inserts the image (or images).

Inserting an image from Drive

If the image you want to use is stored on your Google Drive, you can insert it from there. Here's how:

1. **Place the cursor at the position where you want the image to appear.**
2. **Choose Insert ➪ Image ➪ Drive.**

   Alternatively, click the insert image toolbar icon and then choose Drive.

   Docs displays the Google Drive pane.
3. **Select a tab at the top of the pane.**

   Your choices are Recent, My Drive, Shared with Me, Starred, and Computer.
4. **Select the image you want to use.**

   If you want to use multiple images, don't let me stop you: Select each image you want to insert.
5. **Click Insert.**

   Docs inserts the image (or images).

Inserting an image from Photos

If the image you want to insert is one you've upload to Google Photos, follow these steps to get the image from there to here:

1. **Position the cursor where you want the image to appear and then say "Stay!"**
2. **Choose Insert ⇨ Image ⇨ Photos.**

   Alternatively, click the insert image toolbar icon and then choose Photos.

   Docs displays the Google Photos pane.
3. **If the image resides in an album, select the Albums tab and then double-click the album to open it.**
4. **Select the image you want to use.**

   To insert multiple images, select each image.
5. **Click Insert.**

   Docs inserts the image (or images).

Inserting an image from a URL

If the image you want to use is on the web, and you happen to know the address (also known as the *URL* — Uniform Resource Locator) of the image, you can follow these steps to insert the image:

1. **Use your web browser to copy the address of the image.**
2. **Maneuver the cursor into the position where you want the image to show up.**
3. **Choose Insert ⇨ Image ⇨ By URL.**

   Alternatively, click the insert image toolbar icon and then choose By URL.

   Docs opens the Insert Image dialog.
4. **Paste the image address into the text box.**
5. **Select Insert Image.**

   Docs inserts the image.

Inserting a photo from your computer's camera

If your computer has a camera, you can persuade it to take a photo and then shoehorn that image into your document. Here's how it works:

1. **Get the cursor into the position where you want the photo to appear.**
2. **Choose Insert ⇨ Image ⇨ Camera.**

   Alternatively, click the insert image toolbar icon and then choose Camera.

   The first time you do this, your web browser asks whether it's okay for Docs to access your computer's camera, as shown in Figure 6-13.
3. **Select Allow.**

   Docs connects to the camera and displays a live feed.
4. **Compose your shot as desired.**
5. **Select Insert.**

   Docs inserts the photo.

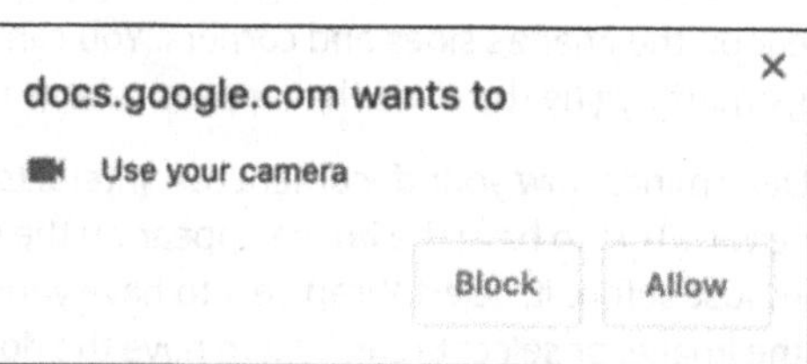

FIGURE 6-13: Sensibly, Docs needs permission to use your computer's camera.

Setting a few image options

After you add an image to your document, you might need to make a few adjustments, such as changing the size, the color, or the way text flows around the image. To make these and other tweaks, first select the image. Docs adds a toolbar icon named image options (you might need to click the more icon — three vertical dots — to see the image options icon), which you can click to display the Image Options pane, shown in Figure 6-14.

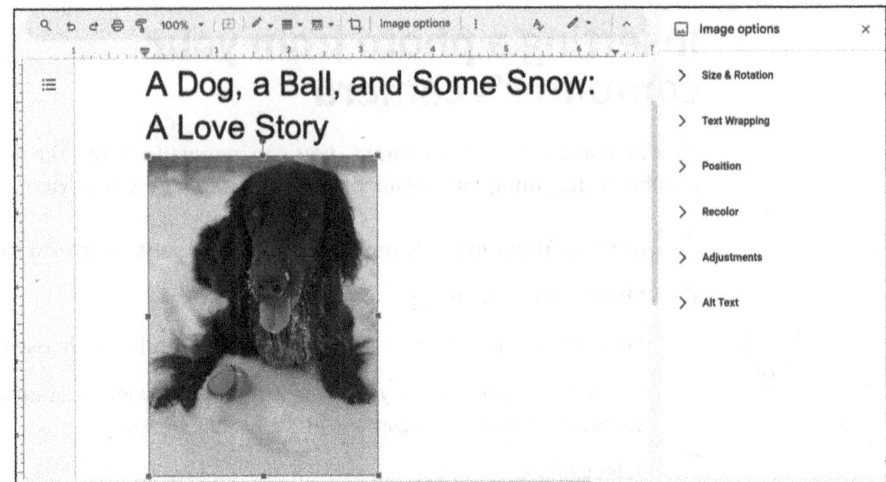

FIGURE 6-14: Select an image and then click Image Options on the toolbar to display the Image Options pane.

Here's a quick look at what you get with each category in the Image Options pane:

- **Size & Rotation:** Enables you to change the width and height of the image or to scale the image larger or smaller. You can also rotate the image.

  REMEMBER

  You can also resize the image directly by clicking-and-dragging any of the square handles that appear on the image's sides and corners. You can rotate the image directly by clicking-and-dragging the circle that appears above the selected image.
- **Text Wrapping:** Determines how your document text interacts with the image. Select Inline with Text to have the image appear on the same line with the text that comes just before it; select Wrap Text to have your document text flow around the image; or select Break Text to have the document text stop before the image and then continue after the image. If you go with Wrap Text or Break Text, you can use the Margins from Text options to set the distance between the text and the image.
- **Position:** Determines how the image is positioned on the page. Note that this category is enabled only if you select either Wrap Text or Break Text in the Text Wrapping category.
- **Recolor:** Enables you to apply a color effect to the image.
- **Adjustments:** Offers sliders that enable you to adjust the image's transparency, brightness, and contrast.
- **Alt Text:** Enables you to add a short description of the image, which will be read aloud by screen readers and similar assistive technologies used by people who might have trouble seeing the image.

You won't use these options all that often, but it's good to know they're waiting patiently for you when you do need them.

IN THIS CHAPTER

» **Constructing sturdy tables for your Docs data**

» **Augmenting your documents with headers and footers**

» **Messing around with margins, breaks, and other page setup chores**

» **Convincing text to display in columns**

» **Making footnotes look easy**

Chapter 7 Fiddling with Document Layout

In Chapter 6, I talk about Docs at the "tree" level of words, sentences, and paragraphs. But getting more out of Docs also requires that you deal with the app at the "forest" level of pages and documents. This means you need to get familiar with the document layout and page setup tools.

The terms *document layout* and *page setup* refer to how text and paragraphs are laid out on each page, and they involve building tables, adding headers and footers, setting margin sizes, specifying the page orientation, choosing the paper size, and so on. In this chapter, you explore these and a few other document layout features.

Building a Table with Your Bare Hands

In this section, you learn a bit of computer carpentry when I show you how to build and work with tables. Don't worry, though, if you can't tell a hammer from a hacksaw: The kinds of tables you deal with are purely digital because, in Docs, a table is a rectangular grid of rows and columns in a document. You can enter all kinds of info into a table, including text, numbers, and graphics.

What is a table?

Most documents consist of text in the form of sentences and paragraphs. However, you may find yourself in situations where you want to include a list of items in a document and, if you want each item in the list to include two or more details, a standard bulleted list (refer to Chapter 6) won't do the job. For a short list with just a few details, the quickest way to add the list to a document is to type each item on its own line and press Tab between each detail. You can then add tab stops to the ruler (check out Chapter 6 for the details on this topic) to line up the subitems into columns.

That works for simple items, but to construct a more complex list in Docs, you can build a *table*, a rectangular structure with the following characteristics:

- Each item in the list gets its own horizontal rectangle, called a *row.*
- Each set of details in the list gets its own vertical rectangle, called a *column.*
- The rectangle formed by the intersection of a row and a column is called a *cell,* and you use the table cells to hold the data.

In other words, a Docs table is similar to a Sheets spreadsheet. Figure 7-1 shows a sample table.

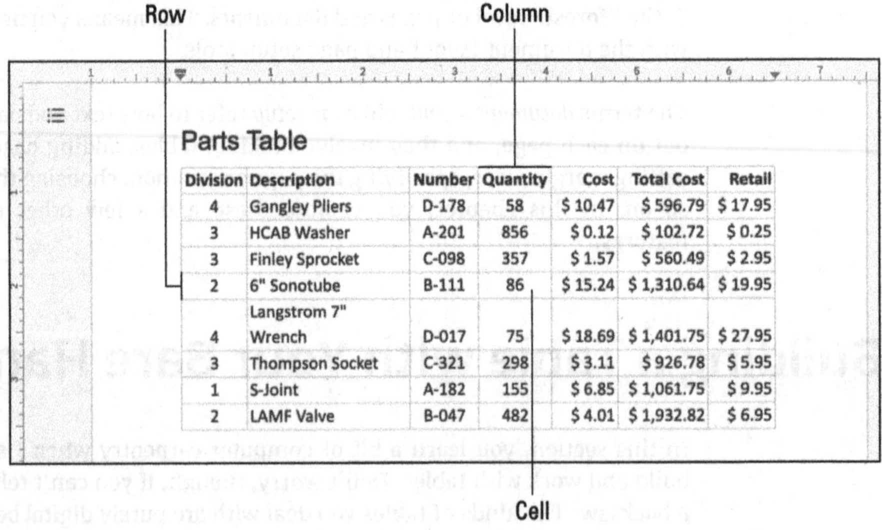

Parts Table

Division	Description	Number	Quantity	Cost	Total Cost	Retail
4	Gangley Pliers	D-178	58	$ 10.47	$ 596.79	$ 17.95
3	HCAB Washer	A-201	856	$ 0.12	$ 102.72	$ 0.25
3	Finley Sprocket	C-098	357	$ 1.57	$ 560.49	$ 2.95
2	6" Sonotube	B-111	86	$ 15.24	$ 1,310.64	$ 19.95
4	Langstrom 7" Wrench	D-017	75	$ 18.69	$ 1,401.75	$ 27.95
3	Thompson Socket	C-321	298	$ 3.11	$ 926.78	$ 5.95
1	S-Joint	A-182	155	$ 6.85	$ 1,061.75	$ 9.95
2	LAMF Valve	B-047	482	$ 4.01	$ 1,932.82	$ 6.95

FIGURE 7-1: A table in a Docs document.

Inserting a table

Here are the are-you-sure that's-all-there-is-to-it? steps to follow to insert a table into a document:

1. **Position the insertion point where you want the table to appear.**
2. **Choose Insert ⇨ Table.**

   Docs displays a grid of squares that you use to define the initial size (that is, the number of rows and columns) of your table.

   TIP

   To start with a basic table all laid out for you, click Table Templates, click one of the prefabricated table types that appears, and then skip the rest of these steps.

3. **Move the mouse pointer over the square that corresponds to the number of rows and columns you want in your table.**

   For example, to create a table with four columns and three rows, move the mouse pointer over the square shown in Figure 7-2. Note that the text below the grid in the figure says 4 x 3, which tells you the number of columns (4) and rows (3) in the current grid selection.

   TIP

   If you need more squares for a big table, as you drag toward the bottom or right or both, Docs expands the grid.

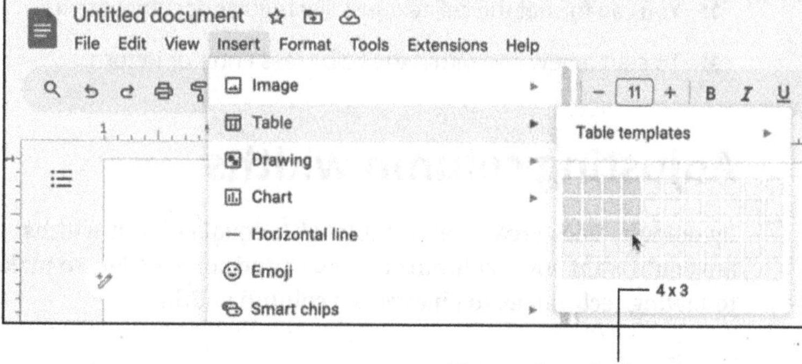

FIGURE 7-2: Use this grid to set the initial number of rows and columns in your table.

4. **Select the square.**

   Docs creates an empty table with the number of rows and columns you specified. (Refer to Figure 7-3, which appears a bit later in this chapter.)

Populating a table

After you've created a table, your next task is to enter the table values. As I mention earlier in this chapter, the intersection between each row and column in a table is called a cell, and you use the table's cells to enter text.

To try this out, either select the cell you want to work with or select any cell and then use the following keyboard techniques to get around:

Press	To Move
Tab	Right one column
Shift+Tab	Left one column
Up arrow	Up one row
Down arrow	Down one row

Now enter the value you want to appear in the cell. Here are some guidelines to keep in mind:

- If your text is longer than the width of the cell, Docs wraps the text and adjusts the height of the cell to accommodate the entry.
- You can format the cell text just like regular document text.
- To start a new line within the cell, press Enter or Return.

Adjusting column widths

By default, Docs creates each table with equal column widths. However, chances are you'll want some columns narrower and some wider, so make use of any of the following techniques to change the column widths:

- On the ruler, drag the column markers (pointed out in Figure 7-3).
- In the table, drag a column's right border.
- In the Table Properties pane (covered in the "Setting table properties" section), set the Column Width value, in inches.

Column markers

FIGURE 7-3: You can set a column's width by dragging its Column marker on the ruler.

Selecting table cells

When you need to work with one or more cells in a table, you need to select those cells in advance. Here are the techniques to use:

- **Select a single cell:** Drag the mouse pointer across the width of that cell.
- **Select two or more cells in a table row:** Move the mouse pointer over the leftmost cell you want to select, and then drag the pointer to the right until you've selected all the cells you need in the row.
- **Select two or more cells in a table column:** Move the mouse pointer over the top cell you want to select, and then drag the pointer down until you've selected all the cells you need in the column.
- **Select multiple cells in multiple rows and columns:** Move the mouse pointer over the first (that is, top-left) cell you want to select, and then drag the pointer down and to the right until you've selected all the cells you need.
- **Select cells with the keyboard:** Position the cursor anywhere inside the first (that is, top-left) cell you want to select, and then use the right and down arrow keys to extend the selection to all the cells you need.

Setting table properties

To change the formatting of table cells, you select the cells you want to work with and then use the standard formatting tools (font, paragraph, and so on). For more table-specific formatting, you can use the Table Properties pane. Here are the steps to follow:

1. **Select which part of the table you want to format:**
   - *To format just a cell,* select that cell.
   - *To format multiple cells,* select those cells.

- *To format a column-related property,* select one or more cells in that column.
- *To format a row-related property,* select one or more cells in that row.

2. **Choose Format ➪ Table ➪ Table Properties.**

   Docs offers up the Table Properties pane, shown in Figure 7-4.

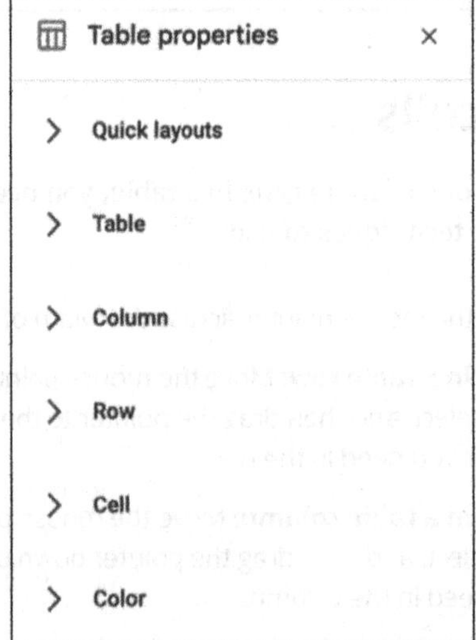

FIGURE 7-4: You can format various table settings in the Table Properties pane.

3. **Click Color and then use the Table Border controls to set the color (left) and width (right) of the table border.**

   If you want your table to be borderless, choose 0 pt for the border width.

4. **In the Cell Background Color palette, set the fill color for the selected cell or cells.**
5. **Click Cell and then use the Cell Vertical Alignment option to set how the data in the selected cell or cells is positioned vertically in its cell:**
   - *Top:* Aligns the cell content vertically with the top edge of the cell.
   - *Middle:* Aligns the cell content vertically with the middle of the cell.
   - *Bottom:* Aligns the cell content vertically with the bottom edge of the cell.
6. **In the Cell Padding text box, set the value, in inches, of the space that Docs adds around the data in the selected cell or cells.**
7. **Click Column, select the Column Width check box, and then enter a value, in inches, in the text box to set the width of the selected column or columns.**

8. **Click Row, select the Minimum Row Height check box, and then enter a value, in inches, in the text box to set the minimum height of the selected row or rows.**

   Minimum height means that the row height can grow taller if needed for the data, but it can't grow smaller than the value you specify.

9. **Click Table, and then use the Style icons to select how you want the table positioned with respect to the rest of the document text:**

   - *Inline:* The table carves out its own horizontal space and the document text continues below the table. Use the alignment icons to align the table horizontally within the document: left, center, or right. If you choose left, use the Left Indent text box to set the value, in inches, that you want Docs to indent the data in the selected cell or cells.
   - *Wrap Text:* The table takes up only the minimum space it requires and the document text flows around the table. Use the wrap icons to determine how the text flows around the table: left only, both sides, or right only. You can also set the size of the margins around the table.

   As you make each change, Docs puts the new table property into effect.

Inserting a new row or column

Unlike real carpentry, building a Docs table doesn't require all kinds of planning (which is good news for folks who wouldn't know a blueprint from a blue moon). This is fortunate because, with many of the tables you create, you won't know in advance how many rows or columns you need. It's easy enough to just create a basic table and then toss in a new row or column whenever you need it. The following steps show you how it's done:

1. **Decide where you want the new row or column to appear and then right-click the table as follows:**

   - *If you're inserting a new row,* right-click any cell in a row that will be adjacent to the new row. If you're adding a new row to the bottom of the table, right-click a cell in the last row of the table.
   - *If you're inserting a new column,* right-click any cell in a column that will be adjacent to the new column. If you're adding a new column to the right of the table, right-click a cell in the rightmost column of the table.

TIP

If you want to insert multiple rows, you can insert them in one operation by first selecting cells in the same number of existing rows. For example, if you want to insert three rows into your table, select cells in three existing rows. Again, you're inserting the new rows either above or below the selection, so select the cells accordingly. Yep, you can do this with columns, too, by selecting cells in the same number of columns as you want to insert. For example, to insert two columns into your table, select cells in two existing columns. Once you've selected the cells, right-click anywhere within the selection.

Docs displays a shortcut menu.

2. **Click the command you want to run:**
   - *Insert Row Above:* Inserts a new row over the current row
   - *Insert Row Below:* Inserts a new row under the current row
   - *Insert Column Left:* Inserts a new column to the left of the current column
   - *Insert Column Right:* Inserts a new column to the right of the current column

The commands you see will be different if you selected multiple cells. For example, if you selected cells in two rows, your choices will be Insert 2 Rows Above and Insert 2 Rows Below.

Need to add a new row to the bottom of a table? Here's the easy way: Position the insertion point in the rightmost cell of the bottom row and then press Tab. Don't mention it.

Deleting a row or column

If you end up with an extraneous column or row in your table, you should remove it to keep things neat and tidy. Here's how:

1. **Right-click a cell in the row or column you want to delete.**

   To delete multiple rows or columns, select at least one cell in each row or column, and then right-click any cell in the selection.

2. **Click the command you want to run:**
   - *Delete Row:* Deletes the current row
   - *Delete Column:* Deletes the current column
   - *Delete Table:* Nukes the entire table — no questions asked

The commands you see will be different if you selected multiple cells. For example, if you selected cells in two columns, to delete those columns you'd click Delete 2 Columns.

Merging table cells

Although most people use tables to store lists of data, using a table to lay out a page in a particular way is also common. For example, if you're building a Docs document that mimics an existing paper form or invoice, you almost certainly need to use a table to do it. However, on most forms, not all the fields — which are the cells in the table you create — are the same width: You might have a small field for a person's age or a much wider field for an address, for example. Changing the column width as I describe earlier doesn't work, because you need to change the size of individual cells.

The best way to control how table data is laid out is to build your table normally and then merge two or more cells. For example, if you merge two cells that are side by side in the same row, you end up with a single cell that's twice the width of the other cells.

To merge cells, follow these steps:

1. **Select the cells you want to merge.**

   You can select cells in a single row, a single column, or in multiple rows and columns. However, the selection must be a rectangle of adjacent cells.

2. **Choose Format ⇨ Table ⇨ Merge Cells.**

   Docs merges the selected cells.

Headers and Footers from Head to Toe

A *header* is a section that appears at the top of each page between the top margin and the first line of text. Any text, graphics, or properties you insert in any header appear at the top of every page in the document. Typical header contents include the document title and the date the document was created or modified.

A *footer* is a section that appears at the bottom of each page between the bottom margin and the last line of text. As with a header, anything you insert in any footer appears at the bottom of every page in the document. Typical footer contents include the page number and document filename.

REMEMBER

It's more precise to say that anything you insert in a *typical* header or footer appears on every page of your document. A bit later in this section, I show you how to set up different headers and footers for the first page of the document and for odd and even pages.

Here are your choices for adding content to a header or footer:

- **Text:** You can type any text, such as a brief document description, a note to the reader, your company name, or a link to a website or another document.
- **Page numbers:** You can insert just the page number, just the page count (that is, the total number of pages in the document), or both. For the last option, you probably want to insert something like the phrase Page *X* of *Y* (where *X* is the current page number and *Y* is the page count).
- **Image or drawing:** You can insert a photo or another image using any of the Docs image options, or you can draw something.

Adding a header

Here are the steps you need to plow through to add a header to your document:

1. **Choose Insert ⇨ Headers and Footers ⇨ Header.**

   You can also insert a header by holding down the Ctrl+Alt key combo (on a Mac, hold down Ctrl+⌘), pressing O, and then pressing H.

   Docs opens the Header section, as shown in Figure 7-5.

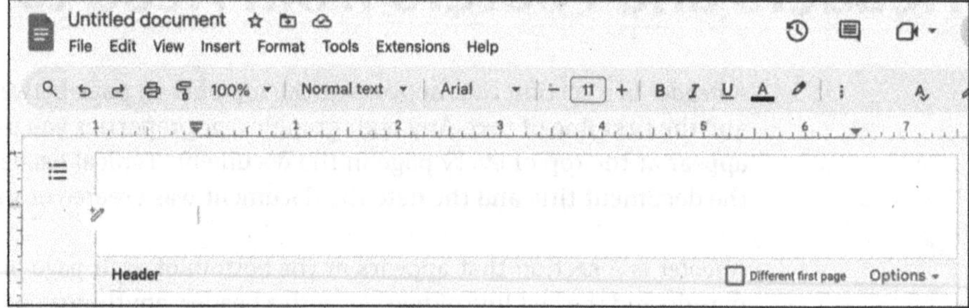

FIGURE 7-5: Running the Header command opens the Header section for editing.

2. **If you want to include page numbers in your header, choose Options ⇨ Page Numbers.**

   Docs opens the Page Numbers dialog, shown in Figure 7-6. Here are some notes:

   - Leave the Header option selected.
   - If you don't want the page number to appear on the first page (this is common), deselect the Show on First Page check box.
   - If you want your page numbers to start with a particular value, enter that value in the Start At text box.

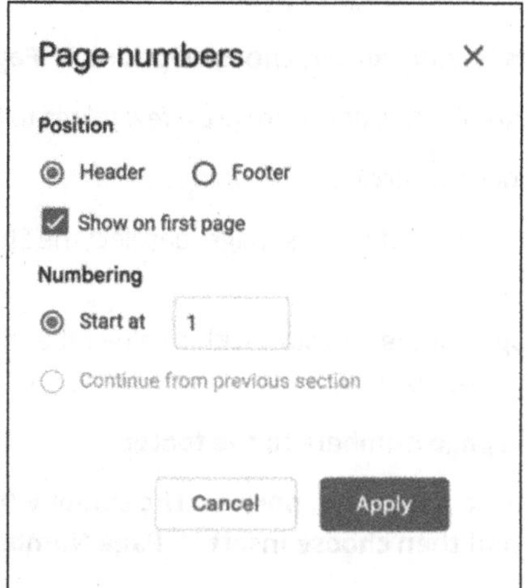

FIGURE 7-6: In the Page Numbers dialog, set up page numbers for your header.

3. **Click Apply to add the page numbers to the header.**
4. **To add the page count to the header, position the cursor where you want the count to appear and then choose Insert ➪ Page Numbers ➪ Page Count.**
5. **To add more stuff to the header, position the insertion point within the header and then enter some text, insert an image, or whatever.**
6. **To close the header, click anywhere in the document outside of the header.**

Adding a footer

Here are the steps to follow to set up your document with a footer:

1. **Choose Insert ➪ Headers and Footers ➪ Footer.**

   Another way to insert a footer is by holding down the Ctrl+Alt key combo (on a Mac, hold down Ctrl+⌘), pressing O, and then pressing F.

   Docs opens the Footer section, as shown in Figure 7-7.

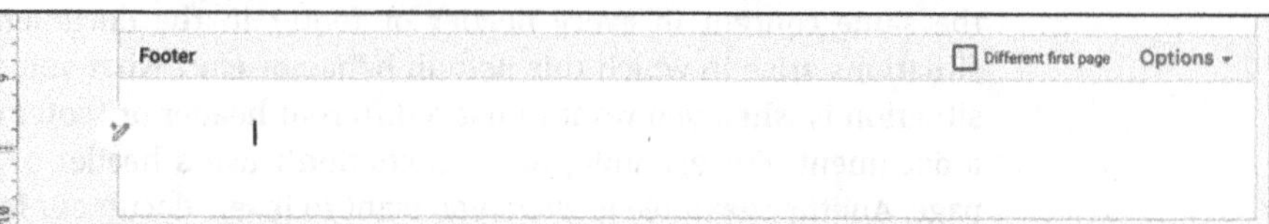

FIGURE 7-7: Running the Footer command opens the Footer section.

2. **To add page numbers to your footer, choose Options ⇨ Page Numbers.**

   Docs opens the Page Numbers dialog. Here are a few things to bear in mind:

   - Leave the Footer option selected.
   - To leave the page number off the first page, deselect the Show on First Page check box.
   - If you want your page numbers to start with a value other than 1, enter that value in the Start At text box.

3. **Click Apply to add the page numbers to the footer.**
4. **To add the page count to the footer, position the cursor where you want the count to appear and then choose Insert ⇨ Page Numbers ⇨ Page Count.**
5. **To add more info to the footer, position the insertion point within the footer and then enter some text, insert images, and so on.**
6. **To close the footer, click anywhere in the document outside of the footer.**

Opening the header or footer for editing

After you close your header or footer, later you might decide to make some changes to the existing text, add some new content, or whatever. To make any changes to a header or footer, you have to open it. Here's how:

» **Opening the header:** Either double-click inside the header or hold down the Ctrl+Alt key combo (on a Mac, hold down Ctrl+⌘), press O, and then press H.

» **Opening the footer:** Either double-click inside the footer or hold down the Ctrl+Alt key combo (on a Mac, hold down Ctrl+⌘), press O, and then press F.

Creating a unique first-page header or footer

By default, when you define the content for one header or footer, Docs displays the same content in every header or footer in the document. However, many situations arise in which this default behavior isn't what you want. One common situation is when you want to use a different header or footer on the first page of a document. For example, many texts don't use a header or footer on the first page. Another example is when you want to insert document instructions or notes in the first header or footer but you don't want that text repeated on every page.

For these kinds of situations, you can tell Docs that you want the first page's header or footer to be different from the headers or footers in the rest of the document:

- **Header:** Open the Header section and select the Different First Page check box. Docs changes the label of the first page header to First Page Header.
- **Footer:** Open the Footer section and select the Different First Page check box. Docs changes the label of the first page footer to First Page Footer.

Now go ahead and create your unique first-page header or footer.

Creating unique odd and even page headers and footers

Many documents require different layouts for the header or footer on odd and even pages. A good example is the printed version of this book, where the even page footer has the page number on the far left, followed by the part number and title, and the odd page footer has the current chapter number and title, followed by the page number on the far right.

To handle this type of situation, you can configure your document with different odd and even page headers or footers by following these steps:

1. **Choose Format ⇨ Headers & Footer ⇨ More Options.**

   Alternatively, either open the Header section for editing and then choose Options ⇨ Header Format, or open the Footer section for editing and then choose Options ⇨ Footer Format.

   Either way, the Headers & Footers dialog pops up.

2. **Select the Different Odd & Even check box.**
3. **Click Apply.**

   Docs changes the labels of the page headers to Even Page Header and Odd Page Header, and the labels of the page footer to Even Page Footer and Odd Page Footer.

4. **Open the Even Page Footer and add or edit the content you want to include on your document's even-numbered pages.**
5. **Open the Odd Page Footer and add or edit the content you want to include on your document's odd-numbered pages.**

Changing the Page Setup

The Docs options and features for setting up pages are legion, but few people use them with any regularity. That's a shame because the Docs page setup tools are often useful and easy to use, after you get to know them. In this section, I walk you through the most useful of the Docs page setup features.

Setting the page margins

The *margins* are the blank spaces to the left and right, as well as above and below, the document text (including the header and footer). The standard margins are 1 inch on all sides, which should be fine for most of your documents.

However, if your document design requires more or less space around the text, you can set specific margin sizes for the top, bottom, left, and right margins by following these steps:

1. **Choose File ⇨ Page Setup.**

   Docs asks the Page Setup dialog to make an appearance and displays the Pages tab (refer to Figure 7-8).

2. **In the following text boxes, set your margins:**
   - *Top:* Sets the top margin.
   - *Bottom:* Sets the bottom margin.
   - *Left:* Sets the left margin.
   - *Right:* Sets the right margin.

3. **Click OK.**

   Docs applies the new margin settings.

You can also use the Docs ruler to adjust the left and right margins. First, make sure the ruler is onscreen by choosing View ⇨ Show Ruler. The left and right ends of the ruler are home to two important controls called *margin markers*, pointed out in Figure 7-9:

- **Left margin marker:** This is the ruler's leftmost vertical marker.
- **Right margin marker:** This is the ruler's rightmost vertical marker.
- **Left margin marker:** This is the ruler's leftmost vertical marker. To adjust the left margin, drag the left margin marker. Dragging left decreases the margin, and dragging right increases the margin.

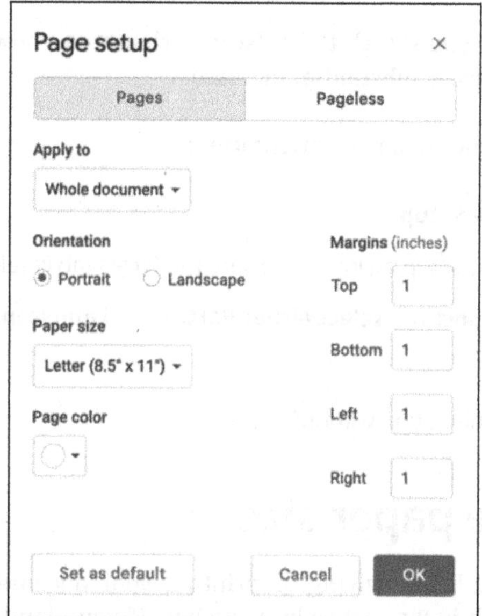

FIGURE 7-8: In the Page Setup dialog box, set margin sizes.

» **Right margin marker:** This is the ruler's rightmost vertical marker. To adjust the right margin, drag the right margin marker. Dragging right decreases the margin, and dragging left increases the margin.

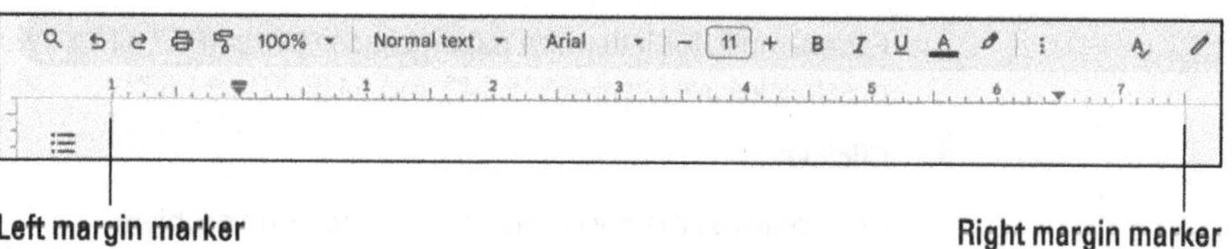

FIGURE 7-9: Drag the margin markers to adjust the left and right margins.

Changing the page orientation

By default, page text runs across the short side of the page and down the long side. This is called *portrait* orientation. Alternatively, you can configure text to run across the long side of the page and down the short side, which is called *landscape* orientation.

What's the use? You'd use landscape orientation mostly when you have text or an image that's too wide to fit across the page in portrait orientation. If you're using letter-size paper and its margins are set to 0.75 inches, you have only 7 inches of usable space across the page. Wide images, a table with many columns, or a long line of programming code are just a few of the situations in which this width might not be enough. If you switch to landscape orientation, however, the usable space grows to 9.5 inches, a substantial increase.

Here's what you do to choose a page orientation:

1. **Choose File ⇨ Page Setup.**

   Docs opens the Page Setup dialog. Make sure the Pages tab is selected.

2. **In the Orientation section, select either Portrait or Landscape.**
3. **Click OK.**

   Docs changes the orientation without protest.

Changing the paper size

Docs assumes that you'll be viewing or printing your documents on standard letter-size paper, which is 8.5 inches by 11 inches. If you plan to use a different paper size, you need to let Docs know so that it can print the document correctly:

1. **Choose File ⇨ Page Setup.**

   Docs opens the Page Setup dialog. Make sure the dialog's Pages tab is displayed.

2. **In the Paper Size list, choose the size you want to use.**

   For example, for letter-size paper, choose Letter (8.5" x 11"). Two other possibilities are Legal (8.5" x 14") and A4 (8.27" x 11.69").

3. **Click OK.**

   Docs changes the document's paper size — no problem.

Adding a page break

As you might know by now, Docs signals the start of a new page by displaying a narrow gap between the previous page and the current page. That gap is called a *page break*. Text that appears above the break prints on one page, and text below the break prints on the next page. This text arrangement isn't set in stone, of course. If you insert a new paragraph or change the margins, the text on both sides of the page break line moves accordingly.

But what if you have a heading or paragraph that must appear at the top of a page? You can fiddle around by, say, pressing Enter above the text until the text appears at the top of the next page, but that strategy is too fragile to be useful.

Instead, Docs gives you an easier and more robust method. Position the cursor at the start of the text that you want to appear at the top of a new page, and then do either of the following:

- » Choose Insert ⇨ Break ⇨ Page Break.
- » Press Ctrl+Enter (⌘+Enter on a Mac).

Docs creates a new page break at the cursor position. Now, no matter how much text you insert earlier in the document, that page break stays in place and the text that follows the break still appears at the top of that page.

Going pageless

Having separate pages in a big document makes sense in many situations because the pages help organize your content and enable you to refer to specific parts of the document (for example, "See the second paragraph on page 57").

However, there are plenty of scenarios where having separate pages just gets in the way:

- » If a document has one or more long tables, there's a good chance a page break will occur in the middle of a table, which makes that table harder to read.
- » In a document with multiple large images, if one of those images can't fit in the space remaining at the bottom of a page, Docs creates a page break and positions the image at the top of the next page. The result? An unsightly gap at the bottom of the preceding page.
- » In a long document with many page breaks, those breaks interrupt the flow of reading.

One way to solve these and similar annoyances is to set up the document so that it's more like a web page. That is, instead of discrete pages of a fixed size, the document scrolls continuously without any page breaks and the content adapts itself to the width of the browser window and to the browser zoom level.

A document with these characteristics is said to be a *pageless* document. You can set one up by following these steps:

1. **Choose File ⇨ Page Setup.**

   Docs opens the Page Setup dialog.

2. **Click the Pageless tab.**
3. **(Optional) In the Background Color palette, select a background hue for your pageless document.**
4. **Click OK.**

   Docs converts your document to pageless without breaking a sweat.

Adding a section break

In Docs-related training sessions and question-and-answer periods, some of the most common complaints and queries center on using multiple page layouts in a single document:

- How can I have different headers (or footers) for different parts of a document?
- I have a long table on one page. How can I set up that one page with smaller margins?

Most people end up splitting a single document into multiple documents to accomplish these and similar tasks. However, you don't have to break up your document just because you want to break up the page layout. Instead, you use a *section*, a document part that stores page layout options such as headers, footers, margins, and columns.

When you create a document, Docs gives it a single section that comprises the entire document. However, you're free to create multiple sections in a single document, and you can then apply separate page layout formatting to each section. The transition from one section to another is called a *section break.*

Docs offers two types of section breaks:

- **Next Page:** Starts a new section on a new page
- **Continuous:** Starts a new section at the insertion point (doesn't add a page break)

Follow these steps to add a section break:

1. **Position the cursor where you want the new section to begin.**
2. **Choose Insert ➪ Break.**

3. **Select a section break:**
   - *Click Section Break (Next Page) for a next-page section break.*
   - *Click Section Break (Continuous) for a continuous section break.*

After you create one or more sections, the Apply To list in the Page Setup dialog (choose File⇨Page Setup) now offers the following choices:

- **Whole Document:** The page setup options apply to the entire document.
- **This Section (Section *X*):** The page setup options apply only to the current section (where *X* is the number of the section).
- **This Section Forward:** The page setup options apply from the current section to the end of the document.
- **Selected Content:** The page setup options apply only to whatever content you selected before opening the Page Setup dialog.

Working with Columns, Just Like the Pros

Docs, of course, is good for more than just the odd letter or memo. All kinds of people are using the program to self-publish things like newsletters, booklets, pamphlets, and fanzines. To give these kinds of documents a more professional appearance, Docs lets you arrange text into columns, just like they do in newspapers and magazines. (Check out Figure 7-10 for an example.) This section shows you how to define columns and enter text in them.

Getting text into columns, part 1: The easy way

Columns are one of those features that many people avoid like the plague because, well, they seem too complicated and so aren't worth the bother. Docs changes all that. It's now easier than ever to set up and use columns. To prove it for yourself, follow these three oh-so-simple steps to define columns for your document:

1. **Select the text that you want to convert into columns.**

   If you want to convert the entire document, don't select anything.

   If you haven't entered the document text yet, that's okay; it's perfectly acceptable to set up columns first and type the text later.

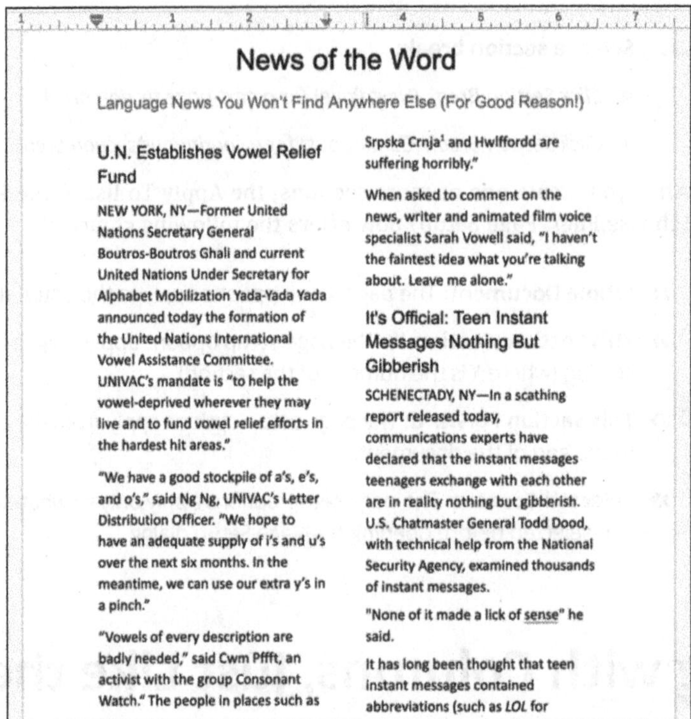

News of the Word

Language News You Won't Find Anywhere Else (For Good Reason!)

U.N. Establishes Vowel Relief Fund

NEW YORK, NY—Former United Nations Secretary General Boutros-Boutros Ghali and current United Nations Under Secretary for Alphabet Mobilization Yada-Yada Yada announced today the formation of the United Nations International Vowel Assistance Committee. UNIVAC's mandate is "to help the vowel-deprived wherever they may live and to fund vowel relief efforts in the hardest hit areas."

"We have a good stockpile of a's, e's, and o's," said Ng Ng, UNIVAC's Letter Distribution Officer. "We hope to have an adequate supply of i's and u's over the next six months. In the meantime, we can use our extra y's in a pinch."

"Vowels of every description are badly needed," said Cwm Pffft, an activist with the group Consonant Watch." The people in places such as Srpska Crnja[1] and Hwlffordd are suffering horribly."

When asked to comment on the news, writer and animated film voice specialist Sarah Vowell said, "I haven't the faintest idea what you're talking about. Leave me alone."

It's Official: Teen Instant Messages Nothing But Gibberish

SCHENECTADY, NY—In a scathing report released today, communications experts have declared that the instant messages teenagers exchange with each other are in reality nothing but gibberish. U.S. Chatmaster General Todd Dood, with technical help from the National Security Agency, examined thousands of instant messages.

"None of it made a lick of sense" he said.

It has long been thought that teen instant messages contained abbreviations (such as *LOL* for

FIGURE 7-10: A document with text finagled into two columns.

2. **Choose Format ⇨ Columns.**

   Docs displays the column options shown in Figure 7-11.

3. **Choose either two columns (the middle option) or three columns (the option on the right).**

   Docs converts your text into columns, just like that.

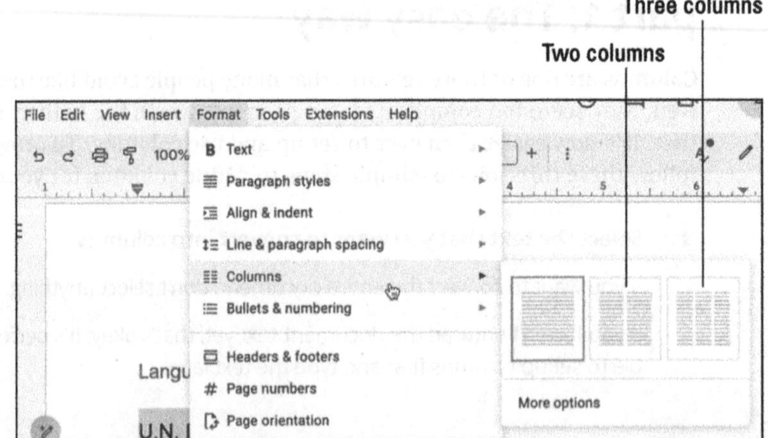

FIGURE 7-11: Select the Columns command, and then choose how many columns you want.

Getting text into columns, part 2: The ever-so-slightly-harder way

Docs has a second column-creation method that gives you slightly more control over the process. Here's how it works:

1. **Select the text that you want to shoehorn into columns.**

   Don't select anything if you want to convert the entire document to columns.

2. **Choose Format ⇨ Columns ⇨ More Options.**

   Docs releases the Column Options dialog, shown in Figure 7-12.

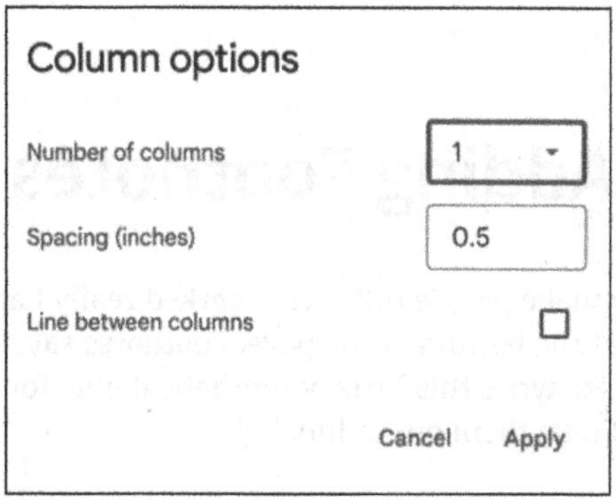

Column options

Number of columns	1
Spacing (inches)	0.5
Line between columns	☐

Cancel Apply

FIGURE 7-12: The Column Options dialog gives you a few extra column-related settings to fiddle with.

3. **In the Number of Columns list, select how many columns you want.**
4. **In the Spacing text box, set the distance, in inches, that you want between each column.**
5. **If you want Docs to add a vertical line between each column, select the Line Between Columns check box.**

   If you're using a somewhat narrow space between your columns (say, anything less than half an inch), adding a line between columns can make your text easier to read.

6. **Click Apply.**

   Docs wastes no time in converting your text into columns.

Entering text in columns

After you have defined your columns, your next step is to fill them in by entering some text (unless, of course, you converted existing text into columns). Here are some guidelines to follow when entering text in columns:

- Entering text in a column isn't all that different from entering text in a normal document. Place the cursor in the column you want to use and start pecking away. If the columns are empty, you have to begin at the top of the first column.
- If you want to move the cursor to the next column before you reach the end of the page (this is called inserting a *column break*), choose Insert ➪ Break ➪ Column Break.

Show Your Work: Adding Footnotes

One of the best ways to make people think you worked really hard on a document is to include footnotes at the bottom of the page. Footnotes say, "Hey, this person took the time and effort to write this little parenthetical note for my edification or amusement. I think I'll take them out to lunch."

To make sure we're on the same page (so to speak), here are some concepts to keep in mind as you work through this section:

- A *footnote* is a short note at the bottom of a page that usually contains asides or comments that embellish something in the regular document text on that page.
- Docs indicates a footnote with a *reference mark*, a number that appears as a superscript in both the regular text and in a special footnote area at the bottom of the page, as shown in Figure 7-13.
- Footnotes are a convenient way to add extra info for the reader, though too many on one page can make your text appear cluttered.

If you've ever tried adding footnotes to a page manually, you know what a nightmare it can be trying to coordinate the size of the note with the regular page text. And if you need to change your footnote numbers? Forget about it.

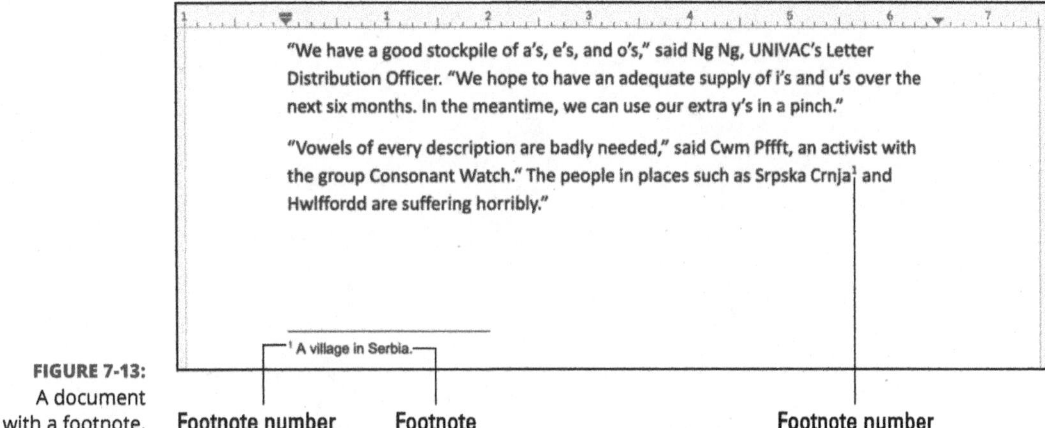

FIGURE 7-13: A document with a footnote.

Docs changes all that by making footnotes as easy as entering text. The program arranges things so that your pages accommodate any footnote size perfectly, and it even manages the footnote numbers for you automatically. Sweet!

Because a footnote always refers to something in the regular text, your first task is to position the insertion point where you want the little footnote number to appear. (Usually, it's at the end of whatever word, phrase, or sentence your footnote will be embellishing.)

After you've done that, choose Insert ➪ Footnote. (You can also press Ctrl+Alt+F or, on a Mac, ⌘+Option+F.) Docs adds a footnote number at the cursor, creates a special footnote area at the bottom of the page, and then inserts the same footnote number there. Now type your footnote text in the footnote area and you're done.

IN THIS CHAPTER

» Getting to know Sheets

» Entering and editing sheet data

» Working with cell ranges

» Making cells fancy with fonts, alignment, and other formatting

» Messing around with rows and columns

Chapter 8

Getting Started with Sheets

If you've never used a spreadsheet, Sheets may seem intimidating, and getting it to do anything useful may seem like a daunting task. However, a spreadsheet is really just a fancy electronic version of a numeric scratch pad. With the latter, you write down a few numbers and then use elementary school techniques to calculate a result. At its most basic level, a Sheets spreadsheet is much the same: You type one or more values and then you create a formula that calculates a result.

The first part of this basic Sheets method is entering your sheet data, and that's what this chapter is all about. After some introductory stuff to get you acquainted with the Sheets interface and file basics, you learn the best ways to get your data into the sheet, some tips and tricks for easier data entry, and some techniques for formatting your data to make it easier to read and understand.

Opening Sheets

If you're ready to get started, use either of the following techniques to get Sheets out into the open:

- Send your trusty web browser to `https://sheets.google.com`. (Note that you end up on `https://docs.google.com/spreadsheets`, but the other address is shorter to type.)
- If you're in a Google Workspace app that has the Google apps icon (such as Mail, Calendar, or the Docs home page), go ahead and click the icon and then choose Sheets from the menu that appears.

Touring the Google Sheets Home Page

When you first land on Sheets, the app's home page appears, which looks somewhat like the page shown in Figure 8-1.

Here's a quick rundown of the main features of the screen:

- **Main menu:** Opens the main menu, which gives you access to other Google Workspace apps (such as Docs and Slides), Settings, and Drive. To close the menu, click any empty space outside the menu (or press Esc).
- **Search:** Enables you to search Sheets for the spreadsheet you want.
- **Google apps:** Displays icons for all the Google apps.
- **Google account:** Gives you access to your Google account.
- **Start a new spreadsheet:** Displays a few templates you can use to start a new spreadsheet. (A *template* is a spreadsheet that comes with predefined text, formatting, and even a formula or two to get you off to a rousing start.)
- **Template gallery:** Displays the complete list of templates.
- **Recent spreadsheets:** Displays the spreadsheets you've worked on most recently.
- **Open file picker:** Displays the Open a File dialog that enables you to open a spreadsheet file from Drive.

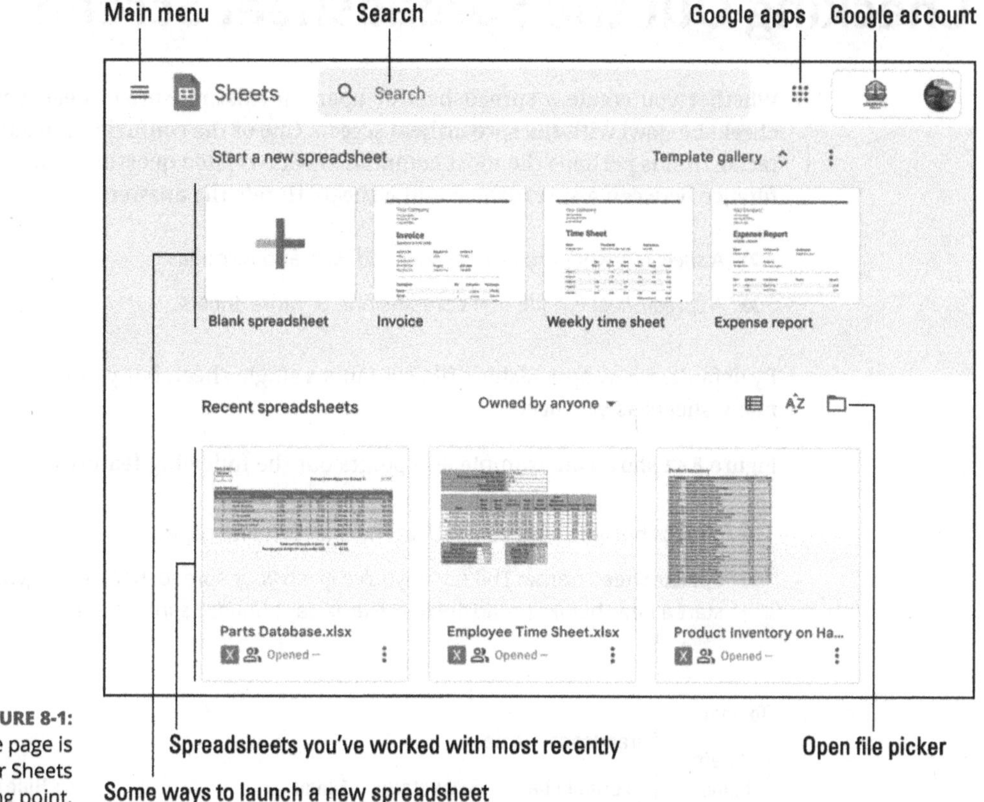

FIGURE 8-1: The home page is your Sheets launching point.

Creating a Spreadsheet

From the Sheets home page, you can open a file you worked on previously (check out the section "Opening an existing spreadsheet," later in this chapter), but you'll often want to create a spreadsheet. You have two ways to crank up a new spreadsheet:

- *To open an empty spreadsheet* (that is, a spreadsheet with no predefined text or formatting), click Blank Spreadsheet in the Start a New Spreadsheet section.
- *To open a spreadsheet that has some ready-to-edit text, formatting, and formulas,* either click one of the template tiles shown in the Start a New Spreadsheet section or click Template Gallery and then choose a template from the long list of possibilities that Sheets displays.

Checking Out the Spreadsheet Screen

Whether you create a spreadsheet or open an existing spreadsheet, you end up cheek-by-jowl with the spreadsheet screen. One of the confusing aspects I should tackle first is perhaps the most common Sheets-related question: What's the difference between a spreadsheet and a sheet? Here's the answer:

- A *sheet* is a work area where you add data and formulas.
- A *spreadsheet* is a file that contains one or more sheets.

By default, a new spreadsheet file contains a single sheet, but you're free to add as many sheets as you need.

Figure 8-2 shows an example and points out the following features:

- **Sheets home:** Takes you back to the Sheets home page.
- **Spreadsheet name:** The name you've given your spreadsheet. When you start a new, blank spreadsheet, the area says *Untitled spreadsheet.*

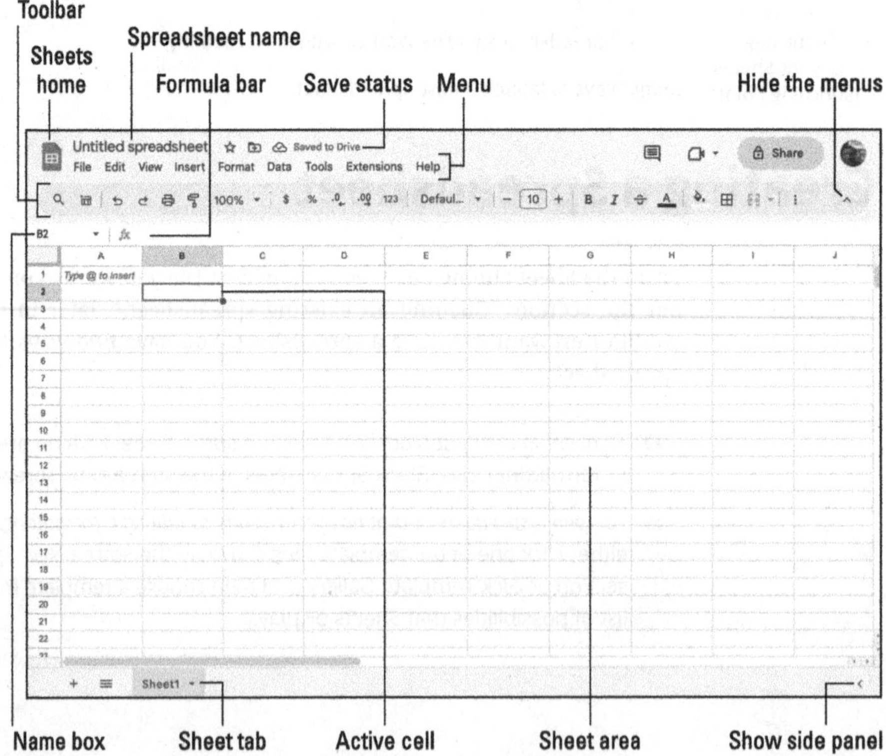

FIGURE 8-2: A blank spreadsheet and the Sheets features that surround it.

» **Save status:** Lets you know when the spreadsheet was last edited (among other info).

» **Menu:** Gives you access to the full arsenal of Sheets commands, features, and tools.

» **Toolbar:** Offers one- or two-click access to the most popular Sheets features.

» **Hide the menus:** Hides the Sheets home icon, the menu, and the spreadsheet name to gain a bit more vertical headroom for your spreadsheet. (You can also toggle the display of the menus by pressing Ctrl+Shift+F.)

» **Name box:** Displays the address of the active cell or the selected range. If the selected cell or range has a name, the name appears here instead of the address.

» **Formula bar:** Shows the formula (if any) entered into the active cell.

» **Active cell:** Represents the cell that you want to edit or format.

» **Sheet area:** The area where you add, edit, and format your sheet data and formulas.

» **Sheet tab:** Represents the current sheet. By default, a blank spreadsheet contains a single sheet named Sheet1, but you can add more, if needed (Sheet2, Sheet3, and so on), by clicking the add sheet icon (shown in the margin). Each sheet gets its own tab, and you display a sheet by selecting its tab.

TIP

If your file has lots of tabs, you can display a sheet also by clicking all sheets (shown in the margin) and then clicking the sheet name in the list that appears.

» **Show side panel:** Displays the side panel, which offers quick access to Calendar, Keep, Tasks, and other tools. Click the arrow again to hide the side panel.

Dealing with Spreadsheets

As you might expect from its name, Sheets is all about spreadsheets. So, before you learn how to add, edit, and format sheet data, it pays to take a few minutes to learn some basic spreadsheet chores.

Sheets saves your work for you

With Sheets, you never have to worry about saving your work, because Sheets takes over the saving duties from here. Every time you make a change to the spreadsheet, the spreadsheet's save status text changes briefly to *Saving. . .*, followed a second or two later by the anxiety-killing message *Saved to Drive* (refer to Figure 8-2).

Naming a new spreadsheet

If you've just started a new spreadsheet, one of your earliest tasks should be to give the spreadsheet a descriptive name. Sheets launches new, blank spreadsheets with the accurate-but-useless name Untitled Spreadsheet. If you use a template, the default is the template name. Follow these steps to give your spreadsheet a proper name:

1. **Click the Untitled Spreadsheet text, which appears near the top-left corner of the page.**

   Alternatively, you can choose File ⇨ Rename.

   Either way, Sheets opens the file name for editing.

2. **Delete the Untitled Spreadsheet text.**
3. **Type the name you want to use for the new spreadsheet.**
4. **Press Enter or Return.**

   Sheets renames the spreadsheet using the new name.

Opening an existing spreadsheet

To return to a spreadsheet you worked on previously, you need to open it by following these steps:

1. **Display the Sheets home page.**

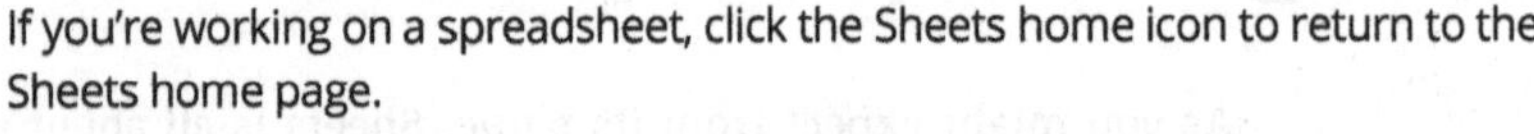

   If you're working on a spreadsheet, click the Sheets home icon to return to the Sheets home page.

2. **If the spreadsheet you want to open appears in the Recent Spreadsheets area, click it and then skip the rest of these steps. Otherwise, click the open file picker icon.**

   Sheets displays the Open a File dialog.

3. **Click the spreadsheet you want to mess with.**
4. **Click Open.**

   Sheets opens the file.

Saving a copy of a spreadsheet

One of the secrets of Sheets productivity is to never reinvent the wheel. That is, if you have an existing spreadsheet and you need a second spreadsheet that's similar, don't go to the time and trouble to re-create the original spreadsheet from scratch. Instead, it's not hard to convince Sheets to make a copy of the original. With that copy in hand, all you need to do is make whatever changes are needed.

Here's how to make a copy of an existing spreadsheet:

1. **Open the spreadsheet you want to copy.**
2. **Choose File ➪ Make a Copy.**

   Sheets opens the Copy Document dialog. The Name text box shows *Copy of* followed by the name of the original spreadsheet.
3. **In the Name text box, enter a descriptive name for the copy.**
4. **Click Make a Copy.**

   Sheets opens a new browser tab and displays the copy you just created.

Understanding Sheet Cells

A sheet is a rectangular arrangement of rows and columns. The rows are numbered, where the topmost row is 1, the row below it is 2, and so on. The columns are labeled with letters, where A is the leftmost column, the next column is B, and so on. After column Z come columns AA, AB, and so on, all the way up to ZZZ; that's 18,278 columns in all.

REMEMBER

"What's the maximum number of rows?" I hear you asking. There isn't one, but the maximum number of *cells* you can have in a spreadsheet is 10 million.

The intersection of each row and column is called a *cell*, and each cell has a unique address that combines its column letter (or letters) and row number. For example, the top-left cell in a sheet is at the intersection of column A and row 1, so its address is A1. When you click a cell, it becomes the *active* cell — which Sheets designates by surrounding the cell with a heavy border and by displaying a small, blue square in the cell's bottom-right corner. You also see the address of the active cell in the name box to the left of the formula bar (as pointed out earlier in Figure 8-2).

You use these sheet cells to enter data, which you learn more about in the next section. For now, you should know that sheet cells can hold three kinds of data:

- **Text:** These entries are usually labels that make a sheet easier to read, such as *August Sales* or *Territory*, but they can also be text and number combinations for items such as phone numbers and account codes.
- **Numbers:** These entries can be dollar values, weights, interest rates, or any other numeric quantity.
- **Formulas:** These are calculations involving two or more values, such as 2*5 or A1+A2+A3. I discuss formulas in more detail in Chapter 9.

Entering Data

A spreadsheet is only as useful — and as accurate — as the data it contains. Even a small mistake can render the results meaningless. Rule number one of good spreadsheet hygiene is to enter your data carefully.

If you're new to spreadsheet work, you'll no doubt be pleased to hear that entering data in a sheet cell is straightforward: Select the cell you want to use and then start typing. Your entry appears in both the cell and the formula bar — the horizontal strip above the column headings. (Refer to Figure 8-2.) When you're done, press Enter or Return. (If you prefer to cancel the edit without adding anything to the cell, press Esc instead.)

REMEMBER

When entering numbers or text, you can also finalize your entry by pressing any of the arrow keys, Tab, Shift+Tab, or by clicking another cell. The active cell moves either in the direction of the arrow or to the selected cell. This feature is handy if you have, say, a lengthy column of data to type.

Entering text

In Sheets, text entries can include any combination of letters, symbols, and numbers. Although text is sometimes used as data, you'll find that you use text mostly to describe the contents of your sheets. These descriptions are important because even a modest-size spreadsheet can become a confusing jumble of numbers without some labels and headings to keep things straight. Text entries can be up to about 50,000 characters long, but in general, you shouldn't use anything too fancy or elaborate; a simple phrase such as Monthly Expenses or Payment Date usually suffices.

TECHNICAL STUFF

Sheets uses the property of *data-type coercion* to determine the data type of a cell entry. For example, Sheets automatically treats any cell that contains only numbers as a numeric type, but if the cell has at least one letter or symbol, Sheets treats it as text. You can use this property to force Sheets to interpret a number as a text entry by preceding the number with a single quote (').

However, not all symbols force Sheets to interpret an entry as text. The exceptions are the forward slash (/), used in dates; the colon (:), used in times; and the following symbols:

```
.,+-()$%
```

I expand on how these symbols affect numeric entries later in this chapter.

How can you tell whether a number in a cell is a text or numeric entry? One way is to examine how Sheets aligns the data in the cell by default. Text entries are automatically aligned on the left, whereas numeric entries are aligned on the right.

Entering numbers

Numbers are what sheets are all about. You add them, subtract them, take their average, or perform any number of mathematical operations on them.

According to the Sheets data-type coercion, a cell entry that contains only numbers is considered a numeric data type. However, Sheets also recognizes that you're entering a number if you start the entry with a decimal point (.), a plus sign (+), a minus sign (–), or a dollar sign ($). Here are some other rules for entering numbers:

- » You can enter percentages by following the number with a percent sign (%). Sheets stores the number as a decimal. For example, an entry such as 15% is stored as 0.15.
- » You can use scientific notation when entering numbers. For example, to enter the number 3,879,000,000, you can type 3.879E+09.
- » You can also use parentheses to indicate a negative number. If you make an entry such as (125), Sheets assumes you mean negative 125.

» You can enter commas to separate thousands, but you have to make sure that each comma appears in the appropriate place. Sheets interprets an entry such as 12,34 as text.

You find out more information about number formatting later in this chapter, in the section "Applying a numeric, date, or time format."

WARNING

A common source of errors in Sheets is to mistakenly enter a lowercase *L (l)* instead of a one (1) or an uppercase *o (O)* instead of a zero (0). Watch for these errors when entering data.

Entering dates and times

Sheets uses serial numbers to represent specific dates and times. To get a date serial number, Sheets uses December 31, 1899, as an arbitrary starting point, so it has a value of 1. Sheets then counts the number of days that have passed since then. For example, the date serial number for January 1, 1900, is 2; January 2, 1900, is 3; and so on. Table 8-1 displays some sample date serial numbers.

TABLE 8-1 Examples of Date Serial Numbers

Serial Number	Date
366	December 31, 1900
16229	June 6, 1944
45527	August 23, 2024

To derive a time serial number, Sheets expresses time as a decimal fraction of the 24-hour day to return a number between 0 and 1. The starting point, midnight, is given the value 0, so 12 noon — halfway through the day — has a serial number of 0.5. Table 8-2 displays some sample time serial numbers.

TABLE 8-2 Examples of Time Serial Numbers

Serial Number	Time
0.25	6:00:00 A.M.
0.375	9:00:00 A.M.
0.70833	5:00:00 P.M.
.99999	11:59:59 P.M.

You can combine the two types of serial numbers. For example, 45527.5 represents 12 noon on August 23, 2024.

The benefit of using serial numbers in this way is that it makes calculations involving dates and times easy. Because a date or time is really just a number, any mathematical operation you can perform on a number can also be performed on a date. This feature is invaluable for sheets that track delivery times, monitor accounts receivable or accounts payable, calculate invoice discount dates, and so on.

Although it's true that the serial numbers make manipulating dates and times easier for the computer, it's not the best format for humans to comprehend. For example, the number 25,404.95555 is meaningless, but the moment it represents (July 20, 1969, at 10:56 P.M. Eastern Time) is one of the great moments in history (the Apollo 11 moon landing). Fortunately, Sheets takes care of the conversion between these formats so that you never have to worry about it. To enter a date or time, use any of the formats outlined in Table 8-3.

TABLE 8-3 **Date and Time Formats in Sheets**

Format	Example
m/d/yyyy	8/23/2024
d-mmm-yyyy	23-Aug-2024
d-mmm	23-Aug (Sheets assumes the current year)
mmm-yyyy	Aug-2024 (Sheets assumes the first day of the month)
h:mm:ss AM/PM	10:35:10 P.M.
h:mm AM/PM	10:35 P.M.
h:mm:ss	22:35:10
h:mm	22:35
m/d/yyyy h:mm	8/23/2024 22:35

TIP

Here are three shortcuts that let you enter dates and times quickly. To enter the current date in a cell, press Ctrl+; (semicolon) in Windows or ⌘+; in macOS; to enter the current time, press Ctrl+Shift+; (semicolon) in Windows or ⌘+Shift+; in macOS; to enter the current date and time in a cell, press Ctrl+Alt+Shift+; (semicolon) in Windows or ⌘+Option+Shift+; in macOS.

Table 8-3 displays the built-in formats, but these aren't set in stone. You're free to mix-and-match these formats, as long as you observe the following rules:

- You can use either the forward slash (/) or the hyphen (-) as a date separator. Always use a colon (:) as a time separator.
- You can combine any date-and-time format as long as you separate them with a space.
- You can specify the month using the number (January is 1, February is 2, and so on), the first three letters of the month name, or the entire month name.
- You can enter date and time values using either uppercase or lowercase letters. Sheets automatically adjusts the capitalization to its standard format.
- To display times using the 12-hour clock, include either am (or just a) or pm (or just p). If you leave these off, Sheets uses the 24-hour clock.

You find out more information on formatting dates and times later in this chapter, in the section "Applying a numeric, date, or time format."

Navigating a sheet

Data entry is much faster if you can navigate your sheets quickly. Table 8-4 lists the most commonly used navigation keys.

REMEMBER

Some keyboards sneakily hide the Home, End, Page Up, and Page Down keys inside other keys (usually the arrow keys). To "press" these hidden keys, you need to hold down the Fn key. That is, to select Home, press Fn+Home, to select End, press Fn+End, to select Page Up, press Fn+Page Up, and to select Page Down, press Fn+Page Down.

Editing cell contents

If you make a mistake when entering data or you have to update the contents of a cell, you need to edit the cell to produce the correct value. One option you have is to select the cell and begin typing the new data. This method erases the previous contents with whatever you type. Often, however, you need to change only a single character or value, so retyping the entire cell is wasteful. Instead, Sheets lets you modify the contents of a cell without erasing it.

TABLE 8-4 **Sheets Navigation Keys**

Press This	To Move Here
An arrow key	Left, right, up, or down one cell
Home	To the beginning of the row
End	To the end of the row
Page Down	Down one screen
Page Up	Up one screen
Ctrl+Home (Mac: ⌘+Home)	To the beginning of the sheet
Ctrl+End (Mac: ⌘+End)	To the bottom-right corner of the sheet
Alt+down arrow (Mac: Option+down arrow)	To the next sheet
Alt+up arrow (Mac: Option+up arrow)	To the previous sheet
Ctrl+arrow key (Mac: ⌘+ arrow key)	In the direction of the arrow to the next nonblank cell if the current cell is blank, or to the last nonblank cell if the current cell is nonblank

To edit a cell, first use any of the following techniques to produce an insertion point for editing:

- Click the cell and then press F2. (Depending on your keyboard layout, you might have to press Fn+F2.)
- Click the cell and then click inside the formula bar. (This technique is the best if you want to edit at a specific point in the cell, because you can click precisely at that position to place the insertion point there.)
- Double-click the cell.

With the insertion point at your command, you can now make changes and press Enter or Return (or press Tab, Shift+Tab, or an arrow key) when you're done to save your work. (Or, you can cancel the procedure without saving your changes, by pressing Esc.)

Working with Ranges

For small sheets, working with individual cells doesn't usually present a problem. However, as your sheets grow larger, you'll find that performing operations cell-by-cell is both time-consuming and frustrating. To overcome this problem, Sheets enables you to work with multiple cells — that is, a range of cells — in a single operation. You can then move, copy, delete, or format the range as a whole.

Understanding ranges

A *range* is defined as any group of related cells. A range can be as small as a single cell or as large as the entire sheet. Most ranges are rectangular groups of adjacent cells, but Sheets allows you to create ranges with noncontiguous cells. Rectangular ranges, like individual cells, have an address, and this address is given in terms of *range coordinates*. Range coordinates have the form UL:LR, where UL is the address of the cell in the upper-left corner of the range, and LR is the address of the cell in the lower-right corner of the range. For example, a range consisting of the intersection of the first four rows (1 to 4) and the first three columns (A to C) would have the coordinates A1:C4. Figure 8-3 shows this range selected. Note, as well, that the range coordinates appear in the name box to the left of the formula bar.

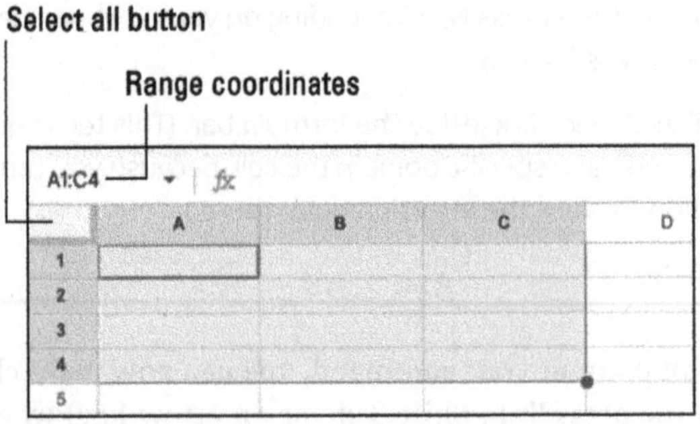

FIGURE 8-3: The range A1:C4.

Ranges speed up your work by enabling you to perform operations or define functions on many cells at once instead of one at a time. Suppose that you want to copy a large section of a sheet to another file. If you work on individual cells, you might have to perform the copy procedure dozens of times. However, by creating a range that covers the entire section, you can do it with a single Copy command.

Similarly, suppose that you want to know the average of a column of numbers running from B1 to B50. You can enter all 50 numbers as arguments in the AVERAGE function, but typing AVERAGE(B1:B50) is decidedly quicker.

Selecting a range

When Sheets requires that you select a range, in some situations you can specify the range by typing the range coordinates. For example, a dialog that requires a range input is common, and you can type the range coordinates in the text box provided. Similarly, you'll often come across a sheet function that requires a range value for an argument, and you can type the range coordinates while you're typing the rest of the formula.

However, using your mouse or keyboard to select the range you want to work with is much more common, so the next few sections take you through a few useful range selection techniques using both devices.

Mouse techniques for selecting a range

The mouse is the standard range-selection tool because it's both flexible and fast. Here are the main techniques:

- **To select a contiguous range:** Drag the mouse pointer over the cells you want to select.
- **To select a noncontiguous range:** Click the first cell, hold down Ctrl, and then either click each of the other cells or drag the mouse pointer over each of the other ranges you want to include in the selection.
- **To select an entire column:** Click the column header. To select multiple adjacent columns, drag the mouse pointer over the column headings. To select nonadjacent columns, click the header of the first column, hold down Ctrl, and then click the header of each of the other columns.
- **To select an entire row:** Click the row header. To select multiple adjacent rows, drag the mouse pointer over the row headings. To select nonadjacent rows, click the header of the first row, hold down Ctrl, and then click the header of each of the other rows.

Mouse tricks for selecting a range

You can save yourself lots of time if you become adept at some of the more esoteric tricks when selecting ranges with the mouse. Here's a list of my favorite mouse range-selection tricks:

- **Using the Shift key:** To select a rectangular, contiguous range, click the top-left cell (this is called the *anchor cell*), hold down Shift, and then click the bottom-right cell. Note that this technique doesn't require that you always use the top-left cell as the anchor. You can just as easily click any corner of the range, hold down Shift, and then click the opposite corner.

- **Scrolling to the anchor cell:** After you select a large range, the anchor cell often gets scrolled off the screen. To bring the anchor cell back onscreen before continuing, you can either use the scrollbars or press Ctrl+Backspace (⌘+Delete on a Mac).
- **Selecting the entire sheet:** Click the select all button near the top-left corner of the sheet (refer to Figure 8-3).

Keyboard techniques for selecting a range

If you're inputting data, you can save time by leaving your hands on the keyboard to select a range. Here are the main techniques you can use to select a range via the keyboard:

- **To select a contiguous range:** Use the arrow keys to select the top-left cell of the range, hold down the Shift key, and then use the arrow keys (or Page Up and Page Down, if the range is a large one) to select the rest of the cells.
- **To select an entire column:** Select a cell in the column and then press Ctrl+spacebar. To select multiple adjacent columns, select a cell in each column and then press Ctrl+spacebar.
- **To select an entire row:** Select a cell in the row and then press Shift+spacebar. To select multiple adjacent rows, select a cell in each row and then press Shift+spacebar.

Keyboard tricks for selecting a range

Do you prefer selecting ranges via the keyboard? Here are a few tricks that can make selecting a range via the keyboard faster and more efficient:

- **Selecting contiguous data:** If you want to select a contiguous range that contains data, begin by selecting the top-left cell of the range. To select the contiguous cells below the top-left cell, press Ctrl+Shift+down arrow; to select the contiguous cells to the right of the selected cells, press Ctrl+Shift+right arrow.
- **Selecting the entire sheet:** Press Ctrl+A (⌘+A on a Mac) or Ctrl+Shift+spacebar (⌘+Shift+spacebar on a Mac).
- **Moving the active cell within a selection:** Use the techniques listed in Table 8-5.

TABLE 8-5 Moving the Active Cell within a Selection

Press This	To Move the Active Cell
Enter/Return	Down one row in the current column. If the cursor is at the bottom of a column, the active cell jumps to the top of the next column. If the cursor is at the bottom-right cell of the selection, the active cell moves to the top-left cell of the selection.
Shift+Enter/Return	Up one row in the current column. If the cursor is at the top of a column, the active cell jumps to the bottom of the previous column. If the cursor is at the top-left cell of the selection, the active cell moves to the bottom-right cell of the selection.
Tab	Right one column in the current row. If the cursor is at the rightmost column of a row, the active cell jumps to the leftmost cell of the next row. If the cursor is at the bottom-right cell of the selection, the active cell moves to the top-left cell of the selection.
Shift+Tab	Left one column in the current row. If the cursor is at the leftmost column of a row, the active cell jumps to the rightmost cell of the previous row. If the cursor is at the top-left cell of the selection, the active cell moves to the bottom-right cell of the selection.

Specifying a range input in a dialog

I mention earlier that dialogs often have controls that require range coordinates as the input value. Again, you can type the range coordinates by hand, but you can also use any of the techniques you learned in the last few sections. Here's the general technique to follow:

1. **Click the select data range icon (shown in the margin.)**

   If a text box requires a range input, the select data range icon appears on the right side of the text box, as shown in Figure 8-4.

   Sheets temporarily hides the dialog or pane and opens the Select a Data Range dialog.

Conditional format rules ×

Single color Color scale

Apply to range

A1:B3

FIGURE 8-4: If a text box requires a range input, it also displays the select data range icon.

2. **In the sheet, use the mouse or keyboard to select the range.**

   As you select the range, Sheet updates the range coordinates in the Select a Data Range dialog, as shown in Figure 8-5.

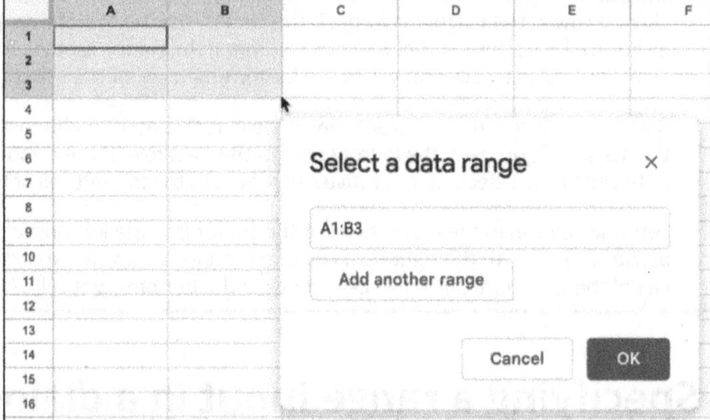

FIGURE 8-5: With the Select a Data Range dialog onscreen, use the mouse or keyboard to select the range you want to use as input.

3. **Click OK.**

   Sheets restores the original dialog or pane, and the coordinates of the range you selected appear in the text box.

Working with named ranges

Working with multiple cells as a range is much easier than working with the cells individually, but range coordinates aren't intuitive. For example, if a formula uses the function AVERAGE(A1:A25), knowing what the range A1:A25 represents is impossible unless you examine the range itself.

You can make ranges more intuitive by using *named ranges*, which are labels you assign to a single cell or to a range of cells. With a name defined, you can use it in place of the range coordinates. For example, assigning the name ClassMarks to a range such as A1:A25 immediately clarifies the purpose of a function such as AVERAGE(ClassMarks).

Sheets also makes named ranges easy to work with by automatically adjusting the coordinates associated with a named range if you move the range or if you insert or delete rows or columns within the range.

Understanding named range restrictions

Named ranges are generally quite flexible, but you need to follow a few guidelines:

- The named range can be no longer than 250 characters.
- The named range must begin with either a letter or the underscore character (_). For the rest of the name, you can use any combination of characters, numbers, or underscore (no spaces, punctuation, or other symbols allowed).
- For multiple-word names, separate the words by using the underscore character or by mixing case (for example, August_Expenses or AugustExpenses). Sheets doesn't distinguish between uppercase and lowercase letters in named ranges.
- Don't use cell addresses (such as Q1).
- Keep names as short as possible to reduce typing but long enough that the name that retains some of its meaning. NetProfit2024 is faster to type than Net_Profit_For_Fiscal_Year_2024, and it's certainly clearer than the more cryptic NtPft24.

Naming a range

Here are the steps to follow to name a range:

1. **Select the range you want to name.**
2. **Choose Data ⇨ Named Ranges.**

   Sheets opens the Named Ranges pane.
3. **Type the name in the text box.**

   Always make at least the first letter of the name uppercase because doing so can help you to troubleshoot formula problems. Later, when you need to include the named range in a formula, you type the name entirely in lowercase letters. When you accept the formula, Sheets then converts the name to the case you used when you first defined it. If the name remains in lowercase letters, Sheets doesn't recognize the name, so it's likely that you misspelled the name when typing it.

4. **If the range address displayed in the range box is incorrect, either type the correct range address or click the select data range icon (shown in the margin) and then use the mouse or keyboard to select a new range on the sheet.**

5. **Click Done.**

   Sheets names the range.

Using a named range

Using a named range in a formula or as a function argument is straightforward: Just replace a range's coordinates with the range's defined name. Suppose that a cell contains the following formula:

```
=B10
```

This formula sets the cell's value to the current value of cell B10. However, if cell B10 is named TotalProfit, the following formula is equivalent:

```
=TotalProfit
```

Similarly, consider the following function:

```
AVERAGE(A1:A25)
```

If the range A1:A25 is named ClassMarks, the following is equivalent:

```
AVERAGE(ClassMarks)
```

Filling a range with data

If you have a range where you want to insert the same value in every cell, typing the value in each cell is time-consuming and boring. You can save a lot of time by telling Sheets to fill the entire range with the value in a single operation. Here are the steps to follow:

1. **Type the value or formula that you want in the first cell of the range.**
2. **Leave the cell from Step 1 selected and then select the rest of the range you want to fill.**

   The range you select must have the cell from Step 1 in the top-left corner.
3. **Press Ctrl+Enter (⌘+Return on a Mac).**

   Sheets fills the entire range with the value or formula you typed.

   Alternatively, you can use these techniques if you want to fill only down or to the right:

   - *Fill down only:* Press Ctrl+D (⌘+D on a Mac).
   - *Fill right only:* Press Ctrl+R (⌘+R on a Mac).

Filling a range with a series of values

Rather than fill a range with the same value, you might need to fill it with a series of values. This might be a text series (such as Sunday, Monday, Tuesday; or January, February, March), a numeric series (such as 2, 4, 6; or 2024, 2025, 2026), or even an alphanumeric series (such as Sample 100, Sample 101, Sample 102; or Quarter1, Quarter2, Quarter3). Again, such series can be time-consuming to insert by hand, particularly for longer series. Fortunately, Sheets has a feature called AutoFill that makes creating a series easy. Here's how it works:

1. **Enter at least the first two values in a series.**

   AutoFill recognizes standard abbreviations, such as Jan (January) and Sun (Sunday).

2. **Select the cells you populated in Step 1.**
3. **Position the mouse pointer over the autofill handle — the blue circle in the bottom-right corner of the selection.**

   The pointer changes to a plus sign (+).

4. **Drag the mouse pointer until the dashed border encompasses the range you want to fill.**

   Dragging the handle down or to the right increases the values according to the pattern you specified in Step 1. Dragging up or to the left decreases the values according to your pattern.

5. **Release the mouse button.**

   Sheets fills in the range with the series.

Copying a range

You often reuse data in sheets. For example, if you set up a range with a particular set of data, you might want to create a second range that uses different data so that you can compare the two. Although the numbers might be different in the second range, the labels and headings probably won't be. You can make this sort of sheet chore go much faster if you start the second range by copying the unchanging data from the first.

Here's how to copy a range:

1. **Select the original range.**
2. **Choose Edit ⇨ Copy (or press Ctrl+C; ⌘+C on a Mac) to copy the range.**

3. **Select the top-left cell of the destination range.**

WARNING

Check out the destination range before copying a range to make sure you aren't overwriting existing data. If you accidentally destroy some data during a copy, immediately choose Edit and then Undo (or press Ctrl+Z) to undo the damage.

4. **Choose Edit ⇨ Paste (or press Ctrl+V; ⌘+V on a Mac).**

   Sheets pastes a copy of the original range.

TIP

In Step 4, rather than paste the copied range, you can insert the copy *within* an existing range. Right-click the destination cell, click Insert Cells, and then choose how you want the existing cells shifted to make room for the copied range: Shift Right or Shift Down.

Moving a range

If you want to move a range, Sheets gives you three methods:

- **Drag-and-drop:** Select the range you want to move, and then hover the mouse pointer over any edge of the selection (except the autofill handle). Drag the mouse pointer to the destination range.
- **Cut command:** Select the original range, choose Edit ⇨ Cut (or press Ctrl+X; ⌘+X on a Mac) to cut it, select the top-left cell of the destination range, and then choose Edit ⇨ Paste (or press Ctrl+V; ⌘+V on a Mac).
- **Insert within a range:** Select the original range, choose Edit ⇨ Cut (or press Ctrl+X; ⌘+X on a Mac) to cut it, right-click the destination cell, choose Insert Cells, and then choose how you want the existing cells shifted to make room for the moved range: Shift Right or Shift Down.

Formatting a Cell

Your sheets must produce the correct answers, of course, so most of your Sheets time should be spent on getting your data and formulas (see Chapter 9) entered accurately. However, you also need to spend some time formatting your work, particularly if other people will be viewing or working with the sheet. Labels, data, and formula results that have been enhanced with fonts, borders, alignments, and other formatting are almost always easier to read and understand than unformatted sheets.

Formatting the cell font

Before moving on to some easier and faster methods for applying formatting, you should know the standard procedures. To begin, select the cell or range you want to format. Then choose your font formatting using any one of the following three methods:

- » On the menu bar, choose Format, choose a menu item, and then choose a command from the submenu that appears.
- » Press a keyboard shortcut.
- » Click a toolbar icon.

Table 8-6 shows the menu commands and their corresponding keyboard shortcuts (if any) that you can press.

TABLE 8-6 **Font Formatting via Menu and Keyboard**

Menu Command	Keyboard Shortcut
Format ⇨ Text ⇨ Bold	Ctrl+B (⌘+B on a Mac)
Format ⇨ Text ⇨ Italic	Ctrl+I (⌘+I on a Mac)
Format ⇨ Text ⇨ Underline	Ctrl+U (⌘+U on a Mac)
Format ⇨ Text ⇨ Strikethrough	Alt+Shift+5 (⌘+Shift+X on a Mac)
Format ⇨ Font Size	None

Table 8-7 shows the Sheets toolbar icons for font-related chores.

Aligning cell data

Sheets has default cell alignments depending on the data, such as left aligned for text and right aligned for numbers, dates, and times. However, you can apply your own alignments. Sheets offers three alignment methods:

- » Choose Format ⇨ Alignment, and then choose a command from the submenu that appears.
- » Press a keyboard shortcut.
- » Click a toolbar icon.

TABLE 8-7 **Font Formatting from the Toolbar**

Toolbar Icon	Icon Name	What It Does
Arial ▾	Font	Displays a list of typefaces
− 11 +	Font Size	Displays a list of font sizes
B	Bold	Applies bold to the text
I	Italic	Applies italics to the text
S	Strikethrough	Applies strikethrough to the text
A	Text Color	Displays a color palette and then applies the color you click to the text
	Highlight Color	Displays a color palette and then applies the color you click to the background of the text
	Border	Applies a border style to one or more cell edges

Table 8-8 shows the Alignment menu commands, their corresponding keyboard shortcuts, and the equivalent toolbar icons for the Sheets alignment options.

Applying a numeric, date, or time format

The numbers — both the raw data and the formula results — are the most important part of a sheet, so applying appropriate numeric formats to your numbers is always worth the time. For example, be sure to format dollar amounts with the appropriate currency symbol, and format large numbers to show commas as thousands separators. If your sheet includes dates or times, you should also format them to make them more readable and to avoid ambiguous dates such as 3/4/2024. (Is that March 4, 2024 or April 3, 2024? It depends on the country!)

TABLE 8-8 Aligning Cells in Sheets

Alignment Menu Command	Keyboard Shortcut	Toolbar Icon	What It Does
Left	Ctrl+Shift+L (⌘+Shift+L on a Mac)		Aligns cell data on the left
Center	Ctrl+Shift+E (⌘+Shift+E on a Mac)		Centers cell data
Right	Ctrl+Shift+R (⌘+Shift+R on a Mac)		Aligns cell data on the right
Top			Aligns cell data vertically with the top of the cell
Middle			Aligns cell data vertically with the middle of the cell
Bottom			Aligns cell data vertically with the bottom of the cell

You won't be the least bit surprised to learn that Sheets offers three methods for applying numeric, date, and time formats:

- Choose Format ⇨ Number, and then choose a command from the submenu that appears.
- Press a keyboard shortcut.
- Click a toolbar icon.

Table 8-9 shows the Number menu commands, their corresponding keyboard shortcuts, and the equivalent toolbar icons for the Sheets numeric formatting options.

Using the paint format tool

Getting a cell formatted just right can take a fair amount of work. That's bad enough, but things get worse if you then have to repeat the entire procedure for another cell. The more times you have to repeat a format, the less likely you are to begin the entire process in the first place.

TABLE 8-9 **Applying Numeric, Date, and Time Formats**

Number Menu Command	Keyboard Shortcut	Toolbar Icon	Format Applied
Number	Ctrl+Shift+!		Two decimal places; using thousands separator
Percent	Ctrl+Shift+%	%	The number multiplied by 100 and with a percent sign (%) to the right
Scientific	Ctrl+Shift+^		Two decimal places
Currency	Ctrl+Shift+$	$	Two decimal places; using the dollar sign; negative numbers surrounded by parentheses
Date	Ctrl+Shift+#		d-mmm-yyyy
Time	Ctrl+Shift+@		h:mm AM/PM
Decrease Decimal		.0 ←	The number of decimal places decreased
Increase Decimal		.00 →	The number of decimal places increased
More Formats	Ctrl+Shift+@	123	All available formats displayed

Fortunately, Sheets has a useful tool that can remove almost all the drudgery from applying the same formatting to multiple cells. It's called the paint format tool, and here are the steps to follow to use the tool to apply existing formatting to another cell:

1. **Select the cell that has the formatting you want to copy.**

2. **Click the paint format icon on the toolbar.**

   The mouse pointer sprouts an icon similar to a paint roller.

3. **Select the cell that you want to receive the formatting.**

   Alternatively, you can drag the mouse pointer across multiple cells.

   Sheets transfers the formatting from the selected cell to the new cell (or cells).

Working with Columns and Rows

One of the easiest ways to improve the appearance of your sheet is to manipulate its rows and columns. This section teaches you how to adjust column widths and row heights and how to hide and unhide entire rows and columns.

Adjusting the column width

You can use column width adjustments to improve the appearance of your sheet in several different ways:

- » If you're faced with a truncated text entry or number, you can widen the column so that the entry appears in full.
- » If your sheet contains lots of numbers, you can widen the columns to create some space to the left of the numbers (since numeric values are right aligned in cells by default) and make the sheet appear less cluttered.
- » You can make your columns narrower to fit the entire sheet on your screen or on a single printed page.
- » You can adjust the column width for the entire sheet to create a custom grid for a specialized model (such as a timeline).

Sheets measures column width in pixels. When you create a sheet, each column uses a standard width of 100 pixels. In the next three sections, I walk you through the Sheets methods for adjusting column widths.

Specifying a column width

Sheets allows column widths as small as 2 pixels and as large as 2,000. To specify a column width, follow these steps:

1. **If you want to resize multiple columns, select them.**
2. **Right-click the column header.**

   If you selected multiple columns in Step 1, right-click the header of any selected column.

   Sheets displays a menu of commands for manipulating columns.
3. **Click Resize the Column.**

   If you selected multiple columns, click Resize Columns *X-Y*, where *X* is the first selected column and *Y* is the last selected column.

   The Resize Column dialog appears.

4. **Select the Enter New Column Width in Pixels radio button.**
5. **In the text box, enter the width you want, in pixels.**
6. **Click OK.**

   Sheets sets the column width and returns you to the sheet.

Using a mouse to set the column width

You can use the mouse to configure a column to the width you want. To give this a whirl, move the mouse pointer to the column header area, position the pointer at the right edge of the column you want to adjust, and then drag the edge to the left (to make the column narrower) or to the right (to make the column wider).

Fitting the column width to the data

If you have a long column of entries of varying widths, getting the optimum column width may take a few tries. To avoid guesswork, you can have Sheets set the width automatically using the Fit to Data feature. When you use this feature, Sheets examines the column's contents and sets the width slightly wider than the widest entry. Sheets gives you two methods to try:

- » Follow the steps outlined earlier, in the "Specifying a column width" section, but rather than specify a width, select the Fit to Data radio button.
- » Position the mouse pointer at the right edge of the column header and double-click.

Adjusting the row height

Sheets normally adjusts row heights automatically to accommodate the tallest character in a row. However, you can make your own height adjustments to give your sheet more breathing room or to reduce the amount of space taken up by unused rows. Sheets measures row height in pixels and sets the default height to 21 pixels. The next three sections take you through the methods Sheets offers to adjust the row height.

WARNING

When reducing a row height, always keep the height larger than the tallest character to avoid cutting off the top of any cell content.

Specifying a row height

Sheets allows row heights of between 2 and 2,000 pixels. To specify a row height, follow these steps:

1. **If you want to resize multiple rows, select them.**
2. **Right-click the row header.**

   If you selected multiple rows in Step 1, right-click the header of any selected row.

   Sheets displays a menu of commands for working with rows.
3. **Click Resize the Row.**

   If you selected multiple rows, choose Resize Rows *M*–*N*, where *M* is the first selected row and *N* is the last selected row.

   The Resize Row dialog appears.
4. **Select the Specify Row Height radio button.**
5. **In the text box, enter the height you want, in pixels.**
6. **Click OK.**

   Sheets sets the row height and returns you to the sheet.

Using the mouse to set the row height

You can use your mouse to set a row to the height you prefer. Move the mouse pointer into the row header area, position the pointer at the bottom edge of the row you want to adjust, and then drag the edge up (to make the row shorter) or down (to make the row taller).

Fitting the row height to the data

If you've made several font changes and height adjustments to a long row of entries, you may need several tries to set an optimum row height. To avoid guesswork, you can use the Fit to Data feature to set the height automatically to the best fit. Sheets gives you two techniques:

- Follow the steps outlined earlier, in the "Specifying a row height" section, but rather than specify a height, select the Fit to Data radio button.
- Position the mouse pointer at the bottom edge of the row header and double-click.

Hiding columns and rows

Your sheets may contain sensitive information (such as payroll figures) or unimportant information (such as the period numbers used when calculating interest payments). In either case, you can hide the appropriate columns or rows whenever you need to show your sheet to somebody else. The data remains intact but isn't displayed on the screen. Here are the techniques to use:

- **Hide one or more columns:** Select the columns, right-click any column header, and then choose Hide Columns. Sheets hides the columns and displays left- and right-pointing arrows where the columns would normally appear, as shown in Figure 8-6.
- **Unhide columns:** In the column headers, click either the left- or right-pointing arrow to unhide the hidden columns.
- **Hide one or more rows:** Select the rows, right-click any row header, and then choose Hide Rows. Sheets hides the rows and displays up- and down-pointing arrows where the rows would normally appear.
- **Unhide rows:** In the row headers, click either the up- or down-pointing arrow to unhide the hidden rows.

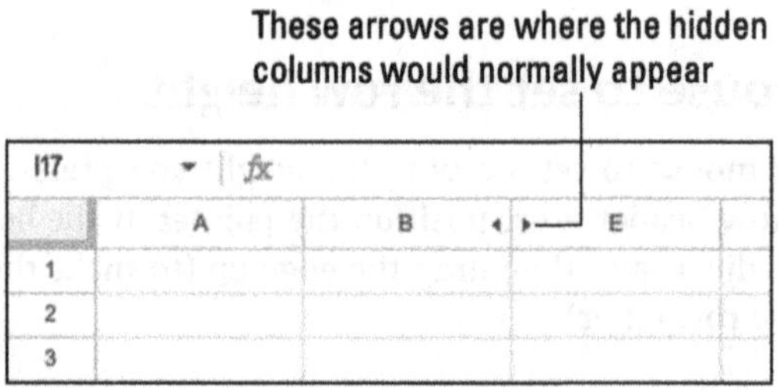

These arrows are where the hidden columns would normally appear

I17	fx		
	A	B ◂ ▸	E
1			
2			
3			

FIGURE 8-6: Sheets replaces hidden columns with arrows.

Inserting columns and rows

When you build a sheet model, you usually work down and to the right, adding new rows of data to the bottom of the model and new columns of data to the right. However, having to add data in the existing model is common, and Sheets offers the following methods for inserting columns and rows within existing data:

- **Inserting one or more columns:** Select the column before or after where you want to insert the new column. (If you want to insert multiple columns, select the same number of columns.) Right-click the column header and then choose either Insert *X* Columns to the Left (to insert *X* columns to the left of the selected columns) or Insert *X* Columns to the Right (to insert *X* columns to the right of the selected columns).

- **Inserting one or more rows:** Select the row above or below where you want to insert the new row. (If you want to insert multiple rows, select the same number of rows.) Right-click the row header and then choose either Insert *X* Rows Above (to insert *X* rows above the selected rows) or Insert *X* Rows Below (to insert *X* rows below the selected rows).

Deleting columns and rows

No sheet is ever built perfectly from scratch, so you often end up with incorrect, old, or unnecessary data that you need to remove. Sheets offers these methods for deleting columns and rows:

- **Deleting one or more columns:** Select the column or columns you want to delete, right-click the column header, and then choose either Delete Column (if you selected a single column) or Delete Columns *X*–*Y* (where *X* and *Y* are the first and last letters of the range of columns you selected).
- **Deleting one or more rows:** Select the row or rows you want to delete, right-click the row header, and then choose either Delete Row (if you selected a single row) or Delete Rows *M*–*N* (where *M* and *N* are the first and last numbers of the range of rows you selected).

IN THIS CHAPTER

» Creating powerful formulas with your bare hands

» Beefing up your formulas with functions

» Sorting and filtering your sheet data

» Creating data eye candy with charts

» Creating a nice, neat summary of your data with a pivot table

Chapter 9
Crunching Numbers

Although you can use Sheets as a simple database for storing text and numbers, that's not what the program is designed to do. At its heart, Sheets is a powerful and sophisticated calculator that can take the raw data on a sheet and summarize it, analyze it, visualize it, and manipulate it in many different ways. In short, Sheets is all about crunching numbers, and that prowess is what this chapter is all about. In the pages that follow, I help you explore such number-crunching features as formulas, functions, sorting and filtering data, visualizing data with charts, analyzing data with pivot tables, and much more. There's a lot of ground to cover, so you had better get started.

Building Formulas

The secret behind Sheets' calculation prowess is the *formula*, a collection of values and symbols that together produce some kind of result. Knowing how to build formulas, particularly if you enhance those formulas with functions, is the royal road to Sheets mastery and to learning everything you can about your data. This section tells you all you need to know to become a master formula builder. After first learning how to make simple calculations, you then learn about operators and cell references and how to control your formulas to produce accurate results.

Creating a simple formula

This section begins with a simple example so that you get the feel of how to build a formula. This example calculates the mortgage principal by subtracting the down payment (in cell B2) from the house price (in cell B1). If you want to follow along, enter values in those cells now (such as $400,000 in B1 and $80,000 in B2). Here are the steps to follow to build the formula:

1. **Select the cell in which you want the formula result to appear (such as B3).**
2. **Enter an equal sign (=).**

   All Sheets formulas begin with an equal sign. Note that the equal sign appears both in the cell itself and in the formula bar. Everything you enter in the cell is mirrored in the formula bar. In fact, you can turn things around and enter stuff in the formula bar and Sheets will automatically mirror that text in the cell.
3. **Click B1.**

   What you're doing here is asking Sheets to include whatever value is in cell B1 to your formula. Sheets does that by adding B1 to the formula, both in the cell and in the formula bar.
4. **Enter a minus sign (-).**

   If you don't have a numeric keypad, enter a hyphen (which is what the minus sign is).

   Sheets adds the minus sign (hyphen) in the cell and in the formula bar.
5. **Click B2.**

   Again, you're asking Sheets to include whatever value is in cell B2 to your formula, which Sheets does by adding B2 to the formula, both in the cell and in the formula bar.

   The formula now reads =B1-B2, which asks Sheets to take whatever value is in cell B1 and subtract whatever value is in cell B2.
6. **Press Enter or Return.**

   Sheets calculates the formula result.

Figure 9-1 shows this example in action. The formula result appears in cell B3, whereas the formula itself appears on the formula bar when you select cell B3.

All Sheets formulas have this basic structure: an equal sign (=) followed by one or more *operands* — which can be a cell reference, a value, a range, a range name, or a function name — separated by one or more *operators* — the symbols that combine the operands in some way, such as the minus sign (-).

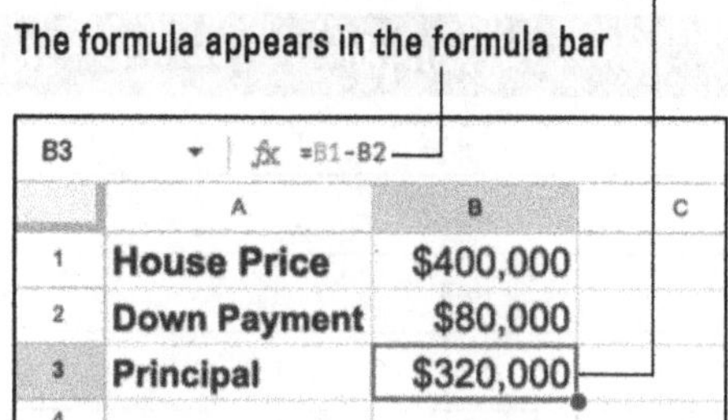

FIGURE 9-1: A simple formula that calculates the difference between two values.

Here are a few notes to keep in mind when entering your formulas:

- *When you need to include a cell reference in a formula,* just typing the cell address is often tempting. However, to ensure accuracy, always click the cell itself instead of typing its address.
- *When you add a cell address to a formula,* Sheets colors the address in the formula and surrounds the cell with a dashed border of the same color. For example, the address might appear as blue, and the cell might be surrounded by a dashed, blue border. These colors are unique (the next cell reference might use green; the next, magenta; and so on), so you can use them to make sure that you've chosen the correct cell.
- *If you need to make changes to the formula before finalizing it by pressing Enter,* you can't use the arrow keys to move the insertion point because Sheets interprets these keystrokes as attempts to select a cell address for inclusion in the formula. To enable the arrow keys for editing rather than for cell selection, press F2 (on some Macs you might have to press Fn+F2) to put the cell into edit mode.

Understanding formula operators

Almost all Sheets formulas fall into one of two categories: arithmetic and comparison. Each category has its own set of operators, and you use each type in different ways, as shown in the rest of this section.

Most of your formulas will be *arithmetic* formulas — that is, they'll combine numbers, cell addresses, and function results with mathematical operators to perform numeric calculations. Table 9-1 lists the operators used in arithmetic formulas.

You use a *comparison* formula to compare two or more numbers, text strings, cell contents, or function results. If the statement is true, the result of the formula is given the logical value `TRUE` (which is equivalent to any nonzero value). If the statement is false, the formula returns the logical value `FALSE` (which is equivalent to 0). Table 9-2 lists the operators you can use in comparison formulas.

TABLE 9-1 **Sheets Arithmetic Operators**

Operator	Example	Result
+ (addition)	=3+2	5
- (subtraction)	=3-2	1
- (negation)	=-3	-3
* (multiplication)	=3*2	6
/ (division)	=3/2	1.5
% (percentage)	=3%	0.03
^ (exponentiation)	=3^2	9

TABLE 9-2 **Sheets Comparison Operators**

Operator	Example	Result
= (equal to)	=3=2	FALSE
> (greater than)	=3>2	TRUE
< (less than)	=3<2	FALSE
>= (greater than or equal to)	="a">="b"	FALSE
<= (less than or equal to)	="a"<="b"	TRUE
<> (not equal to)	="a"<>"b"	TRUE

Avoiding problems with cell references

Cell references in a formula appear to be straightforward. After all, if you reference cell B1, surely that's the end of the story. Unfortunately, the way Sheets interprets cell references in a formula is a bit counterintuitive and can cause problems if you don't understand how it works.

Let's begin with a real-world example. Imagine a conference center with 26 halls, named Room A, Room B, and so on. Imagine further that each hall has three doors — front, middle, and back — and that for security reasons the middle and back doors are always locked. Now imagine, if you will, The Tale of Two Signs:

- All the hall doors appear the same, so you want to put a sign on the (locked) back door that directs people to the front door. For Room A, one possibility is a sign that says "Enter using front door of Room A." That would work, but you have 25 other halls, so you need a different sign for each back door. A better solution is a nonspecific sign such as "Hall entrance two doors up." This way, you need to construct just one sign and make copies for the other doors.

- In the conference center foyer, you want to place a sign for a meeting that's taking place in Room C. One possibility is a sign by the main hallways that says, "Penske meeting: seven doors down." That works (although it's a bit odd), but what if you want to place a second sign just after Room A? Then you'd need a different sign that says, "Penske meeting: four doors down." A better solution is a specific sign such as "Penske meeting: Room C." This way, you just need to construct one sign and make copies for the other locations.

A nonspecific description such as "two doors up" is equivalent to what is called a *relative cell reference* in Sheets. For example, if you're entering a formula in cell B3 and you reference cell B1, Sheets doesn't interpret this directly as "cell B1." Instead, it interprets the reference as "the cell that's two cells above the current cell."

This feature sounds strange, but it can be quite useful. Suppose that you create a second set of House Price and Down Payment data for comparison purposes, and you again want to calculate the principal, as in Figure 9-2. You can reconstruct the formula from scratch, but copying the original formula and then pasting it where you want the new formula to appear is much easier. Figure 9-2 shows the result when the original formula is copied and then pasted into cell B7.

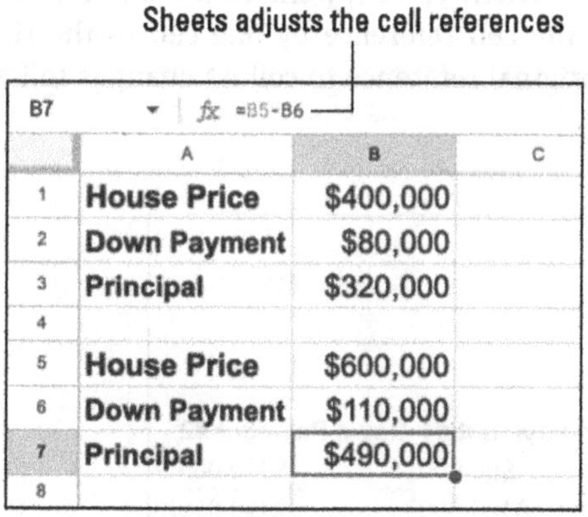

Sheets adjusts the cell references

B7 fx =B5-B6

	A	B	C
1	House Price	$400,000	
2	Down Payment	$80,000	
3	Principal	$320,000	
4			
5	House Price	$600,000	
6	Down Payment	$110,000	
7	Principal	$490,000	
8			

FIGURE 9-2: With relative referencing, Sheets adjusts cell references automatically when you copy a cell containing a formula.

On the formula bar, Sheets has changed the cell references to B5 and B6. That's because the original contained relative cell references, so when the reference "the cell that is two cells above the current cell" is placed in B7, it now refers to cell B5. Thanks to relative referencing, everything comes out perfectly. You'll find that this way of handling copy operations saves you incredible amounts of time when you're building your sheet models.

REMEMBER

Just to keep you on your toes, Sheets adjusts relative cell references when you copy a formula, but it doesn't adjust relative cell references when you move a cell.

However, you need to be a bit careful when copying or moving formulas. To understand why, I'll provide you with a different example. Figure 9-3 shows a sheet that has a fixed house price and two different down payments. The idea here is to display the different principal value that results if you use a different down payment. For Down Payment 1, the sheet uses the formula =A2-B5, as shown on the formula bar in Figure 9-3.

B6 | fx =A2-B5

	A	B	C
1	House Price		
2	$400,000		
3			
4		Down Payment #1	Down Payment #2
5		$80,000	$110,000
6	Principal	$320,000	
7			

FIGURE 9-3: This sheet calculates the principal amount for two different down payments.

Suppose that now you copy the formula from B6 to C6. The result, as shown in Figure 9-4, is incorrect. What happened? The problem is the revised formula in cell C6, which (as shown on the formula bar in Figure 9-4) is =B2-C5. Cell B2 is blank, and Sheets interprets this as 0, so the result is incorrect. The problem is the relative cell references. When you copy the formula and paste it one cell to the right, Sheets adjusts the cell reference by one cell to the right. Unfortunately, this means that the original reference to cell A2 changes to B2, thus resulting in the error.

C6 | fx =B2-C5

	A	B	C
1	House Price		
2	$400,000		
3			
4		Down Payment #1	Down Payment #2
5		$80,000	$110,000
6	Principal	$320,000	-$110,000
7			

FIGURE 9-4: Copying the formula in cell B6 causes the revised formula in cell C6 to be incorrect.

The solution in such cases is to tell Sheets when you want a particular cell reference to remain constant when you copy the formula. Returning to the real-world example from earlier in this section, this is the equivalent of the description "Penske meeting: Room C." In Sheets, this type of explicit direction is called an *absolute cell reference*, and it means that Sheets uses the actual address of the cell.

You tell Sheets to use an absolute reference by placing a dollar sign ($) before both the row number and column letter of the cell address. For example, Sheets interprets the reference $A$2 as "the cell A2." No matter where you copy a formula containing such an address, the cell reference doesn't change. The cell address is said to be *anchored*.

To fix the down payment sheet, you need to anchor the House Price value in cell A2. You do that by opening cell A6 for editing to display the formula, and then changing the original formula in B6 to =$A$2–B5. As shown in Figure 9-5, copying this revised formula produces the correct result in cell C6.

C6 fx =$A$2-C5

	A	B	C
1	House Price		
2	$400,000		
3			
4		Down Payment #1	Down Payment #2
5		$80,000	$110,000
6	Principal	$320,000	$290,000
7			

FIGURE 9-5: When you anchor the House Price value using an absolute cell reference, copying the formula to cell C6 now produces the correct result.

It's also worth noting that Sheets also supports *mixed cell references*, where only the row or only the column is anchored:

- *Anchor just the cell's row* by placing the dollar sign in front of the row number only — for example, A$2.
- *Anchor just the cell's column* by placing the dollar sign in front of the column letter only — for example, $A2.

TIP

To quickly change cell reference formats, place the cursor inside the cell address and keep pressing F4 (on some Macs, you might need to press Fn+F4). Sheets cycles through the various formats.

Using Functions for More Powerful Formulas

Suppose, just for fun, that you want to deposit a certain amount in an investment that earns a particular rate of interest over a particular number of years. Assuming that you start at 0, how much will the investment be worth at the end of the term?

Given a present value (represented by pv), a regular payment (pmt), an annual interest rate (rate), and some number of years (nper), here's the general calculation that determines the future value of the investment:

```
pv(1+rate)^nper+pmt*(((1+rate)^nper)-1)/rate
```

Yikes! This formula is scarily complex, particularly given all those parentheses. That complexity wouldn't be a big deal if this formula were obscure or rarely used. However, calculating the future value of an investment is one of the most common Sheets chores. (It's the central calculation in most retirement planning models.) Having to enter such a formula once is bad enough, but it's one you might need dozens of times. Clearly, entering such a formula by hand multiple times is both extremely time-consuming and prone to errors.

Fortunately, Sheets offers a solution: a function called FV (future value), which reduces the earlier formula to the following:

```
fv(rate, number_of_periods, payment_amount, present_value)
```

This formula is much simpler to use and faster to type, *and* you don't have to memorize anything other than the function name, because, as you'll soon learn, Sheets shows you the full function syntax as you type it.

In general, a *function* is a predefined formula that calculates a result based on one or more *arguments*, which are the function's input values (such as rate and number_of_periods in the FV example). Note that most functions have at least one argument, and that for functions with two or more arguments, in most cases some of those arguments are required (that is, Sheets returns an error if the arguments aren't present) and some are optional.

REMEMBER

Functions not only simplify complex mathematical formulas but also enable you to perform powerful calculations such as statistical correlation, the number of workdays between two dates, and square roots.

Entering functions directly

The quickest way to include a function in a formula is to type the function and its arguments directly into the cell. Here are the steps:

1. **Get your formula off to a flying start by typing an equal sign (=), and then continue entering your formula up to the point where you want to add the function.**

2. **Start entering the function name.**

REMEMBER

Although function names are uppercase, it doesn't matter if you use lowercase or uppercase letters when entering the name. If you use lowercase letters, Sheets helpfully converts the name to uppercase automatically when you complete your formula.

As you type, Sheets displays a list of function names that begin with the characters you've entered so far. Type *f*, for example, and you get a list of functions that begin with *F*.

3. **Use the up- and down-arrow keys to select a function name and display a description of the function.**
4. **To add the selected function name to the formula, press Tab.**

Sheets adds the function name and a left parenthesis: (. If you're typing the function name by hand, be sure to add the left parenthesis after the name.

Sheets now displays a banner displaying the function syntax, as shown in Figure 9-6. Here are two things to note about the syntax:

- The current argument — that is, the one you're about to enter or are in the middle of entering, is highlighted. For example, when you type **fv(** into the cell, the `rate` argument is highlighted. When you enter the current argument and then a comma (,), Sheets highlights the next argument in the list.
- The optional arguments are surrounded by square brackets: [and].

B5 fx =FV(

	A	B	C	D	E
1	Annual Interest Rate	5%			
2	Term (Years)	10			
3	Annual Deposit	-$1,000			
4	Initial Deposit	-$10,000			
5	Future Value	=FV(			
6					
7					
8					
9					
10					

FV(rate, number_of_periods, payment_amount, present_value, [end_or_beginning])

FIGURE 9-6: After you type the left parenthesis, Sheets displays a banner with the function syntax.

5. **Enter the required arguments, separated by commas.**
6. **Enter the optional arguments you want to use, if any, separated by commas.**
7. **Enter the right parenthesis:).**

8. **Complete the rest of your formula, if needed.**
9. **Press Enter or Return.**

   Sheets enters the formula and calculates the result. Figure 9-7 shows the result for the FV function.

B5 fx =FV(B1, B2, B3, B4)

	A	B
1	Annual Interest Rate	5%
2	Term (Years)	10
3	Annual Deposit	-$1,000
4	Initial Deposit	-$10,000
5	Future Value	$28,866.84
6		

FIGURE 9-7: The result of the FV function.

REMEMBER

Note in Figure 9-7 that I used negative numbers for the Annual Deposit and Initial Deposit values. What's up with that? In Sheets, money that you pay out — such as funds paid into an investment or funds used to make a loan payment — is entered as a negative value, while money you receive — such as interest or dividends from an investment — is entered as a positive value.

Entering functions via the Function menu

The pop-up function list and syntax banner that I talk about in the preceding section are so useful that typing functions by hand is almost always the fastest way to incorporate functions into your formulas. However, if you're not sure which function you need, the Function menu might help because it organizes the functions into categories such as financial, logical, math, and statistical.

Here are the steps to follow to include a function in a formula by using the Function menu:

1. **Enter your formula up to the point where you want to add the function.**

2. **Choose Insert ⇨ Function from the menu bar or click the toolbar's functions icon.**

   Depending on the width of your browser window, you might need to first click the more icon (three vertical dots on the right side of the toolbar) to display the functions icon.

   The Functions menu shows a few common functions — SUM, AVERAGE, COUNT, MAX, and MIN — at the top, followed by the function categories.

3. **Either click a common function and then skip to Step 5, or click a function category.**
4. **Click the function you want to insert.**

   Sheets adds the function name followed by left and right parentheses — (and) — and displays a banner like the one shown earlier, in Figure 9-6. Sheets also places the insertion point cursor just after the left parenthesis.
5. **Enter the required arguments, separated by commas.**
6. **Enter the optional arguments you want to use, if any, separated by commas.**
7. **Complete the rest of your formula, if needed.**
8. **Press Enter or Return.**

   Sheets enters the formula and calculates the result.

Using a Range as a Database

Sheets can operate as a simple database, with each column representing a field and each row representing a record. When you use a range to store data in this way, you can also perform several database-like operations on the data, including sorting the range and filtering the range. This section shows you how to perform these operations on your data.

Sorting a range

One benefit of using Sheets as a database is that you can rearrange the records so that they're sorted alphabetically, numerically, or by date. This feature enables you to view the data in order by customer name, part number, order date, or any other field. You can even sort on multiple fields, which would enable you, for example, to sort a client list by country and then by city within each state.

If you want to sort the range on the data in a single column, select any cell within that column and then use one of the following techniques:

- **To sort in ascending order:** Choose Data ⇨ Sort Sheet ⇨ Sort Sheet by Column *X*, A to Z (where *X* is the letter of the column).
- **To sort in descending order:** Choose Data ⇨ Sort Sheet ⇨ Sort Sheet by Column *X*, Z to A (where *X* is the letter of the column).

If you prefer to sort on the data in two or more columns, follow these steps instead:

1. **Select the range you want to sort.**

   If you want to sort on multiple columns, select those columns.

2. **Choose Data ⇨ Sort Range ⇨ Advanced Range Sorting Options.**

   Sheets displays the Sort Range dialog.

3. **If the selected range has a header row that you don't want Sheets to include in the sort, select the Data Has Header Row check box.**

   Selecting this check box also means that Sheets populates the Sort By list with the column names from the range's header row.

4. **In the Sort By list, select the column you want to use for the sort.**
5. **Select the sort order for the column: A to Z (ascending) or Z to A (descending).**
6. **Click Add Another Sort Column, and then repeat Steps 4 and 5 to set the sort options for the new column.**

   Note that when you click Add Another Sort Column, Sheets adds a Then By list for you to select the next column on which to sort.

7. **If you want to sort on other fields, repeat Step 6.**

   Figure 9-8 shows the Sort Range dialog, set up to sort first on the Country field, then on the Region field, and then on the PostalCode field.

   WARNING

   Be careful when you sort list records that contain formulas. If the formulas use relative addresses that refer to cells outside their own record, the new sort order might change the references and produce erroneous results. If your list formulas must refer to cells outside the list, be sure to use absolute addresses.

8. **Click Sort.**

   Sheets sorts the range.

Filtering a range

If your range has a large amount of data, finding what you want can be difficult. Sorting can help, or you can use the Edit menu's Find and Replace command to locate data. However, in some cases, what you really need to do is work with just a subset of the data. You can do so by *filtering* the data so that you display only the records that meet your criteria. This section shows you how to filter data in Sheets.

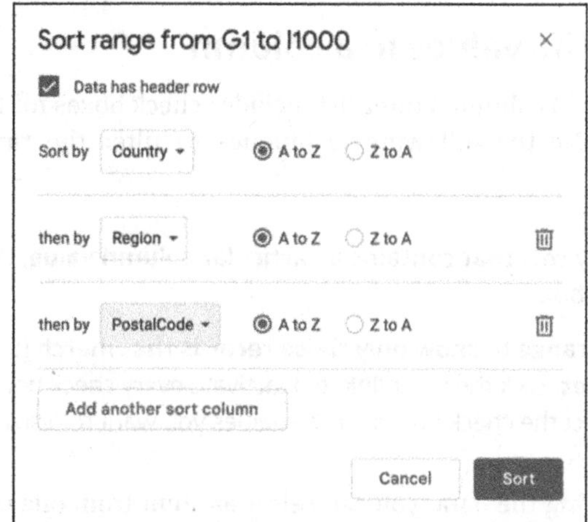

FIGURE 9-8: You can sort a range using multiple columns.

Activating the filter

The Filter feature makes filtering out subsets of your data as easy as choosing an option from a drop-down list. In fact, that's literally what happens. First, click anywhere inside the table, and then turn on Filter by choosing Data ⇨ Create a Filter from the menu bar. Sheets adds Filter icons in the cells containing the data's column labels. Clicking one of these icons displays a list of filtering options for that column. For example, Figure 9-9 shows the filter list for the Country field in a database of customers.

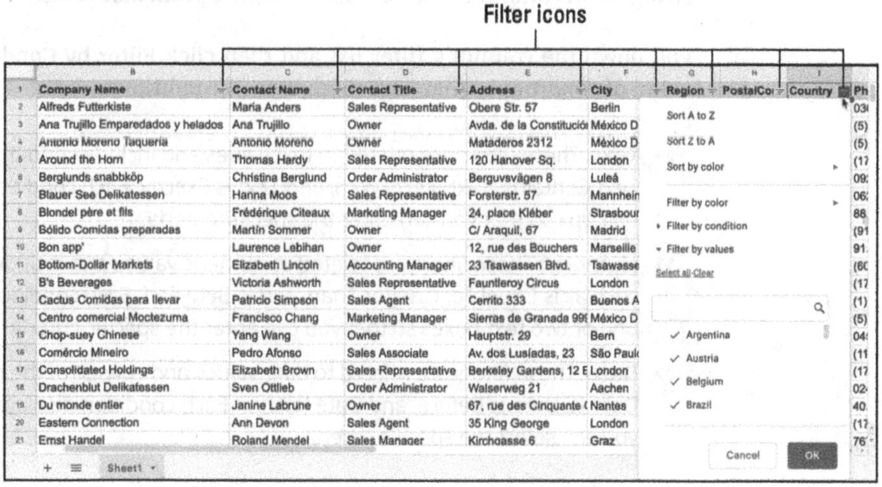

Filter icons

FIGURE 9-9: For each column, Filter adds an icon that opens the list of that column's filtering options.

Filtering by the values in a column

The bottom part of a column's filter list includes check boxes for the unique items in the column. Use the following techniques to filter the range using these check boxes:

- **To hide every row that contains a particular column value,** deselect that value's check box.
- **To filter the range to show only those records that match just a few column values,** click the Clear link to deactivate every check box in the list, and then select the check boxes for the values you want to display.

To continue filtering the data, you can select an item from one of the other lists. For example, after filtering by country, you can choose a state from the Region field to display only the customers from that state. When you're done, click OK to apply the filter.

To remove a filter, click the filter icon to display the filter list and then choose Select All.

Filtering by condition

The filter lists enable you to filter the range based on the values in a column. However, you can also filter the range based on less-stringent criteria. For example, you can filter based on column text values that begin or end with a particular string or on column numeric values within a particular range.

Pull down the column's filter list and then click Filter by Condition to open the menu of conditions. There are three type of conditions:

- **Text:** These filters are related to text values and include conditions such as Text Contains, Text Starts With, and Text Is Exactly. Each condition displays a text box so that you can enter the specific criteria.
- **Numeric:** These filters are related to numeric values and include conditions such as Is Equal To, Greater Than, and Is Between. Each condition displays one or two text boxes so that you can enter the specific criteria.
- **Date:** These filters are related to date values and consist of the conditions Date Is, Date Is Before, and Date Is After. Each condition displays a list so that you can select the specific criteria.

When you're ready, click OK to apply the filter.

Visualizing Data with Charts

One of the best ways to analyze your sheet data — or get your point across to other people — is to display your data visually in a chart. Sheets gives you tremendous flexibility when creating charts; it enables you to place charts in separate sheets or directly on the sheet that contains the data. Not only that, but you also have dozens of different chart formats to choose from, and if none of Sheets' built-in formats is just right, you can customize these charts to suit your needs.

Getting to know the chart elements

Before getting down to the nitty-gritty of creating and working with charts, there's some chart terminology that you need to become familiar with. Figure 9-10 points out the various parts of a typical chart. I explain each part in Table 9-3.

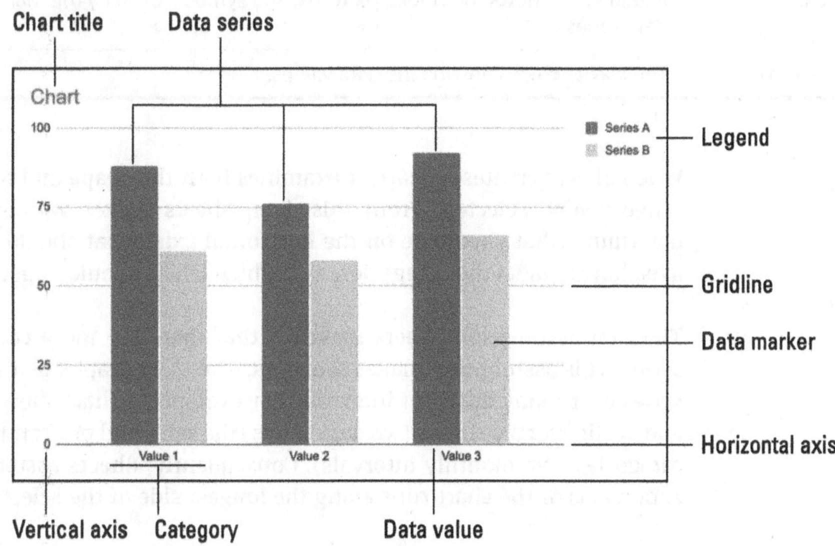

FIGURE 9-10: The elements of a Sheets chart.

How Sheets converts sheet data into a chart

Creating a Sheets chart usually is straightforward, and often you can create one in only a few mouse clicks. However, a bit of background on how Sheets converts sheet data into a chart can help you avoid some charting pitfalls.

TABLE 9-3 **The Elements of a Sheets Chart**

Element	Description
Category	A grouping of data values on the horizontal axis. Figure 9-10 shows three categories: Value 1, Value 2, and Value 3.
Horizontal axis	The X axis, which contains the category groupings.
Chart title	A word or short phrase that describes the chart.
Data marker	A symbol that represents a specific data value. The symbol used depends on the chart type. In a column chart such as the one shown in Figure 9-10, each column is a marker.
Data series	A collection of related data values. Normally, the marker for each value in a series has the same pattern. Figure 9-10 has two series: Series A and Series B. These are identified in the legend.
Data value	A single piece of data. Also called a *data point.*
Gridlines	Optional horizontal and vertical extensions of the axis tick marks. These make data values easier to read.
Legend	A guide that shows the colors, patterns, and symbols used by the markers for each data series.
Vertical axis	The Y axis, which contains the data values.

When Sheets creates a chart, it examines both the shape and the contents of the range you've selected. From this data, Sheets makes various assumptions to determine what should be on the horizontal axis, what should be on the vertical axis, how to label the categories, and which labels should appear in the legend.

The first assumption Sheets makes is that there are more categories than data series. This assumption makes sense because most graphs plot a small number of series over many different intervals. For example, a chart showing monthly sales and profit over a year has two data series (the sales and profit numbers) but twelve categories (the monthly intervals). Consequently, Sheets assumes that the horizontal axis of the chart runs along the longest side of the selected sheet range.

The chart shown in Figure 9-11, left is a plot of the range A1:D3. In this case, the range has more columns than rows, so Sheets uses each column as a category. Conversely, Figure 9-11, right shows the plot of the range A1:C4, which has more rows than columns. In this case, Sheets uses each row as a category.

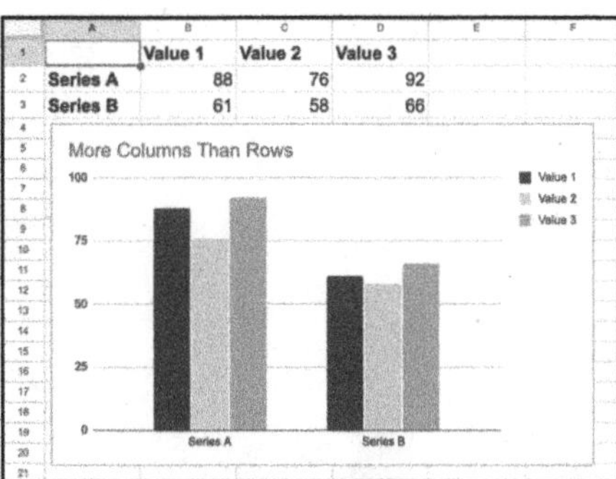

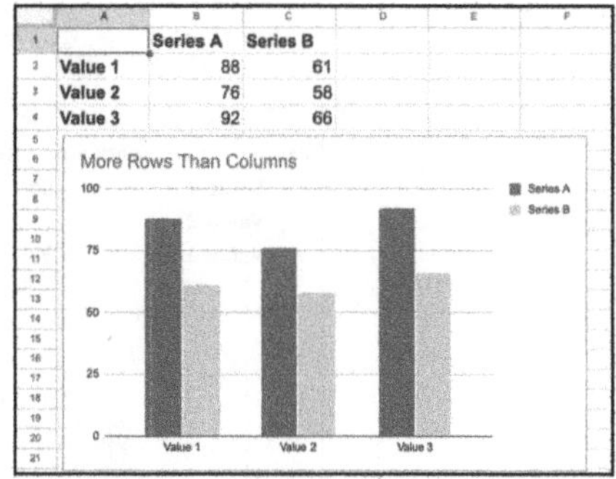

FIGURE 9-11: Charts created from a range with more columns than rows (left) and more rows than columns (right).

The second assumption Sheets makes involves the location of labels for categories and data series:

- **For a range with more columns than rows** (such as in Figure 9-11, left), Sheets uses the contents of the top row (row 1 in Figure 9-11, left) as the category labels, and the far-left column (column A in Figure 9-11, left) as the data series labels.
- **For a range with more rows than columns** (such as in Figure 9-11, right), Sheets uses the contents of the far-left column (column A in Figure 9-11, right) as the category labels, and the top row (row 1 in Figure 9-11, right) as the data series labels.

REMEMBER

If a range has the same number of rows and columns, Sheets uses the columns as categories. Also, Sheets uses the top row for the category labels and the far-left column for the data series labels.

Creating a chart

When plotting your sheet data, the resulting chart sits on top of your sheet and can be moved, sized, and formatted. The chart is linked with the sheet data, so any changes you make to the data are automatically updated in the chart. Nice!

The basic steps for creating a chart require just a few mouse moves, as the following steps show:

1. **Select the range you want to plot.**

   Be sure to include the row and column labels, if there are any. Also, make sure that no blank rows are between the column labels and the data.

2. **Choose Insert ➪ Chart.**

   Sheets creates a default chart, opens the Chart Editor pane, and displays the Setup tab, shown in Figure 9-12.

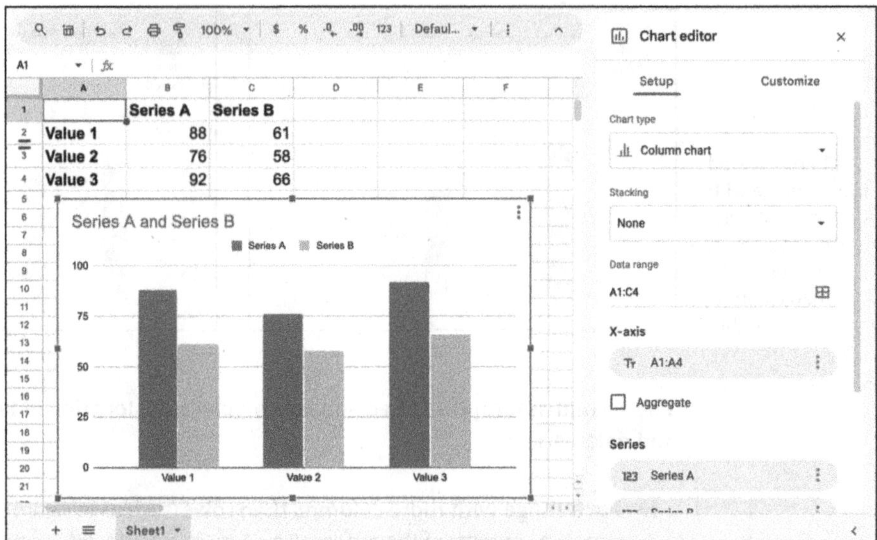

FIGURE 9-12: Use Chart Editor to set up your new chart.

3. **In the Chart Type list, select the kind of chart you want to use.**
4. **If you want to mess around with fonts, colors, and other chart formatting fun, click the Customize tab, click the name of the chart element you want to tweak (Chart Style, Chart & Axis Titles, or Series, for example), and make your changes.**

   In each case, clicking a chart element name reveals the available controls for customizing that chart element.

   Sheets updates the chart as you make your changes.
5. **When you're done with Chart Editor, click X (close).**
6. **Position the chart on the sheet using the following techniques:**
   - *To move the chart,* drag any empty section of the chart.
   - *To size the chart,* drag a chart corner or the middle of any side of the chart border.

Moving a chart to its own sheet

After you create a chart, you might decide later that you want to move the chart to its own sheet. Easier done than said:

1. **Select the chart you want to move.**
2. **Click the more icon (shown in the margin).**

3. **Click Move to Own Sheet.**

   Sheets moves the chart to a separate sheet, which you're free to rename as you see fit.

Editing the chart

After you've created a chart, you may decide that the existing chart type doesn't display your data the way you want. Or, you may want to experiment with different chart types to find the one that best suits your data. Fortunately, the chart type isn't set in stone — you can change it at any time. You can also change the formatting and perform any other tasks in Chart Editor. Here's how:

1. **Select the chart you want to edit.**
2. **Click the more icon.**
3. **Click Edit Chart.**

   Sheets opens Chart Editor.

   TIP

   If you know which chart element you want to edit, double-click that element to open the Chart Editor pane with the element's editing controls displayed.

4. **Make your changes to the chart type, chart settings, chart formatting, and so on.**

   Sheets updates the chart as you make your changes.

5. **Click X (close).**

Building Pivot Tables

It's not that unusual for a sheet to contain thousands of rows. Let's face it: Figuring out how to glean useful insights from that much data will either keep you awake at night or cause nightmares if you do sleep. Want to get some quality shut-eye? No need for sleeping pills when Sheets offers a powerful and versatile data analysis tool called a *pivot table*, which enables you to take those thousands of rows and summarize them in a concise tabular format. You can then manipulate the layout of — or *pivot* — the pivot table to display different views of your data.

This section shows you everything you need to know to get started with what is arguably the most useful data-analysis tool in Sheets. You learn how to create pivot tables, refresh them, pivot them, group them, filter them, and more.

Understanding pivot tables

In a general sense, pivot tables take a large amount of information and condense that data into a report that tells you something useful or interesting. For example, examine the table shown in Figure 9-13. This table contains well over 100 records, each of which is an order from a sales promotion. That's not a ton of data in the larger scheme of things, but trying to make sense of even this relatively small dataset just by examining the table's contents is futile. For example, how many earbuds were sold via social media advertising? Who knows?

SUMMER SALES PROMOTION - ORDERS

Date	Product	Quantity	Net $	Promotion	Advertisement
6/1/2024	Smartphone case	11	$119.70	1 Free with 10	Social media
6/1/2024	HDMI cable	6	$77.82	Extra Discount	Blog network
6/1/2024	USB-C car charger	15	$100.95	Extra Discount	Search
6/1/2024	HDMI cable	11	$149.71	1 Free with 10	Blog network
6/2/2024	USB-C car charger	22	$155.40	1 Free with 10	Blog network
6/2/2024	USB-C car charger	3	$20.19	Extra Discount	Search
6/2/2024	Earbuds	5	$33.65	Extra Discount	Social media
6/2/2024	Smartphone case	22	$239.36	1 Free with 10	Search
6/2/2024	HDMI cable	10	$129.70	Extra Discount	Blog network
6/5/2024	USB-C car charger	22	$155.40	1 Free with 10	Blog network
6/5/2024	Smartphone case	8	$82.96	Extra Discount	Social media
6/5/2024	Smartphone case	22	$239.40	1 Free with 10	Social media
6/5/2024	Earbuds	55	$388.50	1 Free with 10	Blog network
6/5/2024	USB-C car charger	25	$168.25	Extra Discount	Search
6/5/2024	HDMI cable	22	$299.42	1 Free with 10	Blog network

Orders

FIGURE 9-13: Some great data, but how do you make sense of it?

Ah, but now check out at Figure 9-14, which shows a pivot table built from the order data. This report tabulates the number of units sold for each product based on each promotion. From here, you can quickly learn that 322 earbuds were sold via social media advertising. *That* is what pivot tables do.

SUM of Quantity	*Advertisement*			
Product	Blog network	Search	Social media	Grand Total
Earbuds	555	562	322	1439
HDMI cable	719	587	402	1708
Smartphone case	546	460	338	1344
USB-C car charger	1596	1012	752	3360
Grand Total	**3416**	**2621**	**1814**	**7851**

FIGURE 9-14: The pivot table creates order out of data chaos.

Pivot tables help you analyze large amounts of data by performing three operations: grouping the data into categories, summarizing the data using calculations, and filtering the data to show just the records you want to work with:

- **Grouping:** A pivot table is a powerful data-analysis tool in part because it automatically groups large amounts of data into smaller, more manageable chunks. Suppose that you have a data source with a Region field in which each item contains one of four values: East, West, North, and South. The original data may contain thousands of records, but if you build your pivot table using the Region field, the resulting table has just four rows — one each for the four unique Region values in your data.

  You can also create your own grouping after you build your pivot table. For example, if your data has a Country field, you can build the pivot table to group all the records that have the same Country value. Then you can further group the unique Country values into continents: North America, South America, Europe, and so on.

- **Summarizing:** In conjunction with grouping data according to the unique values in one or more fields, Sheets also displays summary calculations for each group. The default calculation is Sum, which means that for each group, Sheets totals all the values in some specified field. For example, if your data has a Region field and a Sales field, a pivot table can group the unique Region values and display the total of the Sales values for each one. Sheets has other summary calculations, including Count, Average, Maximum, Minimum, and Standard Deviation.

  Even more powerful, a pivot table can display summaries for one grouping broken down by another. Suppose that your sales data also has a Product field. You can set up a pivot table to show the total sales for each product, broken down by region.

- **Filtering:** A pivot table also enables you to view just a subset of the data. For example, by default, the pivot table's groupings show all the unique values in the field. However, you can manipulate each grouping to hide those that you don't want to view. Each pivot table also comes with a feature that enables you to apply a filter to the entire pivot table. For example, your sales data may also include a Customer field. By placing this field in the pivot table's filter, you can filter the pivot table report to show just the results for a single customer.

Exploring pivot table features

You can get up to speed with pivot tables quickly after you learn a few key concepts. You need to understand the features that make up a typical pivot table, particularly the four areas — row, column, data, and filter — to which you add fields from your data. Figure 9-15 points out the following pivot table features:

- **Rows area:** Displays vertically the unique values from a field in your data.
- **Columns area:** Displays horizontally the unique values from a field in your data.
- **Values area:** Displays the results of the calculation that Sheets applied to a numeric field in your data.
- **Rows field header:** Identifies the field contained in the Rows area. You also use the rows field header to filter the field values that appear in the Rows area.
- **Columns field header:** Identifies the field contained in the Columns area. You also use the columns field header to filter the field values that appear in the Columns area.
- **Values field header:** Specifies both the calculation (such as Sum) and the field (such as Quantity) used in the Values area.

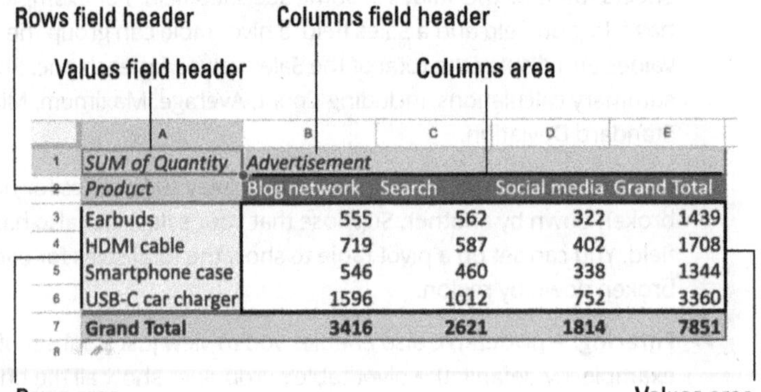

SUM of Quantity	Advertisement			
Product	Blog network	Search	Social media	Grand Total
Earbuds	555	562	322	1439
HDMI cable	719	587	402	1708
Smartphone case	546	460	338	1344
USB-C car charger	1596	1012	752	3360
Grand Total	3416	2621	1814	7851

FIGURE 9-15: The features of a typical pivot table.

Building a pivot table

If the data you want to analyze exists as a Sheets table, you can use the Pivot Table command to quickly build a pivot table report based on your data. You need to specify only the location of your source data and then choose the location of the resulting pivot table.

Here are the steps to follow:

1. **Select a cell within the data you want to use as the basis for your pivot table.**
2. **Choose Insert ➪ Pivot Table.**

   The Create Pivot Table dialog shows up. The Data Range box displays the range address of your data. Double-check the address to make sure it's correct, and adjust the address as needed before moving on.
3. **Select the New Sheet radio button.**

   Alternatively, if you want to add the pivot table to an existing location, select the Existing Sheet radio button and then use the range box to select the sheet and cell where you want the pivot table to appear.
4. **Click Create.**

   Sheets creates a blank pivot table and displays the Pivot Table Editor pane, as shown in Figure 9-16. This pane is divided vertically into two main areas:

   - The left side of the pane contains a Suggested list that offers a few ready-made pivot table layouts, as well as four boxes representing the four areas of the pivot table: Rows, Columns, Values, and Filters. To complete the pivot table, your job is to add one or more fields to some (or even all) of these areas.
   - The right side of the pane contains a searchable list of the columns in your data.

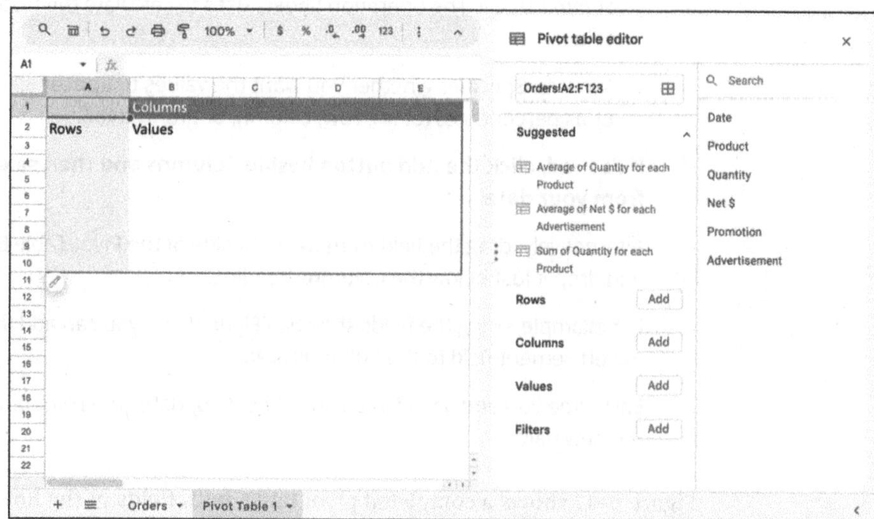

FIGURE 9-16: You start with a blank pivot table and the Pivot Table Editor pane.

5. **In the Pivot Table Editor pane, click the Add button beside Rows and then select a field from your data.**

   Alternatively, drag the field from the right side of the Pivot Table Editor pane and drop it just below the Rows heading.

   For example, using the fields shown in Figure 9-13, you can add the Product field to the Rows area.

   Sheets adds the field's unique values to the pivot table's Rows area.

   Sheets also displays three controls associated with the field:

   - *Order:* How the items are sorted. Choose either Ascending or Descending.
   - *Sort by:* The field on which to sort the Rows area.
   - *Show Totals:* A check box you select to have Sheets add a Grand Total row to the bottom of the pivot table.

6. **In Pivot Table Editor, click the Add button beside Values and then select a numeric field from your data.**

   Alternatively, drag the field from the right side of the Pivot Table Editor pane and drop it just below the Values heading.

   For example, using the fields shown in Figure 9-13, you can select the Quantity field.

   Sheets sums the numeric values based on the row values.

   Sheets also displays two controls associated with the field:

   - *Summarize By:* The operation Sheets uses to calculate the pivot table's values.
   - *Show As:* Specifies whether you want the values to appear as raw numbers or as percentages (of the row, column, or grand total).

7. **If desired, click the Add button beside Columns and then select a field from your data.**

   Alternatively, drag the field from the right side of the Pivot Table Editor pane and drop it just below the Columns heading.

   For example, using the fields shown in Figure 9-13, you can add the Advertisement field to the Columns area.

   Each time you add a field in an area, Sheets updates the pivot table to include the new data.

Figure 9-17 shows a completed pivot table, with fields in the Rows, Columns, and Values areas.

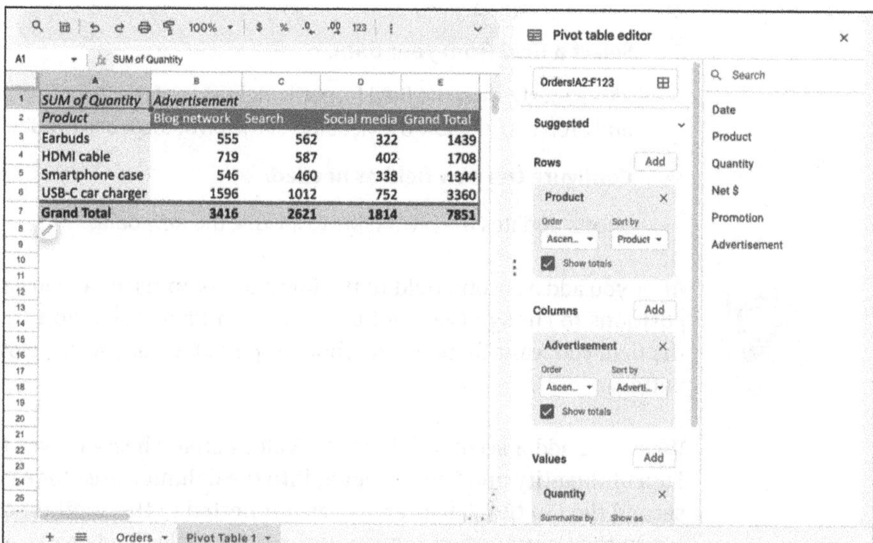

SUM of Quantity	Advertisement			
Product	Blog network	Search	Social media	Grand Total
Earbuds	555	562	322	1439
HDMI cable	719	587	402	1708
Smartphone case	546	460	338	1344
USB-C car charger	1596	1012	752	3360
Grand Total	3416	2621	1814	7851

FIGURE 9-17: A pivot table built from the data in Figure 9-13.

REMEMBER

To remove a field from a pivot table, click the X that appears in the top-right corner of the field in Pivot Table Editor.

Adding multiple fields to a pivot table area

You can add two or more fields to any pivot table area. Having multiple fields is a powerful feature that enables you to perform further analysis of your data by viewing the data differently. Suppose that you're analyzing the results of a sales campaign that ran different promotions in several types of advertisements. A basic pivot table might show you the sales for each product (the Rows field) according to the advertisement used (the Columns field). You might also be interested in displaying, for each product, the breakdown in sales for each promotion. You can do that by also adding the Promotion field to the Rows area.

REMEMBER

Sheets doesn't restrict you to just two fields in any area. Depending on your data analysis requirements, you're free to add three, four, or more fields to any pivot table area.

Follow these steps to add another field to a pivot table area:

1. **Select a cell within the pivot table to display Pivot Table Editor.**
2. **Click the Add button for the field you want to work with.**

3. **Select a field from your data.**

   Alternatively, drag the field from the right side of the Pivot Table Editor pane and drop it just below the heading of the pivot table area you're working with.

4. **Configure the new field as needed.**

   Sheets updates the pivot table to include the new data.

TIP

After you add a second field to the Rows or Columns area, you can change the field positions to change the pivot table view. In Pivot Table Editor, drag the name of the field you want to move and then drop the field above or below an existing field button.

When you add a second field to the Values area, Sheets moves the labels, such as Sum of Quantity and Sum of Net $, into the Columns area for easier reference. The second field in the Values area is also reflected in the addition of a Values As button in the Columns box section of the pivot table Fields pane. You use the Values As button to pivot the values within the report, as I describe in the next section.

Pivoting a field to a different area

A pivot table is a powerful data-analysis tool because it can take hundreds or even thousands of records and summarize them into a compact, comprehensible report. However, a pivot table isn't a static collection of sheet cells. Instead, you can move a pivot table's fields from one area of the pivot table to another. Moving fields to various areas enables you to view your data from different perspectives, which can greatly enhance the analysis of the data. Moving a field within a pivot table is called *pivoting* the data.

The most common way to pivot the data is to move fields between the Rows and Columns areas. However, you can also pivot data by moving a Rows or Columns field to the Filters area. Either way, you perform the pivot by dragging the field from its current box in the pivot table Fields pane and then dropping it inside the area where you want it moved.

You can move any Rows, Columns, or Filters field to the pivot table's Values area. Moving a field to this location may seem strange because Rows, Columns, and Filters fields are almost always text values, and the default value area calculation is Sum. How can you sum text values? You can't, of course. Instead, the default Sheets pivot table summary calculation for text values is CountA (which counts text values). For example, if you drag the Promotion field and drop it inside the Values area, Sheets creates a second value field named CountA of Promotion.

Grouping pivot table values

To make a pivot table with a large number of row or column items easier to work with, you can group the items. For example, you can group months into quarters, thus reducing the number of items from twelve to four. Similarly, if you use a numeric field in the Rows or Columns area, you may have hundreds of items, one for each numeric value. You can improve the report by creating just a few numeric ranges.

Grouping numeric values

Grouping numeric values is useful when you use a numeric field in a row or column field. Sheets enables you to specify numeric ranges into which the field items are grouped. For example, you might have a pivot table of invoice data that shows the extended price (the Row field) and the salesperson (the Column field). It would be useful to group the extended prices into ranges and then count the number of invoices each salesperson processed in each range.

Follow these steps to group numeric values in a pivot table field:

1. **Right-click any item in the numeric field you want to group.**
2. **Choose the Create a Pivot Group Rule option from the menu that appears.**

   The Grouping Rule dialog appears.
3. **In the Minimum Value text box, enter the starting numeric value.**

   The value you enter will be the starting value for the lowest range.
4. **In the Maximum Value text box, enter the ending numeric value.**

   The value you enter will be the ending value for the highest range.
5. **In the Interval Size text box, enter the size you want to use for each grouping.**

   Figure 9-18 shows the Grouping Rule dialog set up to create ten intervals: 1 to 100, 101 to 201, up to 901 to 1000.
6. **Click OK.**

   Sheets groups the numeric values.

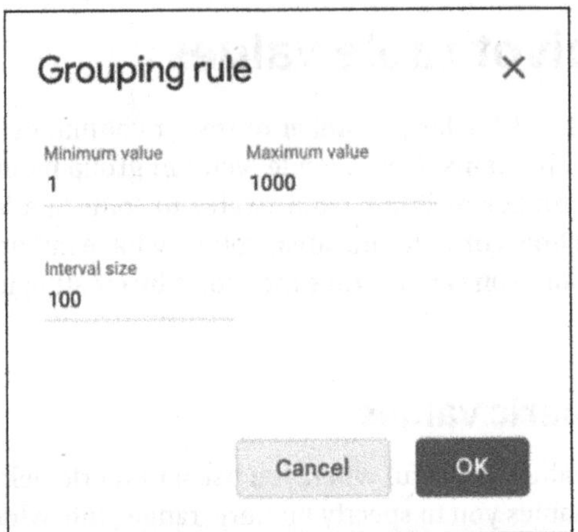

FIGURE 9-18: In the Grouping Rule dialog, specify the numeric ranges you want to use to group your data.

Grouping date and time values

If your pivot table includes a field with date or time data, you can use the grouping feature to consolidate that data into more manageable or useful groups. Follow these steps:

1. **Right-click any item in the date or time field you want to group.**
2. **Choose the Create Pivot Date Group option from the menu that appears.**

   Sheets displays a menu of the date-and-time grouping options.

3. **Select the grouping option you want to apply to your data.**

   Sheets groups the date or time values.

Filtering pivot table values

By default, each pivot table report displays a summary for all the records in your source data, which is usually what you want. However, you may have situations in which you need to focus more closely on some aspect of the data. You can focus on a specific item from one of the source data fields by taking advantage of the pivot table's Filters field.

Suppose that you're dealing with a pivot table that summarizes data from thousands of customer invoices over a certain period. A basic pivot table might tell you the total amount sold for each product you carry. That's interesting, but what if you want to display the total amount sold for each product in a specific country?

If the Product field is in the pivot table's Rows area, you can add the Country field to the Columns area. However, you may have dozens of countries, so adding the field to the Columns area isn't an efficient solution. Instead, you can add the Country field to the filter and tell Sheets to display the total sold for each product for the specific country you're interested in.

Follow these steps to apply a pivot table filter:

1. **Select a cell in the pivot table to display Pivot Table Editor.**
2. **Click the Add button for the Filters field.**
3. **Select a field from your data.**
4. **Select the Status drop-down list.**

   Sheets displays the filter options for the field.
5. **Choose your filter options.**

   You can use the same filtering techniques as I discuss earlier in this chapter, in the "Filtering a range" section.

IN THIS CHAPTER

» Getting comfy with Slides

» Adding and manipulating slides

» Formatting your slides

» Adding transitions and animations

» Mastering the Master slide

» Running your slide show

Chapter 10
Creating Eye-Popping Presentations

Presentations let you communicate your ideas to groups of people. Using a variety of formats and techniques, you can present textual material, tables, graphs, drawings, and other types of information to your audience to inform, persuade, train, or otherwise influence their thinking. In Google Workspace, Slides provides the framework and engine for creating eye-catching presentations.

The Slides presentational building blocks are, appropriately enough, *slides*, which are individual chunks of information in the form of text, graphics, tables, charts, and other objects. People generally convey information on slides in telegraphic or shorthand style — short phrases or bursts of text, pictures, charts, or graphs. Save long sentences and flowing prose for reports — presentations use short, pithy lines to make text easy to grasp.

In this chapter, you explore the creation of a Slides presentation with an emphasis on design and learning to consciously choose the elements of an effective presentation. My goal here is to present a middle way that avoids the two most common slide show faults: drab, lifeless presentations that are ineffective because they bore the audience to tears and overly fancy presentations that are festooned with formats, transitions, sounds, and other effects that have no discernible purpose, use, or benefit. With the middle way, you learn how to create attractive presentations that offer visual interest without sacrificing clarity.

Opening Slides

If you're ready to get the presentation party started, use either of the following techniques to get Slides on the dance floor:

- Send your favorite web browser to `https://slides.google.com`. (Note that you'll end up at `https://docs.google.com/presentation`, but the other address is shorter to type.)
- If you're in a Google Workspace app that has the Google apps icon (such as Mail or Calendar), select Google Apps and then choose Slides from the menu that appears.

Touring the Google Slides Home Page

When you first get to Slides, the app's home page appears, looking somewhat like the page shown in Figure 10-1.

Here's a fast review of the main features of the screen:

- **Main menu:** Opens the main menu, which gives you access to other Google Workspace apps (such as Docs and Sheets), Settings, and Drive. To close the menu, select any empty space outside the menu.
- **Search:** Enables you to search Slides for the presentation you want.
- **Google apps:** Displays icons for all Google apps.
- **Google account:** Gives you access to your Google account.
- **Start a new presentation:** Displays a few templates you can use to start a new presentation. (A *template* is a presentation that comes with predefined slides, text, formatting, and even an image or two to get you off to a quick start.)
- **Template gallery:** Displays the complete list of templates.
- **Recent presentations:** Lists the presentations you've worked on most recently.
- **Open file picker:** Enables you to open a presentation file from Drive.

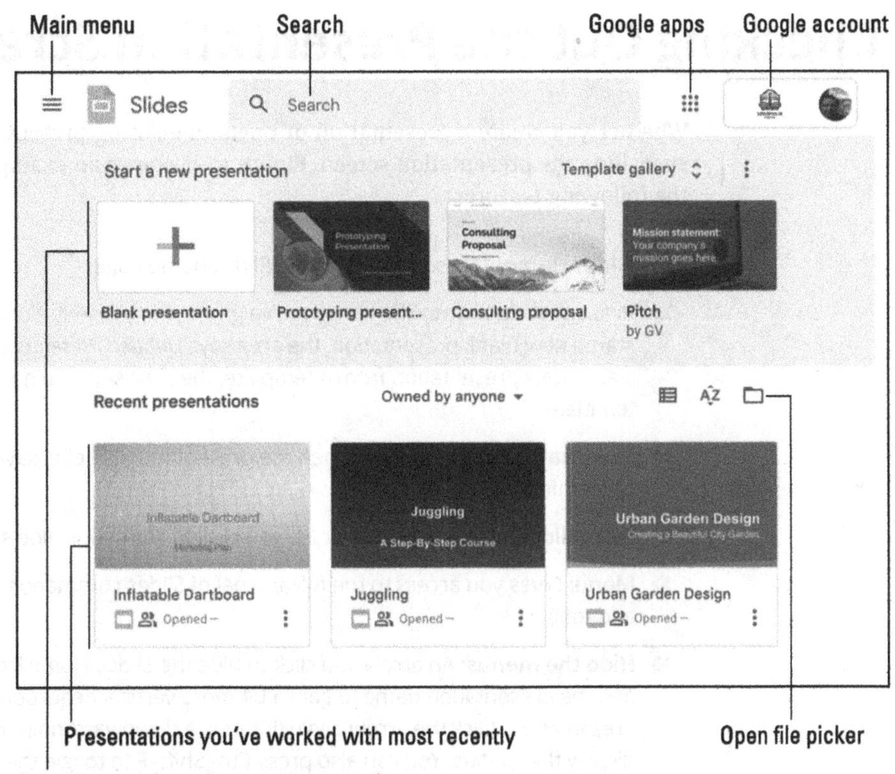

FIGURE 10-1: The home page is your Slides launching point.

Creating a New Presentation File

From the Slides home page, you can open a file you worked on previously (refer to the later section "Opening an existing presentation"), but you'll often want to create a presentation. You have two ways to crank out a new presentation file:

- **To open an empty presentation** (that is, a presentation with no predefined text or formatting), click Blank Presentation in the Start a New Presentation section.
- **To open a presentation that has some ready-to-edit text, formatting, and images,** either choose one of the template tiles shown in the Start a New Presentation section or click Template Gallery and then choose a template from the long list of possibilities that Slides displays.

Checking Out the Presentation Screen

Whether you create a presentation or open an existing presentation, you end up eyeballing the presentation screen. Figure 10-2 shows an example and points out the following features:

- **Slides Home:** Takes you back to the Slides home page.
- **Presentation name:** The name you've given your presentation. When you start a new blank presentation, the area says *Untitled Presentation;* when you start a new presentation from a template, the area says the name of the template.
- **Save status:** Lets you know when the presentation is being saved (among other info).
- **Start slideshow:** The button or list you click to start your slide show.
- **Menu:** Gives you access to the full arsenal of Slides commands, features, and tools.
- **Hide the menus:** An arrow you click to hide the Slides Home icon, the menus, and the presentation name to gain a bit more vertical headroom for your presentation. Click the arrow again (it's now a downward-pointing arrow) to display the menus. You can also press Ctrl+Shift+F to toggle the menus.
- **Toolbar:** Offers one- or two-click access to the most popular Slides features.
- **Filmstrip:** Displays a vertical list of your presentation's slides.
- **Current slide:** Contains the presentation content. This is where you add, edit, and format your slide's content.
- **Grid view:** Display the slides as a grid, which displays a larger view of your slides that takes up most of the Slides screen.
- **Hide filmstrip:** Hides the filmstrip to give the current slide a bit more horizontal legroom.
- **Show side panel:** Displays the side panel, which gives you access to quick actions associated with Calendar, Keep, Tasks, Contacts, and Maps.

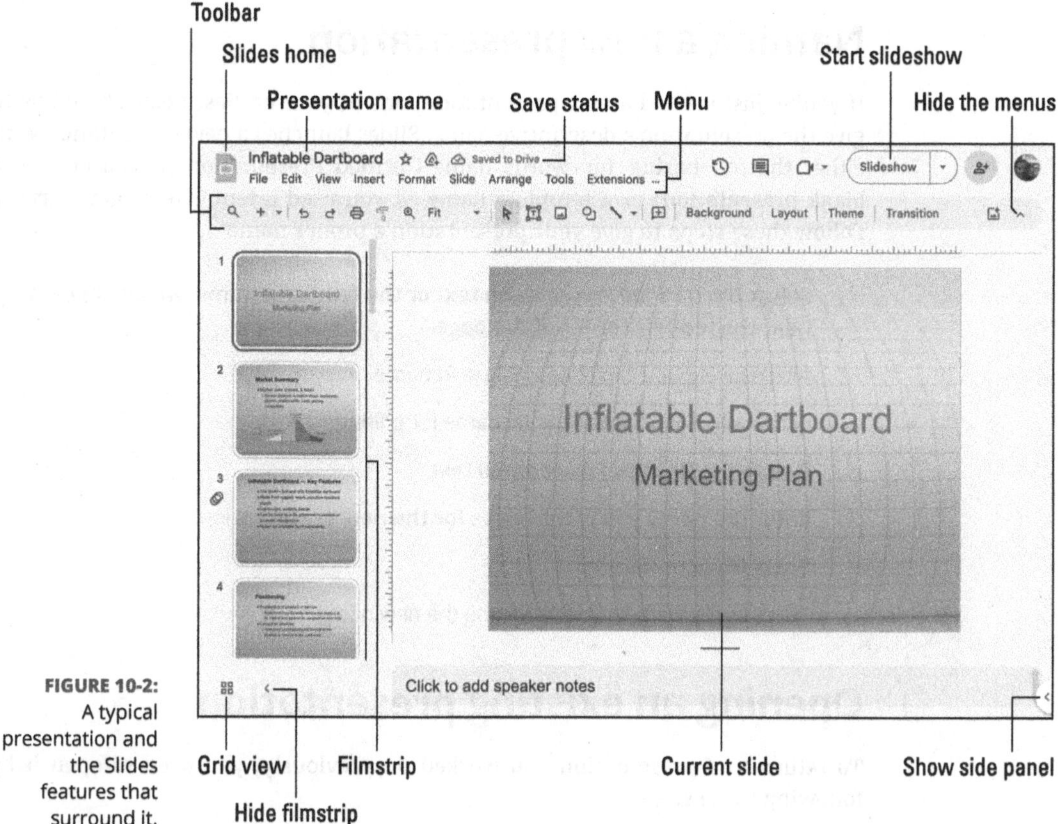

FIGURE 10-2: A typical presentation and the Slides features that surround it.

Dealing with Presentations

Before you learn how to add, edit, and format slides, it pays to take a few minutes to learn some basic presentation chores.

Slides saves your work for you

As you work in Slides, with each change you make, the presentation's save-status text changes to *Saving. . . .* When the save is complete, the status changes to *Saved to Drive.* In other words, Slides takes care of the vital task of saving your work for you, so you never have to worry about it. Sweet!

Naming a new presentation

If you've just started a new presentation, one of your earliest tasks should be to give the presentation a descriptive name. Slides launches a new presentation with either the too-boring-for-words name Untitled Presentation (if you created a blank presentation) or a template name (if you used a template to get started). Follow these steps to give your presentation a proper name:

1. **Select the *Untitled Presentation* text or the template name, which appears near the top-left corner of the page.**

   Alternatively, you can choose File ⇨ Rename.

   Either way, Slides opens the filename for editing.

2. **Delete the *Untitled Presentation* text.**
3. **Enter the name you want to use for the new presentation.**
4. **Press Enter or Return.**

   Slides saves the presentation using the new name.

Opening an existing presentation

To return to a presentation you worked on previously, you need to open it by following these steps:

1. **Open the Slides home page.**

   If you're working on a presentation, click the Slides home icon to return to the Slides home page.

2. **If the presentation you want to open appears in the Recent Presentations area, click it and then skip the rest of these steps. Otherwise, click the open file picker icon.**

   Slides displays the Open a File dialog.

3. **Choose the presentation you want to mess with.**
4. **Click Open.**

   Slides opens the file.

Saving a copy of a presentation

One of the secrets of Slides productivity is to never reinvent the wheel. That is, if you have an existing presentation and you need a second presentation that's similar, don't go to the time and trouble to re-create the original presentation from scratch. Instead, it's not hard to convince Slides to make a copy of the original. With that copy in hand, all you need to do is make whatever changes are needed.

Here's how to make a copy of an existing presentation:

1. **Open the presentation you want to copy.**
2. **Choose File ⇨ Make a Copy ⇨ Entire Presentation.**

   Slides opens the Copy Document dialog. The Name text box shows *Copy of,* followed by the name of the original presentation.
3. **In the Name text box, give a descriptive name to the copy.**
4. **Click Make a Copy.**

   Slides opens a new browser tab and displays the copy you just created.

Applying a presentation theme

A *theme* is a predefined collection of formatting options that control the colors, fonts, and background used with each slide in the presentation. Slides comes with more than two dozen ready-to-present themes.

To apply a theme to your presentation, first choose Slide ⇨ Change Theme (or click Theme on the toolbar). In the Themes pane that appears (see Figure 10-3), click the theme you want to apply to your presentation.

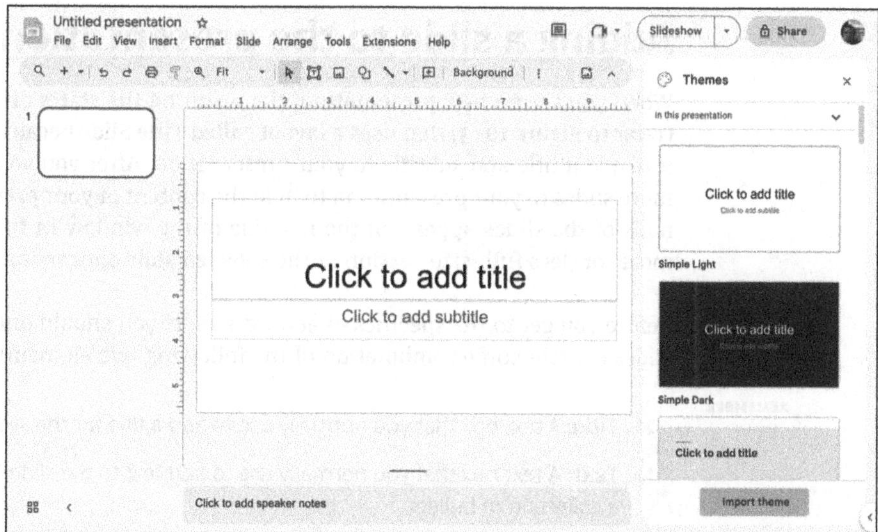

FIGURE 10-3: In the Themes pane, choose a theme.

REMEMBER

If another presentation has a theme you want to reuse, display the Themes pane and then click the Import Theme button. In the Import Theme dialog, either use the Recent, My Drive, or Shared with Me tab to choose an online presentation or use the Upload tab to choose a presentation file from your computer.

Working with Slides

The heart and soul of any presentation is the collection of slides that make up the bulk of its content and serve as both the focal point and the organizing structure of your talk. The slides serve as the bridge between your audience — who, for the most part, have no idea what you're going to talk about — and yourself — who (presumably) knows exactly what you want to say. Building an effective presentation consists mostly of creating and organizing slides, which in turn involves four things:

REMEMBER

- The content — text and graphics — presented on each slide
- The organization of the content presented on each slide
- The formatting applied to each slide: fonts, colors, and background, for example
- The organization of the slides in the context of the entire presentation

In most of what follows in this chapter, I talk about various Slides techniques and tricks that support these four design ideas.

Adding a slide to the presentation

When you start a new presentation, the resulting file starts off with a single slide (refer to Figure 10-3) that uses a layout called Title Slide because you normally use it to add a title and subtitle to your presentation. After you've done that, you add more slides to your presentation to hold the content of your presentation. Thumbnails of the slides appear on the left side of the window in filmstrip view, and a more-or-less full-size version of the selected slide appears on the right.

REMEMBER

Before you get to the specifics of adding a slide, you should understand that most slides contain some combination of the following two elements:

- **Title:** A text box that you normally use to add a title for the slide
- **Text:** A text box that you normally use to add text to the slide, which is usually a collection of bullets

In each case, the new slide contains one or more *placeholders*, and your job is to fill in the placeholder with your text. Most slides use some combination of Title and Text placeholders, and the arrangement of these placeholders on a slide is called the *slide layout*.

Inserting a new slide

Here are the steps to follow to add a slide with a predefined layout:

1. **In filmstrip view on the left, click the slide after which you want the new slide to appear.**
2. **Choose Slide ⇨ New Slide.**

   Slides inserts a new slide that uses the same layout as the slide you selected in Step 1. If that's the layout you want for your new slide, skip the rest of these steps.
3. **Choose Slide ⇨ Apply Layout.**

   Alternatively, click Layout on the toolbar.

   Either way, a gallery of slide layouts appears.
4. **Click the slide layout you want to apply to the new slide.**

   Slides applies the new layout.

Duplicating a slide

If you have a slide in the current presentation that has similar content and formatting to what you want for your new slide, you can save yourself a great deal of time by inserting a duplicate of that slide and then adjusting the copy as needed. Here are the steps to follow to duplicate a slide:

1. **In filmstrip view on the left, click the slide you want to duplicate.**

   If you have multiple slides you want to duplicate, you can save time by selecting all the slides at one time. I talk about selecting multiple slides later in this chapter, in the "Selecting slides" section.
2. **Choose Slide ⇨ Duplicate Slide (or Slide ⇨ Duplicate Slides if you have multiple slides selected).**

   Slides creates a copy of the slide and inserts the copy below the selected slide.

TIP

A quicker way to duplicate a slide is to select it, press Ctrl+C to copy it, and then press Ctrl+V to paste it. If you want the copy to appear in a particular place in the presentation, select the slide after which you want the copy to appear and then press Ctrl+V. The slide you copied appears below the slide you selected.

TIP

Yet another way to create a duplicate of a slide is to hold down Ctrl (Option on a Mac) and then click-and-drag the slide. When you drop the slide, Slides creates a copy of the slide in the new location.

Importing slides from another presentation

One of the secrets of Slides productivity is to avoid redoing work you've performed in the past. If you have a slide with boilerplate legal disclaimer text, why re-create it in each presentation? If you create an organization chart slide and your organization hasn't changed, you don't need to build the chart from scratch every time you want to add it to a presentation.

In the preceding section, you learn how to duplicate a slide from the current presentation. However, the far more common scenario is that the slide you want to reuse exists in another presentation. Here are the steps to follow to import one or more slides from an existing presentation into the current presentation:

1. **In filmstrip view on the left, select the slide after which you want the imported slides to appear.**
2. **Choose File ⇨ Import Slides.**

   Slides opens the Import Slides dialog.
3. **Click the Recent, My Drive, or Shared with Me tab and choose the online presentation that has the slides you want to import.**

   If the presentation you want to use isn't online, select the Upload tab instead, and then choose the presentation file on your computer.
4. **Click Insert.**

   Slides displays all slides that are in the selected presentation.
5. **Click each slide you want to import.**
6. **If you want to preserve the formatting of the imported slides, select the Keep Original Theme check box.**

   If you deselect Keep Original Theme, Slides applies the theme of the current presentation to the imported slides.
7. **Click Import Slides.**

   Slides inserts the slides into the presentation below the slide you selected in Step 1.

Adding data to a slide

After you've added one or more slides, the next step is to fill in the slide data. How you do this depends on whether you're filling in an existing slide placeholder or inserting another object, such as an image.

Adding slide text

With a Title or Text placeholder, click inside the placeholder to enable editing and then enter your text. Strangely, when you're filling in a Text placeholder, Slides does *not* assume that you'll add bullet points, despite the fact that 99.99 percent of all nontitle text in every presentation ever made consists of bullet points. This means you have to endure the extra steps of creating a bulleted list. You have two choices:

- Choose Format ➪ Bullets & Numbering ➪ Bulleted List Menu and then choose the style of bullets you want to use.

- Click the toolbar's bulleted list icon to insert a standard bulleted list. To choose a different list style, click the icon's drop-down arrow and then select the list style you want.

Type your bullet text, press Enter to start a new bullet, and repeat as needed.

REMEMBER

You can have multilevel bulleted lists, where an item in the list can have one or more sub-bullets, those items can have one or more sub-sub-bullets, and so on. The original list items are at the top level of this hierarchy, sub-bullets are on the second level, sub-sub-bullets are on the third level, and so on.

You can also use the keyboard shortcuts in Table 10-1 to work with bullet items.

TABLE 10-1 Keyboard Shortcuts for Working with Slide Bullets

Press This	To Do This
Tab	Demote a bullet to a lower level
Shift+Tab	Promote a bullet to a higher level
Alt+Shift+down arrow (Control+Shift+down arrow on a Mac)	Move a bullet down one position in the list
Alt+Shift+up arrow (Control+Shift+up arrow on a Mac)	Move a bullet up one position in the list

REMEMBER

If you've completed your list and you want to add some regular text below the list, press Enter twice to tell Slides you're done with your bulleted list.

Adding slide objects

To insert content outside any slide placeholder, click the Insert menu and then choose the content type: Image, Text Box, Audio, Video, Shape, Table, Chart, Diagram, Word Art, or Line. No image to insert? No problem if your Google Workspace account includes Google's Gemini AI because you can generate just about any image you want from a simple text prompt. Check out "Generating Images with AI," at the end of the chapter.

Adding speaker notes

When determining the content of your presentation, you keep to a minimum the amount of information on a slide — just the high-level points to provide the framework for the topics you want to present. How then do you keep track of the details you want to cover for each slide? What if you want to provide these details to your audience, too? The answer to both questions is to use slide notes.

Notes let you have paper printouts that contain both your slides and additional information you enter in notes. Consider the following ways you can use notes:

- **As presentation notes:** Notes that only you can refer to while you're making the presentation.
- **As additional detailed handouts for your audience:** Notes that you print and pass around to your audience so they have something to refer to during and after your presentation.
- **As a student guide:** Notes where you can put additional information for your learners when you use a presentation as a teaching tool.
- **As an instructor's guide:** Notes where you include additional points you want to make or other information that would be beneficial to your learners when you use a presentation as a teaching tool.

To create notes, select the notes box below the slide — the box that has *Click to add speaker notes*. If this box doesn't appear, choose View ⇨ Show Speaker Notes.

TIP

If you want more room to type, drag the separator bar at the top of the notes box. Drag the bar up until the notes box is the size you want, and then release the bar. This gives you less room for the slide, but you can also return the notes box to its original size after you've added your note.

Selecting slides

To work with slides, you must first select one or more. Here are the techniques you can use in the filmstrip:

- **To select a single slide,** click it in the filmstrip on the left.
- **To select multiple, consecutive slides,** click the first slide you want in the filmstrip, hold down Shift, and then click the last slide.
- **To select multiple, nonconsecutive slides,** click the first slide you want in the filmstrip, hold down Ctrl, and then click each of the other slides.
- **To select all slides,** click any slide in the filmstrip and then press Ctrl+A (⌘+A on a Mac; you can also choose Edit ➪ Select All).

Rearranging slides

If you need to change the order in which your slides appear in the presentation, Slides gives you two different methods, either of which you can use in the filmstrip or in grid view (choose View ➪ Grid View):

- Select the slide you want to move, press Ctrl+X, select the slide after which you want the moved slide to appear, and then press Ctrl+V.
- Drag the slide and drop it either below the slide after which you want it to appear or above the slide before which you want it to appear.

Changing the layout of a slide

If the original layout you applied to a slide just isn't cutting it for you, you can change the layout by following these steps:

1. **Select the slide or slides you want to change.**
2. **Choose Slide ➪ Apply Layout.**

   You can also click the toolbar's Layout button.

   Slides displays a gallery of slide layouts.
3. **Choose the layout you want to use.**

   Slides applies the new layout. If the slide contains items for which the new layout doesn't have placeholders, Slides leaves those placeholders on the slide.

Changing the slide background

Most themes offer a solid color background, which is usually a good choice because you don't want your background to interfere with the slide content. However, each theme gives you a choice of background colors and gradients, or you can use an image.

Here are the steps to follow to change the slide background style:

1. **If you're applying the background to only certain slides, select the slides.**
2. **Choose Slide ⇨ Change Background.**

   Alternatively, click the toolbar's Background button.

   Slides opens the Background dialog.
3. **Choose the background you want to apply:**
   - *To apply a color or gradient,* use the Color palette.
   - *To apply an image,* click Choose Image.
4. **Click Done.**

   Alternatively, if you want to apply your new background to all the slides in the presentation, click Add to Theme.

   Slides applies the new background to the selected slides.

Working with Theme Builder

One of the Slides themes might be just right for your presentation. If so, great! Your presentation's design will be one less thing to worry about on your way to an effective presentation. Often, however, a theme is just right except for the background color, title alignment, or font. Or, perhaps you need the company's logo to appear on each slide. Using the theme as a starting point, you can make changes to the overall presentation so that it's just right for your needs.

However, what do you do if your presentation already has a number of slides? It'll probably require a great deal of work to change the background, alignment, or font on every slide. Fortunately, Slides offers a much easier way: Theme Builder, which is available for every presentation. Theme Builder acts as a kind of design center for your presentation. Theme Builder's typefaces, type sizes, bullet styles, colors, alignment options, line spacing, and other options are used on each slide in your presentation. Not only that, but any object you add to Theme Builder — a piece of clipart or a company logo, for example — also appears in the same position on each slide.

REMEMBER

The beauty of Theme Builder is that any change you make to this single slide is propagated to all slides in your presentation. Need to change the background color? Just change the background color of the theme's master slide. Prefer a different type size for top-level items? Change the type size for the top-level item shown on the theme's master slide. Theme Builder also has master slides for each type of layout.

To display Theme Builder onscreen, choose View ⇨ Theme Builder. Figure 10-4 shows Theme Builder using the Simple Light theme.

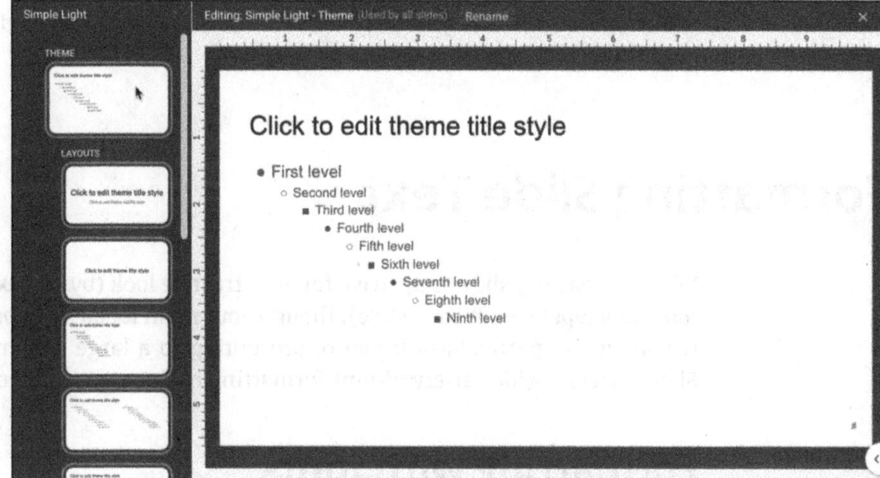

FIGURE 10-4: Theme Builder acts as a design center for the current presentation's theme.

Theme Builder shows several layout masters on the left, with the theme master slide at the top and the masters for the standard layouts below it. Choose the master you want to work with, and then use the following techniques to customize it:

- **To work with a placeholder,** select it.
- **To delete a placeholder,** select it and then press Delete.
- **To size a placeholder,** position the mouse pointer over one of the placeholder's sizing handles (the squares that appear at the corners and border midpoints). Drag the sizing handle to the position you want.
- **To move a placeholder,** position the mouse pointer over one of the placeholder borders (but not over a sizing handle). The pointer changes to a four-headed arrow. Drag the placeholder to the position you want.

- **To display an object (such as an image or a text box) on every slide,** click the Insert menu and then insert the object into the master.

Note, too, that after you select a master, you can format the text, background, bullets, and colors as if you were working on a regular slide. When you finish, choose X (close) in the top-right corner of Theme Builder.

Now one of the following will happen:

- If you made a change to the theme's master slide, that change gets reflected in every slide in your presentation. The exception here is that Slides doesn't overrule layout master modifications, so if you've already made the same change to a layout master, your theme master slide change doesn't appear in that layout.
- If you made a change to a layout master, that change is reflected in every slide that uses that layout.

Formatting Slide Text

When formatting slide text, strive for an attractive look (by, for example, avoiding too many typefaces in each slide), though your main focus must be on maximizing readability — particularly if you're presenting to a large audience. Fortunately, Slides offers a wide variety of font formatting options, as this section shows.

Formatting with fonts

To apply font formatting, select the block of text you want to format. You then choose your font formatting using any one of the following three methods:

- Choose Format ⇨ Text and then click a formatting option from the submenu that appears.
- Press a keyboard shortcut.
- Click a toolbar icon.

Table 10-2 shows the Text menu commands and their corresponding keyboard shortcuts.

If you do a lot of work with fonts, you'll appreciate the pushbutton convenience of the font-related buttons on the Slides toolbar. Table 10-3 shows you the available icons for font-related chores.

TABLE 10-2 Font Formatting via Menu and Keyboard

Text Menu Command	Keyboard Shortcut
Bold	Ctrl+B (⌘+B on a Mac)
Italic	Ctrl+I (⌘+I on a Mac)
Underline	Ctrl+U (⌘+U on a Mac)
Strikethrough	Alt+Shift+5 (⌘+Shift+X on a Mac)
Superscript	Ctrl+. (period; ⌘+. on a Mac)
Subscript	Ctrl+, (comma; ⌘+, on a Mac)
Size, Increase Font Size	Ctrl+Shift+. (period; ⌘+Shift+. on a Mac)
Size, Decrease Font Size	Ctrl+Shift+, (comma; ⌘+Shift+. on a Mac)
Color	N/A
Highlight Color	N/A
Capitalization	N/A

TABLE 10-3 Font Formatting from the Toolbar

Toolbar Icon	Icon Name	What It Does
Arial ▾	Font	Displays a list of typefaces
− 11 +	Font size	Displays a list of font sizes
B	Bold	Applies bold to the text
I	Italic	Applies italics to the text
U	Underline	Underlines the text
A	Text color	Displays a color palette and then applies the color you select to the text
	Highlight Color	Displays a color palette and then applies the color you select to the background of the text

Aligning paragraphs

Aligning stuff is about getting your paragraphs dressed up so that they look all prim and proper. Specifically, I'm talking about lining up the left and right ends of your text with respect to the left or right margins — or both. Slides offers three alignment methods:

- Choose Format ⇨ Align & Indent and then click a formatting option from the submenu that appears.
- Press a keyboard shortcut.
- Click a toolbar icon.

Table 10-4 shows the Align & Indent menu commands, their corresponding keyboard shortcuts, and the equivalent toolbar icons for the four Slides alignment options.

TABLE 10-4 Aligning Paragraphs in Slides

Align & Indent Menu Command	Keyboard Shortcut	Toolbar Icon	What It Does
Left	Ctrl+Shift+L (⌘+Shift+L on a Mac)		Aligns each line on the left margin
Center	Ctrl+Shift+E (⌘+Shift+E on a Mac)		Centers each line between the left and right margins
Right	Ctrl+Shift+R (⌘+Shift+R on a Mac)		Aligns each line on the right margin
Justified	Ctrl+Shift+J (⌘+Shift+J on a Mac)		Aligns each line on both the left and right margins; ignores the last line in a paragraph if the line is too short to justify
Increase Indent	Ctrl+] (⌘+] on a Mac)		Shifts the selected text to the right
Decrease Indent	Ctrl+[(⌘+[on a Mac)		Shifts the selected text to the left

Align & Indent Menu Command	Keyboard Shortcut	Toolbar Icon	What It Does
Top			Aligns data vertically with the top of the placeholder
Middle			Aligns data vertically with the middle of the placeholder
Bottom			Aligns data vertically with the bottom of the placeholder

Slide formatting considerations

Slides has many tools and features for tweaking the formatting of your slides. Like any program with a large number of options, the temptation is to try them all to develop a feel for what Slides is capable of. However, *trying* the formatting features is one thing, but actually *using* all of them is quite another. If you lay on the formatting too thick, you run the risk of hiding the slide content under too many layers of fonts, colors, images, and effects.

To help you avoid that all-too-common fate, here are a few formatting considerations to keep in mind when working on your slides:

- **When in doubt, opt for simplicity.** The most effective presentations are almost always the simplest presentations. This doesn't mean that your slides must be dull, plain affairs. A judicious use of fonts, colors, effects, and (particularly) images can greatly enhance your message. *Simplicity* in presentations just means that whatever formatting you add must not interfere with your content and must not overwhelm the senses of your audience.
- **Remember your message.** Before even opening a new Slides file, think about the overall message you want your presentation to convey. Then, when you format each slide, ask yourself whether each formatting tweak is an enhancement of your message or, at worst, a neutral effect on it. If the answer is no, don't add the formatting.
- **Consider your audience.** Some designs suit certain audiences better than others. For example, if you're presenting to children, a bright, happy design with kid-friendly images will work, whereas a plain, text-heavy design will induce naptime. If, however, you're presenting to managers or the board of directors, you need a design that gets straight to the point and has little in the way of design frills.
- **Preserve your company's image.** I mean this in two ways: First and most obviously, if your company has a set color scheme or style, your presentation

should reflect it. Second, if your company is known as one that's staid or bold, serious or fun, your presentation should not conflict with that image.

- **Be consistent across all slides.** Use the same typeface and type size for all your titles, use consistent bullet styles throughout the presentation, use the same or similar background images on all slides, and have the company logo in the same place on each slide. The more consistent you are, the less work your audience has to do to interpret the formatting for each slide, so the more they can concentrate on your content.
- **Remember, however, not to use the same layout on every slide.** To help keep your audience interested, vary the layout from slide to slide.
- **Remember typeface considerations.** For the typeface, use sans serif fonts (the ones without the little "feet" at the letter tips), such as Arial, Montserrat, Roboto, and Verdana. These typefaces are easier to read than serif typefaces (the ones with the little feet) and are much better choices than fancy, decorative typefaces, which are very difficult to decipher from a distance.
- **Remember type size considerations.** For the type size of your slide content, don't use anything smaller than the default sizes. In particular, never use a type size smaller than 20 points because it's nearly impossible for your audience to read. If your audience is older or you're presenting in a large hall, consider using type sizes even larger than the Slides defaults.
- **Remember color considerations.** For maximum readability, be sure to have significant contrast between the text color and the slide's background color. Dark text on a light background is best for most presentations. Finally, don't use a background image unless it's relatively faint and the text stands out well against it.
- **Design slide content.** Finally, and perhaps most important, design your slides so that they don't include too much information. Each slide should have, at most, four or five main points; anything more than that and you're guaranteed to lose your audience by making them work too hard.

Animating Your Slides

Many years ago, someone defined *fritterware* as any software program that offered so many options and settings that you could fritter away hours at a time tweaking and playing with the program. The animation features certainly put Slides into the fritterware category because it isn't hard to while away entire afternoons playing with transitions, entrance effects, and other animation features. Consider yourself warned that the information in this section might have adverse effects on your schedule.

Learning a few animation guidelines

Before you learn how to apply slide transitions and object animations, it's worth taking a bit of time now to run through a few guidelines for making the best use of slide show animations:

REMEMBER

- **Enhance your content.** The goal of any animation should always be to enhance your presentation, either to emphasize a slide object or to hold your audience's interest. Resist the temptation to add effects just because you think they're cool or fun, because chances are good that most of your audience won't treat them that way.
- **Remember that transitions can be useful.** Using some sort of effect to transition from one slide to the next is a good idea because it adds visual interest, gives the audience a short breather, and helps you control the pacing of your presentation.
- **Remember that transitions can be distracting.** A slide transition is only as useful as it is unremarkable. If everybody leaves your presentation thinking, "Nice transitions!" you have a problem, because they *should* be thinking about your message. Simple transitions such as fades, wipes, and dissolves add interest but don't get in the way. On the other hand, if you have objects flying in from all corners of the screen, your content will seem like a letdown.
- **When it comes to transitions and animations, remember that variety is *not* the spice of life.** Avoid the temptation to use many different transitions and animations in a single presentation. Just as slide text looks awful if you use too many fonts, your presentations will look amateurish if you use too many animated effects.
- **Keep up the pace.** For transitions, use the Fast setting (or one close to it) to ensure that the transition from one slide to another never takes more than a few seconds. Also, avoid running multiple object animations at the same time, because it can take an awfully long time for the effect to finish, and audiences *never* like having their time wasted on such things.
- **Match your animations to your audience.** If you're presenting to sales and marketing types, your entire presentation will be a bit on the flashy side, so you can probably get away with more elaborate animations. In a no-nonsense presentation to board members, animations and transitions should be as simple as possible.

Setting up a slide transition

A *slide transition* is a special effect that displays the next slide in the presentation. For example, in a *fade in* transition, the next slide gradually materializes, while in

a *flip* transition, the next slide appears with an effect similar to turning over a card. Slides has seven transition effects, and for each one you can control the transition speed.

Here are the steps to follow to apply a slide transition to one or more slides:

1. **If you want to apply the transition to only certain slides, select the slides you want to work with.**
2. **Choose View ➪ Motion.**

   Alternatively, click the toolbar's Transition button or press Ctrl+Alt+Shift+B (⌘+Option+Shift+B on a Mac).

   Slides displays the Motion pane.
3. **In the Slide Transition group, click None (or the name of the transition if you've previously applied one) to expand the group, and then click the drop-down menu and choose the transition effect you want.**

   The Motion pane sprouts several controls related to the transition, as shown in Figure 10-5.

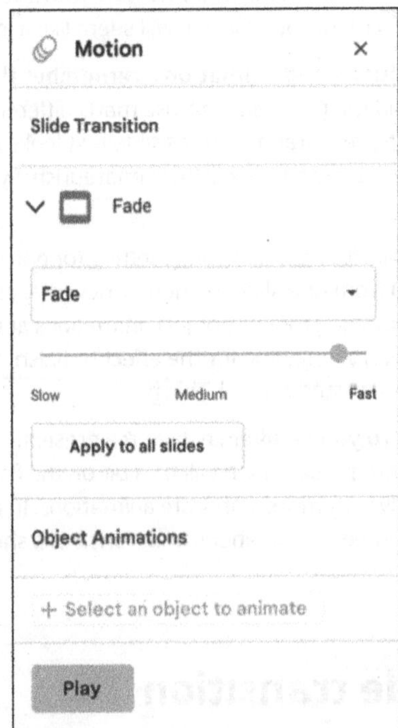

FIGURE 10-5: In the Motion pane, use the Slide Transition controls to apply a built-in slide transition to the selected slides.

4. **Use the slider to select the transition speed.**

   Drag the slider to the left for a slower transition speed; drag the slider to the right for a faster speed.

5. **If you want to use the transition for all slides in the presentation, click Apply to All Slides.**

   If you don't choose this option, the transition applies to only the selected slides.

6. **To preview the transition, click Play.**

7. **Click X (close) in the top-right corner of the Motion pane.**

REMEMBER

Slides indicates that a slide has an applied transition by adding the animation icon (three overlapping circles) below the slide number in filmstrip view.

Animating slide objects

Whereas a slide transition is a visual effect that plays during the switch from one slide to another, an *object animation* is a visual effect applied to a specific slide element, such as the slide title, bullet text, or an image.

Here are the steps to follow to apply an animation to a slide object:

1. **Select the slide object.**

   If you want to apply the same animation to multiple objects, go ahead and select them.

2. **Choose View ⇨ Motion.**

   Alternatively, click the toolbar's Animate button or press Ctrl+Alt+Shift+B (⌘+Option+Shift+B on a Mac).

   Slides displays the Motion pane.

3. **In the Object Animations group, click Add Animation.**

4. **On the Animation Type drop-down menu, choose the animation effect you want.**

5. **On the Start Condition drop-down menu, choose how you want the animation to start:**

   - *On Click:* The animation starts when you click the mouse.
   - *After Previous:* The animation starts immediately after the previous animation is complete.
   - *With Previous:* The animation starts at the same time as the previous animation.

6. **To animate bullet points individually, select the By Paragraph check box.**

   If you deselect By Paragraph, Slides animates the entire list.

7. **Use the slider to select the animation speed.**

   Note that this slider doesn't appear for all animation types, including Appear and Disappear.

   Drag the slider to the left for a slower animation speed; drag the slider to the right for a faster speed.

8. **If you want to apply multiple animations (easy now), select Add Animation and then repeat Steps 3-6 to configure the new animation.**
9. **To preview the animation, click Play.**
10. **Click X (close) in the top-right corner of the Motion pane.**

Slides indicates that a slide has an applied animation by adding the animation icon (three overlapping circles) below the slide number in filmstrip view.

Running a Slide Show

With your slides laid out, the text perfected, the formatting just right, and transitions and animations tastefully applied, it looks like you're good-and-ready to present your slide show. This section shows you how to start and navigate a slide show.

Starting the slide show

Slides gives you two ways to launch a slide show:

» *To start the slide show from the first slide,* click the Start Slideshow button (refer to Figure 10-2) and then choose Start from Beginning from the menu that appears. You can also press Ctrl+Shift+F5 (⌘+Shift+Return on a Mac).

» *To start the slide show from a particular slide,* select that slide and then click the Start Slideshow button. You can also press Ctrl+F5 (⌘+Return on a Mac).

Navigating slides

With your slide show running, you now need to navigate from one slide to the next. By far the easiest way to do so is to use the mouse, and Slides gives you two choices:

» Click the mouse to advance to the next slide.

» Turn the mouse wheel forward — or, if you have a trackpad, swipe up with two fingers — to advance to the next slide.

If you have animations defined in a slide, clicking the mouse or turning the wheel forward (or swiping up with two fingers on a trackpad) also initiates those animations in the order you defined.

For other navigation techniques and slide show controls, move the mouse pointer toward the lower-left corner of the screen to display a toolbar with the following controls (from left to right):

» **Previous (<):** Moves to the previous slide in the presentation. (You can also turn the mouse wheel backward.)

» **Go to Slide:** Displays a menu of the slides in the presentation. Click the slide you want to view.

» **Next (>):** Moves to the next slide in the presentation.

» **Open the Options menu:** Displays a menu with quite a few commands (see Figure 10-6), of which the following are the most useful:

- **Open Speaker Notes:** Opens the Presenter View window with the Speaker Notes tab displayed, which shows you the speaker notes for each slide.
- **Turn On/Off the Laser Pointer:** Toggles the laser pointer on and off.
- **Turn On/Off the Pen:** Toggles the pen on and off. You can use the pen to annotate the slides during the presentation.
- **Exit/Enter Full Screen:** Toggles full screen mode on and off.
- **Exit Slideshow:** Stops the slide show.
- **Auto-Play ⇨ Play:** Runs the slide show automatically.

TIP

To set the duration that Slides uses for each slide when you turn on Auto-Play, choose Auto-Play ⇨ Play and then choose a time interval. You can also click Loop to have Slides automatically start over when it reaches the end.

- **Captions Preferences:** Enables you to toggle closed captions on and off as well as customize the caption position (Top or Bottom) and size (Small, Medium, Large, or Extra Large).
- **More ⇨ Q & A:** Opens the Presenter View window with the Audience Tools tab displayed. You can then click Start New to accept questions from your audience. (Slides displays a web address that audience members can use to submit their questions.)
- **More ⇨ Keyboard Shortcut:** Displays a list of keyboard shortcuts.

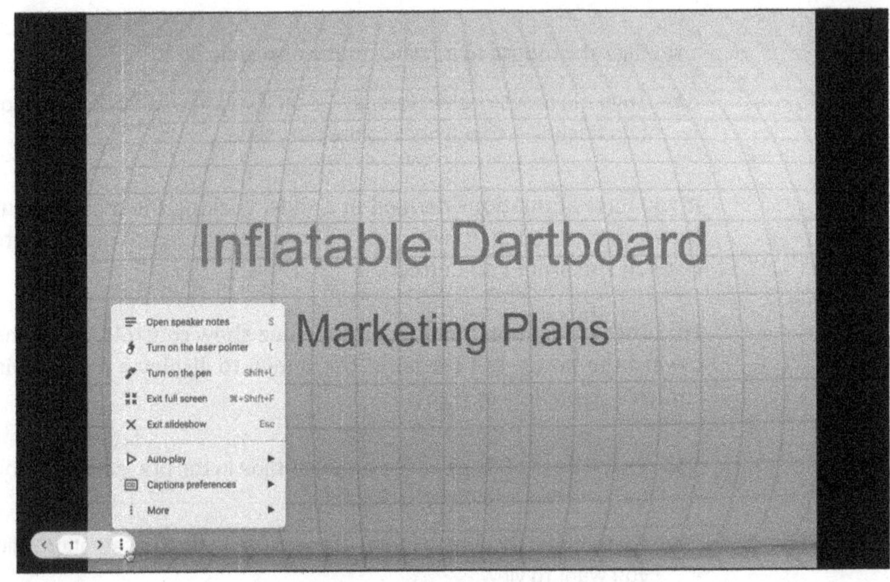

FIGURE 10-6: Move the mouse pointer to the left edge of the slide show to view the toolbar and its navigation controls.

Navigating the slide show from the keyboard

Slides gives you quite a few keyboard alternatives for navigating and controlling the slide show. These are useful alternatives because displaying the toolbar can seem unprofessional, and pressing a key or key combination is usually faster. Table 10-5 lists the available keyboard shortcuts for navigating a slide show.

TABLE 10-5 Slide Show Keyboard Navigation Techniques

Press This	To Do This
N	Advance to the next slide or animation. (You can also press the spacebar or the Enter, Return, right arrow, down arrow, or Page Down keys.)
P	Return to the previous slide or animation. (You can also press the Backspace, left arrow, up arrow, or Page Up keys.)
n, Enter	Navigate to slide number *n*.
Home	Navigate to the first slide.
End	Navigate to the last slide.
A	Display the audience tools.
B	Toggle the black screen on and off. (You can also press the period [.].)
L	Toggle the laser pointer. (You can also press Ctrl+Shift+P or ⌘+Shift+P.)

Press This	To Do This
S	Display the speaker notes.
W	Toggle the white screen on and off. (You can also press the comma [,].)
Shift+L	Toggle the pen.
Shift+A	Erase all annotations.
Ctrl+Shift+C (⌘+Shift+C)	Toggle closed captions.
Ctrl+Shift+F	Toggle full screen view. (You can also press F11 on a PC, or ⌘+Shift+F on a Mac.)
Ctrl+/ (⌘+/)	Display the list of keyboard shortcuts.
Esc	End the slide show.

Generating Images with AI

Although it's likely that most of your slides will be text, it's important to throw in a bit of eye candy every now and then in the form of an image that augments the text, supports the text, or just adds a decorative touch to the slide.

Adding an image is a no-brainer if you have a ready-made image or you have the artistic or design chops to create your own image. No image or artistic skills in sight? No problem! If your Google Workspace account includes access to Google's Gemini AI service, you can use artificial intelligence to generate the image you need from a simple text prompt.

Here are the steps to follow:

1. **Create or navigate to the slide in which you want to insert the image.**

   If you've just opened or created the presentation, you might already see the Create Image with Gemini pane displayed to the right of the current slide. If so, scurry down to Step 3 to continue.

2. **Choose Insert ⇨ Image ⇨ Create Image with Gemini.**

   Alternatively, click the toolbar's create image with Gemini icon.

   Either way, the Create Image with Gemini pane appears.

3. **In the large text box near the top of the pane, type a prompt that describes the image you want Gemini to generate.**

   Your prompt text depends on the type of image you need, but it will generally include some or all of the following:

   - The main object you want to include in the image. If you need more than one object, feel free to include anything you need.
   - The environment or location in which you want the object to appear.
   - One or more colors you want applied.
   - Any other details that you think are relevant to the image you want.

4. **In the Add a Style list, select an overall look you want for the image, such as Photography or Vector Art.**

   If you want Gemini to choose a random style, click I'm Feeling Lucky. If you don't want a style applied, click No Style.

5. **Click Create.**

   Gemini takes a few seconds to generate a few images, as shown in Figure 10-7.

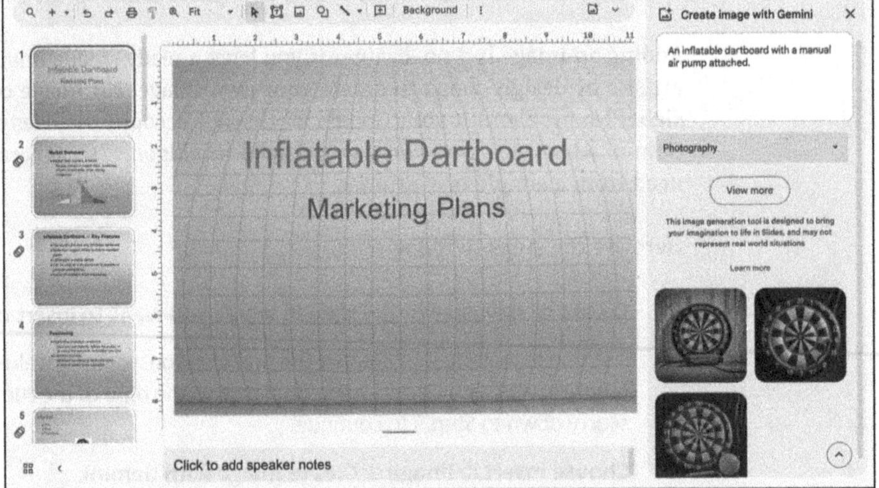

FIGURE 10-7: Gemini generates images based on a simple text prompt.

6. **To generate a new set of images, click View More.**
7. **When you see an image you want to use, click it.**

   The image appears in the slide, where you can move and resize the image as needed.

3 Collaborating with Your Team

IN THIS PART . . .

Learn how to collaborate on documents, spreadsheets, and presentations.

Share calendars and set up video meetings.

Collaborate with chat, groups, forms, and more.

IN THIS CHAPTER

» Inviting other people to edit, comment on, or view your files

» Controlling file access

» Editing and commenting on other people's files

» Accepting or rejecting suggested edits

» Dealing with comments

Chapter 11
Collaborating on Files

Whether you're a company employee, a consultant, or a freelancer, you almost certainly work with other people in one capacity or another. Most of the time, your work with others is likely pretty informal and consists of ideas exchanged during video meetings, chats, or email messages. However, the modern work world often calls upon people to work with others more closely by collaborating with them on a file, such as a document, a spreadsheet, or a presentation. This work can involve commenting on another person's spreadsheet, editing someone else's document, or dividing a presentation among multiple authors. For all these situations, Google Workspace offers a number of powerful collaborative tools. This chapter shows you how to use, and get the most out of, these tools.

Sharing a File

If you want to let other folks examine a file, make snarky comments about a file, suggest changes to a file, or even edit a file directly, you need to *share* the file with those people. Note that when I use the word *file* here (and throughout this chapter), I'm talking about a Docs document, a Sheets spreadsheet, or a Slides presentation.

What do I mean by sharing a file? I'm talking about collaborating in one or more of the following ways:

- **Viewing:** Examining the file but not making any changes to it.
- **Commenting:** Giving feedback about the file as a whole or about sections of the file.
- **Suggesting:** Making proposed changes to the file. The owner of the file (or other people who are allowed to edit the file) can then either accept or reject those changes individually.

  REMEMBER

  If you've used Microsoft Word in the past, suggesting mode is similar to Word's Track Changes feature.

- **Editing:** Making changes directly to the file.

  When you share a file, Google Workspace asks you to specify the level of *permission* you want to apply to each person or group you want to share the file with. A user's permission level defines, among other things, which of the collaboration modes in this list the user can work in. You can play around with three permission levels:

  - *Editor:* Can make changes to the file, add comments to the file, suggest changes to the file, accept and reject changes suggested by other people, change collaborators' permissions, and share the file with others
  - *Commenter:* Can only add comments to the file and suggest changes to the file
  - *Viewer:* Can only view the file

Google Workspace gives you two ways to share a file:

- **Via email:** You specify the email address of each collaborator (or the group address of multiple collaborators) and Google Workspace emails an invitation that includes an Open in *App* button (where *App* is Docs, Sheets, or Slides, depending on the file) that the collaborator selects to load the file into the specified app.
- **Via a link:** Google Workspace provides you with a unique link address that you can copy and then paste into a chat message, a Groups post, a social media post, an email message, a web page, or whatever. You can restrict the link to specified email addresses, or you can make the link public so that anyone can view (but only view) the file via the link.

REMEMBER

Amazingly, you can have up to 100 people collaborate on a single file in Docs, Sheets, or Slides.

Sharing a file for editing

The highest level of collaboration occurs when you ask another person to make changes to a document. That is, rather than suggest changes or add comments, the other person performs the changes directly in the file. Giving a person Editor permission can save you a lot of time and effort but should be reserved for people you trust explicitly, because you're giving that person a great deal of power over your document.

Follow these steps to share a file for editing:

1. **Open the file in Docs, Sheets, or Slides, or select the file in Drive.**
2. **Start the sharing process:**
   - *In Docs, Sheets, or Slides,* click the Share button in the top-right corner of the page.

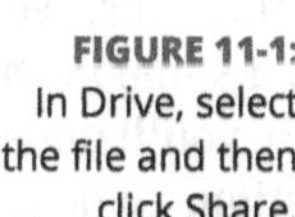

   - *In Drive,* click the share icon, which appears in the toolbar above the selected file, as shown in Figure 11-1.

   Either way, you're confronted with the Share "*Name*" dialog (where *Name* is the filename of the file you're sharing).

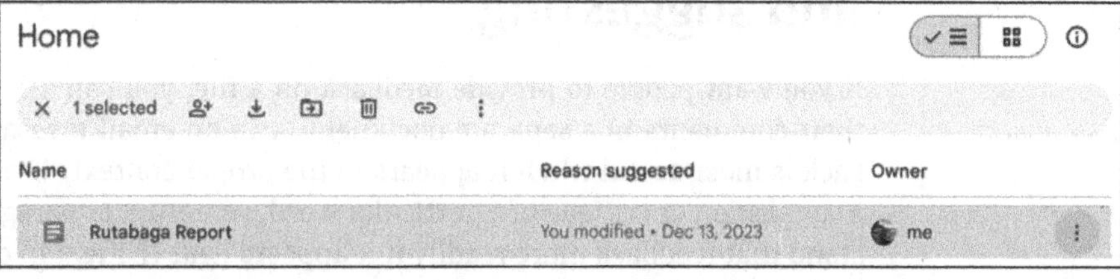

FIGURE 11-1: In Drive, select the file and then click Share.

3. **In the Add People and Groups text box, enter the names or email addresses of the people or groups you want editing the file.**
4. **In the Permission list to the right, make sure the Editor permission is selected, as shown in Figure 11-2.**
5. **In the Message box, enter a short note that appears in the body of your invitation email.**

   If you don't want to send the email for some reason, deselect the Notify People check box.

FIGURE 11-2: To give your collaborators Editor permission, make sure Editor is selected.

TIP

To prevent editors from changing the file's sharing permissions and from sharing the file with others, click the settings icon (gear) and then deselect the Editors Can Change Permissions and Share check box.

6. **Click the Send button.**

   If you deselected the Notify People check box, click Share instead.

   Your file is now shared for editing with the specified users.

Sharing a file for commenting and suggesting

If you want people to provide feedback on a file, you can ask them each to write their comments in a separate document or in an email message. However, feedback is most useful when it appears in the proper context. That is, if someone has a suggestion or critique of a particular word, sentence, or paragraph, you'll understand that feedback more readily if it appears near the text in question. To do that in Docs, Sheets, or Slides, you insert a *comment*, a separate section of text associated with some part of the original document.

Alternatively, if you're working in Docs, you might prefer that collaborators make changes to a document. You can give people Editor permission, but that can lead to problems if you want to know what parts of the document the user edited. For example, if you don't know what the user changed, you have no way of checking the changes for style or for factual errors. To avoid such problems, you can give users Commenter permission, which enables them to collaborate not only by commenting but also by suggesting. Docs tracks all changes made to a document.

Tracking means that any time a Commenter makes suggested changes to the original text — including adding, editing, deleting, and formatting the text — Docs records the changes and shows not only what changes were made but also who made them and when. You, as the document owner, can then accept or reject those suggested changes.

Here are the steps to follow to share a file for commenting and (in Docs) suggesting:

1. **Open the file in Docs, Sheets, or Slides, or select the file in Drive.**
2. **Start the sharing process:**
   - *In Docs, Sheets, or Slides,* click the Share button in the top-right corner of the page.
   -  *In Drive,* click the share icon.

   Either way, the Share *"Name"* dialog appears (where *Name* is the filename of the file you're sharing).
3. **In the Add People and Groups text box, enter the names or email addresses of the people or groups you want to comment on the file.**
4. **In the Permission list to the right, select the Commenter permission.**
5. **In the Message box, enter a short note that will appear in the body of your invitation email.**

   If you don't want to send the email for some reason, deselect the Notify People check box.

   TIP: To prevent commenters (and viewers) from being able to download, copy, and print the file, click the settings icon (gear) and then deselect the Viewers and Commenters Can See the Option to Download, Print, and Copy check box.
6. **Click Send.**

   If you deselected the Notify People check box, click Share instead.

   Your file is now shared for commenting and suggesting with the specified users.

Sharing a file for viewing

Sometimes you just want some people to examine a file. You don't need feedback or suggestions or any other type of two-cents'-worth. When you just want to allow some people to take a peek at a file, you need to follow these steps to share the file with Viewer permission:

1. **Open the file in Docs, Sheets, or Slides, or select the file in Drive.**
2. **Start the sharing process:**
   - *In Docs, Sheets, or Slides,* click the Share button in the top-right corner of the page.
   - *In Drive,* click the share icon.

   The Share "*Name*" dialog appears (where *Name* is the filename of the file you're sharing).
3. **In the Add People and Groups text box, enter the names or email addresses of the people or groups you want to edit the file.**
4. **In the Permission list to the right, select the Viewer permission.**
5. **In the Message box, enter a short note that will appear in the body of your invitation email.**

   If you don't want to send the email for some reason, deselect the Notify People check box.
6. **Click Send.**

   If you deselected the Notify People check box, click Share instead.

   Your file is now shared for viewing with the specified users.

Sharing a link to a file

In the previous few sections, I talk about emailing an invitation to share a file as an editor, a commenter, or a viewer. Nothing wrong with the email invitation, but it isn't always the best choice. Specifically, in some situations you want to offer people a simple link to click to initiate a file collaboration.

For example, if you're chatting with a few people and the subject of collaborating on a file comes up, it would be better if you could just send a collaboration link in a chat message. Similarly, you might want to ask for volunteers to view or comment on a file. Rather than guess at who ought to receive an email invitation, post the link to, say, an internal web page.

You can share a collaboration link with people in your company, with specific users, or with the public. The next three sections show you how it's done.

Sharing a link with your organization

Here are the steps to follow to share a link to a file with everyone in your organization who has access to the link:

1. **Open the file in Docs, Sheets, or Slides, or select the file in Drive.**
2. **Start the sharing process:**
   - *In Docs, Sheets, or Slides,* click the Share button in the top-right corner of the page.
   - *In Drive,* click the share icon.

   The Share "*Name*" dialog appears (where *Name* is the filename of the file you're sharing).
3. **Click the General Access list and then click the name of your organization.**

   You now get a version of the Share dialog that appears like the one shown in Figure 11-3.

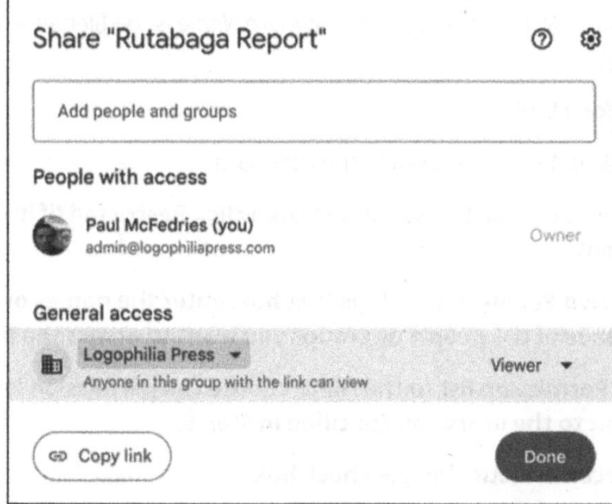

FIGURE 11-3: Use this version of the Share dialog to select the permission level you want to give people in your organization.

4. **In the General Access section, use the list on the right to select the permission level you want to give:**
   - *Viewer:* Everyone at your organization who was access to the link can view the file.
   - *Commenter:* Everyone at your organization who was access to the link can comment on and add suggestions to the file.

- *Editor:* Everyone at your organization who was access to the link can edit the file.

5. **Click the Copy Link button.**

   The link to the file is copied to the clipboard.

6. **Share the link by pasting it where the people you want to give access to the file can view and click the link, such as an email or chat message.**

Sharing a link with selected users

If you'd rather restrict access to just a few users, here are the steps to follow to share a link with specific people:

1. **Open the file in Docs, Sheets, or Slides, or select the file in Drive.**
2. **Start the sharing process:**
   - *In Docs, Sheets, or Slides,* click the Share button in the top-right corner of the page.
   - *In Drive,* click the share icon.

   The Share "*Name*" dialog appears (where *Name* is the filename of the file you're sharing).

3. **Click Copy Link.**

   The link to the file is copied to the clipboard.

4. **Click the General Access list and then click Restricted (if it's not already selected).**
5. **In the Add People and Groups text box, enter the names or email addresses of the people or groups you want to access the file.**
6. **In the Permission list to the right, choose the permission level you want to grant to the users you specified in Step 5.**
7. **Deselect the Notify People check box.**

   The assumption here is that you'll be sharing the link with people in some other way (via, say, a text message), so no need to send the sharing invitation.

8. **Click the Share button.**

   Your file is now shared with specific people. All that's left to do is provide those people with a link to the shared file.

9. **Share the link by pasting it where the people you selected in Step 5 can view and click the link, such as a chat or email message.**

Sharing a link with the public

Here are the steps to follow to share a link to a file with everyone who has access to the link:

1. **Open the file in Docs, Sheets, or Slides, or select the file in Drive.**
2. **Start the sharing process:**
   - *In Docs, Sheets, or Slides,* click the Share button in the top-right corner of the page.
   - *In Drive,* click the share icon.

   The Share "*Name*" dialog appears (where *Name* is the filename of the file you're sharing).
3. **Click the General Access list, and then click Anyone with the Link.**
4. **In the General Access section, use the list on the right to specify the permission level.**

   The default here is Viewer, which is safest. However, you can also choose Editor or Commenter, if either one seems reasonable to you.
5. **Click the Copy Link button.**

   The link to the file is copied to the clipboard.
6. **Click the Done button.**
7. **Share the link by pasting it where the people you want to give access to the file can view and click the link, such as in an email message or in a chat message.**

Emailing your collaborators

If you've shared a file via an email invitation (not via a link to a file), you can reach out to your collaborators by sending them an email message directly from the file's app. Here's how it works:

1. **Open the shared file in its app.**
2. **Choose File ➪ Email ➪ Email Collaborators.**

   The Email People on the File dialog appears.
3. **Edit the Subject line and fill in the Message text box.**
4. **If you want to skip a collaborator, click the X that appears in that person's box in the Recipients list.**

5. **If you want to receive a copy of the message yourself, select the Send Yourself a Copy check box.**
6. **Click the Send button.**

   The app fires off the message.

Setting an access expiration date

By default, the sharing access you give each user is indefinite and remains in effect until you revoke a user's access (as I describe in the later section "Removing a user's sharing access"). If you prefer that a user have access to your file for only a limited time, you can set an access expiration date. Here's how:

1. **Open the file you shared.**
2. **Click the Share button in the top-right corner of the page.**

   The Share "*Name*" dialog appears (where *Name* is the filename of the file you're sharing).

3. **Click the permissions list to the right of the user you want to work with, and then click the Add Expiration command.**

   REMEMBER

   When you give a user an access expiration date, you can give that user permission to only comment on and view the file. That is, you can't give the user Editor permission.

   The app automatically sets the user's access to expire in 30 days. If this works for you, feel free to skip Step 4.

4. **Click the edit expiration icon that appears to the right of the Access Expires *date* text (where *date* is the date 30 days from now; refer to Figure 11-4), select an expiration date using the calendar that appears, and then click Done.**
5. **Click the Save button.**

   The app will expire the user's access at the specified time.

Changing a user's sharing access

If you've given a user a particular level of sharing permission, you might change your mind later and decide to give that user either a higher or lower permission level. Here's what you have to do to change a collaborator's permission level:

1. **Open the shared file.**
2. **Click the Share button.**

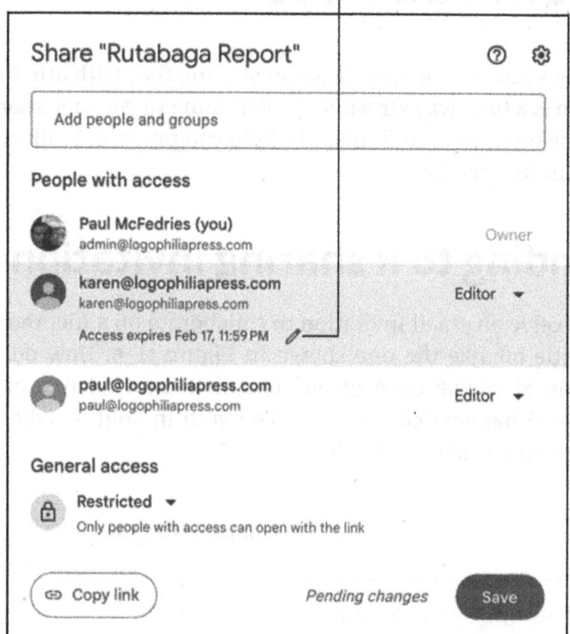

FIGURE 11-4: In the Access Expires list, set when the user's sharing access is no more.

3. **To the right of the user you want to modify, click the Permission list and choose the new permission level.**
4. **Click the Save button.**

   The app updates the user's access permission.

Removing a user's sharing access

Sometimes you come to regret giving a user *any* level of permission. Hey, these things happen. If expiring the user's access isn't feasible (for example, if you want this user gone *now*), you can revoke the user's access. Here's what's needed:

1. **Open the shared file.**
2. **Click the Share button.**
3. **To the right of the user you want to yank, click the Permission list and then click Remove.**

   The app removes the user.
4. **Click the Save button.**

   The app revokes the user's access permission.

Dealing with Shared Files

In the previous few sections, I talk about sharing files with other people. However, collaboration is a two-way street, so you're going to get your share (pun intended) of shared-file invitations and links. To help you prepare, I talk about dealing with shared files in this section.

Responding to a sharing invitation

When you receive an email invitation to collaborate on a file, the message appears at least a little bit like the one shown in Figure 11-5. How do you know which permission level you've been given? Examine the first line of the message — *Person (address)* has invited you . . . . The verb in bold — edit, comment on, or view — tells you the permission level.

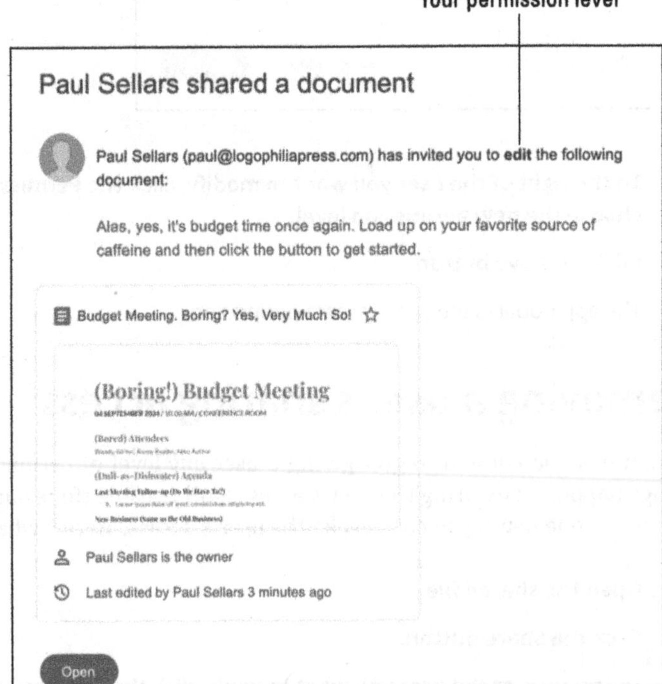

FIGURE 11-5: The sharing invitation email tells you your access level and offers a button to open the file.

When you're ready to begin your collaboration, click the Open button to launch the shared file in its native app (Docs, Sheets, or Slides).

Viewing which files have been shared with you

If you receive a ton of sharing invitations, it can be tough keeping them all straight. Fortunately, that's one chore you can leave off your to-do list because Google Workspace has your back on this one. Specifically, the Drive app has your back because it maintains a list of all the files folks have shared with you.

To access this list, head over to `https://drive.google.com` and then select the Shared with Me folder. As shown in Figure 11-6, Drive displays your shared files with a few recent files at the top and then all the rest organized by the date they were shared with you.

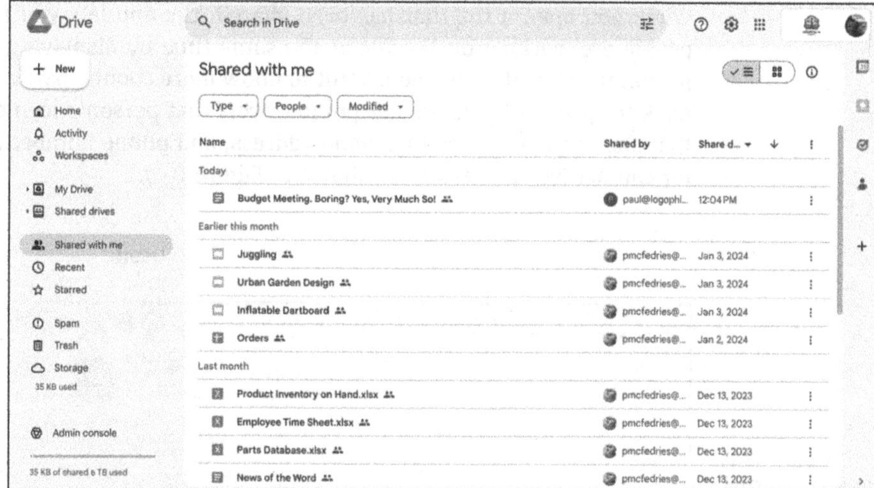

FIGURE 11-6: Open Drive's Shared with Me folder to examine every file that people have been generous enough to share with you.

Working on a Shared File

After you've shared a file with one or more of your colleagues, or after any of those colleagues has invited you to edit or comment on a file, it's time to get to work and do some actual collaborating. Unfortunately, Google Workspace makes file collaboration overly confusing, because what you can do with a file depends on the app and the user's permission level. Here's a summary to help you get sharing straight in your head:

- **Docs document:** People can collaborate as follows:
  - *Editors:* Can edit the document directly, make suggested changes, and comment on the document

- *Commenters:* Can make suggested changes and comment on the document

» **Sheets spreadsheet:** People can collaborate as follows:

- *Editors:* Can edit the spreadsheet directly and comment on the spreadsheet
- *Commenters:* Can comment on the spreadsheet

» **Slides presentation:** People can collaborate as follows:

- *Editors:* Can edit the presentation directly and comment on the presentation
- *Commenters:* Can comment on the presentation

In all cases, people with Viewer permission can only examine the file.

When you open a file that has been shared, the app lets you know when other people are working on the file at the same time by displaying an icon for each person who has the file open. Want to know more about a particular collaborator? Click (or just hover the mouse pointer over) that person's icon to open a pop-up that shows the user's name, email address, and phone number and several icons for contacting that person, as shown in Figure 11-7.

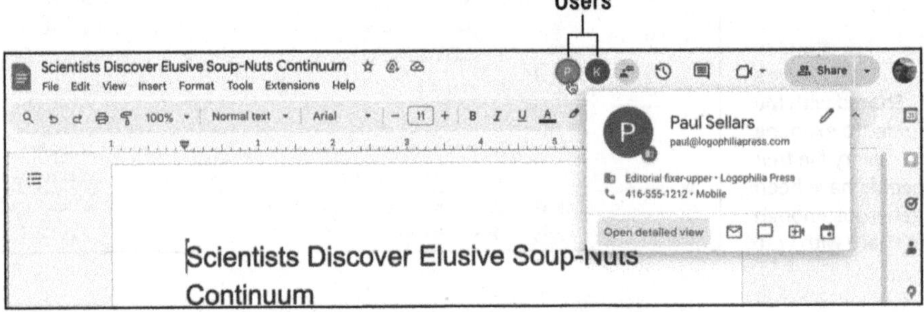

FIGURE 11-7: Click a user's icon to display details for that user.

REMEMBER

If lots of people are collaborating on the file, there isn't enough room to display an icon for every user, so the app displays a single icon with the number of users. Click that icon to display the list of users who have the file open.

The app also gives you a visual indication of where each person is working within the file:

» **Docs:** For each user, you see a pin — a vertical bar with a square top —that's the same color as the user's icon. When the user moves the cursor or makes an edit (or a suggested change), Docs displays the person's name at the top of the pin, as shown in Figure 11-8. You can also hover the mouse pointer over a user's pin to display the user's name.

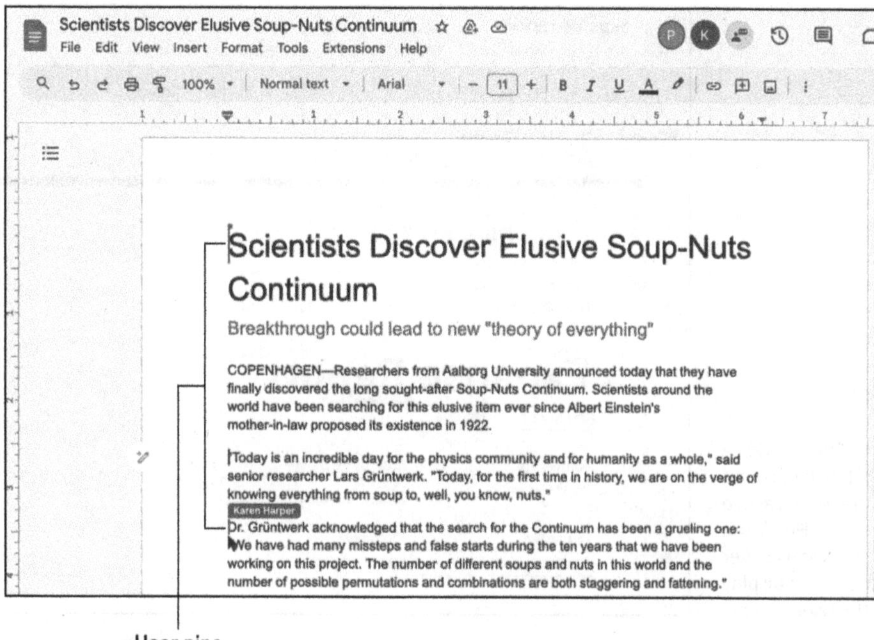

FIGURE 11-8: Docs displays a pin for each user and adds the person's name to the pin when the person moves the cursor or makes an edit.

- **Slides:** This app uses the same system as Docs (that is, for each user, a pin appears showing the user's current position in the presentation).
- **Sheets:** Displays a border around whatever cell is active for the user, and that border is the same color as the user's icon. (If the user has selected a range, Sheets adds the border to the first cell of the range.) To display the name of the user, hover the mouse pointer over the cell, as shown in Figure 11-9.

Making suggested edits to a shared Docs document

If you have Editor permission for a Docs document, you're free to make whatever changes you see fit in the document (this is called working in *editing mode*). However, if you're not sure about an edit, the prudent thing to do is to make a *suggested edit,* which is a proposed change to the document that the document owner (or another person with Editor access) can later accept or reject. (This process is called working in *suggesting mode;* see "Accepting or rejecting suggested changes in Docs," later in this chapter.)

To switch from editing mode to suggesting mode, click the editing mode icon on the right side of the toolbar and then choose Suggesting from the menu that appears, as shown in Figure 11-10.

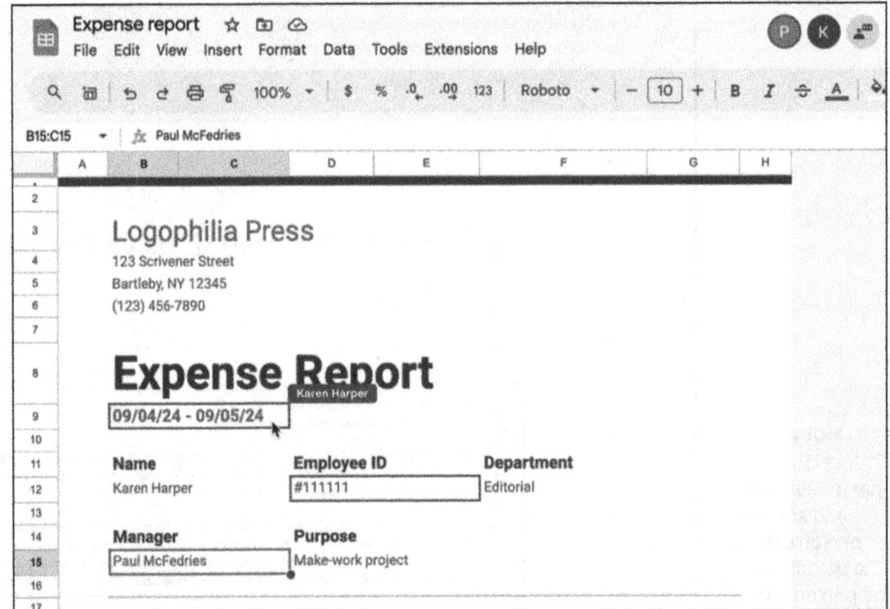

FIGURE 11-9: Sheets adds a border around the user's active cell. Hover the mouse over the cell to display the user's name.

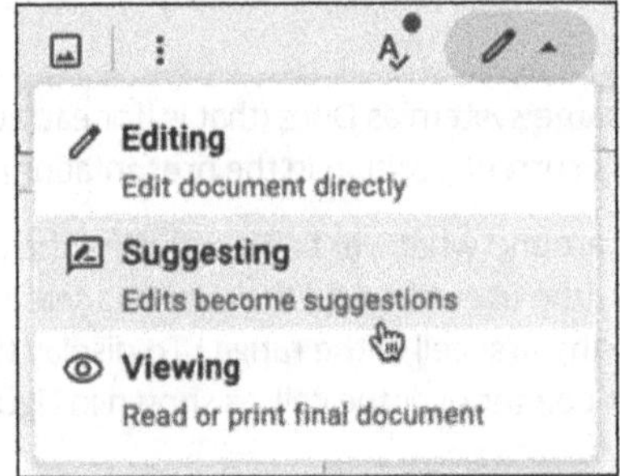

FIGURE 11-10: Click the editing mode icon and then select Suggesting to switch to suggesting mode in Docs.

Adding comments to a file

If you're working on a shared file with Editor or Commenter access, you can add comments to the file. Comments are separate from the file content itself and are useful if you want to provide feedback, ask (or answer) questions, make suggestions, and so on. Here are the steps to follow to add a comment to a shared file:

1. **Select, or position the cursor at the file location that contains, the content you want to comment on. (In Sheets, make the cell you're interested in the active cell.)**

2. **Choose Insert ➪ Comment.**

You can also click the add comment icon; press Ctrl+Alt+M (⌘+Option+M on a Mac); or right-click the content and then choose Comment.

The app highlights the content and displays a comment box.

3. **In the text box, enter your comment (see Figure 11-11).**
4. **Click Comment.**

The app adds the comment to the file.

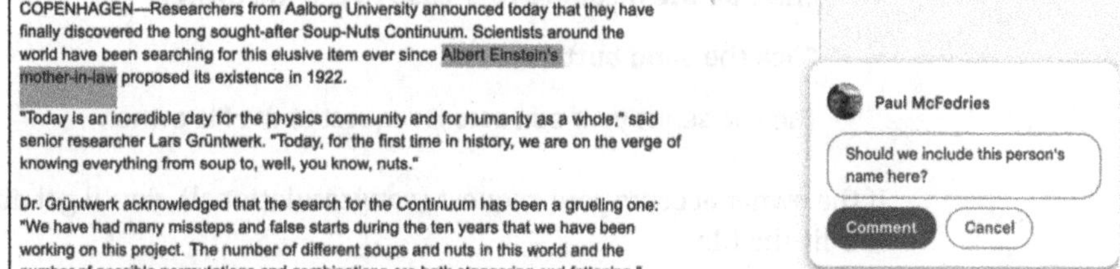

FIGURE 11-11: A comment, ready to be added to a document.

Requesting Editor access

If you've been given Commenter access to a spreadsheet or presentation, the app disables most menu bar commands and displays a toolbar with a radically downsized set of buttons and an extra button labeled Comment Only. Figure 11-12 shows the reduced toolbar and Comment Only button as they appear in Sheets. (If you have just Viewer access to the file, the View Only button appears.)

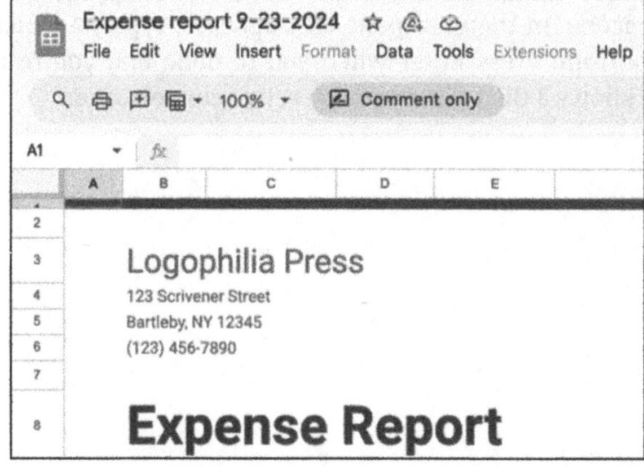

FIGURE 11-12: With Commenter access, you get a reduced app toolbar.

If you feel someone has done you wrong by giving you only Commenter access, you can ask the file owner to hike your privileges to Editor access by following these steps:

1. **Click the Comment Only button.**

   If you just have Viewer access, click the View Only button instead.

2. **Click Request Edit Access from the menu that appears.**

   The Ask Owner to Be an Editor for "*Name*" dialog shows up (where "*Name*" is the name of the file.

3. **Enter a note pleading your case to the file owner.**
4. **Click the Send button.**

   The app sends your edit access request to the file owner.

If the owner accepts your request (congratulations!), you'll get an email invitation to edit the file.

Chatting with your fellow collaborators

I point out earlier (refer to Figure 11-7) that you can click a collaborator's icon to display various ways to communicate with that user, including sending an email or text or connecting with a video call. However, if the person's icon appears in the file, that person is right there with you, so to speak, so why communicate in a roundabout way? Instead, you can "talk" to the person directly, by conducting a chat right in the file.

Just go ahead and click the show chat icon, which appears to the right of the collaborator icons. In the Chat pane that appears, type your message in the text box at the bottom. Press Enter when you're done and you're off and chatting. Figure 11-13 shows a Chat pane with an active conversation.

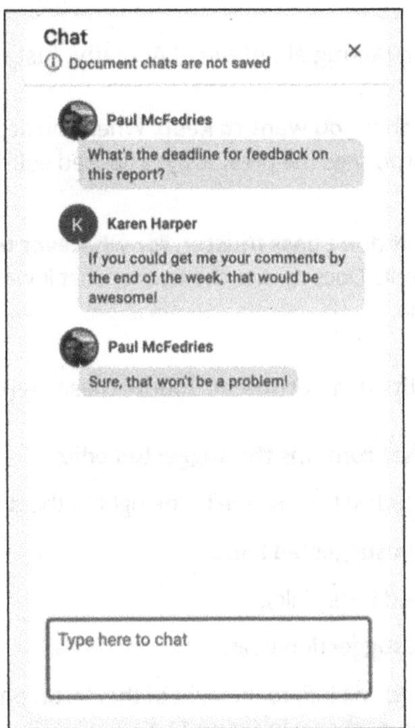

FIGURE 11-13: Click the show chat icon to start a chat with your collaborators.

Reviewing a Shared File

If you've given people Commenter access to a file, having those folks add their comments or, in Docs, make suggested edits is only the first part of the sharing process. After your collaborators have had their say, it's your turn to review those suggestions and comments. In this section, I walk you through all the important reviewing tools and techniques.

Accepting or rejecting suggested changes in Docs

One of the unique features in Docs is suggesting mode, whereby collaborators make proposed changes to document text, layout, and formatting. The operative word here is *proposed* because each person's suggestions are just that: potential changes, not (yet) actual ones. You then review the changes and incorporate into the final version the ones that are useful and remove those that aren't. The point is to give you, in a word, *control* over a person's edits.

What kind of control are we talking about here? Actually, just two things:

- **Accepting those edits that you want to keep:** When you accept a suggested edit, Docs officially incorporates the previously proposed edit into the document.
- **Rejecting any edits that don't pass muster, for whatever reason:** When you reject a suggested edit, Docs reverts the text to what it was before the proposed edit was made.

To review the suggested edits in a document, follow these steps:

1. **Open the document that contains the suggested edits.**

   Docs displays all suggested edits in a pane to the right of the document.

2. **Choose Tools ➪ Review Suggested Edits.**

   Docs opens the Suggested Edits dialog.

3. **Click the move to next suggestion icon.**

   Docs opens the suggested edit info to the right of the document and highlights the edit in the document, as shown in Figure 11-14.

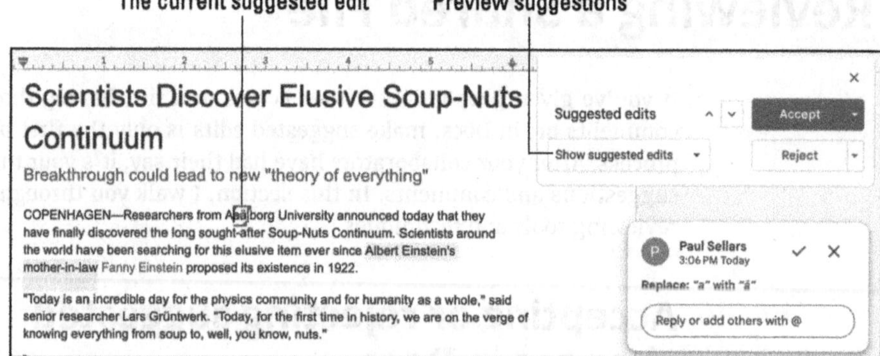

FIGURE 11-14: When you move to a suggestion, Docs displays the edit info and the edit itself.

4. **Review the suggested edit. You have three choices:**
   - *Reply to the edit:* If you have a question about the edit, want more information, or are in some other way not ready to finalize the edit, use the Reply box to send a message to the collaborator who made the edit.

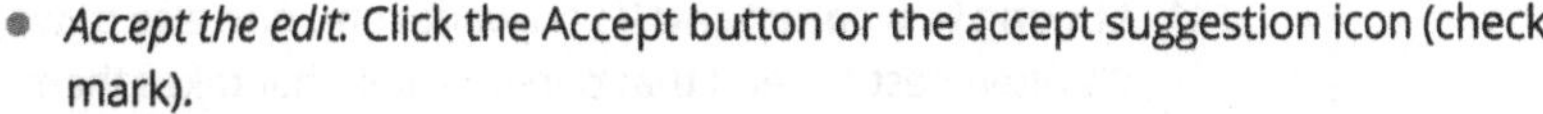

- *Accept the edit:* Click the Accept button or the accept suggestion icon (check mark).

- *Reject the edit:* Click the Reject button or the reject suggestion icon (X).

5. **Repeat Steps 3 and 4 until you've reviewed all suggested edits.**

REMEMBER

If you're sure you want to either accept or reject every suggested edit, let me save you a whack of time:

- **To accept every edit in the document:** If no suggested edit is currently selected, click Accept All. Otherwise, pull down the Accept list in the Suggested Edits dialog and then click Accept All.
- **To reject every edit in the document:** If no suggested edit is currently selected, click Reject All. Otherwise, pull down the Reject list in the Suggested Edits dialog and then click Reject All.

TIP

If clicking Accept All or Reject All strikes you as rash, I hear you. Before accepting or rejecting all suggestions willy-nilly, pull down the Preview Suggestions list in the Suggested Edits dialog and then select either Preview "Accept All" or Preview "Reject All." If you don't like how the preview appears, you can revert the document by pulling down the Preview Suggestions list and choosing Show Suggested Edits. Otherwise, you can make the previewed edits permanent by clicking either Accept All or Reject All.

Working with comments

If your co-conspirators — er, I mean, collaborators — have been busy loading up a file with helpful comments, you'll almost certainly want to review those comments before finalizing your file. Docs, Sheets, and Slides give you no fewer than three ways to work with file comments:

- **Replying to a comment:** To ask a question or solicit more info from a commenter, click the comment, enter a response in the Reply text box (see Figure 11-15), and then click Reply.

- **Resolving a comment:** If you're done with a comment, select the comment and then click the icon shown in the margin (mark as resolved and hide discussion). The app removes the comment from the file.

» **Linking to a comment:** If you want someone else to weigh in on a comment, it's often best to send that person a link that takes them directly to the comment. (This is particularly true for very long files.) Click the more options icon and then click Get Link to This Comment to put a copy of the link on the clipboard. Now paste the link in an email, a text, or whatever other communications medium works best, and send the link to the person you want to review it.

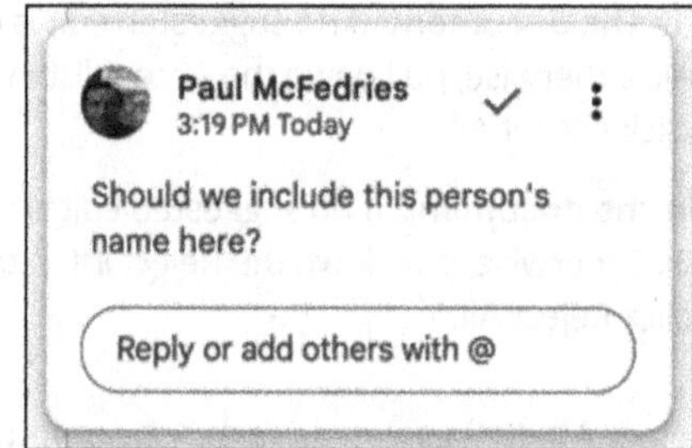

FIGURE 11-15: You can reply to, resolve, or get a link to a comment.

IN THIS CHAPTER

» **Inviting colleagues to an event**

» **Coordinating schedules**

» **Letting other people view your calendar**

» **Subscribing to calendars that other people have shared**

» **Importing and exporting events**

Chapter 12
Collaborating with Calendar

In these "whatever-comes-after-busy" days, a common comedic trope is for two people to spend an inordinate amount of time trying to coordinate their schedules to come up with a time for some simple activity, such as having coffee. "No, Monday's no good. How about Tuesday morning at 5:30?" "That doesn't work for me, but I could do Wednesday afternoon at 3:47." A popular cartoon from *The New Yorker* shows a busy executive on the phone, pointing to his calendar and saying "No, Thursday's out. How about never — is never good for you?"

Never getting together with anyone would certainly simplify everyone's lives, but the extroverts of the world simply won't allow it. So, if we must both meet *and* greet, the least we can do is make the scheduling part faster and more efficient. Fortunately, the Calendar app is chock-full of collaboration features for helping busy people (that would be all of us) to coordinate their schedules and meet up with a minimum of fuss.

In this chapter, you delve into Calendar's collaboration features for inviting guests to events, sharing your calendar, subscribing to calendars other people have shared, importing and exporting events, and much more.

Inviting Guests to a Meeting

The appointments and events that I yammer on about in Chapter 3 don't require you to work directly with anyone else in your organization. Sure, you might informally ask a colleague to lunch or to a watercooler meet-up, and you might go to the trouble of actually entering those get-togethers as events in Calendar, but the events themselves don't merit mentioning the person you're meeting.

However, you'll have plenty of meetings that are more official, where you have a list of people you want to attend, a place to meet, an agenda, and so on. For these more formal gatherings, you don't want to invite people via chat, a cubicle drop-in, or some other loosey-goosey method. Instead, you need to take advantage of Calendar's add guests feature, which enables you to specify who you want to attend and then send out email invitations to each guest.

Inviting guests to a new meeting

Follow these steps to send out guest invitations to your next meeting:

1. **Create your event, give it a snappy title, and make sure the start and end times are what you want.**

   If you're not sure about any of this, head on back to Chapter 3 to get the details.

2. **Click in the Add Guests text box, and then start entering the name of a person you want to attend your meeting.**

   Calendar displays a list of people in your address book who match what you've typed, as shown in Figure 12-1.

3. **Choose the name you want to add.**

   Alternatively, use the arrow keys to highlight the name you want and then press Tab or Enter.

4. **Repeat Steps 2 and 3 to add all your guests.**
5. **Fill out the rest of your meeting details, such as the location and description.**

REMEMBER

When you add one or more guests to a meeting, Calendar automatically sets up a Google Meet videoconference URL. If you don't need a videoconference component in your meeting, click the X to the right of the Join with Google Meet button. Refer to Chapter 13 for the details on using Meet for videoconferencing.

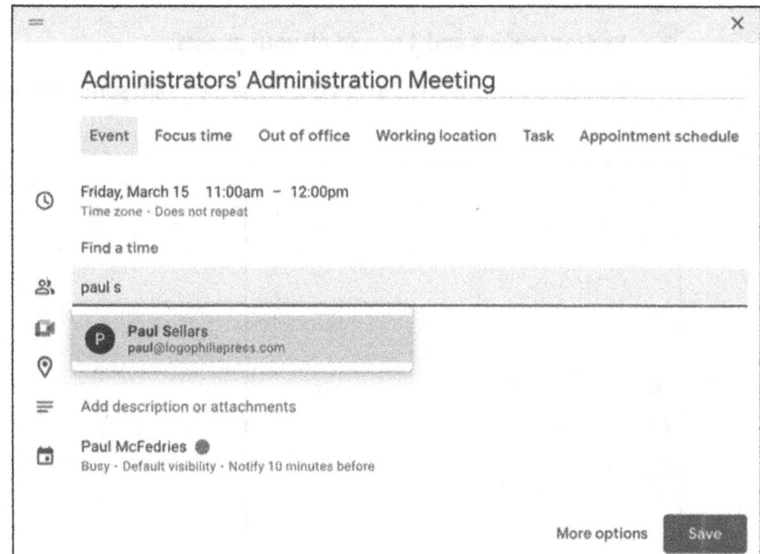

FIGURE 12-1: Start typing a guest's name and Calendar displays a list of folks who match.

6. **Click Save.**

   Calendar asks if you want to send invitation emails to the guests you added.

7. **Click Send.**

   Calendar sends out the invites and saves your event.

Inviting guests to an existing meeting

If you've already added your meeting to Calendar, the procedure for inviting guests is a bit different than inviting guests as part of creating a new meeting. Here's what you need to do:

1. **In Calendar, click your meeting.**
2. **Click the edit event icon.**

   Calendar opens the meeting for editing and displays a separate Guests section.

3. **Click in the Add Guests text box and start entering the name of a person you want to attend your meeting.**

   Calendar displays a list of people in your address book who match what you've typed.

4. **Choose the name you want to add.**

   Alternatively, use the arrow keys to highlight the name you want and then press Tab or Enter.

5. **Repeat Steps 3 and 4 to add all your guests.**

   Figure 12-2 shows a meeting's Guests section with some attendees added.

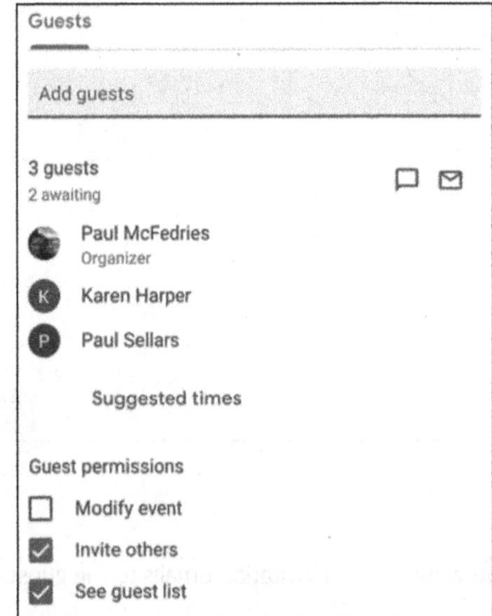

FIGURE 12-2: Open an existing meeting for editing and use the Guests section to invite attendees.

6. **Click the email guests icon.**

   Calendar opens the Email Guests dialog.

7. **Enter a message to the guests and then click Send.**

   Calendar sends the invitation to each guest.

8. **Click Save.**

   Calendar saves your changes.

Controlling your guest list

After you've added a few guests to your meeting, you might find that you need to make some changes to your guest list. Easier done than said. Select your meeting and then click the edit event icon to open the meeting for editing. You can then use the following techniques:

» **Mark a guest as optional:** If a guest's attendance at the meeting would be nice but isn't necessary, hover the mouse pointer over the guest's name and click the mark as optional icon.

- **Uninvite a guest:** If you change your mind about having a guest attend the meeting, you can take that person off the guest list by hovering the mouse pointer over the guest's name and clicking the remove icon.

By default, Calendar allows meeting guests to view the meeting's full guest list and to invite other people to the meeting. If these privileges seem like too much, you can rein in your guests by opening the meeting for some selective editing. The Guests section includes a Guest Permissions area with three settings:

- **Modify event:** Select this check box (it's deselected by default) to allow guests to make changes to your meeting details, such as the time, location, and duration.
- **Invite others:** Deselect this check box to prevent guests from inviting other people to the meeting.
- **See guest list:** Deselect this check box to prevent guests from viewing the other people you've invited to the meeting.

Coordinating attendee schedules

There are certainly times when you need to coordinate schedules with other people to arrange a meeting or similar gathering.

The old-fashioned method of checking schedules involved a phone or text conversation in which everyone consulted their day planners to try to find a mutually free time. You might still be able to get away with that method if just two or three people are involved, but what if there are a dozen? Or a hundred? You could try sending out email messages, but you've still got a coordination nightmare for a large group of people.

The new-fashioned method of checking schedules is to ask Calendar to show you the availability of the people you're inviting. You end up at a calendar that shows the schedule of each guest, which lets you know at a glance whether your meeting time will work (and, if not, to find a time that does work).

Calendar can perform the seemingly amazing feat of showing you your guest's schedules because, by default, Calendar configures each user's main calendar to be available to everyone in your organization. (It doesn't do this for folks outside your organization.) To learn more about calendar permissions, check out "Sharing Your Calendar," later in this chapter.

Follow these steps to take a peek at your guest's schedules:

1. **Create the meeting and add all your guests.**

   Alternatively, for an existing meeting, click the meeting and then click the edit event icon to open the meeting for editing.

2. **Click the Find a Time tab.**

   The app displays in day view a calendar that shows the events that each guest has scheduled for the day of your meeting. Figure 12-3 offers an example.

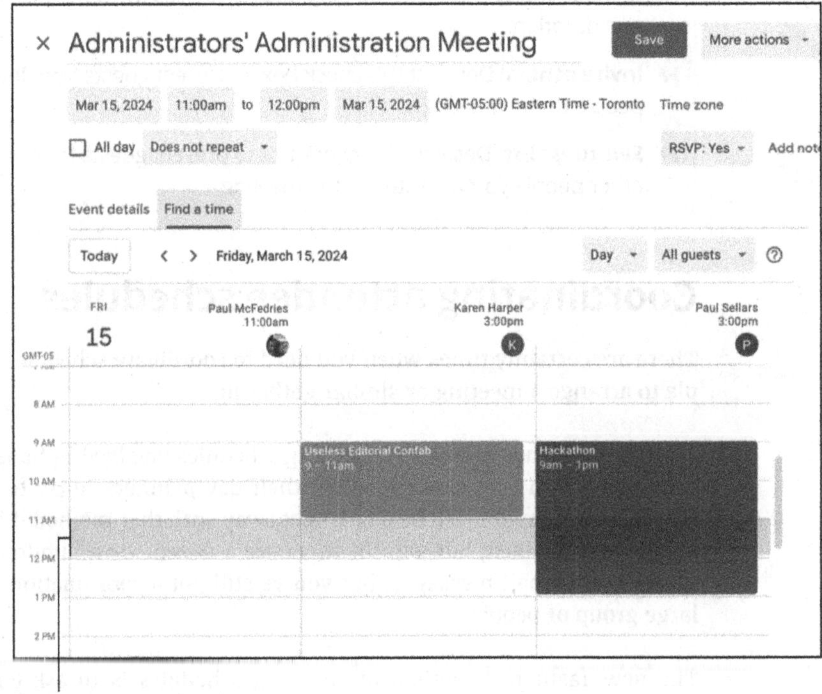

FIGURE 12-3: Click the Find a Time tab to peruse a calendar that shows the scheduled events for your meeting guests.

3. **Adjust your meeting start time (and end time, if necessary) to one that allows each guest to attend.**
4. **Fill out the rest of the meeting details, save your meeting, and then send the invitations.**

Getting suggested meeting times

If you're inviting just a few people to your meeting, viewing each guest's availability, as I describe in the preceding section, will probably work just fine because you can use the displayed calendar to figure out a meeting time that works for everyone.

However, once your meeting attendee list grows beyond just a few guests, trying to find a time that works for everyone can be a real time suck. Forget that. Instead, let Calendar do all the hard work by showing you a list of times when everyone can attend. Here's how it works:

1. **Create the meeting and add all the guests you want to attend.**

   Alternatively, for an existing meeting, click the meeting, and then click the edit event icon to open the meeting for editing.

2. **Click the Suggested Times button.**

   Calendar displays a list of times before and after your meeting times when every guest can attend. Figure 12-4 shows an example.

3. **Select a meeting time that works for you.**

   Calendar adjusts your meeting start and end times.

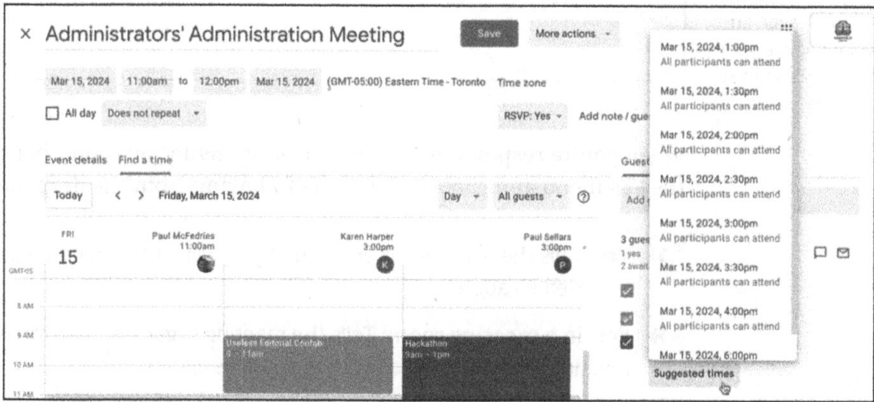

FIGURE 12-4: Click Suggested Times to display a list of meeting times when all your guests can attend.

Responding to a Meeting Invitation

If you receive a meeting invitation, you should respond as soon as you can so that the meeting organizer knows who's coming and who's not. Here are three ways you can respond to a meeting invite:

- In your Gmail inbox, hover the mouse pointer over the invitation, and Gmail displays an RSVP list. Click the RSVP button and then choose your response: Yes, Maybe, or No. (See Figure 12-5.)

» In Gmail, open the invitation email to display the meeting details, and then choose a response: Yes, Maybe, or No. (See Figure 12-6.)

» In Calendar, select the meeting (which Calendar adds temporarily, pending your response), and then in the Going? section, click Yes, No, or Maybe.

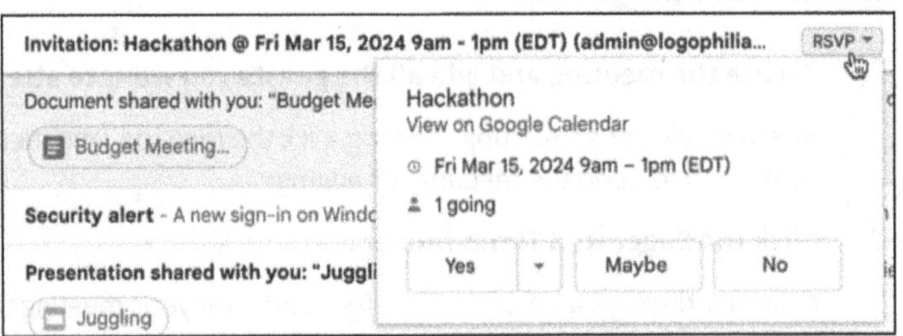

FIGURE 12-5: In your Gmail Inbox, choose your response in the invitation's RSVP list.

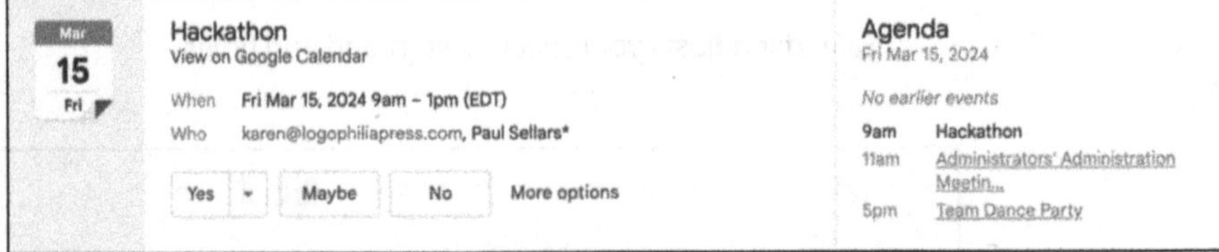

FIGURE 12-6: Open the invitation and then choose your response.

When you're responding Yes to a meeting invitation, note that you can pull down the Yes menu and choose one of the following from the drop-down menu:

» **Yes:** Tells the meeting organizer that you will attend the meeting in the specified location.

» **Yes, in a meeting room:** Tells the meeting organizer that you will attend the meeting, but you need a meeting room assigned.

» **Yes, joining virtually:** Tells the meeting organizer that you will attend the meeting, but you'll be joining virtually from another location.

Sharing Your Calendar

Earlier in this chapter, I talk about how you can view the schedules of people you invite to a meeting and display suggested meeting times that fit into each attendee's schedule. These timesaving techniques seem nearly magical. Ah, but that magic is just Calendar taking advantage of a useful fact: For each Google

Workspace user in an organization, Calendar automatically makes that user's main calendar available to everyone else in the organization. This is called *sharing* a calendar, and the Calendar app gives you a few techniques and settings for controlling how your calendar is shared, both inside and outside your organization.

Controlling access to your calendar in your organization

Google Workspace automatically shares your calendar with everyone in your organization, but that sharing isn't set in stone. In fact, you have two ways to control how your calendar is shared with your co-workers:

- **You can hide the details of your calendar's events.** This makes sense in many cases because, for the most part, all your colleagues need to know is whether you're free or busy at a particular time. The fact that you're busy because you've scheduled a video call with your astrologer is no one's business but your own.
- **You can turn off calendar sharing altogether.** Do you find the fact that *everyone* in your organization can access your schedule to be, well, intrusive — and maybe even a little creepy? I sympathize, I really do. If that's how you feel, go ahead and disable organization-wide calendar sharing. The downside to this will likely be lots of back-and-forth pre-meeting emails as your colleagues struggle to find a time when you're available. Your call.

Follow these steps to configure the access permissions for your calendar in your organization:

1. **In Calendar, click the Settings menu icon and then choose Settings from the menu that appears.**

   The Settings page appears.

2. **On the left side of the Settings page, under the Settings for My Calendars heading, click your calendar.**

   If you have multiple calendars, select your main work calendar.

3. **If you want to prevent others at work from accessing your schedule, deselect the Make Available for *Organization* check box (where *Organization* is the name of the place where you work) in the Access Permissions for Events section (see Figure 12-7).**

   Calendar saves your setting and you can skip Step 4.

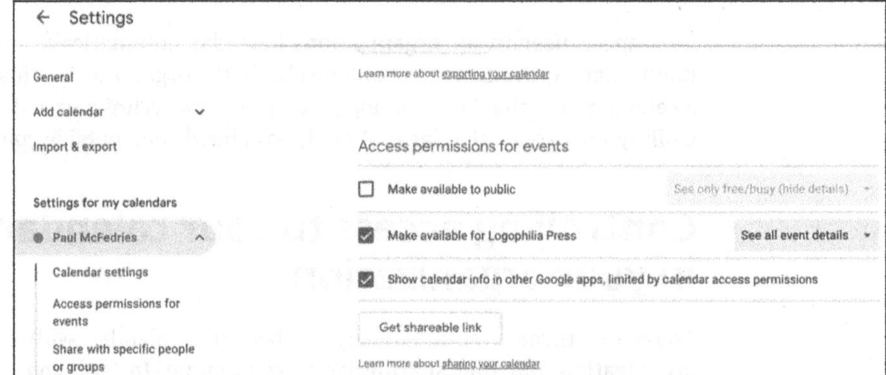

FIGURE 12-7: In the Access Permissions for Events section, control sharing access to your calendar.

4. **If you leave the Make Available for *Organization* check box selected, use the associated drop-down list to choose what people in your organization can view:**
   - *See Only Free/Busy (Hide Details):* Select this item to show co-workers only whether you're available at a specified time.
   - *See All Event Details:* Select this item to make your event specifics available to your colleagues.

   Calendar saves your settings as soon as you change them.

Making your calendar available to the public

Are you an exhibitionist at heart? If so, then, boy oh boy, does Calendar have just the thing for you: sharing your calendar with the entire world! If the thought fills you with dread, go ahead and skip the rest of this section. If the thought fills you with excitement, follow these steps to make it so:

1. **In Calendar, click the Settings menu icon and then choose Settings from the menu that appears.**

   The Settings page appears.
2. **On the left side of the Settings page, under the Settings for My Calendars section, click your calendar.**

   If you have multiple calendars, select your main work calendar.

3. **In the Access Permissions for Events section, select the Make Available to Public check box.**

   Sensibly, Calendar displays a warning about making your events visible to the entire universe and asks whether you're sure you want to continue with this crazy idea.

4. **If you're still okay with sharing your schedule publicly, click OK.**

   If your feet suddenly become ice-cold at the thought of public sharing, you'll get no judgment from me if you click Cancel instead and forget the whole idea.

   If you do end up leaving the Make Available to Public check box selected, know that Calendar once again shows its common sense by enabling only the See Only Free/Busy (Hide Details) item in the associated drop-down list.

   Calendar saves your settings automatically.

Making your calendar unavailable to other Google Workspace apps

Sometimes your calendar info might be needed in other Google Workspace apps. By default, Calendar shares your schedule throughout Google Workspace, but you can turn off this setting by following these steps:

1. **In Calendar, click the Settings menu icon and then choose Settings from the menu that appears.**

   The Settings page appears.

2. **On the left side of the Settings page, under Settings for My Calendars heading, click your calendar.**

   If you have multiple calendars, select your main work calendar.

3. **In the Access Permissions for Events section, deselect the Show Calendar Info in Other Google Apps, Limited by Calendar Access Permissions check box.**

   Calendar saves the new setting.

Sharing your calendar on an ad hoc basis

If you want to share your schedule online with a particular person or a small group, making your calendar publicly available is overkill, to say the least. A much safer approach is to ask Calendar to forge a link to your calendar that you can then share via email, text, or whatever. Here's what you do:

1. **In Calendar, click the Settings menu icon and then choose Settings from the menu that appears.**

   The Settings page appears.

2. **On the left side of the Settings page, under Settings for My Calendars heading, click your calendar.**

   If you have multiple calendars, select your main work calendar.

3. **In the Access Permissions for Events section, click the Get Shareable Link button.**

   Calendar opens the Shareable Link to Your Calendar dialog, which displays the link to your calendar.

4. **Click the Copy Link button.**

   Calendar copies the link address to your computer's clipboard.

5. **Paste the link into an email, a text, a web page, or whatever other medium you prefer to use to share the link.**

   When someone with access to the link clicks the link, your calendar appears in that person's Calendar app and a dialog asks whether they want to add your calendar. If they do, they can click Add to make it so.

Sharing your calendar with only specific people

Calendar enables you to share your schedule with specific people. How is that useful? Here are three ways:

- If you turned off organization-wide access to your calendar (as I discuss a bit earlier, in the section "Controlling access to your calendar in your organization"), you can then make your calendar available to a few lucky people you work with.
- If you have an assistant, a partner, a protégé, or another co-worker whom you want to allow to manage your calendar, you can *delegate* calendar access to that person.
- If you know someone who doesn't use Google Calendar, you can invite that person to view your calendar's free and busy times.

Here are the steps to follow to invite specific people to share your calendar:

1. **In Calendar, click the Settings menu icon and then choose Settings from the menu that appears.**

   The Settings page appears.

2. **On the left side of the Settings page, under Settings for My Calendars heading, click your calendar.**

   If you have multiple calendars, select your main work calendar.

3. **In the Share with Specific People or Groups section, click Add People and Groups.**

   Calendar opens the Share with Specific People dialog.

4. **Click in the Add Email or Name text box, and then start typing the name of a person with whom you want to share your calendar.**

   Calendar displays a list of people in your address book who match what you've typed.

5. **Click the name you want to add.**

   Alternatively, use the arrow keys to highlight the name you want and then press Tab or Enter.

6. **Repeat Steps 4 and 5 to add the other people you want to invite.**
7. **Use the Permissions drop-down list to choose the permission level you want to grant the invitees:**
   - *See Only Free/Busy (Hide Details):* Click this item to show only whether you're available at a specified time.

   The following three permissions are available only to people in your organization. However, if you add one or more people who aren't in your organization, Calendar disables all permissions except See Only Free/Busy. Therefore, if you want to set any of the permissions that follow, invite only people in your organization to your calendar.

   - *See All Event Details:* Click this item to make your event specifics available.
   - *Make Changes to Events:* Click this item to allow the invitees to edit your events.
   - *Make Changes and Manage Sharing:* Click this item to allow the invitees to not only edit your events but also share your calendar with other people.

8. **Click Send.**

   Calendar sends a sharing invitation to the people you added.

Calendar adds your invitees to the Share with Specific People or Groups section of the Settings page, as shown in Figure 12-8. Note that if you change your mind about the permission level you assigned to a particular person, you can change the level using that person's drop-down list. You can also remove a person from sharing your calendar by clicking the X to the far right of the person's name.

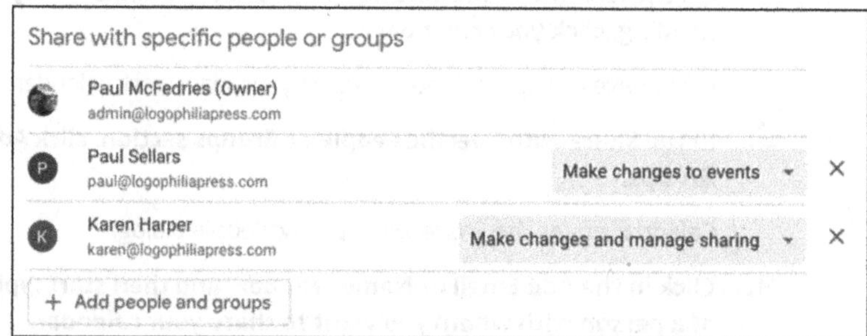

FIGURE 12-8: Folks with whom you've shared your calendar appear in the Share with Specific People or Groups section.

Subscribing to a Shared Calendar

It's one thing to view another person's availability when you're setting up a meeting, but it's quite another to always have that person's events visible in the Events area of your Calendar app. If that person's calendar is shared and you want to see the person's events alongside your own in the Calendar app, you need to *subscribe* to that person's calendar.

Once you subscribe to someone's shared calendar, that person's events appear side-by-side with yours. However, what appears depends on how the other person has shared their calendar:

- If the other person chose the See Only Free/Busy (Hide Details) access permission (which I describe earlier, in the "Controlling access to your calendar in your organization" section), the word *busy* appears in place of the event title, and selecting the event shows only the scheduled date and time.
- If the other person chose the See All Event Details access permission, the event title appears, and selecting the event shows its details.

Here are the steps to run through to subscribe to someone's shared calendar:

1. **In Calendar's Other Calendars section, located near the bottom of the navigation menu running down the left side of the page, click + (add other calendars icon).**

2. **Click Subscribe to Calendar from the menu that appears.**

   Calendar opens the Add Calendar page.

3. **Click in the Add Calendar text box, and then start typing the name of a person to whose calendar you want to subscribe.**

   Calendar displays a list of people in your address book who match what you've typed.

4. **Click the name you want to add.**

   Alternatively, use the arrow keys to highlight the name you want and then press Tab or Enter.

   Calendar subscribes you to the calendar and displays the calendar's settings.

5. **Adjust the calendar's settings as needed.**

   You can edit the calendar's name and a bunch of notification settings.

6. **Click the back icon.**

   Calendar adds the other person's calendar to the Other Calendars section and displays that person's scheduled events alongside yours in the events area. Figure 12-9 shows an example.

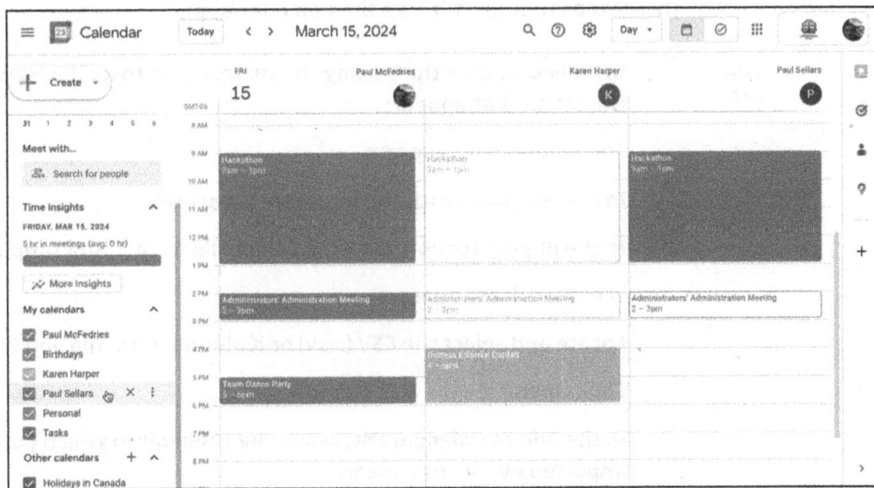

FIGURE 12-9: Calendar, subscribed to a couple of shared calendars.

TIP

To change a subscribed calendar's color and other settings, click the calendar's options icon.

REMEMBER

To unsubscribe from a calendar, locate the calendar in the Other Calendars section and then click the calendar's unsubscribe icon.

Importing Events

If someone you know uses a calendar program other than Google Calendar, you might be able to share that person's events by having the person export their calendar to a file that you can then import into Calendar. You can import these two calendar file formats:

- **CSV:** Contains the event data in a row-and-column format, where each row is an event and the event details are separated by commas. (CSV stands for *c*omma *s*eparated *v*alues.) Most calendar apps can export a calendar's events as a CSV file.
- **iCalendar:** Contains event data in a special iCalendar file that uses the .ics file extension. Many calendar apps, including Apple Calendar and Microsoft Outlook, can export a calendar's events to an iCalendar file.

Assuming that you have a CSV or iCalendar file stored on your computer, follow these steps to import it into the Calendar app:

1. **In Calendar, click the Settings menu icon and then choose Settings from the menu that appears.**

   The Settings page appears.

2. **In the left pane, click the Import & Export tab.**
3. **In the Import section, click the Select File from Your Computer button.**

   The Open dialog appears.

4. **Locate and select the CSV (.csv) or iCalendar (.ics) file you want to import.**
5. **Click Open.**
6. **In the Add to Calendar list, select the calendar in which you want the imported events to appear.**
7. **Click Import.**

   Calendar displays a dialog after it has completed the import.

8. **Click OK.**

   The imported events now appear in the calendar you chose in Step 6.

Exporting Events

If you want to share one or more of your calendars with someone who doesn't use Google Calendar, you can export your calendars and then send the other person the resulting iCalendar files. Here's what needs to happen:

1. **In Calendar, click the Settings menu icon and then choose Settings from the menu that appears.**

   The Settings page appears.

2. **In the left pane, click the Import & Export tab.**
3. **In the Export section, click Export.**

   Calendar creates and downloads a ZIP archive file that contains an iCalendar (.ics) file for each of your calendars.

IN THIS CHAPTER

» Learning what equipment you need to use Google Meet

» Setting up a video meeting

» Joining someone else's video meeting

» Fiddling with video meeting features and settings

» Presenting your screen

Chapter 13 Setting Up Video Meetings

A very long time ago, most people worked in the place where they lived. Farmers had their fields and livestock right outside the door, and tradespeople of all descriptions had their tools inside the house. Home was work and work was home, and separating the two would never have occurred to most people. All that changed when the Industrial Revolution came rumbling along. Its muscular machinery mass-produced goods formerly crafted by hand, and the great bulk of its hulking factories and warehouses required huge tracts of land outside cities and towns. The world's butchers, bakers, and candlestick makers had no choice but to leave their homes to ply their trades (or, more likely, some repetitive and soul-destroying subset of a trade) in these faraway enterprises. As a result, for the better part of 200 years, most workers have been leaving their homes and hi-ho, hi-hoing their way to work.

But now a post-industrial revolution is taking shape as a steady stream of workers abandon their traditional employment locales and bring their work home. The result is the *remote workforce*, where people toil at home, in a shared office space, hunkered down at the local coffee shop — anywhere but in a standard office.

Nothing wrong with that, but how do these so-called *office-free* workers get some face time? How do they meet? Well, if their organization uses Google Workspace, they can create video meetings using the Google Meet app. In this chapter, you get to know Meet, find out what it can do, use it to start or join meetings, and explore its features. An office? Who needs it?

What Do You Need to Use Meet?

A *video meeting* is, by definition, multiple simultaneous video and audio streams where everyone in the meeting needs to see and hear everyone else. That's a tall order, so Google Meet asks a lot from your computer and your internet connection to get its job done. "Asking a lot" means that Meet comes with a few important requirements that must be met before you can start or join a meeting. Here's a summary:

- **A recent version of your operating system:** Meet supports the current version and the two previous major versions of Windows, macOS, Chrome OS, and Ubuntu or other Debian-based Linux distributions.
- **The current version of your web browser:** Meet supports Chrome, Firefox, Edge, and Safari. Be sure to update your browser to the latest version before using Meet.
- **A video camera:** Make sure your computer has a built-in or an external USB video camera or web camera.
- **A high-speed internet connection:** For the best video quality, your internet connection should have at least 3.2 Mbps per meeting participant for upload (outbound data) and at least 2.6 Mbps (1.8 Mbps minimum) per meeting participant for download (inbound data). Your internet service provider probably has an online tool that will let you know your connection's upload and download speeds. If not, search Google for *internet speed test* and then click the Run Speed Test button.
- **A modern processer and a decent amount of memory:** To stream HD video, your computer's CPU (central processing unit) should be at least a dual-core processor and your computer should have at least 2 GB of memory. For larger meetings, you'll need a faster quad-core processor and at least 4 GB of memory. Is all this just gobbledygook to you? If so, don't give it a second thought. As long as your computer is less than ten years old or so, you'll be fine.

Allowing Meet to use your camera and microphone

You won't be even the teensiest bit surprised to learn that videoconferencing apps require access to video and audio hardware to do their thing. Meet is no different, so before you can use the app to start or join a meeting, you must give Meet permission to use your computer's camera and microphone.

To allow Meet access to your equipment, surf over to the Meet home page at `https://meet.google.com` and try any of the following:

- **Access Meet settings:** Click the Settings menu icon.
- **Start a new meeting:** Click New Meeting, click the type of meeting you want to create (refer to "Starting a Video Meeting" to learn more about these options), enter an optional nickname, and then click Continue.
- **Join an existing meeting:** In the Enter a Code or Nickname text box, type the meeting code, and then click Continue.

Whichever method you choose, a dialog lets you know that Meet needs to use your camera and microphone. Click Allow Microphone and Camera. A browser pop-up now asks whether you want to allow `meet.google.com` to use your camera and microphone, as shown in Figure 13-1. Click Allow to grant access to your equipment. You're good to go!

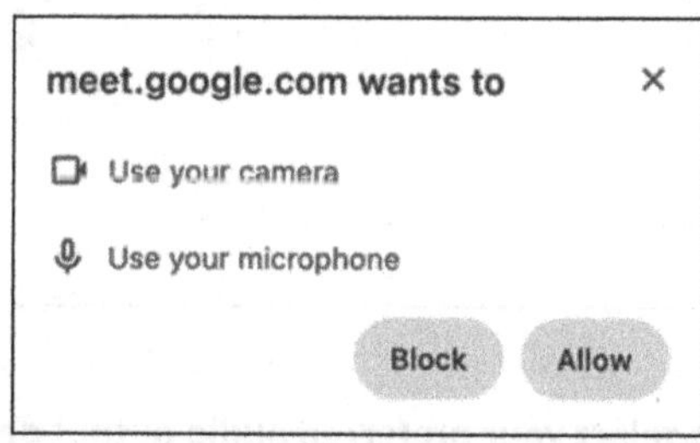

FIGURE 13-1: Click Allow to give Meet access to your computer's camera and microphone.

REMEMBER

Another browser pop-up might also ask whether you want to allow `meet.google.com` to show notifications (such as reminders about upcoming events). If you're cool with that, click Allow; if not, click Block.

If you clicked the Settings menu icon earlier, you end up at the Settings dialog. Either leave the dialog onscreen if you plan to continue with the next section or click X (close) to shut down the dialog.

Making sure Meet is using the equipment you want

If your computer happens to have multiple cameras, microphones, speakers, or headphones, Meet chooses the default devices on your system. If the defaults aren't what you want to use, it's best to check now to avoid embarrassing "We can't see you!" or "We can't hear you!" admonishments in your next meeting.

Follow these steps to double-check, and if necessary change, the audio and video equipment that Meet is using:

1. **On the Meet home page at `https://meet.google.com/`, click the Settings menu icon.**

   Meet opens the Settings dialog.

2. **On the Audio tab (check out Figure 13-2), click the Microphone list and select your preferred audio input device.**

   REMEMBER

   No microphone or speakers? No problem! You can still participate in meetings by using your phone as your audio device, as I describe later in the "Dialing in to a video meeting and using the phone for audio" section.

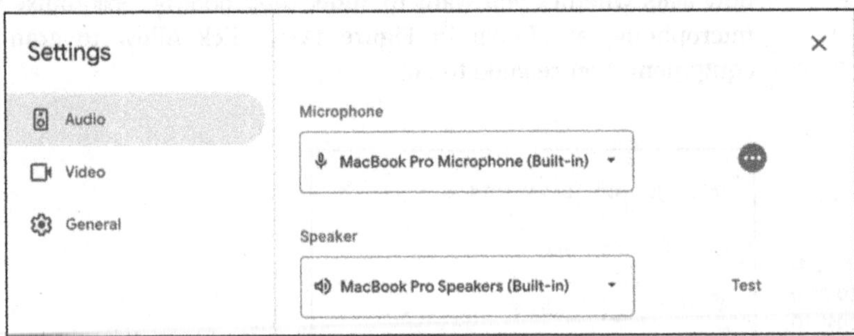

FIGURE 13-2: Use the lists on the Audio tab to choose your preferred audio input and output devices.

3. **Use the Speaker list to select your preferred audio output device.**

   To ensure that your chosen speakers are working, click the Test icon to hear some sample audio.

4. **On the Video tab (check out Figure 13-3), click the Camera list and select the device you want to use for your video feed.**

   Meet shows a camera preview to the right of the Camera list, so after you select a device, make sure the preview is displaying live video.

5. **Click X (close).**

   Meet uses your selected devices for current and future meetings.

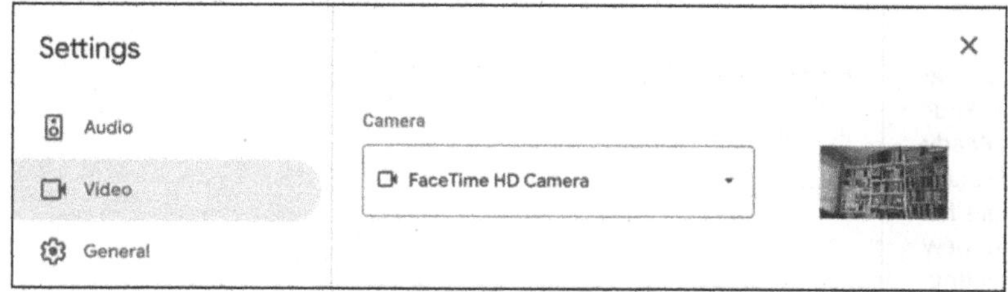

FIGURE 13-3: In the list on the Video tab, choose your preferred camera.

Starting a Video Meeting

One of the awesome features of Meet is that it has very few features! As long as your computer and internet connection meet the minimum requirements (which I drone on about earlier, in the section "What Do You Need to Use Meet?"), creating a fresh meeting from scratch requires just a few steps. Even better, you don't have to use the Meet home page because you can fire up a meeting from the friendly confines of Gmail or schedule a meeting using the Calendar app.

REMEMBER

Yet another way to crank out a video meeting is from a Google Chat conversation. To learn how this works, head over to Chapter 14.

Using the Meet home page to start an instant video meeting

Here are the relatively few steps you have to follow to crank up an instant video meeting from the Meet home page:

1. **Send your favorite web browser to `https://meet.google.com`.**
2. **Click New Meeting.**

   Meet displays a list of ways to create a meeting. One of the options in the list is Schedule in Google Calendar. To learn how to use Calendar to set up a meeting, refer to "Using Calendar to schedule a video meeting," later in this chapter.
3. **Click Start an Instant Meeting.**

   Google Meet creates the meeting, adds you to it, and displays the Your Meeting's Ready dialog, shown in Figure 13-4.

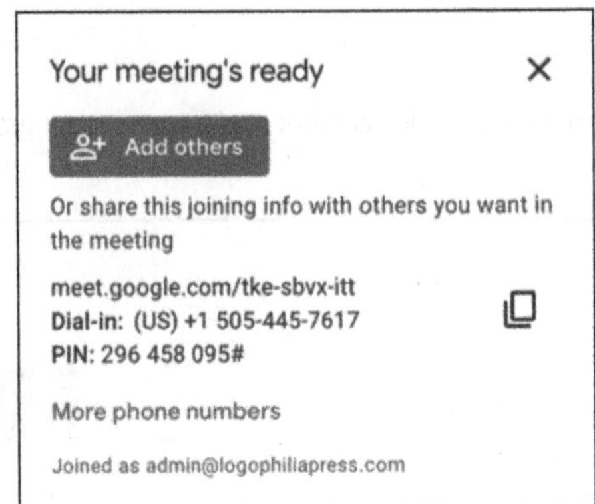

FIGURE 13-4: The Your Meeting's Ready dialog displays the details for your new meeting.

To find out how to populate your meeting, refer to the "Adding people to your video meeting" section, a bit later in this chapter.

Using the Meet home page to set up a video meeting to start later

If you don't want to start your meeting right now, you can create the meeting and save the details to distribute to the participants later when you're ready to meet. Here are the steps to follow to create a meeting for later from the Meet home page:

1. **Send the nearest web browser to `https://meet.google.com`.**
2. **Click New Meeting.**

   Meet displays a list of ways to create a new meeting.
3. **Click Create a Meeting for Later.**

   Google Meet displays the Here's Your Joining Info dialog, shown in Figure 13-5.

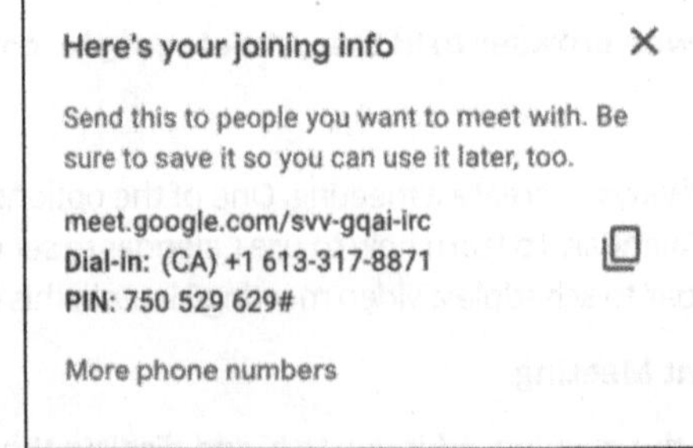

FIGURE 13-5: The Here's Your Joining Info dialog displays the joining data for your meeting.

4. **Click the copy joining info icon.**

   Meet copies the joining information to your computer's clipboard. You should paste the info somewhere handy so that you can send it to your meeting invitees when you're ready to start your meeting.

Refer to the "Adding people to your video meeting" section, a bit later in this chapter, to find out how to invite people to your meeting.

Using Gmail to start a video meeting

Forging a new video meeting from Gmail requires just the following steps:

1. **Head on over to `https://mail.google.com`.**
2. **In the navigation menu on the left side of the page, click Meet.**

   The Meet pane appears.

3. **Click New Meeting.**

   The Share Your New Meeting dialog appears, as shown in Figure 13-6.

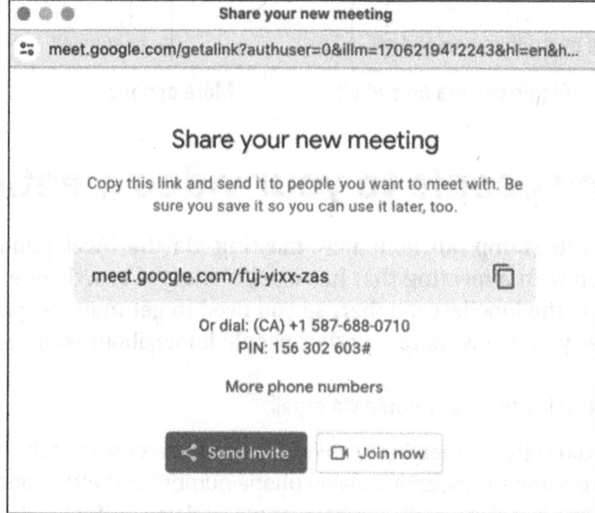

FIGURE 13-6: Use the Share Your New Meeting dialog to share a link or start a new meeting.

4. **You have two ways to proceed:**

   - *Start the new meeting right away:* Click Join Now and then, when you see the Ready to Join? page, click Join Now. Meet adds you to your own meeting and you end up at the meeting screen, a typical example of which is shown in Figure 13-7. Refer to the "Adding people to your video meeting" section, next, to find out how to populate your meeting.

- *Share a link to the meeting:* Click the copy joining info icon. Meet copies the joining information to your computer's clipboard. Paste the info somewhere safe so you can send it to your meeting invitees when you're ready to start your meeting. Refer to the next section, "Adding people to your video meeting" section, to find out how to invite people to your meeting.

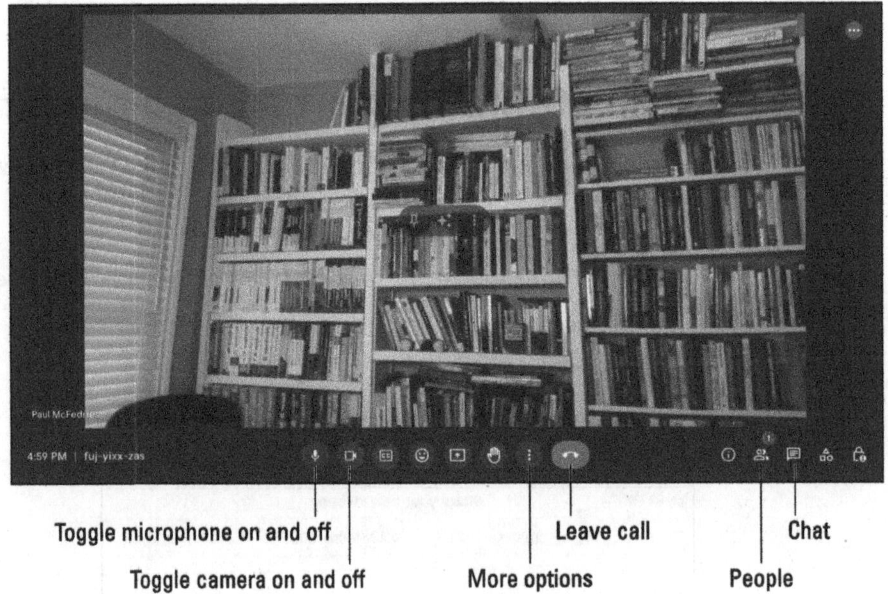

FIGURE 13-7: A typical meeting window.

Adding people to your video meeting

Whether you stamp out your new meeting via the Meet home page or Gmail, you end up with a meeting that has a population of exactly one: you. As the song says, one is the loneliest number, so you need to get more people in there — fast. Meet gives you two ways to let other people know about your meeting:

- You can invite other people via email.
- You can copy the meeting's *joining info* — which consists of the meeting address and the meeting's dial-in phone number and PIN — and then paste that info in a text, email, or whatever method you prefer for sharing.

The next two sections cover both methods.

Inviting people to join your video meeting via email

The simplest and easiest way to ask people to join your meeting is to send them an email invitation. You have two ways to do this:

- » If the Your Meeting's Ready dialog is onscreen (this dialog appears when you first join your own meeting; refer to Figure 13-4), click Add Others.

- » In the meeting window, click the show everyone icon and then click Add People in the People pane that appears on the right.

You end up at the Add People dialog. Enter the name or address of the person you want to invite (or select that person from the list provided), repeat as needed, and then click Send Email. Your invitees receive an email message with a big Join Call button that gets them to the Ready to Join? page, and they then click Join Now to enter your meeting — just like that.

Sending the video meeting joining info to people

The joining info for your meeting consists of two bits of data:

- » The meeting address, which takes the following general form:

  ```
  https://meet.google.com/meeting-code
  ```

  Here, *meeting-code* is a code that uniquely identifies your meeting.

TIP

- » The dial-in phone number and PIN that people who dial in need to enter. By default, Meet displays a phone number for US callers. If you have people calling in from elsewhere, select More Phone Numbers to view numbers from other countries, as well as a PIN those people can use.

The basic idea is that you copy your meeting's joining info and then share that info with would-be participants by pasting the info in an email, a text, a web page, or another text-based medium. Meet gives you two methods for copying the joining info:

- » *If the Your Meeting's Ready dialog is onscreen* (which shows up when you first join your own meeting; refer to Figure 13-4), click the copy joining info icon (shown in the margin).

- » *In the meeting window,* click Meeting Details to open the Meeting Details pane, shown in Figure 13-8, and then click the meeting details icon (shown in the margin).

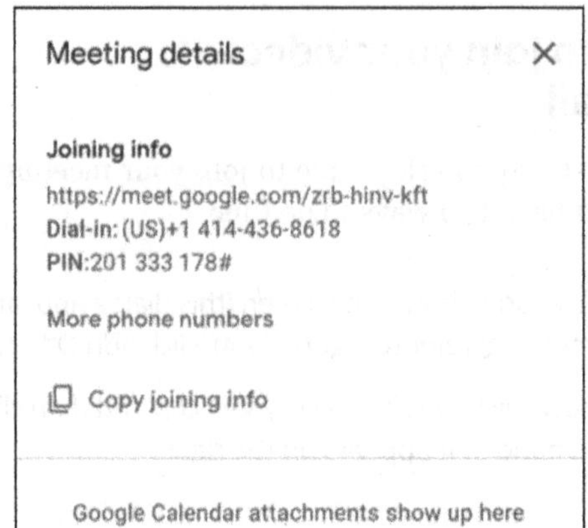

FIGURE 13-8: Click Meeting Details to display this pane with, you know, the meeting details.

Using Calendar to schedule a video meeting

Starting a video meeting and then inviting people to join you is fine for quick get-togethers or impromptu chinwags. However, most of the time it makes more sense to schedule a video meeting in advance. That way, you give your attendees plenty of notice, you can pick a time that works for everyone, and you know going into the meeting who will attend.

When you schedule a regular meeting in Calendar, you can turn it into a video meeting by doing either of the following on the Event tab:

- Click the Add Google Meet Video Conferencing button.
- Add at least one guest to the meeting.

The Event tab then shows the Join with Google Meet button (which you can click later to join your meeting) as well as the address of the video meeting. To display more joining info for the meeting, click the downward-pointing arrow (view conference details). Calendar expands the video meeting info to display the meeting ID, a dial-in phone number, and a PIN, as shown in Figure 13-9. You can click the More Phone Numbers link to display the dial-in numbers for other countries.

TIP

If you use Microsoft Outlook, you can schedule a Google Meet videoconference from Outlook's Calendar if you install the Google Meet add-in to Outlook. Surf over to Microsoft's AppSource (`https://appsource.microsoft.com`) and search for *Meet* to locate the add-in.

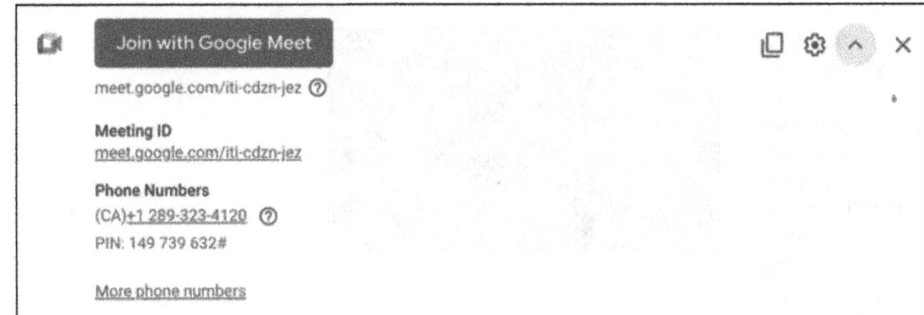

FIGURE 13-9: The joining info for the scheduled video meeting.

Joining a Video Meeting

Before getting to the specifics of the myriad methods that Meet offers for joining a video meeting, you need to get straight exactly *who* can join automatically and who needs to request permission to join.

Three types of people can join video meetings automatically:

- » People in your organization who are signed in to their Google Workspace account
- » People outside your organization who have been invited to the meeting via Calendar and who have a Google account
- » People outside your organization who are invited during the meeting by a participant

And these three types of people require permission to join video meetings:

- » People who weren't invited to the meeting via Calendar
- » People who don't have a Google account and are attempting to join the meeting using the meeting's web address
- » People outside your organization who are using Google Workspace for Education accounts

When a person who requires permission tries to access the meeting, they land on the Ready to Join? page and must click the Ask to Join button. In the meeting itself, the Someone Wants to Join This Call dialog appears, shown in Figure 13-10.

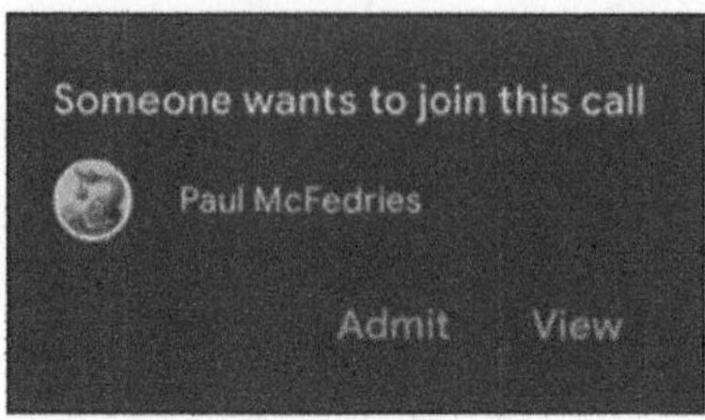

FIGURE 13-10: This dialog appears to the meeting participants when a user who requires permission asks to join the meeting.

Any meeting participant can then do one of the following:

- **Admit the user:** Click Admit to welcome the user into the meeting.
- **Deny the user:** Click View to open the People pane, click the more actions icon to the right of the user asking to be admitted, and then click Deny Entry to block the interloper.

JOIN A MEETING JUST TO PRESENT

TECHNICAL STUFF

In some cases, you might prefer to join a meeting only to present something. For example, if you're teaching a course via Meet, you probably want to skip the conversation part and go right into your presentation. Even if you stop presenting, you don't end up in the regular meeting space; instead, you just get a button that enables you to resume presenting.

Here's how to join a meeting only to present something on your screen:

1. **Select the meeting you want to join.**

   The Ready to Join? page appears.

2. **Click Present (instead of Join Now).**

   Meet opens the Choose What to Share dialog.

3. **Select what you want to share (an entire screen, an application window, or a Chrome tab, if you're running Chrome).**
4. **Click Share.**

   Meet shares your screen with the meeting.

Joining a video meeting from the Meet home page

Follow these steps to join an existing video meeting from the Meet home page:

1. **Surf to `https://meet.google.com`.**
2. **In the Enter a Code or Link text box, paste (or type) the meeting code.**

   The meeting code consists of the characters that appear in the meeting address after `https://meet.google.com` (for example, `abc-defg-hij`). If you're entering the code manually, note that you can skip the hyphens.

   If the meeting has a nickname, you can enter the nickname instead.
3. **Click Join.**

   Meet opens the Ready to Join? page.
4. **Click Join Now.**

   If you don't have permission to join the meeting, you have to click Ask to Join, instead, and then wait for some good Samaritan to let you in.

   Meet connects you to the meeting.

Joining a video meeting from Gmail

Joining an in-progress video meeting via Gmail requires just a few steps:

1. **Surf to `https://mail.google.com`.**
2. **In the navigation menu on the left side of the page, click Meet.**

   The Meet pane appears.
3. **Click Join a Meeting.**

   Gmail displays the Join a Meeting dialog.
4. **Paste (or type) the meeting code in the text box.**

   The meeting code consists of the characters that appear in the meeting address after `https://meet.google.com` (for example, `abc-defg-hij`). If you're entering the code manually, note that you can skip the hyphens.
5. **Click Join.**

   Meet opens the Ready to Join? page.

6. **Click Join Now.**

   If you don't have permission to join the meeting, you must click Ask to Join, instead, and then wait for a kind meeting participant to let you in.

   Meet connects you to the meeting.

Dialing in to a video meeting and using the phone for audio

It's not technically impossible to participate in a meeting without a microphone or speakers, but what on Earth are you even doing there if you can't say anything or hear anything? Sure, you can use the chat feature, but you don't need the full power of a video meeting just to chat with people.

So, if your computer lacks the necessary audio equipment, your equipment is on the fritz, or you left your headset at home, you might as well not join the meeting, right? Not so fast. You can still participate if you have access to a phone because Meet has a feature that enables you to dial in to the meeting and then use your phone's built-in microphone and speaker to speak and listen.

Here's how it works:

1. **Tell Meet you want to use your phone:**
   - *If you're at the Ready to Join? screen,* click the link named Join and Use a Phone for Audio.
   - *If you're already in a meeting,* click the more options icon and then click Use a Phone for Audio from the menu that appears.

   The Use a Phone for Audio dialog appears, as shown in Figure 13-11.

2. **On the Dial In tab, select your country from the Country list.**

   Meet displays a phone number and a PIN.

3. **Use your phone to dial the displayed phone number.**

   An automated service welcomes you to Google Meet and prompts you to enter the PIN.

4. **Use your phone's dial pad to enter the PIN, followed by the pound symbol (#).**

   You can now use your phone for talking and listening.

Use a phone for audio

Call me | Dial in

Meet calls your phone so you can use it to listen and speak to the video call. When you answer the call, press 1 to connect to the call.

Select your country and enter your number.

Country | Phone number

Remember the phone number on this device
Don't use on a public device

Dismiss | Call me

FIGURE 13-11: Use this dialog if you have to switch to your phone for audio during a meeting.

Customizing Video Meeting Settings

After you're safely ensconced in a video meeting, you can use a few techniques to customize the meeting to suit your style. These techniques include changing the meeting layout, turning on captions, and pinning, muting, and removing participants.

Changing the meeting layout

By default, Meet chooses a meeting layout that (at least in Meet's opinion) best displays the meeting's video feeds and other content. Meet chooses one of the following layouts:

- **Sidebar:** The video feed of the person who is speaking or presenting takes up most of the meeting window, and smaller versions of the other video feeds appear along the right side of the window.
- **Spotlight:** The video feed of the person who is speaking or presenting takes up the entire meeting window. If you pin a participant (refer to "Messing around with meeting participants," next), that person's video feed takes up the entire window, no matter who is speaking or presenting.
- **Tiled:** The video feeds for each participant are arranged in equal-sized tiles to fill the meeting window. Meet can display up to 16 video feeds this way.

If you don't like the layout Meet chooses, you can change the layout as follows:

1. **In the meeting window, click an empty part of the screen.**

   Meet displays its toolbar.

2. **Click the more options icon and then choose Change Layout from the menu that appears.**

   Meet opens the Change Layout dialog, shown in Figure 13-12.

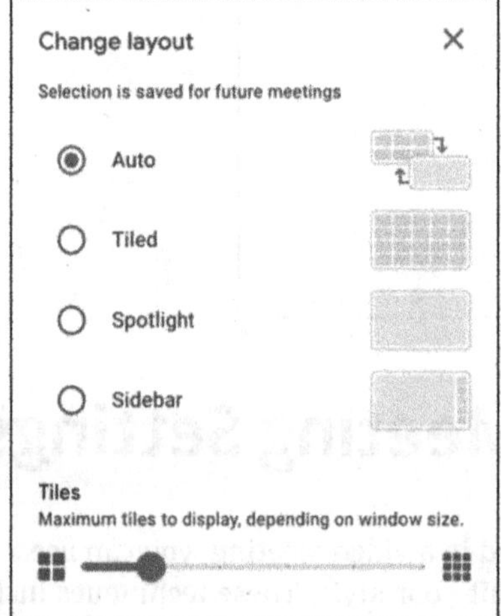

FIGURE 13-12: In the Change Layout dialog, choose your preferred meeting layout.

3. **Select the layout you prefer.**

   If you want Meet to choose a layout for you, click Auto.

   Meet switches to the layout you chose.

4. **Use the Tiles slider to select the maximum number of tiles you want Meet to display.**

   The Tiles slider is enabled only if you select the auto or tiles layout.

5. **Click X (close).**

TIP

To apply effects or a background to your video feed, click the more options icon, and then click Apply Video Effects to open the Effects pane. Here you can blur the background, change the background, add a filter, or apply a style. If your Google Workspace account has access to Duet AI, you can click Generate a Background, type a prompt specifying the type of background you want, choose an optional style, and then click Create Samples to see what the AI comes up with. If you see something you like, click the sample to make it your background.

Messing around with meeting participants

If you're the creator of the meeting, you can call upon some extra features to lord it over the other participants. To learn what you can do, follow these steps:

1. **Click the people icon.**

   Meet displays the People pane.

2. **Click the mute icon to the right of the person you want to manage to turn off that person's volume for all meeting participants.**

   REMEMBER

   For privacy reasons, you can't unmute the person's (or any participant's) volume; the muted person must unmute their own volume.

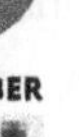

3. **Click the more actions icon to the right of the person you want to manage.**

   The menu shown in Figure 13-13 appears.

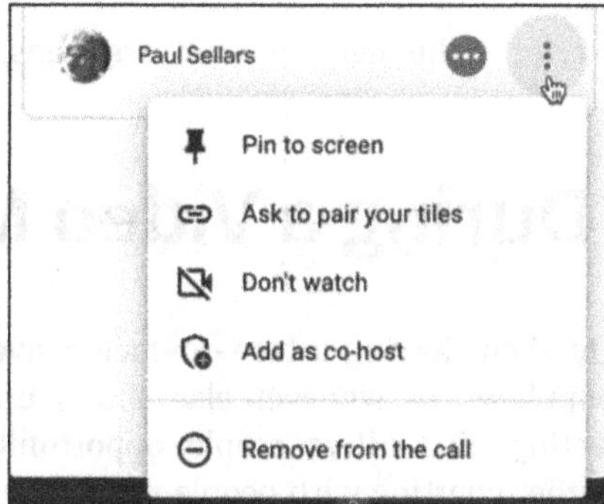

FIGURE 13-13: Click a participant's more actions icon to display the list shown here.

Here's what each icon does:

- **Pin to Screen:** Makes this person's video feed the main tile in the sidebar and spotlight layouts.
- **Ask to Pair Your Tiles:** Sends a request to the participant to pair your tile with theirs. If the person accepts your request, each time one of you speaks, both your tiles appear as the main tile in the sidebar and spotlight layouts.
- **Add as Co-host:** Promotes the participant to be another host of the meeting, which means the person now has the same hosting privileges as you.
- **Remove from the Call:** Kicks the person out of the meeting. This is a drastic step, to be sure, but it might be your only option if the person is belligerent, abusive, or in some other way too unpleasant to tolerate.

Displaying captions

If you're having trouble following what meeting participants are saying, hey, no judgment — it happens to the best of us. Meetings with two or three other people aren't usually a problem, but once a meeting's population swells much beyond that, the difficulty of keeping track of what's being said increases along with the size of the meeting.

You can make it easier to follow what's happening by turning on captions, which display a transcription of the meeting conversation. Meet gives you three ways to turn on captions:

- Click an empty part of the Meet window to display the toolbar, and then select the toolbar's Turn on Closed Captions option.
- Press C.

- Click the more options icon, and then click Turn on Captions from the menu that appears.

Meet now displays a transcript of the meeting's conversations.

Sharing Resources During a Video Meeting

A video meeting is mostly about having a face-to-face conversation with your colleagues, customers, suppliers, or whoever else shows up. I said "mostly" because every video meeting also offers ample opportunity to share other resources, which means either chatting with people in the meeting or presenting your screen to the meeting.

Chatting with meeting participants

Every meeting has what the corporate cognoscenti call the *back channel*, which refers to an informal communications channel that happens, as it were, behind the scenes of the meeting. In olden times (say, the early 2000s), the back channel might have been handwritten notes passed between participants. In the modern world of Google Meet videoconferences, the back channel takes the form of chat messages (Google Meet also calls them *in-call messages*) exchanged between meeting participants.

Why chat during a meeting? There are as many reasons as there are participants, but here are some of the most popular:

- To share a link to something mentioned during the meeting conversation

» To answer a question that comes up during the meeting without having to interrupt the current conversation
» To ask a question about something said during the meeting
» To let people know you have to leave the meeting, either temporarily or permanently
» To comment on something said during the meeting

Bear in mind that everyone in the meeting can view every chat message, so be cool with any comments or questions.

To send a chat message, follow these steps:

1. **In the Meet window, click the chat with everyone icon.**

   Meet opens the In-Call Messages pane, which you can then use to view existing chat messages and post your own messages.

2. **In the Send a Message text box, type the message you want to post to everyone in the meeting.**

3. **Click the send icon or press Enter.**

   Meet posts the message to each participant.

Presenting your screen

Suppose you want to impart some information, run through a technique, convey the results of something, or describe something visual. Although you can certainly try to do these things within the meeting conversation, your words are likely to fall short, even if you have the proverbial gift of gab. It's much better to *show* your meeting friends what you mean rather than describe it (pictures, despite inflation, still being worth the usual thousand words).

How do you show something in a meeting? Not by holding it up to the camera (although that's fine if you're showing off a new puppy). No, you *present* it, which means broadcasting to everyone in the meeting a live feed of your computer screen, which you then control as needed. (You can scroll up and down, select things, choose menu items, and so on.) And if you need to show people only part of your screen, you can present just a particular window (or a browser tab, if you're using the Chrome web browser).

Follow these steps to present to the meeting:

1. **In the meeting window, click an empty part of the screen.**

   Meet displays its toolbar.

2. **Click the present now icon.**

   If someone else is currently presenting, Meet displays a dialog letting you know that this will allow you to take over the presenting duties. Say "My evil plan is working!" and then click Share Now.

   Meet opens the Choose What to Share dialog. Figure 13-14 shows the version that appears if you're using the Chrome web browser.

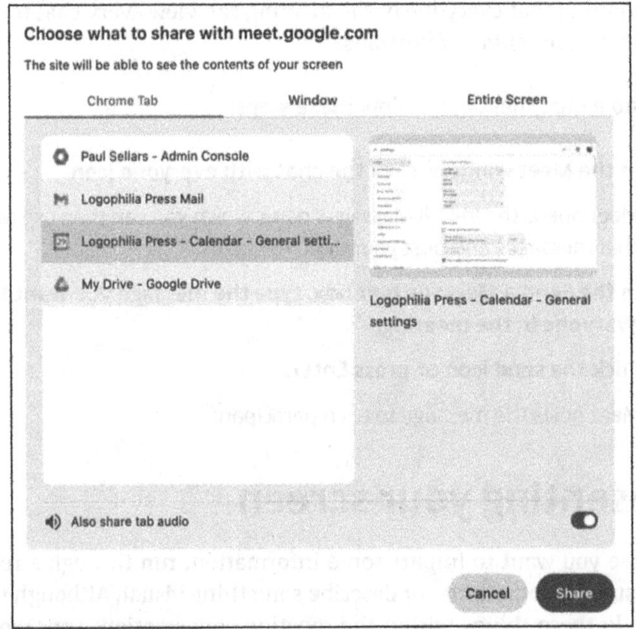

FIGURE 13-14: Use this dialog to choose what you want to present to the meeting.

3. **Select one of the following tabs to choose what you want to present:**
   - *Chrome Tab* (Chrome only): Displays a list of your open Chrome tabs. Select the tab you want to present. If you don't want to share the tab's audio output, click the Also Share Tab Audio switch off. Click Share to make it so.
   - *Window:* Displays thumbnail versions of your open application windows. Select the window you want to present, and then click Share.
   - *Entire Screen:* Displays a thumbnail version of your screen. Click the thumbnail and then click Share. (If you're using a web browser other than Google Chrome, a dialog might appear that asks you to set up your browser permissions so you can share your screen. In most cases, you need to click the Share button to give the browser access.)
4. **Share your content to the meeting.**
5. **When you're done, return to the Meet window and click Stop Presenting.**

IN THIS CHAPTER

» How do I chat with thee? Let me count the ways

» Exchanging messages with your co-workers

» Setting up your very own chat space

» Using Chat to collaborate with colleagues

Chapter 14
Chatting with Your Team

Chatting — that is, exchanging simple text messages with one or more people — is so easy and so convenient that it's quickly becoming (if it isn't already) the de facto communication choice for Google Workspace users. Not that long ago, chat was the medium you used for quick-and-short communiqués. Nowadays, it's not unusual for people to exchange messages that consist not just of a short phrase or two but also multi-sentence — even multi-paragraph mini-essays. This ain't your father's chat.

In this chapter, you dig into Google Workspace's messaging features, with a special emphasis on its flagship chat app, Google Chat. You learn not only how to exchange direct messages but also how to create chat spaces, use Chat to collaborate with your co-workers, and more.

Chatting, Google Workspace Style

Proof of chat's ascendance in the corporate communications realm is the myriad ways that Google Workspace enables its users to message each other: Gmail, Docs, Sheets, Slides, and Meet. Before moving on to Google Chat, the next few sections examine these alternative chat methods.

Chatting with Gmail

When you're hanging around in Gmail, you can use Google Chat to exchange messages with people you know, including people outside your organization. You can set up a classic one-on-one text conversation, or you can organize (or join) a group chat of up to 100 people.

Here are the steps to follow to start a chat in Gmail:

1. **In the navigation menu down the left side of the page, click Chat.**

   You can also just hover your mouse pointer over the Chat button.

2. **Click New Chat.**

   A dialog appears, prompting you to specify someone to chat with.

3. **In the Add 1 or More People text box, start typing the name, email, or phone number of the person you want to chat with.**

   Chat displays a list of names (refer to Figure 14-1) that match what you've typed so far. You usually see one or more apps followed by the names or email addresses of one or more people. If a person is outside your organization, Chat displays an external icon, as pointed out in Figure 14-1.

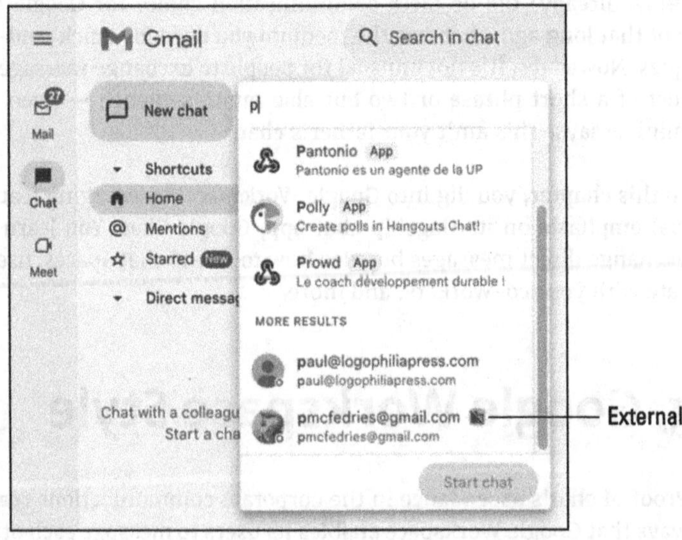

FIGURE 14-1: As you enter a name or an address, a list of matching names appears.

4. **When the person you want appears, click that name in the list.**
5. **Click Start Chat.**

   Google Chat opens a chat window.

6. **In the large text box near the bottom of the window, type your initial message and then click the send icon or press Enter or Return.**

   Chat sends the message and you're off and chatting.

Chatting with Meet

During a meeting, you might want to make a comment to another participant without interrupting the meeting, ask a question, or share a link with everyone. You can do all that and more by clicking the Chat icon to open the Chat pane (refer to Chapter 13 to learn more about chatting during a meeting).

Remember that all Meet chats are public, meaning that anyone else in the meeting can read the messages you exchange with someone. Therefore, Meet chats are definitely *not* the place to rag on your boss or make snarky comments about someone in the meeting!

Chatting with Google Chat

The rest of this chapter covers Google Chat, which is the main messaging app for Google Workspace users. To get you started, here are the three ways you can access Google Chat (which I call Chat from here on out):

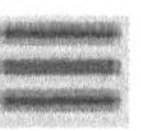

- **On the web:** Take your web browser by the hand and guide it gently to `https://chat.google.com`. Figure 14-2 shows the Chat landscape that appears when you first open the site. Click Main Menu if you don't see the full navigation menu on the left.
- **On the desktop:** A Google Chat app is available for Windows and Mac. Head over to `https://chat.google.com/download` and click the Get the App button.
- **On your mobile device:** A mobile version of the Google Chat app is available for Android, iOS, and iPadOS. Use Google Play (Android) or the App Store (iOS or iPadOS) to install the app on your device.

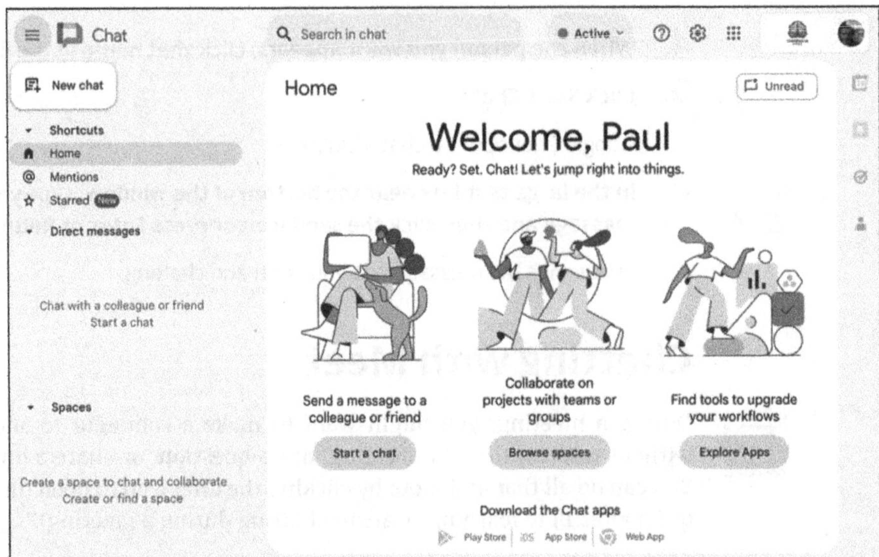

FIGURE 14-2: Google Chat's web home.

Exchanging Messages

When you're ready to start a conversation, here are the steps to follow on the Chat website to get a chat off the ground:

1. **Click the New Chat button in the navigation area on the left side of the page.**

   If you still have the Welcome page onscreen (the page shown earlier in Figure 14-2), you can also click Start a Chat.

2. **In the Add 1 or More People text box, start typing the name of the person you want to converse with.**

   Chat displays a list of people in your organization who match what you've entered so far.

TIP

   If you want to chat with someone outside your organization, you need to enter that person's email address.

3. **When the name of the person you want appears, click that name.**
4. **Click Start Chat.**

   Chat launches a new conversation.

5. **Enter your initial message in the text box that's provided, as shown in Figure 14-3.**

6. **Click the send message icon or press Enter or Return.**

   Chat tosses the message at the other person.

7. **Read the response you get from the other person.**
8. **Repeat Steps 6 and 7 until you can't take it anymore.**

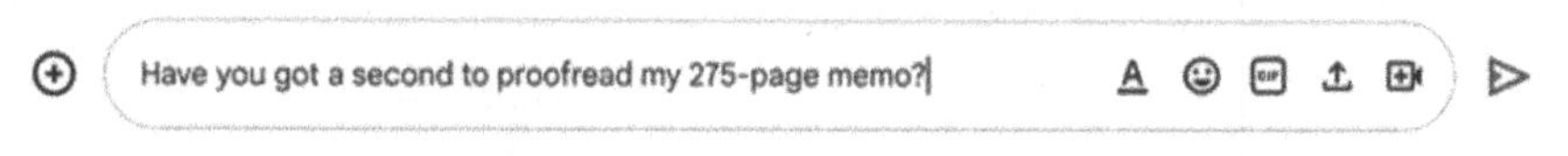
Have you got a second to proofread my 275-page memo?

FIGURE 14-3: Type your message in the big text box provided.

Formatting chat text

The vast majority of your messages will use plain old text, but you'll occasionally want to spice up your chats with a little formatting: bold to make a word or phrase stand out; italics to emphasize something; even an emoji or two to give your message that certain visual oomph that only well-chosen pictograms can give. Here's what you can do:

- **Making text bold:** Surround the word or phrase with asterisks (*). For example, entering `To make it rain cats and dogs, clicking the *Poodle* button` would be displayed as `To make it rain cats and dogs, click the` **`Poodle`** button.
- **Making text italic:** Surround the word or phrase with underscores (_). For example, entering `That is a _terrible_ idea!` would display as `That is a` *`terrible`* `idea!`

- **Formatting text:** Click the formatting options icon to display the extra controls shown in Figure 14-4. Select the text you want to format, then click the icon for the formatting you want (from left to right): bold, italic, underline, bulleted list, strikethrough, and insert link.

- **Adding an emoji:** Click the add emoji icon to display the dialog shown in Figure 14-5, and then select the emoji that does the job for you.

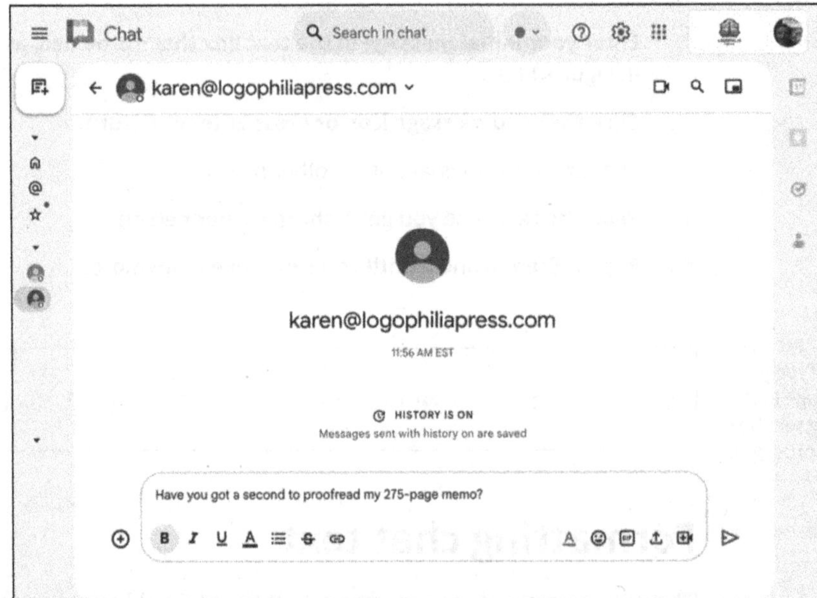

FIGURE 14-4: Click the formatting options icon to display a few icons for formatting text.

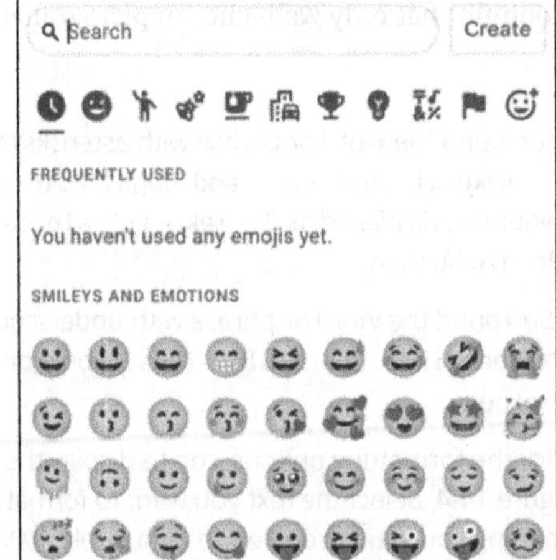

FIGURE 14-5: Click the add emoji icon to enhance your message with a just-so emoji.

Messing around with messages

Did you make a typo, a grammatical gaffe, or a factual error in a text? Hey, it happens. You might think, after you toss a message out into the ether, that the message becomes a fixed, unchangeable, un-mess-with-able thing. Not so. In fact, Chat gives you a host of ways to mess with a message, including fixing any errors.

In the list of sent chat messages, move your mouse pointer over (or click) the message you want to do something with. Chat displays the icons shown in Figure 14-6.

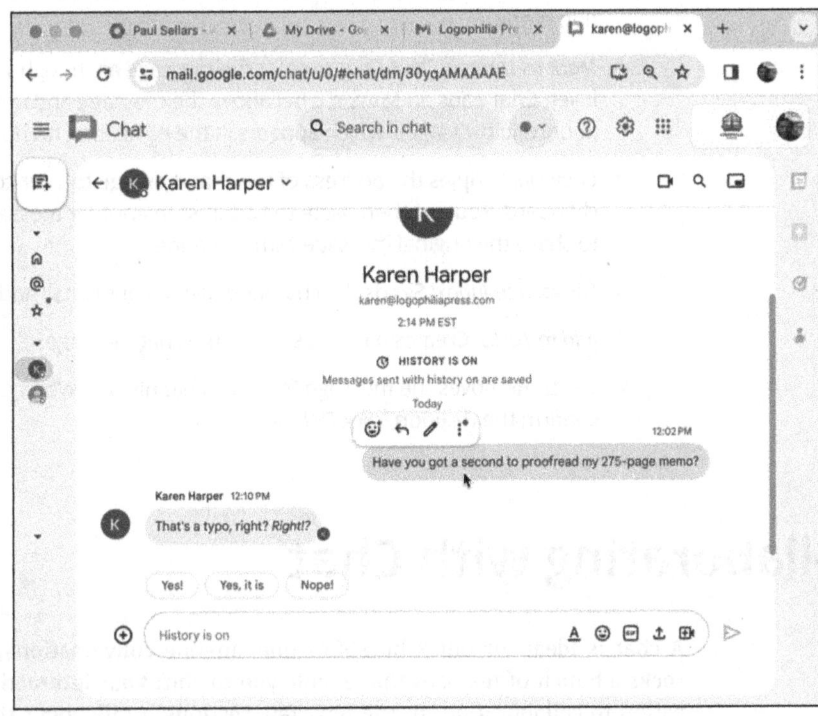

FIGURE 14-6: Select a message in your chat history to display the icons shown here.

REMEMBER

The icons shown in Figure 14-6 are the ones that Chat displays when you select one of your own messages. If you select another person's message, Chat shows replaces the edit icon with the mark as unread icon.

Here are the four icons that appear when you select one of your messages:

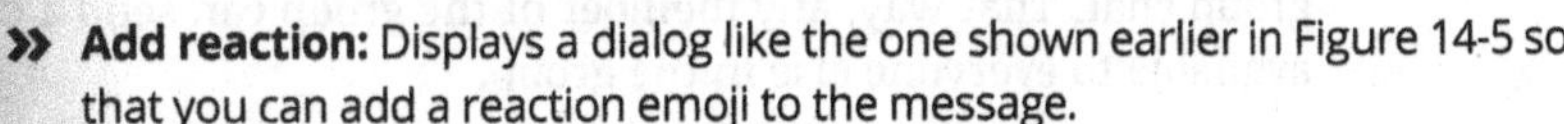

» **Add reaction:** Displays a dialog like the one shown earlier in Figure 14-5 so that you can add a reaction emoji to the message.

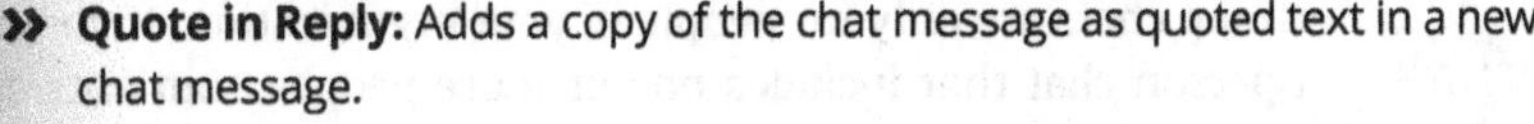

» **Quote in Reply:** Adds a copy of the chat message as quoted text in a new chat message.

» **Edit:** Opens the message for editing. Make your changes and then click Update.

» **More Actions:** Displays a menu with the following commands:
   - *Star:* Adds a star icon to the right of the chat message time, which is a handy way to remind yourself to do something with the message. All your starred messages appear in the Starred folder, accessible via the navigation menu.
   - *Mark as Unread:* Tells Chat to treat the message as though you haven't read it yet. Chat adds an *Unread* label above the message and updates the total of unread messages, which appears in the navigation menu.
   - *Copy Link:* Copies the address of the chat message to your computer's clipboard. You can then paste the address in another message or an email to share the original message with someone.
   - *Forward to Inbox:* Sends the chat message to your Gmail address.
   - *Add to Tasks:* Creates a new task from the chat message.
   - *Delete:* Removes the message from the chat history. When Chat asks you to confirm the deletion, click Delete.

Collaborating with Chat

A chat is ideal for quick bursts of one-on-one conversations, but Google Chat rocks a bunch of features that enable you to shift your interactions from conversation to collaboration. In the next few sections, I talk about these collaboration features.

Chatting with a group

If you have a question to answer, a controversy to settle, or a detail to hash out, the quickest and easiest way to get it done is to gather everyone involved into a group chat. That way, any member of the group can send a direct message that's available to everyone else in the group.

REMEMBER

Group chats are only for people in your organization. If you need to create a multiperson chat that includes one or more people from outside your organization, you need to create a chat space. Refer to "More Collaboration: Congregating in a Chat Space," later in this chapter.

Here are the steps to follow to organize a group chat:

1. **Click the New Chat button in the navigation area on the left side of the page.**

   If you still have the Welcome page onscreen (refer to Figure 14-2), you can also click Start a Chat.

2. **In the Add 1 or More People, start typing the name of a person you want to include in the group.**

   Chat displays a list of people in your organization who match what you've entered so far.

3. **When the name of the person you want appears, click that name.**

   Chat adds the person to the list.

4. **Repeat Steps 2 and 3 until you've added all the people you want to the group chat.**

5. **Click Start Chat.**

   Chat opens a chat window for the group.

   REMEMBER

   Chat automatically supplies a name for the chat, which is usually the first names of the first few participants.

6. **Enter your message in the text box that's provided.**

7. **Click the send message icon or press Enter or Return.**

   Chat distributes the message to each person in the group.

8. **Read the responses you get from the other members.**

9. **Repeat Steps 6 through 8 as needed.**

TIP

To add people to the group chat, click the group name at the top of the chat window, and then choose Add People. In the Add People or Groups dialog that appears, start typing the name of a person you want to add to the group. Then, when the name of the person you want appears, click that name. Repeat as needed if you want to add multiple people, and then click Add.

Uploading a file to a chat

If you want your chat mate (or mates) to examine a file, you can upload the file into the chat, where anyone can then select the file to view it. Note that you can upload any file to the chat, not just files you created in a Google Workspace app.

Here are the steps required to upload a file midchat:

1. **In the chat text box, type a message explaining that you're going to upload a file.**

2. **Click the upload file icon.**

   Chat displays the Open dialog.

3. **Select the file you want to upload, and then click Open.**

   Chat adds the file to your message.

4. **Click the send message icon or press Enter or Return.**

   Chat adds a thumbnail image of the file to the chat transcript, as shown in Figure 14-7.

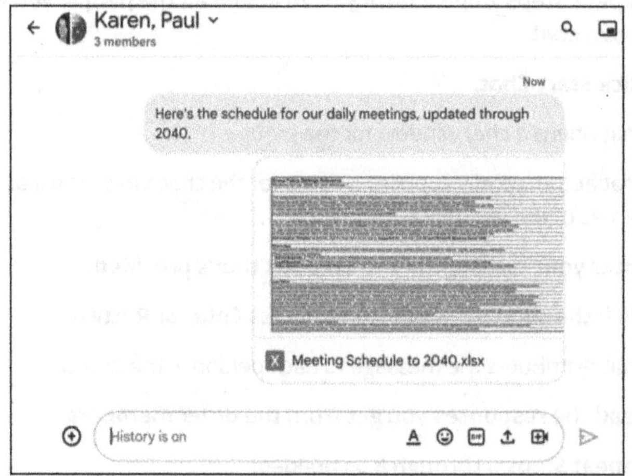

FIGURE 14-7: A file, uploaded to a chat.

Adding a video meeting to a chat

A common chat scenario is to be mid-conversation and realize that you need to show or demonstrate something to the other person (or other people, if you're in a group chat). Yep, you can upload a file, as I describe in the preceding section, but that doesn't help if you need to perform some action.

For these and similar scenarios, the best thing to do is to create an on-the-fly Meet video meeting. That enables both you and the other chat participants to quickly join the meeting and view the presentation (or just each other).

Here's what you do to add a Meet video meeting to a chat:

1. **In the chat text box, type a message explaining that you're going to add a video meeting.**

2. **Click the add video meeting icon.**

   Chat adds a link to a new video meeting to your message.

3. **Click the send message icon or press Enter or Return.**

   Chat adds the video meeting link to the chat transcript. Refer to Figure 14-8.

4. **Each person in the chat can click Join Video Meeting and then Join Now.**

   Meet starts the videoconference. If you need more info on using Meet for video conferencing, see Chapter 13.

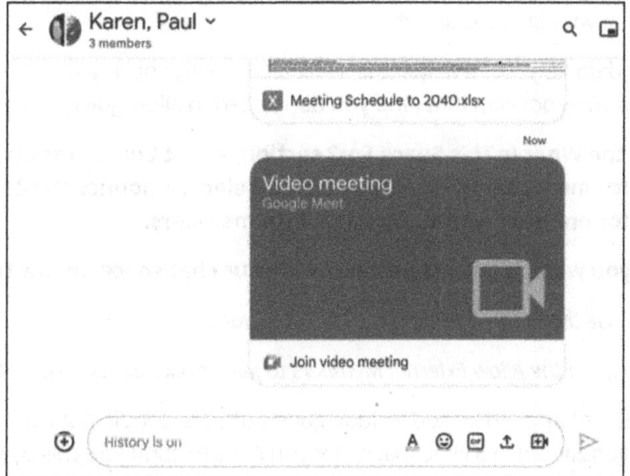

FIGURE 14-8: A video meeting link added to a chat transcript.

More Collaboration: Congregating in a Chat Space

Chat and collaboration combine in a big way with the concept of a *chat space*. This special Chat area enables you to not only exchange messages with your team but also organize those messages into multiple conversation threads, share files and other resources, add chat apps, include people from outside your organization, and more.

Creating a space

When you're ready to build a chat space with your bare hands, follow these steps:

1. **Click the New Chat button in the navigation area on the left side of the page, then click Create a Space in the menu that appears.**

   Alternatively, click Main Menu to open the full navigation menu, click the Spaces heading to open it, and then click Create or Find a Space ⇨ Create a Space.

   Chat opens the Create a Space dialog.

2. **In the Space Name text box, type the name you want to use for your chat space.**

   Space names can be a maximum of 128 characters. Optionally, in the Description text box, you can type a short (up to 150 characters) summary of what your space is about.

   By default, your new space is available to everyone in your entire organization. If you're cool with that (and you don't need to allow guests), skip to Step 7.

3. **In the What Is This Space For? section, select Collaboration if your space is for members to work together or select Announcements if your space is for one-way communication with members.**

4. **If you want to allow guests to join your chat space, follow these substeps:**

   a. *Use the Access Settings list to select Private.*

   b. *Select the Allow External Members to Join check box, as shown in Figure 14-9.*

REMEMBER

   Chat is happy to let you include guests (that is, people not from your organization) in a chat space, but you have to configure this by selecting the Allow People Outside Your Organization to Join check box. If you leave this check box deselected, there's no way to reconfigure the space later to allow people from outside your organization to join the space.

5. **Click Create.**

   Chat creates your new space. If you selected the Allow External Members to Join check box in Step 4, External appears to the right of the space name.

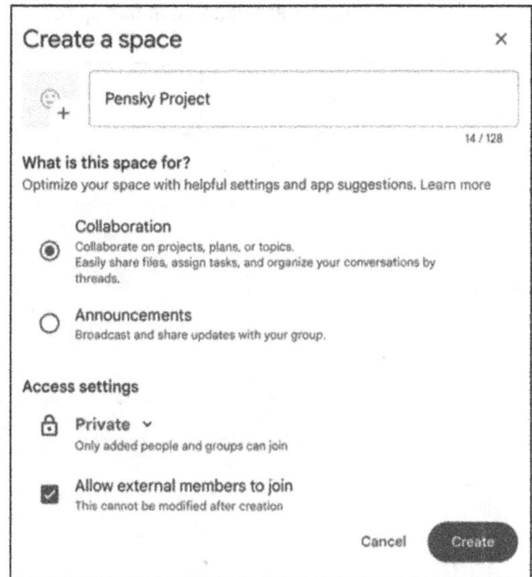

FIGURE 14-9: Configuring the space to allow guests to join in the fun.

Managing a space

Figure 14-10 shows a freshly minted chat space and points out a few features.

Here's a list of the things you can do in your new chat space:

- **Add more people to the space:** Either click the Add Members button, or click the space name at the top of the window and then choose Manage Members ⇨ Add.
- **Send a direct message to a space member:** Click the space name, and then choose Manage Members from the menu that appears to display a list of the space's current members. Click the more options icon to the right of the person you want to message, and then choose Message from the menu that appears.
- **Remove someone from the space:** Click the space name, and then choose Manage Members from the menu that appears to display the Members list. Click the more options icon to the right of the person you want to kick out, and then choose Remove from Space from the menu that appears.
- **Change the space name:** Click the space name, choose Space Details from the menu that appears to open the Space Details pane. Modify the space name in the text box and then click Save.

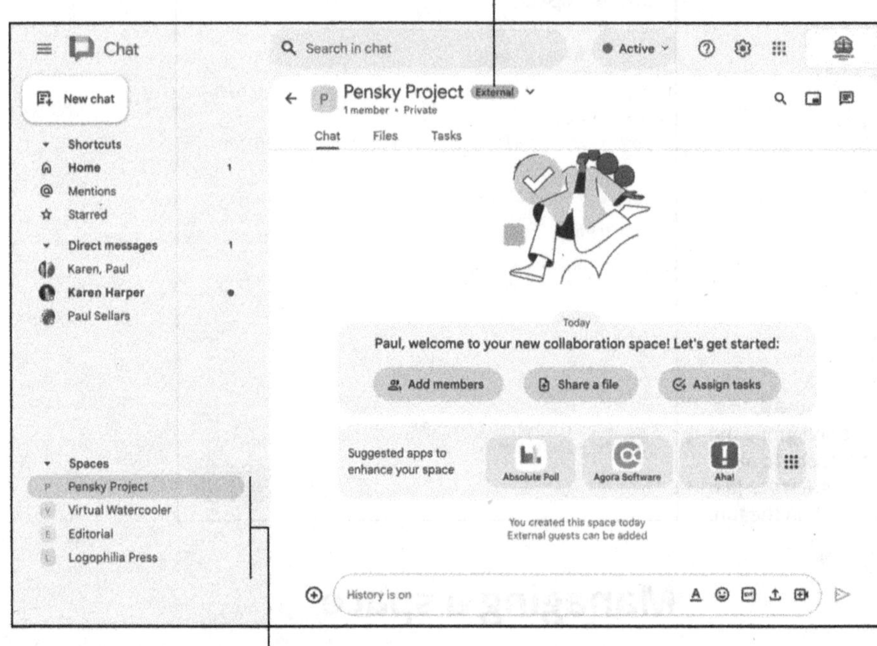

FIGURE 14-10: A brand-new chat space, ready for the team.

- **Promoting a member to space manager:** Click the space name, and then choose Manage Members to display the Members list. Click the more options icon to the right of the person you want to anoint, and then choose Make Space Manager from the menu that appears. Note that you and this person are now both space managers (that is, it's okay to have multiple space managers).
- **Changing space settings:** Click the space name, and then choose Space Settings to display the configuration options for the space. Make your changes and then click Save.
- **Sharing a file:** Either click Share a File in the Chat tab, or click the Files tab and then click Add File. Either way, the Select an Item dialog appears. Select a file from your Google Drive or your computer, and then click Insert.
- **Assigning a task:** Either click Assign Tasks in the Chat tab, or click the Tasks tab and then click Add Space Task. Either way, fill in the details for the task and then click Add.
- **Leaving the space:** Click the space name, choose Leave from the menu that appears, and then click the Leave button when Chat asks you to confirm. (If you're the space manager, before you leave the space you must assign

another member to be the manager. Click the space name, click Manage Members, click the more options icon to the right of the person you want to promote, and then click Make Space Manager.)

- **Rejoining a space:** Click the New Chat button, click Browse Spaces from the menu that appears, and then click the space's join icon (+). Note that, by default, Chat shows only spaces you've never joined, so you won't see the space you want to rejoin. Click the first drop-down list (the one with Spaces I Haven't Joined as the currently selected value), and then click either All Spaces or Spaces I Have Joined.
- **Deleting the space:** Click the space name, choose Delete from the menu that appears, and then click the Delete button when Chat asks if you're sure you know what you're doing.

Joining an existing space

The usual way you get access to a space is when the space manager (usually the person who created the space) adds you. However, if the space is open to the entire organization, you can join the space yourself by following these steps:

1. **Click the New Chat button.**
2. **Click Browse Spaces.**

   The Browse Spaces page appears and displays a list of the spaces you haven't joined.

TIP

   To get a sneak peek at a space before joining it, click the space's Preview button.
3. **Locate the space you want to crash and then click the space's Join button.**

   Chat makes you a member of the space.

IN THIS CHAPTER

» Checking out Google Groups for yourself

» Understanding group roles

» Joining groups that will have you as a member

» Posting and replying to group messages

» Creating your own groups for fun and (no) profit

Chapter 15 Collaborating with Groups

Workers in the modern world are almost always part of some larger collective. The word most often used these days for such a collective is a *team*, but employees can also be part of a department, a section, a unit, a task force, a committee, or even a crew. Whatever moniker they use, they're all *groups* of employees who are connected in some way.

That connection is crucial because it means that these collections of employees are working on a common cause, such as a project or product. In short, the employees in a collection need to collaborate with each other, and that collaboration is where Google Groups comes in. When you add employees to a group, a whole new world of collaborative tools becomes available. In this chapter, you explore these collaboration features and learn how they can make your team (or whatever) more efficient and more cohesive.

Why Create a Group?

With so many other Google Workspace collaboration tools at your disposal, why bother with Google Groups? The simple answer is that when you create a group and then add the connected employees to that group, collaboration suddenly becomes much easier. Why? Because now you can treat the group as a single entity, which means you can communicate with everyone in the group just by communicating with the group itself. Here are some examples:

- You can email everyone in a group by sending the email to the group's email alias.
- You can invite everyone in a group to a Calendar event by adding the group to the event's guest list.
- You can ask everyone in a group to collaborate on a file by sharing that file with the group.
- You can invite an entire group to a chat room by making the group a member of the room.
- You can use the group's online forum to have group discussions.

Sure, none of these examples is a big deal if you're only talking about 2 or 3 employees. But if a group contains 20 or 30 employees, or 200 or 300, dealing with just the group rather than all those individuals is a timesaver.

Investigating the Groups Home Page

Are you intrigued by Groups? Curious? Just want to get it over with? Whatever your state of mind, you can use either of the following techniques to take yourself to the Groups home page:

- Whistle for your favorite web browser and then ask it to load `https://groups.google.com`.
- In a Google Workspace app that has the Google Apps icon (such as Calendar or Docs), click Google Apps and then click Groups.

The Groups home page that materializes out of the ether will probably display the message *You are not a member of any groups yet.* Once you are a member of one or more groups (refer to "Joining a Group," a tad later in this chapter), the Groups home page will be similar to the page shown in Figure 15-1. The My Groups section is a list of the groups in which you're a member.

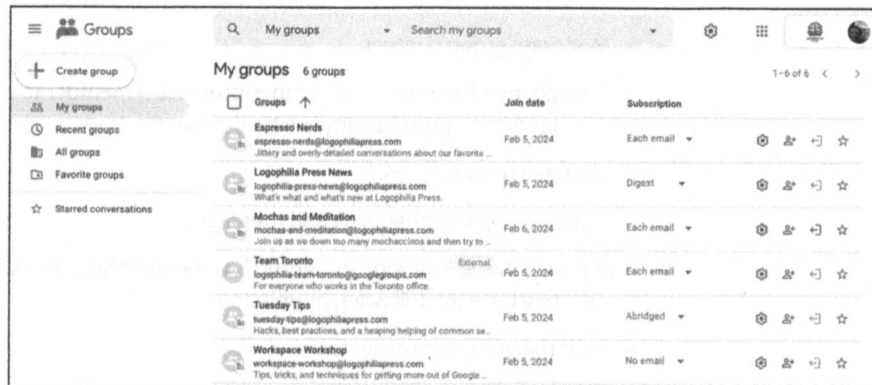

FIGURE 15-1: The Groups home page lists the groups in which you're a member.

Understanding Group Roles

When you work with groups, particularly if you create your own groups, you constantly bump up against the idea of who does what in a group and what permissions each of these roles has. There are four roles to consider in any group:

- **Group owners:** The owner of the group is the person who created the group. However, that person can also assign the owner role to other people. The owner role has the following default permissions:
  - All member permissions (refer to the "Group members" entry).
  - Post original messages and replies as the group (that is, by using the group's email address).
  - Add or remove group members, managers, and owners.
  - Moderate group content.
  - Change member roles (for example, promote a manager to an owner).
  - Change group settings.
  - Delete the group.
  - Export group memberships and messages.
- **Group managers:** The manager role has the following default permissions:
  - All member permissions (refer to the "Group members" entry).
  - Post original messages and replies as the group (that is, by using the group's email address).
  - Add or remove group members and managers (but not owners).

    - Moderate group content.
    - Change member roles (for example, promote a member to a manager; managers can't promote anyone to an owner).
    - Change group settings.
    - Export group memberships and messages.
- **Group members:** Everyone in a group has the member role by default, which means they have the following permissions:
    - View the group's messages.
    - Post messages to the group.
    - Post private replies to the author of a message.
    - Moderate post metadata (such as assigning topics).
    - Send files to the group.
    - View the group's membership list.
- **Entire organization (internal groups only):** Everyone in your Google Workspace organization, even folks who aren't members of the group, have the following permissions by default:
    - View the group's messages.
    - Post messages to the group.
    - Contact the group owners.
    - View the group's membership list.

REMEMBER

An *internal group* is one where all the members come from your organization and nobody outside the organization is allowed to join. An *external group* is one where people from both inside and outside the organization are allowed to join.

- **Anyone on the web (external groups only):** Everyone who has web access has just the following permission by default:
    - Contact the group owners.

If you're a group owner or manager, you can make changes to any of these permissions by following these steps:

1. **Click the Group Settings icon to the right of the group you want to work with.**

   If you don't see the Group Settings icon, click the more icon to the right of the group you want to work with, and then click Group Settings in the menu that appears.

Or click the group to open it, and then click Group Settings in the main menu.

The settings page for the group appears.

2. **For each of the following permission settings (the first few of which are shown in Figure 15-2), click the role that you want to assign: Group Owners, Group Managers, Group Members, or either Entire Organization (for internal groups) or Anyone on the Web (for external groups):**
   - *Who can view conversations?*
   - *Who can post?*
   - *Who can view members?*
   - *Who can manage members?*
   - *Who can modify custom roles?*
   - *Who can contact the group owners?*
   - *Who can view member email addresses?*
   - *Who can reply privately to authors?*
   - *Who can attach files?*
   - *Who can moderate content?*

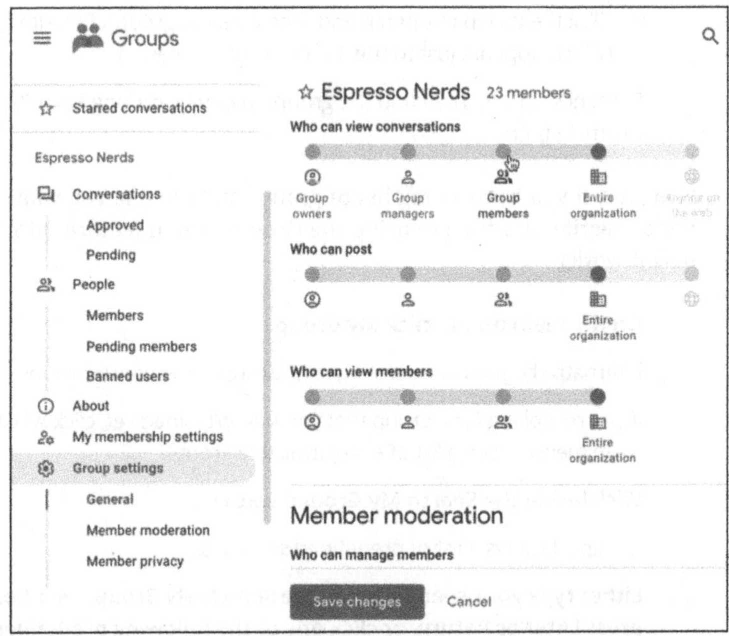

FIGURE 15-2: In the group's settings page, assign roles to each permission.

- *Who can moderate metadata?*
- *Who can post as the group?*

3. **Click Save Changes.**

   Groups applies the new roles to each permission you modified.

Finding a Group

If you own or have joined just a few groups, locating the group you want isn't too much of a bother. That is, you click My Groups on the Groups main menu and then click the group you want in the list that appears. Even if your My Groups list is quite long, you can do a couple of things to make finding a particular group easier:

» If you joined or created the group relatively recently, click Recent Groups on the main menu.

» If you access the group frequently, favorite the group by using either of the following techniques:

- Click the group's more icon and then click Favorite Group in the menu that appears.
- Click the group to open it and then click the group's favorite group icon (which appears just to the left of the group name).

From now on, you can find the group quickly by clicking Favorite Groups on the main menu.

However, if you have a long list of groups and the one you want is neither recent nor a favorite, it's time to bring the Groups search feature into the game. Here's how it works:

1. **On the main menu, click My Groups.**

   Alternatively, you can search Recent Groups or Favorite Groups.

   If you're looking for a group that you haven't joined yet, click All Groups on the main menu to see a list of every available group.

2. **Click inside the Search My Groups text box.**

   Groups displays a list of predefined searches.

3. **Either type your search text in the Search My Groups text box and then press Enter or Return, or click one of the following predefined searches:**

- *Groups I Own/Manage:* Searches for the groups that you own or for which you're a manager.
- *Groups Within Org:* Searches for only internal groups.
- *Groups Outside Org:* Searches for only external groups.
- *Joined Within a Day:* Searches for all the groups that you joined within the past 24 hours.
- *Joined Within a Week:* Searches for all the groups that you joined within the past seven days.

Groups displays a list of groups that match your criteria.

Joining a Group

Once you've located a group that sounds promising, it's time to join the group and get involved. Wait — not so fast! Joining a group isn't as straightforward as you might think. How you join (and even *whether* you can join) depends on how the group owner configured the group's Who Can Join Group setting. You have to consider three possibilities: Join a group directly, ask to join a group, or wait to be contacted by the owner if the group is invitation-only.

For the last of these possibilities, there's not much you can do except wait to receive an invitation. I cover the other two possibilities in the next two sections.

Joining a group directly

If the owner has configured the group's Who Can Join Group setting to Anyone in the Organization Can Join, it means that anyone in the group's organization can join directly. Here are the steps required to join such a group directly:

1. **In the group search results or the All Groups list (for the latter, click All Groups on the main menu), click the group you want to join.**
2. **Click the Join Group button, shown in Figure 15-3.**

   The Join *Name* dialog appears, where *Name* is the group's name. Figure 15-4 shows an example.
3. **If you don't want group members to view your Google Workspace profile, deselect the Link to My Google Account Profile check box.**

☆ Mochas and Meditation 13 members Join group

FIGURE 15-3: The Join Group button appears for groups you can join directly.

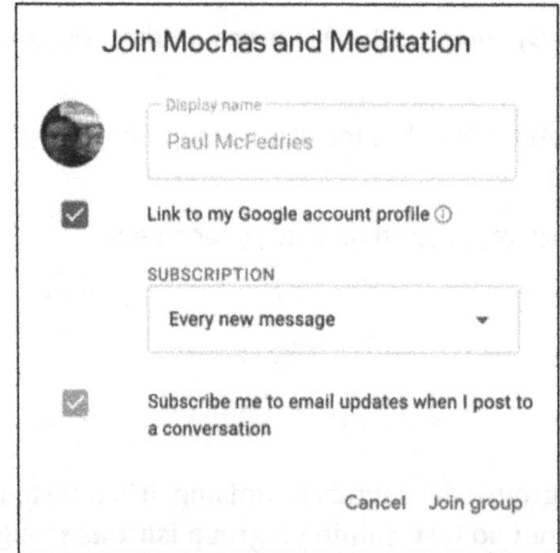

FIGURE 15-4: Fill in this dialog to join the group.

4. **If you elected to not link to your Google account in Step 3, the Display Name text box is enabled, and you can use that text box to specify a different display name to use in this group.**

5. **In the Subscription list, select how you want group emails delivered to you:**

   - *Every new message:* You receive all the group's messages, emailed individually as they're posted to the group.
   - *Send daily summaries:* You receive up to 25 complete messages combined into a single email and delivered once per day.
   - *Combined updates:* You receive abridged versions of up to 150 messages combined into a single email and delivered once per day.
   - *Don't send email updates:* You receive no email messages from the group.

6. **Click the Join Group button.**

   Groups adds you as a member of the group.

Asking to join a group

If the owner has configured the group's Who Can Join Group setting to Anyone in the Organization Can Ask, it means that anyone in the group's organization can ask the owner whether they can join. (Any group owner or manager can approve the join request.) Here are the steps to follow to ask to join such a group:

1. **In the group search results or the All Groups list (for the latter, click All Groups on the main menu), click the group you want to join.**
2. **Click the Ask to Join Group button, shown in Figure 15-5.**

   The Ask to Join *Name* dialog appears, where *Name* is the group's name. Figure 15-6 shows an example.
3. **If you don't want group members to view your Google Workspace profile, deselect the Link to My Google Account Profile check box.**
4. **If you elected to not link to your Google account in Step 3, the Display Name text box is enabled and you can use that text box to specify a different display name to use in this group.**

☆ The Slush Pile 11 members Ask to join group

FIGURE 15-5: The Apply to Join Group button appears for groups you have to ask to join.

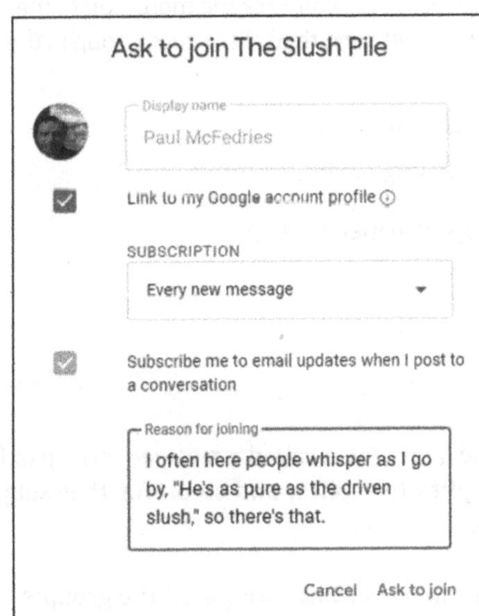

FIGURE 15-6: Fill in this dialog to ask to join the group.

5. **In the Subscription list, select how you want group emails delivered to you.**

   Refer to Step 5 in the preceding section for the details about each option.

6. **In the Reason for Joining text box, provide one or more reasons why you should be allowed to join the group.**
7. **Click the Ask to Join button.**

   Groups sends your request to the group, where it will be reviewed by the group's owners and/or managers and either approved or rejected.

Leaving a group

If you find that a particular group's conversations have become tiresome, annoying, useless, or all of the above, you're free to leave at any time. Here's what you need to do:

1. **On the main menu, click My Groups.**

   Alternatively, you can click Recent Groups or (unlikely, given the circumstances) Favorite Groups.

2. **Click the group's leave group icon.**

   If you don't see the leave group icon, click the more icon to the right of the group you want to work with, and then click Leave Group in the menu that appears.

   Groups asks you to confirm.

3. **Click the Yes, Leave Group button.**

   Groups revokes your group membership.

Posting Messages

In a group, you can send a *post* (also called a *message*) on a particular subject. The collection of replies, replies to replies, and so on for that subject is known as a *conversation* (or a *topic*).

It's possible that the group owner has configured the group's permissions to not allow posts from certain cohorts, such as members. If you open a group and the New Conversation button (refer to the steps that follow) is disabled, it means you don't have posting permission for the group.

Here are the steps involved in starting a new conversation in a group:

1. **Navigate to the group where you want your post to appear.**
2. **On the main menu, click New Conversation.**

   If there are no conversations in the group, click the Start a Conversation link instead.

   If the New Conversation button (or the Start a Conversation link) is disabled, it means you don't have permission to post to the group.
3. **In the Subject text box, type a title for the conversation.**
4. **In the large text box, type your message.**
5. **Click the Post Message button.**

   Groups sends your message to the group.

Responding to Posts

If someone has started a conversation and you want to chime in, no problem. Just follow these steps:

1. **Navigate to the group where you want your reply to appear.**
2. **Click the conversation that includes the post you want to respond to.**
3. **Click the post you want to respond to.**

   Groups assumes that you want to reply to the most recent post, so you can skip this step if that's the post you're responding to.
4. **Select the type of reply you want to make:**
   - *Reply All:* Click this button to send your response to the group.
   - *Reply to Author:* Click this button to send an email response to the person who sent the post. If you're replying to a post other than the most recent one, you must first click the post's more icon (three vertical dots) and then click Reply to Author.
5. **In the large text box, type your message.**
6. **Click the Post Message button.**

   Groups sends your reply.

Creating a Group

Joining existing groups is all well and good, but if you're getting a project off the ground, organizing an event, leading a committee, or doing something new in your organization, you'll want to set up your own group.

Preparing to add a group

Groups makes it easy (if a tad time-consuming) to forge fresh groups, but before you dive in, you should ask yourself (and, ideally, answer) a few questions:

- **What name should I give the group?** You need a name that's both descriptive and an accurate reflection of the group's purpose.
- **Do I want multiple owners?** If one or more colleagues are running the project, event, or whatever alongside you, you probably want those people to also be owners of the group.
- **Do I want group managers?** If you expect your group to be busy, you can save oodles of time by sharing the burden of managing the group with a manager or two.
- **How do I want to add people to the group?** You can add people directly, which means that once you specify someone's name or email address, that person is automatically a group member; alternatively, you can invite people to join. The latter is the way to go if you want to give people the option of joining.

Creating the group

When you're good and ready to proceed, follow these steps to create your group:

1. **Surf to `https://groups.google.com`.**
2. **On the main menu, click Create Group.**

   Groups displays the Enter Group Info page.
3. **In the Group Name text box, type an identifier for the group.**

   The name can be up to 73 characters long.

   Groups uses the name to populate the Group Email field by replacing spaces with hyphens and by removing most nonalphanumeric characters (except hyphens and underscores) that would be illegal in an email address. Figure 15-7 shows an example.

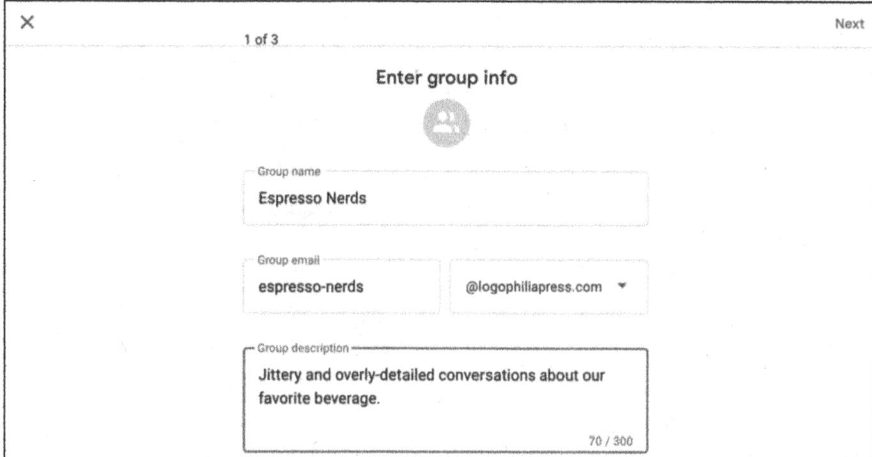

FIGURE 15-7: Enter a group name and Groups automatically populates the Group Email field.

4. **If the email address proposed by Groups rubs you the wrong way for some reason, click in the Group Email text box and edit the name to put your mind at ease.**

   Bear in mind that this part of the group email address can't be any longer than 63 characters.

   In the list to the right of the Group Email text box, you can select either your organization's domain name or `@googlegroups.com`. Which one to choose? Use your organization's domain if only people from your organization will be members of your group; if your group will have people from outside your organization, the `@googlegroups.com` domain is the way to go.

5. **In the Group Description text box, type a short description of the group's purpose, content, members, or whatever.**
6. **Click Next.**

   Groups displays the Choose Privacy Settings page, as shown in Figure 15-8.

7. **Set the new group's privacy settings:**
   - *Who can search for group (external groups only):* Select who is allowed to find the group via search: Group Members or Anyone on the Web.
   - *Who can join group:* Select who is allowed to join the group. The default is Anyone in the Organization Can Join, which means that any Tom, Dick, and Harriet in your organization can add themselves to the group directly; if you prefer that people in your organization must ask to join (that is, they can't add themselves directly), click Anyone in the Organization Can Ask; finally, if you want people to join your group by invitation only (that is, folks can't add themselves directly or even ask to join), click Only Invited Users.

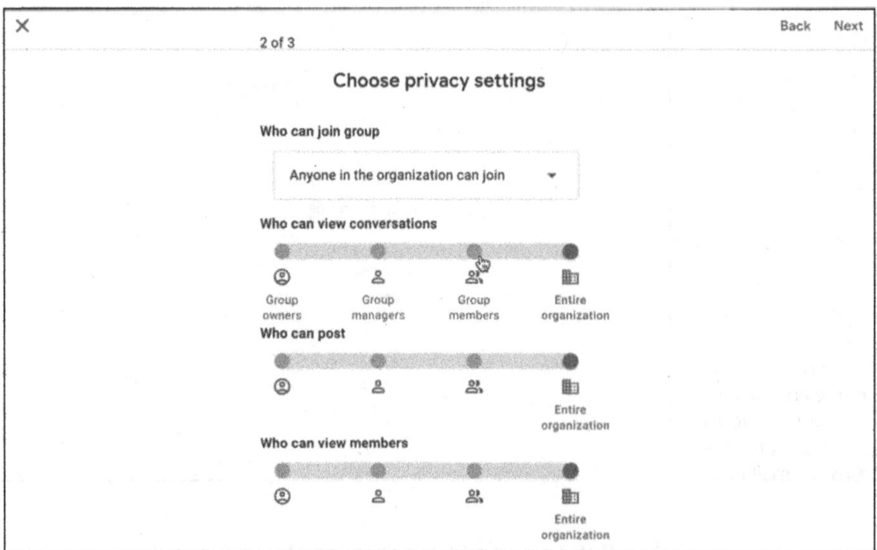

FIGURE 15-8: Use this page to set your group's main privacy permissions.

- *Who can view conversations:* Select which category of users can view your group's conversations. By default, Entire Organization is selected for an internal group and Group Members is selected for an external group. If your group contains sensitive or not-ready-for-prime-time material, consider selecting Group Members for an internal group.
- *Who can post:* Select which categories of users can post messages to your group's conversations. By default, Entire Organization is selected for an internal group and Group Members is selected for an external group. If you want to restrict posting to members, consider selecting the Group Members category for an internal group. If your group posts only announcements, you'll want to select either Group Owners or Group Managers.
- *Who can view members:* Select which categories of users can view your group's membership list. By default, Entire Organization is selected for an internal group and Group Members is selected for an external group. If you want to keep your group membership within the group itself, consider selecting the Group Members category for an internal group. If you don't even want members to see the list, select either Group Owners or Group Managers.

8. **Click Next.**

   Groups displays the Add Members page, as shown in Figure 15-9.

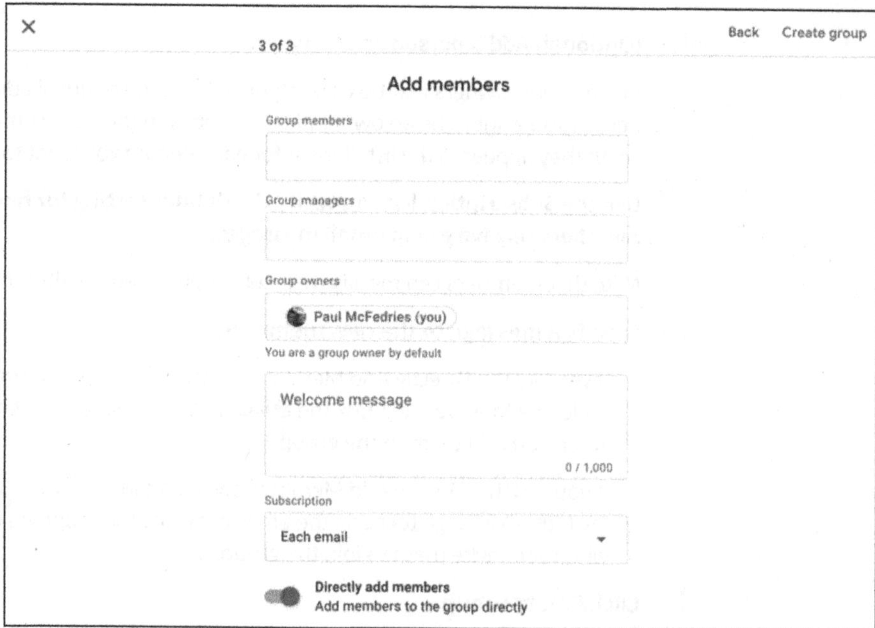

FIGURE 15-9: Use this page to add members to your group.

9. **Add a person as a member.**

   In the Group Members text box, start typing the name or email address of someone you want to be a member of the group, and then select that person when they appear in the list. Repeat for each person you want to be a member.

10. **Decide whether to add members directly or by invitation:**

   - *If you want to add members directly to the group,* slide the Directly Add Members switch on.
   - *If you want to invite members to join the group,* click the Directly Add Members switch off. If you change Directly Add Members to off, Groups hides the Group Managers, Groups Owners, and Subscription controls, so skip to Step 14.

11. **(Optional) Add a person as a manager.**

   In the Group Managers text box, start typing the name or email address of a person you want to be a manager of the group, and then select that person when they appear in the list. Repeat for each person you want to be a manager.

12. **(Optional) Add a person as an owner.**

    In the Group Owners text box, start typing the name or email address of a person you want to be an owner of the group, and then select that person when they appear in the list. Repeat for each person you want to be an owner.

13. **Use the Subscription list to specify the default setting for how new members receive group email messages.**

    Note that members can modify their subscription setting after they join.

14. **Specify a message to the new members:**

    - If you slid the Directly Add Members switch on in Step 10, enter in the Welcome Message text box the email message that appears to members when you add them to the group.
    - If you slid the Directly Add Members switch off in Step 10, enter in the Invitation Message text box the email message that appears to members when you invite them to join the group.

15. **Click Create Group.**

    Groups, at long last, creates your new group. When it's done, Groups displays a dialog to let you know the good news.

16. **Click Go to Group.**

    Groups opens your new group.

Adding more people directly to the group

You can directly add up to ten people at a time to your group by following these steps:

1. **Navigate to your group.**
2. **Choose Members on the navigation menu that runs down the left side of the screen.**

    Groups displays a list of your group's members.

3. **Click the Add Members button.**

    Groups displays the Add Members dialog.

4. **Slide the Directly Add Members switch on.**

    This switch is on by default, but it's best to make sure.

5. **Add a person to be a member.**

In the Group Members text box, start typing the name or email address of someone you want to be a member of the group, and then select that person when they appear in the list. Repeat for each person you want to be a member.

6. **(Optional) Add a person as a manager.**

   In the Group Managers text box, start typing the name or email address of a person you want to be a manager of the group, and then select that person when they appear in the list. Repeat for each person you want to be a manager.

7. **(Optional) Add a person as an owner.**

   In the Group Owners text box, start typing the name or email address of a person you want to be an owner of the group, then select that person when they appear in the list. Repeat for each person you want to be an owner.

8. **(Optional) Enter a welcome message.**

   This message appears in the email that new members receive to let them know they've been added to your group.

9. **Use the Subscription list to specify the default setting for how new members receive group email messages.**

10. **Click the Add Members button.**

    Groups adds the new members and sends them email notifications.

Inviting people to your group

If your group operates by invitation-only, follow these steps to invite more people to join:

1. **Navigate to your group.**

2. **Choose Members on the navigation menu that runs down the left side of the screen.**

   Groups displays a list of your group's members.

3. **Click the Add Members button.**

   Groups displays the Add Members dialog.

4. **Slide the Directly Add Members switch off.**

5. **Add a person as a member.**

   In the Group Members text box, start typing the name or email address of someone you want to invite to be a member of the group, and then select that person when they appear in the list. Repeat for each person you want to invite to be a member.

6. **(Optional) Enter an invitation message.**

   This message appears in the email that prospective members receive to invite them to join your group.

7. **Click the Send Invites button.**

   Groups sends out the group invitations.

Managing group requests and invitations

If your group is configured either to allow people to ask to join or as invitation-only, you need to stay on top of those requests and invitations. Here's how to manage group requests and invitations:

1. **Navigate to your group.**
2. **Choose Members on the navigation menu that runs down the left side of the screen.**
3. **Click the Pending Members tab.**
4. **In the Join Requests section, you can do either of the following:**
   - *Approve a join request:* Click the approve request icon that appears to the right of the request.
   - *Reject a join request:* Click the reject request icon that appears to the right of the request.
5. **In the Pending Invitations section, you can do any of the following:**
   - *Resend one invitation:* Hover the mouse pointer over the invitation and then click the resend invitation icon.
   - *Resend multiple invitations:* For each invitation you want to resend, hover the mouse pointer over the invitation and then select the invitation's check box. After you've selected the invitations, click the resend invitation icon.
   - *Cancel one invitation:* Hover the mouse pointer over the invitation and then click the cancel invitation icon.
   - *Cancel multiple invitations:* For each invitation you want to rescind, hover the mouse pointer over the invitation and then select the invitation's check box. After you've selected the invitations, click the cancel invitation icon.

IN THIS CHAPTER

» Getting to know the Forms and Keep apps

» Constructing a form to gather information

» Sending out a quiz or survey

» Creating notes that contain text, images, drawings, and more

» Collaborating with other people on forms and notes

Chapter 16
Collaborating with Forms and Notes

This chapter completes my tour of Google Workspace's extensive collaboration tools by taking you on a quick tour of two more apps that enable you to work with people both inside and outside your organization. The first app I investigate is called Forms and, as its name implies, you use it to construct a form that gathers information from people. It might be a form that enables people to register for an event, order a product or service, give feedback about something, take a survey, or test their knowledge with a quiz. Whatever the content of the form, the Forms app gathers the responses automatically so that you can later analyze them.

The second app I discuss in this chapter is called Keep and, as its name doesn't imply, you use it to store relatively simple notes. These notes can include short text snippets, a list of check boxes (for, say, a to-do list), images, drawings, and more.

With both forms and notes, you can split the workload by having multiple people collaborate with you. This chapter tells you everything you need to know.

Gathering Info with Forms

One of the simplest, yet most useful, ways to collaborate with others is to ask them for information. For example, you might ask your customers for feedback about a product or service, or you might ask co-workers for feedback about an event you hosted. Want to know what people think about a topic? Send them a survey. Want to measure how much people know about a subject? Give them a quiz.

"Sounds great," I hear you thinking, but it also sounds like a ton of work. It certainly would be if you had to build the necessary forms with the sweat of your own brow. Fortunately, you can build forms sweat-free with Google Forms. Whether you modify an existing template or construct a form from scratch, Forms makes it easier than you might think to publish professional-looking feedback forms, registration forms, evaluations, surveys, quizzes, and much more.

Loading the Forms website

When you feel up to it, use either of the following techniques to get the Forms home page onscreen:

- Convince your web browser to take you to `https://forms.google.com`. (Note that you actually end up at `https://docs.google.com/forms`, but the first address is shorter to type.)
- If you're in a Google Workspace app that has the Google Apps icon (such as Mail or Calendar), click Google Apps and then click Forms.

Touring the Forms home page

When you first get to Forms, the home page appears, which is similar to the page shown in Figure 16-1.

Let's take a quick trip around the screen so that you know what's what here:

- **Main menu:** Opens the main menu, which gives you access to other Google Workspace apps (such as Docs and Sheets), Settings, and Drive. To close the menu, click any empty space outside the menu.
- **Search:** Searches Forms for the item you want.

- **Google Apps:** Displays icons for all Google apps.

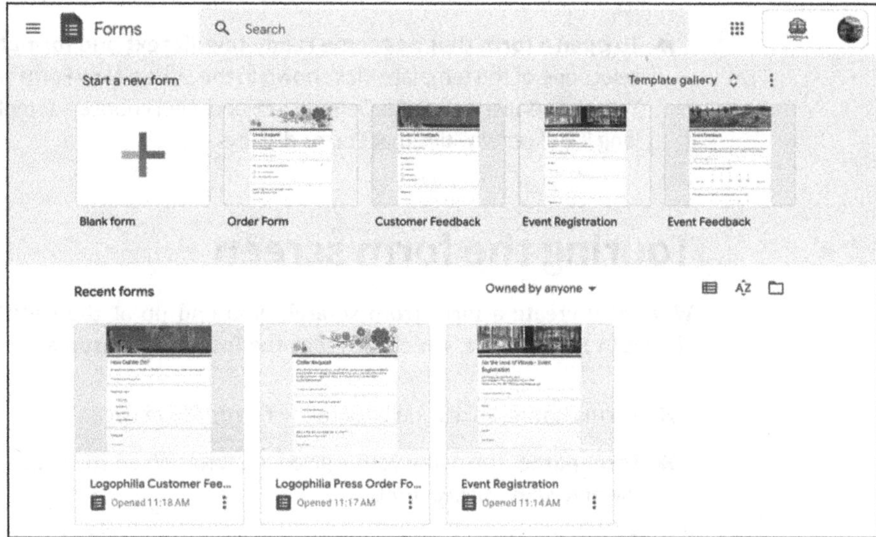

FIGURE 16-1: The home page is your Forms jumping-off point.

- **Start a New Form:** Displays a few templates that you can use to start a new form. A *template* is a document that comes with predefined text, formatting, and (sometimes) images to get you off to a good start.
- **Template gallery**: Displays the complete list of Forms templates.
- **More:** Displays a menu with a single item — Hide All Templates — that, when clicked, hides the Start a New Form section of the home page. (If you hide that section and later change your mind about it, display the main menu, click Settings, select the Display Recent Templates on Home Screens check box, and then click OK.)
- **Recent forms:** Shows you the forms you've worked on most recently.
- **Open file picker:** Displays a dialog that enables you to open a file from Drive or upload a file from your computer.

Creating a form

Once you land on the Forms home page, you'll want to create a form. You have two ways to ask Forms to create a document for you:

- **To open an empty form** (that is, a form with no predefined text or formatting), click Blank Form.

» **To open a form that has some ready-to-edit text and formatting,** either select one of the template tiles shown in the Start a New Form section or click Template Gallery, click the General tab, and then choose a template from the long list of possibilities that Forms displays.

Touring the form screen

When you create a form from scratch, you end up at the Untitled Form screen, shown in Figure 16-2, which includes the following features:

» **Forms home:** Takes you back to the Forms home page.

» **Form name:** The name you've given the form. When you start a new form, the area says *Untitled form.*

» **Customize theme:** Enables you to modify the overall design of the form.

» **Preview:** Enables you to try out the form before sending it.

» **Undo:** Reverses your most recent action.

» **Redo:** Reverses your most recent undo.

» **Send:** Ships out the form when you're done.

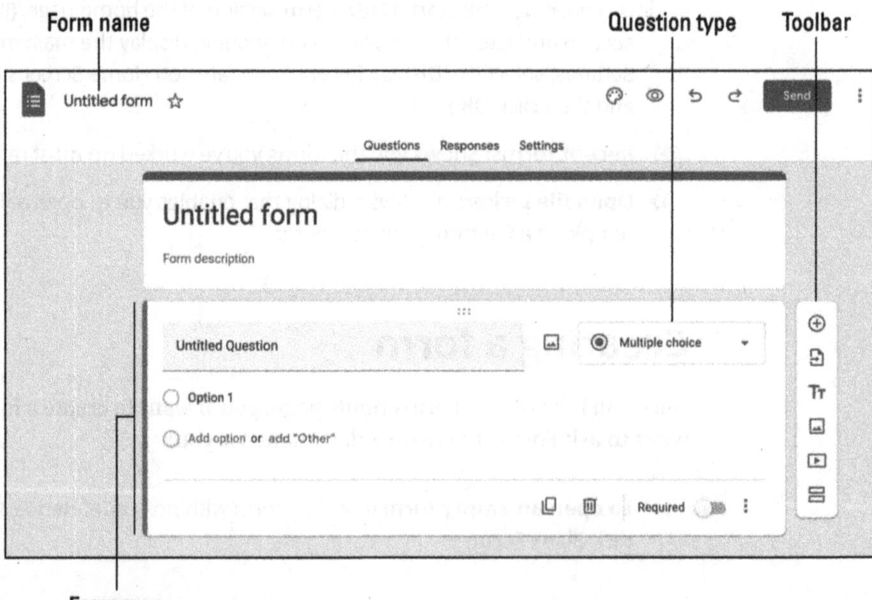

FIGURE 16-2: A new form and the features that surround it.

» **More:** Displays a menu of commands.

» **Untitled form:** The default title that Forms applies to a new, blank form. If you use a template, the default title is the name of the template.

» **Form description:** The default description that Forms applies to a new, blank form. Templates usually come with a description related to the type of template.

» **Form area:** Displays the controls that define your form. A new, blank form offers an initial question and an Option button; a new form based on a template will have a complete form related to the type of template. The form area is where you build and modify your form.

» **Toolbar:** Offers quick access to some useful form features.

Fabricating a form

With your new form waiting for your input, here are the general steps to go through to build a working form:

1. **In the text box that contains the new form's default title (such as *Untitled form*), type a title for the form.**
2. **In the text box that contains the new form's default description (such as *Form description*), type a description for the form.**
3. **Replace the Untitled Question text with the question you want to ask.**
4. **In the question type list (refer to Figure 16-2), select the format of the question.**

   There are 11 question formats in all, including Multiple Choice (respondents choose one out of a group of possible answers), Checkboxes (toggle answers on and off), Dropdown (choose an answer from a list), Short Answer (type a shorter answer), and Paragraph (type a longer answer).

   The response controls that appear depend on the question format. (For example, Multiple Choice uses radio buttons.)

TIP

If you want to reuse questions you added to a previous form, don't enter them from scratch. Instead, click the toolbar's import questions icon (shown in the margin), click the form that contains the questions, and then click Insert.

5. **In the text box that contains the first answer (the default is usually *Option 1*), enter the text for the first answer option, if required by the question format.**
6. **Add more options, as needed for the question.**

7. **Click the toolbar's add question icon.**

For longer forms, or forms that cover multiple subjects, it often helps to break up the form into multiple sections. To add a section to your form, click the add section icon, at the bottom of the toolbar.

8. **Repeat Steps 3–6 for the added question.**
9. **Repeat Steps 7 and 8 until your form is complete.**
10. **Give your new form a trial run by clicking the preview icon.**

Constructing a quiz

If you want your form to be a quiz, you need to make a couple of adjustments:

REMEMBER

» Click the Settings tab and then click the Make This a Quiz toggle on. By default, Forms shows the user their score immediately after they submit the quiz. If you prefer to review the quiz first, select the Later, After Manual Review option. You can now return to the Questions tab to build your quiz.

If you're starting your quiz from scratch, the easiest way to go is to select the Blank Quiz template in the Template Gallery.

» For each question, an Answer Key link now appears. Click Answer Key, set the number of points you want to assign to the question, choose which option is (or options are) the correct answer, and then click Done.

Adding form collaborators

Why build a form yourself when you can cajole other people inside (and outside) your organization to chip in and help? I can't think of a reason! To bring one or more collaborators on board, click the more icon and then click Add Collaborators from the menu that appears. In the dialog that drops by, you have two ways to entice people to work on your form:

» **Share a link:** Click the Copy Responder Link button to copy the address to the clipboard, and then paste the address in an email, a text, a web page, or wherever.

» **Invite people via email:** In the Add People, Groups, and Calendar Events text box, start typing the name or email address of a person you want to invite to collaborate, and then click the person's name when it appears in the list. Repeat as needed until you've selected everyone you want to invite. If you want to include a custom message in your email, enter your text in the Message text box. Click Send to fire off the invitations.

Sending your form

When you've completed and previewed your form (or quiz), it's time to make it available to its respondents. You have three ways to make a form available: email, link, and web page.

REMEMBER

Actually, there's a fourth way to share your form: via social media. As pointed out in Figure 16-3, you can click either the Facebook icon or the X (formerly Twitter) icon to share a link to your form on those sites.

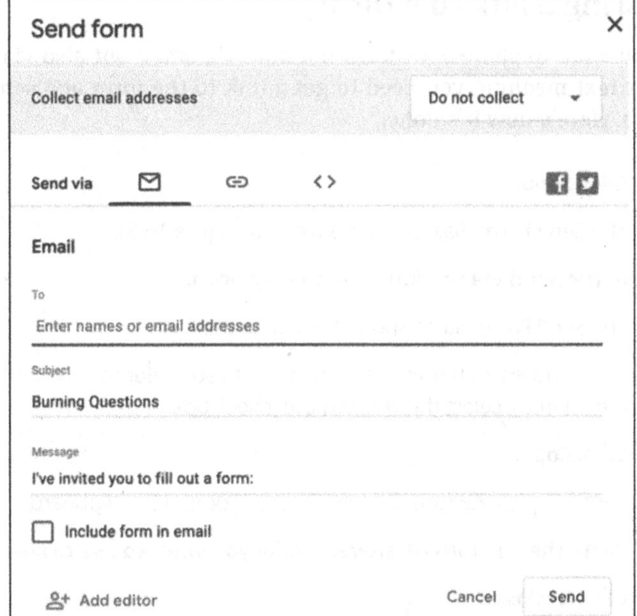

FIGURE 16-3: In the Send Form dialog, use the Email interface to share your form via email.

Emailing a form

If you want only select people in your organization to fill out the form, send the form via email by following these steps:

1. **Click Send.**

   The Send Form dialog appears (refer to Figure 16-3).

2. **In the Send Via section, click the email icon.**
3. **In the To field, start typing the name or email address of a person or group you want to fill out the form, and then click the person's name when it appears in the list.**

4. **Repeat Step 3 as needed until you've selected everyone you want to fill out the form.**
5. **(Optional) Edit the Subject line, if needed.**
6. **(Optional) Edit the Message field, if you want to.**
7. **Click Send.**

   Forms ships out the email, which includes a Fill Out Form button that users click to go to the form.

Sharing a link to a form

If you want to share your form not only via email but also via text, chat, or any other text medium, you need to get a link to the form and send the link to your peeps. Here's how it's done:

1. **Click Send.**

   The Send Form dialog appears (refer to Figure 16-3).

2. **In the Send Via section, click the link icon.**

   The Send Form dialog shows the link to the form.

   TIP

   Form addresses tend to be quite long. If you prefer to send a shorter version of the address, select the Shorten URL check box.

3. **Click Copy.**

   Forms copies the form address to your computer's clipboard.

4. **Paste the link into whatever media you want to use to share the form.**
5. **Click X (close).**

Embedding the form in a web page

If you want to make your form available to anyone who has access to a particular web page, and you know how (or know someone who knows how) to add HTML to the page, follow these steps to embed the form's HTML code in the page:

1. **Click Send.**

   The Send Form dialog appears (refer to Figure 16-3).

2. **In the Send Via section, click the embed HTML icon.**

   The Send Form dialog shows the HTML code for the form.

3. **In the Width and Height text boxes, specify the dimensions of the frame that holds the form.**
4. **Click the Copy button.**

   Forms copies the form HTML to your computer's clipboard.
5. **Paste the HTML into your web page code.**
6. **Click X (close).**

Checking out the form responses

When your respondents complete your form and click Submit, the submitted forms start showing up on the form's Responses tab. That tab includes a summary of the responses, question-by-question results, and user-by-user responses. You also get a Link to Sheets button to load the responses into a Sheets file for data analysis. Sweet!

Sharing Notes with Keep

A word processing app such as Docs is useful for creating complex and lengthy documents. However, this powerful tool feels like overkill when all you want to do is jot down a few notes or make a to-do list. For these simpler text tasks, the Keep app that comes with Google Workspace is perfect because it offers a simple interface that keeps all your notes together.

Checking out the Keep home page

Are you ready to learn what Keep can do? That's the spirit. Accompanied by an optional fist pump, use either of these techniques to land safely on the Keep home page:

- Whisper the following address into your web browser's ear: `https://keep.google.com`.
- If you're using a Google Workspace app that has the Google Apps icon (such as Forms or Groups), click the icon and then click Keep.

When you're just getting started with Keep, the home page appears as shown in Figure 16-4. (Note that Figure 16-4 shows the Keep home page as it appears in the Google Chrome web browser. Other web browsers might not offer every feature shown here.)

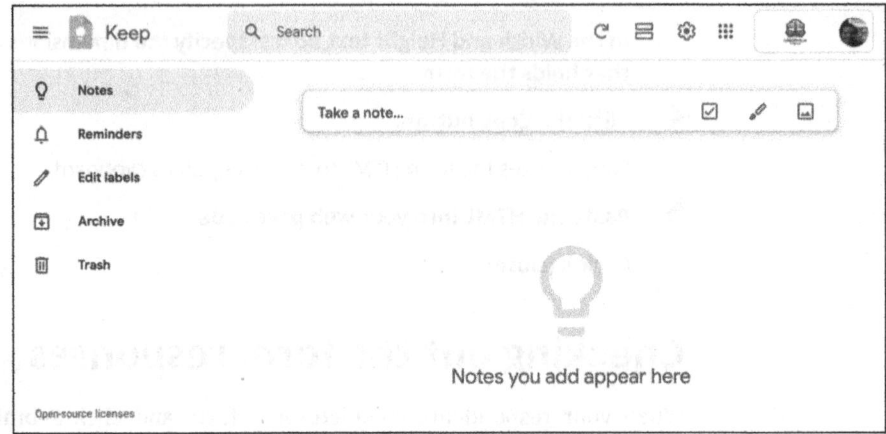

FIGURE 16-4: The Keep home page.

Let's take a quick trip around the screen so that you know what's what here:

- **Main menu:** Click this icon to toggle Keep's Main menu between icons only and icons with titles.
- **Search:** Search Keep for the note you want.

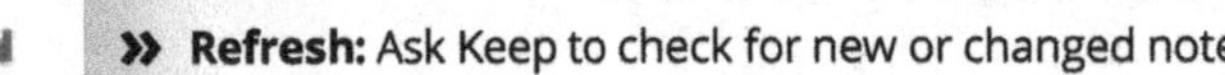

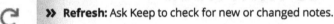

- **Refresh:** Ask Keep to check for new or changed notes.
- **List/grid view:** Toggle the notes display between a list and a grid.
- **Settings:** Display a menu of Keep settings.
- **Google apps:** Display icons for all Google apps.

Creating a new note

As shown in Figure 16-4, the Keep home page includes a box with the text *Take a note* that's awfully tempting. When you can't take it any longer, follow these steps to create a note:

1. **Click inside the Take a Note text box.**

   Keep opens the new note for editing, as shown in Figure 16-5.

2. **In the Title text box, type a title for your note.**
3. **In the Take a Note text box, type your note text.**

FIGURE 16-5: An empty note, yearning to be filled.

4. **To take your note to a higher level, you can add one or more of the following features:**

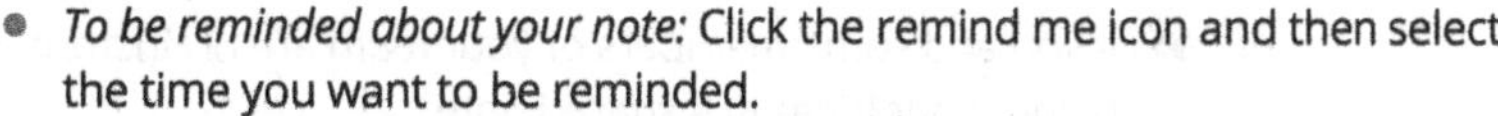

- *To be reminded about your note:* Click the remind me icon and then select the time you want to be reminded.

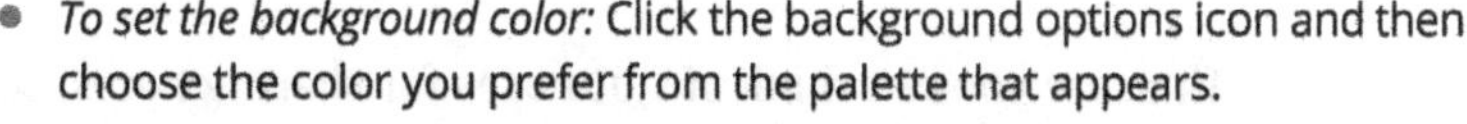

- *To set the background color:* Click the background options icon and then choose the color you prefer from the palette that appears.

- *To insert an image:* Click the add image icon, select the image file in the Open dialog that appears, and then click Open.

- *To add a label:* Click the more icon, choose Add Label from the menu that appears, enter your label name, and then press Enter.
- *To add a drawing:* Click the more icon, choose Add Drawing from the menu that appears, create your drawing in the window that appears, and then click the back icon (left-pointing arrow).
- *To add check boxes:* Click the more icon and choose Show Checkboxes from the menu that appears.

5. **When you're done, click Close.**

   Keep saves your note.

If a note contains information you want to refer to often, or if you know you need to add info to a note frequently, you can keep the note handy by clicking the pin note icon. Keep creates a new Pinned section at the top of the window and adds the note to that section.

If you want to create a note that includes elements other than plain text, Keep gives you three slightly quicker methods to get the note off the ground:

- To start a new note that has a list of check boxes, click the new list icon.

- To start a new note that has a drawing, click the new note with drawing icon.

- To start a new note that has an image, click the new note with image icon.

Adding note collaborators

Notes are such simple affairs that the idea of collaborating on a note might seem odd. However, consider these ideas:

- » If you have no artistic skill whatsoever but a colleague does, it would make sense to ask that colleague to add a drawing to a note.
- » If a colleague has an image you need for a note, the easiest way to use that image would be to add that colleague as a collaborator.
- » If you and some members of your team are brainstorming a topic, you can all record your ideas in a shared note.

I'm sure you can think of 1,001 uses for sharing notes, so here's how you actually do it:

1. **Click the note you want to share.**
2. **Click the collaborator icon.**

   Keep opens the Collaborators dialog.
3. **In the Person or Email to Share With text box, start typing the name or email address of a person you want to invite to collaborate, and then click the person's name when it appears in the list.**
4. **Click the add collaborator icon.**

   You can also press Enter or Return.
5. **Repeat Steps 3 and 4 until you've specified all the collaborators you want to work on your note.**
6. **Click Save.**

   Keep shares the note with the people you specified. For people in your organization or people with a Google account, the note appears automatically in the person's Keep window.

TIP

If someone shares a note with you but you don't want to contribute to the note, you can take yourself off the list of collaborators. Select the note, click the more icon, choose Remove Myself from the menu that appears, and then, when Keep asks you to confirm, click Delete.

4

The Part of Tens

IN THIS PART . . .

Get useful tips for using Google Workspace when working from home.

Take Gmail to the next level.

Beef up your Google Workspace privacy and security settings.

IN THIS CHAPTER

» Keeping sane by defining your working hours and availability

» Staying in touch with remote colleagues

» Adding multiple time zones and clocks to Calendar

» Reading email from more than one account

» Setting up your home video meeting space

Chapter 17 Ten Tips for Working from Home

As I write this edition of the book, The Great Shutdown is slowly fading from our collective memory. I speak, of course, of the entire world coming to a virtual halt to stop — or at least slow down — the spread of the novel coronavirus that emerged in late 2019. Literally overnight, those of us who were used to spending our working days in bustling offices located in faraway skyscrapers were now forced to stay home, quarantined from our colleagues and bosses. Some of us have now returned to those skyscrapers, but for many people, one of the ongoing changes brought about by The Great Shutdown is the opportunity to still work at home, either part-time or full-time.

Being at home means watching Netflix all day, right? Fat chance! No, our work still cries out to get done, and those colleagues and bosses still clamor for our attention. Ah, but working from home isn't as easy as it sounds. Distractions abound, work is no longer bookended by commutes to and from the office, and it's just harder to get things done when the people you rely on or collaborate with are at the office or hunkered down in their own homes. Fortunately, Google

Workspace has your back here. In this chapter, I take you through ten Google Workspace tips and techniques that can help the working-from-home work effectively from home.

Set Your Working Hours

One of the biggest problems with working from home is that the working part of your day doesn't have a set beginning and end. At least when you work at the office, the morning commute acts as a transition into your working day, and the commute home is a signal to your mind and body that the working part of the day is done. (Yes, I know that our modern workdays are really 24/7, but humor me here.) At home, where your commute is, at best, a walk down a hallway or up a flight of stairs, you don't get that same sense of separation between your work life and the rest of your life.

Even worse, your colleagues and managers also have that same lack of work-life boundaries, so they end up sending you requests for meetings and chats pretty much any time of day or night. It's madness!

You can fight back and inject a little sanity into your work-from-home life by setting your *working hours*, which are the days of the week you work and the times on those days that you've set aside for work. Any go-getter without a personal life who tries to invite you to a meeting at some insane time of the morning or evening gets notified that the event occurs outside your working hours, as shown in Figure 17-1.

You set your working hours using the Calendar app:

1. **Navigate to `https://calendar.google.com`.**

   Alternatively, if you're in a Google Workspace app that has the Google apps icon (such as Mail), click Google Apps and then click Calendar.

2. **Click the Settings menu icon and choose Settings.**

3. **On the Settings page that appears, click Working Hours & Location from the navigation menu on the left.**
4. **Select the Enable Working Hours check box.**

   Calendar adds the Working Hours controls for each workday, as shown in Figure 17-2.

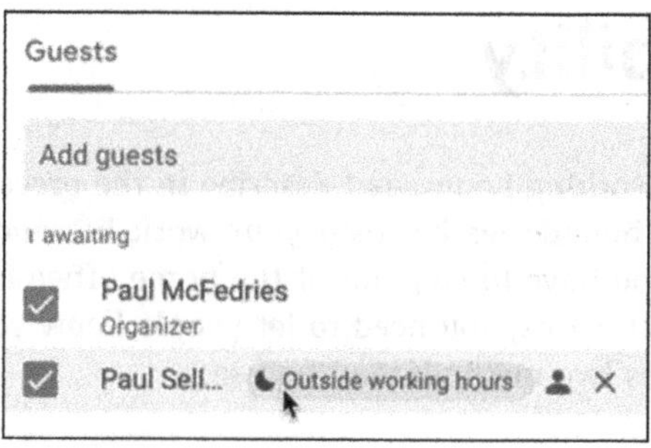

FIGURE 17-1: Calendar lets people know when they're trying to invite you to an event that occurs outside of your working hours.

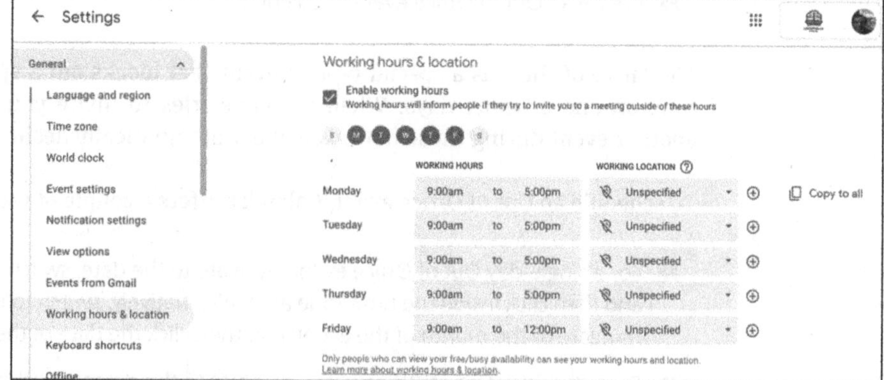

FIGURE 17-2: Define your workdays by specifying your working hours.

5. **Deselect the icon for each day of the week that you don't work.**

   By default, the icons for Saturday and Sunday are deselected.

6. **Using the controls for the first day of your workweek, set the start and end times of your workday.**

7. **To apply the same hours to each of your other workdays, click the Copy to All link.**

   If you work different hours each day, set the start and end times for each workday instead.

REMEMBER

For members of your team to get notified when they try to rope you into an event that's outside your working hours, you must share your calendar with the team. To learn how to share a calendar, check out Chapter 12.

Show Your Availability

Setting your standard working hours, as I describe in the preceding section, is a great start for setting boundaries between your work life and your home life. However, sometimes you have to step out of the home office for a few hours or even a few days. In such cases, you need to let people know you're unavailable. Google Workspace offers two methods you can use:

- Set up a vacation responder in Gmail, as I describe in Chapter 2.
- Create an Out of Office event in Calendar.

The latter of these is a special type of event that blocks out a specified chunk of time on one or more days. When someone tries to invite you to a meeting or another event during those hours, Calendar automatically declines the invitation.

To schedule an Out of Office event, Calendar offers a couple of ways to get started:

- For a single-day Out of Office event, navigate to the date, switch to day view, and then click inside the time zone area. Alternatively, switch to month view, navigate to the month of the event, and then click the date of the event.
- For a multiday Out of Office event, navigate to the dates, switch to week view, and then click-and-drag across the time zone area for each day of the event. Alternatively, switch to month view and then click-and-drag across each day of the event.

Calendar creates a new event and you follow these steps to complete the Out of Office event:

1. **Select the Out of Office tab.**

   Calendar switches to the interface shown in Figure 17-3.

2. **If the Out of Office start time, end time, or both are incorrect, click each incorrect time and then either edit it to the correct time or choose the time you want from the list.**
3. **If you don't want Calendar to decline invitations for you, deselect the Automatically Decline Meetings check box.**
4. **If you scoffed at Step 3 (good for you!), you can use the following options to control how Calendar performs its automatic declines:**
   - *Only New Meeting Invitations:* Select this option to tell Calendar to send out a decline message only when you receive an invitation for a new meeting.

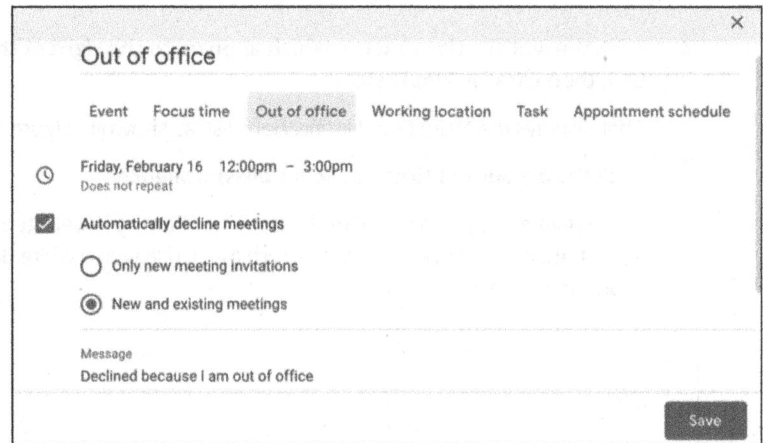

FIGURE 17-3: On the Out of Office tab, set up an Out of Office event in Calendar.

- *New and Existing Meetings:* Select this option to tell Calendar to ship a decline message both for new meetings and for existing meetings.
- *Message:* Use this text box to write the decline message that Calendar sends back to the meeting organizers.

5. **Click Save.**

   If you left the Automatically Decline Meetings check box selected, Calendar asks you to confirm that you want the app to decline meetings on your behalf.

6. **Click Save & Decline.**

   Calendar adds the Out of Office event to the Events area.

Tell Chat to Chill for a While

One of the unique challenges of working from home is that you often have to perform other tasks around the house during work hours: Empty the dishwasher, fill the dishwasher, put in a load of laundry, wax the dog, and so on.

If your co-workers are a chatty bunch, you probably don't want a fistful of chat notifications to come rolling in while you're taking care of the homestead. To silence chat notifications for a while, follow these steps:

1. **Head on over to** `https://chat.google.com` **to open Chat.**

   Alternatively, if you're in a Google Workspace app that has the Google apps icon (such as Mail or Calendar), click the Google apps icon and then click Chat.

2. **Click the Notifications menu, which appears to the right of the search box, then click Do Not Disturb.**

   Chat displays the Mute Chat Notifications list, as shown in Figure 17-4.

3. **Click the amount of time you want blissful silence.**

   Chat activates do not disturb for the amount of time you selected and changes your status from active to do not disturb (red circle with a white dash), as shown in Figure 17-5.

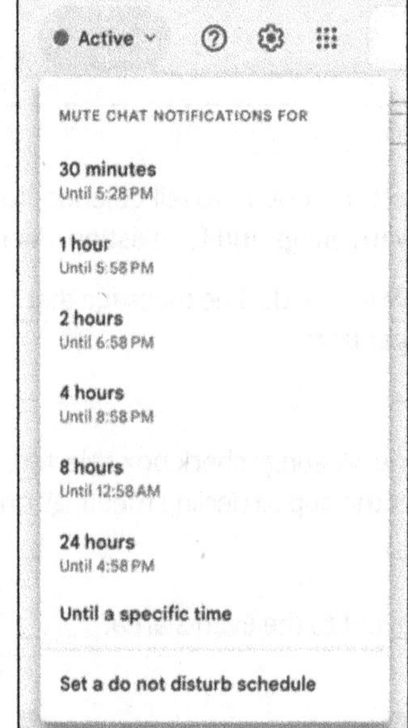

FIGURE 17-4: In the Mute Chat Notifications list, specify how long you want to turn on Do Not Disturb.

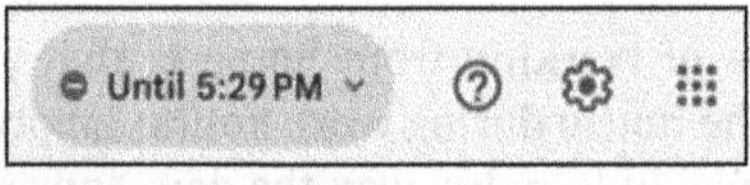

FIGURE 17-5: After you mute notifications, Chat changes your status to do not disturb.

Keep Up the Face-to-Face Communication

When you're at home and everyone you deal with every day is "out there" somewhere, it can be easy to fall into the trap of responding to requests, questions, and discussions using text-based communication channels such as email, messaging, and chat. These methods are convenient and quick but come with a significant downside: When you're out of sight, you're out of mind. That is, communicating with co-workers via only the written word can quickly erode your relationships and can make all your communications feel increasingly impersonal and formal.

How do you prevent your work relationships from going south in this way? Easy: Connect via video as often as you can (or as often as you're comfortable). There's no substitute for face-to-face conversation as a way of staying in the loop, keeping relationships friendly and cordial, and responding empathetically (because you can read facial expressions and hear tone of voice).

Fortunately, Google Workspace makes a video get-together a no-brainer, thanks to Google Meet's easy video meeting setups. To learn more, head over to Chapter 13.

Know Which Communications Tools to Use

Google Workspace gives you lots of ways to reach out to your co-workers, but not every communications tool is right for every task. After all, you wouldn't use a hammer to peel an orange. (At least, I *think* you wouldn't.)

Here are the main Google Workspace communications apps, along with some suggestions about when it's appropriate to use each one:

- **Chat (text):** Useful for short conversations, time-sensitive updates, urgent messages, and quick feedback.
- **Chat (video call):** Useful for conversations that consist of sensitive topics, constructive criticism, or any other matter where facial expressions are important.
- **Groups:** Useful for most day-to-day communications, question-and-answer sessions, status updates, and so on.
- **Meet:** Useful for longer discussions, larger groups, or ad hoc meetings to discuss issues too complex for Groups posts.
- **Gmail:** Useful for longer, more thoughtful, and less time-sensitive messages and replies.

Add Time Zones in Your Calendar

If you have colleagues, customers, or suppliers who work in a different time zone, it's often important to know the correct time in that zone. For example, you probably won't have much luck calling someone at work at 9 a.m. your time if that person lives in a time zone that's three hours behind you. Similarly, if you know that a business colleague leaves work at 5 p.m. and that person works in a time zone that's seven hours ahead of you, you know that any calls you place to that person must occur before 10 a.m. your time.

If you need to be sure about the current time in another time zone, you can customize Calendar's display to show not only your current time but also one or more *world clocks*, each of which displays the current time in another time zone. Follow these steps to add one or more world clocks to Calendar:

1. **Cajole your web browser into displaying** `https://calendar.google.com`**.**

   Alternatively, if you're in a Google Workspace app that has the Google apps icon (such as Mail), choose Google Apps ⇨ Calendar.

2. **Click the Settings menu icon and choose Settings.**
3. **In the World Clock section, select the Show World Clock check box.**
4. **Click the Add Time Zone button.**

   Calendar adds a Time Zone list.
5. **In the Time Zone list, select a time zone you want to display in your world clock.**
6. **To add more world clocks, repeat Steps 4 and 5 as needed.**

   Calendar saves your settings automatically.

Figure 17-6 shows Calendar with a couple of world clocks on the go.

Knowing the current time elsewhere is great, but it's not a big help when it comes to setting up events and meetings. Fortunately, Calendar can help by displaying a second time zone in day view and week view. Here's how to set this up:

1. **Ask your web browser to please take you to** `https://calendar.google.com`**.**

   Alternatively, if you're in a Google Workspace app that has the Google apps icon (such as Mail), choose Google Apps ⇨ Calendar.

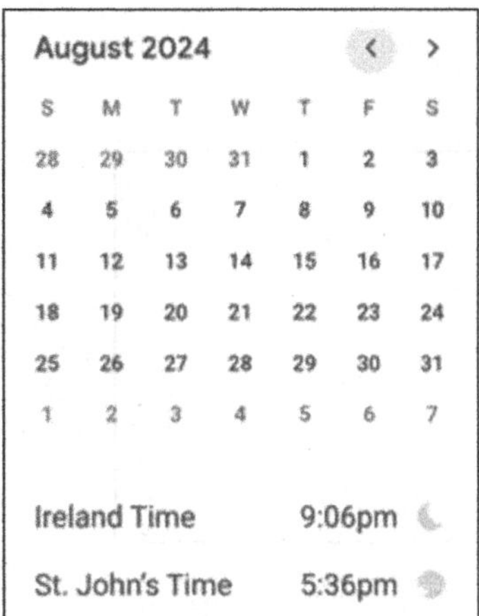

FIGURE 17-6: Calendar, rocking a couple of world clocks.

2. **Click the Settings menu icon and choose Settings.**
3. **In the Time Zone section, select the Display Secondary Time Zone check box.**
4. **In the Label text box to the right of the Primary Time Zone list, type a short name for your main time zone.**

   While you're at it, double-check that the Primary Time Zone list is set to your time zone.
5. **In the Secondary Time Zone list, select the other time zone you want to display.**
6. **In the Label text box to the right of the Secondary Time Zone list, type a short name for the second time zone.**

   Figure 17-7 shows the Time Zone section with a secondary time zone all set up and ready to go. Figure 17-8 shows how the two time zones appear in Calendar (in week view, in this case).

   Calendar saves your settings automatically.

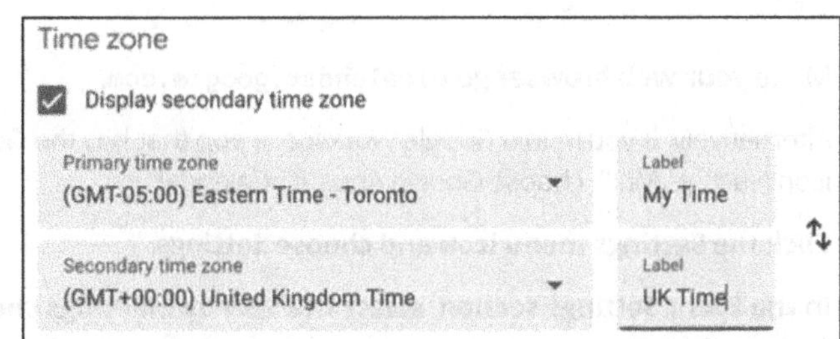

FIGURE 17-7: Calendar's Time Zone settings with a secondary time zone added.

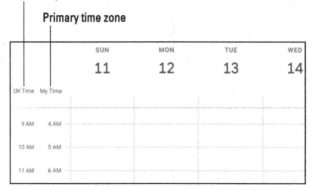

Secondary time zone

Primary time zone

UK Time	My Time	SUN 11	MON 12	TUE 13	WED 14
9 AM	4 AM				
10 AM	5 AM				
11 AM	6 AM				

FIGURE 17-8: How the two time zones appear in week view.

Configure Calendar for Speedy Meetings

The biggest problem with working from home is not only that you have multiple hats to wear — besides your work hat, you might also have a spouse hat, a parent hat, a cook hat, a taking-out-the-garbage hat, and many more — but you also often need to switch from one hat to another throughout the day. That's life in the big city, but you can give yourself a bit more time to change hats by configuring Calendar to schedule slightly shorter meetings by default. Using the Speedy Meetings settings, Calendar automatically schedules meetings as follows:

- *When you create a 30-minute meeting,* Calendar schedules the meeting for just 25 minutes. For example, if you create a 30-minute meeting to start at 3:00 p.m., Calendar schedules the meeting to end at 3:25 p.m.
- *When you create any meeting longer than 30 minutes,* Calendar sets the end time for 10 minutes less than what you selected. (For example, if you select a 60-minute meeting, Calendar schedules it for only 50 minutes.)

I ask you: Who doesn't like shorter meetings? If you're loving the sound of all this, follow these steps to configure Calendar to automatically schedule shorter meetings:

1. **Make your web browser go to `calendar.google.com`.**

   Alternatively, if you're in a Google Workspace app that has the Google apps icon (such as Mail), choose Google Apps ⇨ Calendar.

2. **Click the Settings menu icon and choose Settings.**
3. **In the Event Settings section, select the Speedy Meetings check box.**

   Calendar saves the new setting automatically.

Read Email from Another Account

When you're working from home, you might have to monitor email messages from one or more accounts besides your Gmail account. Normally, monitoring another email account means configuring an email client or accessing a website where that account is configured. However, you can avoid all that hassle by configuring Gmail to check for messages from that account. If Gmail finds any messages on the other server, it helpfully imports them into your Gmail inbox for leisurely reading.

To set up Gmail to check mail from another account, here's a rundown of the information you should have at your fingertips:

- The account email address.
- The username and password for the email account. (Note that in most cases the username is the account email address.)
- The address used by the email provider's incoming mail server. This address often takes the form `mail.`*`provider`*`.com` or pop.*provider*.com, where *provider* is the name of the email provider. Gmail calls this address the *POP server* (POP is short for Post Office Protocol).

  REMEMBER

  A *mail server* is a computer that your ISP uses to store and send your email messages.
- Whether your email provider requires a secure connection to check for and retrieve mail. Secure connections are handled via a protocol called Secure Sockets Layer (SSL).
- Whether the email provider requires you to use a special port number for incoming mail. You can think of a port as a communications channel, and Gmail and your provider must be tuned to the same channel for things to work. If you don't have any info on this, your provider probably uses the standard port number: 110 if you don't use SSL; 995 if you do use SSL.

With all that info at your fingertips, follow these steps to add the other account to Gmail:

1. **Head on over to `mail.google.com` `https://mail.google.com`.**

   Alternatively, if you're in a Google Workspace app that has the Google apps icon (such as Calendar), choose Google Apps ⇨ Gmail.

2. **Click the Settings menu icon and choose See All Settings.**

   Gmail opens its settings.

3. **Select the Accounts tab.**
4. **In the Check Mail from Other Accounts section, click Add a Mail Account.**

   Gmail opens the Add a Mail Account window.
5. **In the Email Address text box, type the account address and then click Next.**

   Gmail asks you to enter the settings for the account. Note that Gmail makes a few guesses about the info, most of which should be accurate, or close to it.
6. **In the Username text box, type the account username (usually, the email address).**
7. **In the Password text box, type the account password.**
8. **In the POP Server text box, type the address of the server that your provider uses for incoming mail.**
9. **In the Port list, select the port number your provider uses for incoming mail.**

   Again, this is 110 if your provider doesn't require SSL (refer to Step 11 in this list); if your provider does want you to use SSL, select 995 in the Port list.
10. **If you want Gmail to leave a copy of any imported message on the original server, select the Leave a Copy of Retrieved Message on the Server check box.**

    If you still want to access the account's messages using another email client, selecting the Leave a Copy of Retrieved Message on the Server check box is a good idea. If you'll access the messages only in Gmail, leave the check box deselected so that after Gmail retrieves your messages, it deletes the messages from the original server.
11. **If your email provider requires that incoming mail connections be secure, select the Always Use a Secure Connection (SSL) When Retrieving Mail check box.**
12. **It's a good idea to label the account's messages in some way, so select the Label Incoming Messages check box.**

    By default, Gmail labels the messages using the account's email address. If you prefer to use a different label, select New Label in the drop-down list, enter the label in the dialog that appears, and then click OK.
13. **If you want Gmail to bypass the inbox and send the account's incoming messages straight to the label you specified in Step 12 (or to the All Mail label, if you skipped Step 12), select the Archive Incoming Messages check box.**

    Figure 17-9 shows a filled-in version of the Add an Email Account window.

FIGURE 17-9: To import incoming messages from another account, fill in the settings in the Add an Email Account window.

14. Click the Add Account button.

Gmail adds the account and then asks whether you also want to be able to send email from the account.

15. Select the No radio button and then click Next.

Gmail now regularly checks your account for messages.

Handle Microsoft 365 Documents

Because you're a full-fledged Google Workspace user, there's a good chance your organization has decided to go all in with Docs, Sheets, and Slides for productivity apps. That makes exchanging files with your colleagues easier, but when you're working from home, you might have to deal with people who haven't gone all-Google and still use Microsoft's productivity stalwarts: Word, Excel, and PowerPoint. Fortunately, Google Workspace understands this and is happy to work with Microsoft 365 documents. Here are the three main techniques you need to know:

- **Opening Microsoft 365 documents:** Google Workspace gives you a few different ways to open Microsoft 365 documents in their corresponding Google apps:
  - In a Google app, choose File ⇨ Open (or, if you're on the home page of an app such as Docs, click Open File Picker), select the Microsoft 365 document, and then click Open.

  - If you receive an Microsoft 365 document as an email attachment, select the attachment's Edit with Google *App* icon (where *App* is Docs, Sheets, or Slides, depending on the file type).

- If the Microsoft 365 document is in Drive, select the document, click the more actions icon (three vertical dots), choose Open With from the menu that appears, and then select the Google app that works with the file type.

  Whichever method you use, the Microsoft 365 document appears in the Google app. To remind you that this is a Microsoft 365 file and not a native Google file, the Microsoft 365 document's file extension appears beside the document name. For example, Figure 17-10 shows a Word document open in Docs, so the `.DOCX` file extension appears.

- **Converting a Microsoft 365 document to Google format:** If you only ever use Google apps but you have a bunch of Microsoft 365 documents lying around, you should convert those files to their Google-equivalent formats to make it easier to work with the files. To convert a Microsoft 365 document, first open it in the corresponding Google app: Docs for a Word document; Sheets for an Excel spreadsheet; or Slides for a PowerPoint presentation. Choose File ⇨ Save As Google *App* (where *App* is Docs, Sheets, or Slides, depending on the file type) from the menu bar.
- **Sharing a Google file as a Microsoft 365 file:** If you've created a file using a Google app but you want to email that file to a Microsoft 365 user, you're out of luck, right? Nope. You can actually attach the Google file as a Microsoft 365 file, which enables your recipient to view and work with the file — no problem. To share a file in this way, open the file in its native Google app, and then choose File ⇨ Email This File. In the Email This File dialog's File Type list, select the Microsoft 365 format (such as Microsoft Excel for a Sheets spreadsheet file). Fill in the To, Subject, and Message fields in the usual email way and then click Send.

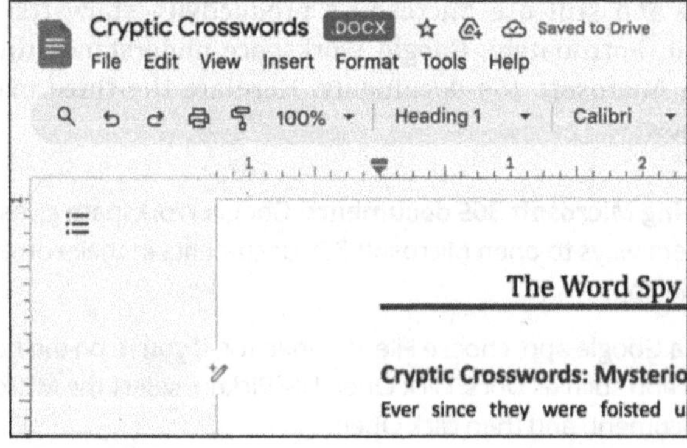

FIGURE 17-10: Google displays the Microsoft 365 file extension beside the document name to remind you that you're working with a Microsoft 365 document.

Set Up Your Video Conference Space

Conducting video meetings at the office is easy enough because you almost always have the right equipment, the right space, and the right environment. Holding video meetings at home, on the other hand, is a bit trickier. I close this chapter with a few tips borne out of hard-won experience with home-based video meetings.

First, here are some things to consider, equipment-wise:

- To minimize the disturbance for others in your household, consider wearing headphones or earbuds. This not only prevents meeting noises from leaking to other rooms in your house but also has the benefits of giving you the best audio experience and preventing potential echoes.
- You'll almost certainly be taking notes during the meeting, so to avoid subjecting your meeting buddies to the noise of your typing, mute your microphone when you're not talking.
- What's that? You often type while you talk? Wow, good on you! In that case, however, you should think about using an external microphone instead of your computer's built-in mic, to minimize the typing noises.
- Okay, so now that you're in the market for an external microphone, you should get a wireless mic or headset, right? Not so fast. Wireless mics are convenient and easier to manage in the heat of the call, but the sound quality is often not that great. For the best audio, go for a wired headset or mic.
- Make sure Meet is using the microphone and camera that you prefer. I talk about how to check this in Chapter 13.

Now get a load of these tips for setting up your home environment:

- The room you use should have good lighting — preferably, natural light from a nearby window.
- Don't sit with the light behind you, which turns your head and upper body into a silhouette. Try to position yourself so that the light is in front of you.
- Don't rely on your camera feed to judge your lighting and position. Cajole a colleague or friend into running a test call to learn how things really appear.
- Ideally, the wall or space behind you should be blank or, at least, not distracting.
- Make sure that whatever section of the room people can see is neat and tidy. This is a *business* call, after all.

- Ideally, the space you use should have little to no ambient noise. Do not — I repeat do *not* — play music or talk radio during the meeting.
- If you can't avoid noise, or if noise is always a potential danger (parents with children under 10 nod their heads knowingly), be sure to mute your microphone when you're not speaking.

Finally, here are some ideas for eking out the best video performance:

- Connect your computer to your internet router directly with an Ethernet cable, if possible.
- If you need to use Wi-Fi, try to move your device as close as possible to the wireless access point.
- For the best Wi-Fi performance, use a 5 GHz network, if you have one.
- Politely ask the other members of your family to hold off on heavy-duty internet activities (such as streaming video or online gaming) for the duration of the meeting. Be prepared to buy everyone pizza as compensation.

IN THIS CHAPTER

» Sending a message as plain text

» Configuring how you reply to messages

» Customizing Gmail's default text style

» Taking Gmail out of conversation view

» Telling Gmail to let you know when it labels a message as Important

» Giving Gmail permission to display desktop notifications

Chapter 18
Ten Really Useful Gmail Settings

Gmail offers a relatively simple interface on the surface, but dig a little deeper and you learn that the app has a more sophisticated side. I'm talking about the Settings page and its seemingly endless supply of options, configurations, and customizations. I mean, there's a *lot* of stuff in there.

Yep, sure, many of the settings should be labeled For Nerds Only. However, a veritable treasure trove of settings are actually useful in the real world and can help you be more productive, more efficient, healthier, wealthier, and wiser. (Well, maybe not those last three; but you never know!)

In this chapter, I take you on a tour of ten eminently useful and practical Gmail settings related to the two main Gmail tasks: sending messages and reading messages. Prepare to be amazed!

Five Splendiferous Send Settings

Sending email seems like such a simple thing: You click Compose, insert an address or three, conjure up a snappy Subject line, write the message itself, and then click Send. What more could there be to say about such a straightforward procedure?

Well, quite a bit, as it turns out. Gmail actually comes with many settings that can make sending stuff even more useful. This section takes you through close to a half dozen settings and features that you'll want to add to your sending toolkit.

Sending a message as plain text

You can use one of two message modes when you send an email:

- **Rich text:** This mode enables you to dress up your message text with fonts, colors, and styles such as bold and italics. Rich text is Gmail's default format, and almost all messages these days use this format.
- **Plain text:** This mode doesn't offer any formatting for your text — no fonts, no type sizes, no italics.

What's the use of this plain-text mode? It's rare nowadays, but there are still some very old or very simple email programs that choke when faced with rich text. If you send a rich text email to someone and that person complains that your text is just a gumbo of incomprehensible symbols, you need to resend your message using plain-text mode. Here's how it's done:

1. **Create, address, and compose your email.**
2. **Click the more options icon.**
3. **From the menu that appears, select the Plain Text Mode setting.**

   Gmail adds a check mark to the left of the command, as shown in Figure 18-1. Gmail also removes all formatting from your message text.

   WARNING

   When you choose the Plain Text Mode command, Gmail strips out all your existing text formatting and throws it away. You might think that turning off plain-text mode (by repeating Steps 2 and 3 to deselect the Plain Text Mode setting) would restore your previous formatting, but no, that's not happening. Therefore, if you have an elaborately formatted message, think twice before turning on the Plain Text Mode command.
4. **Click Send.**

   Gmail sends your plain-text message.

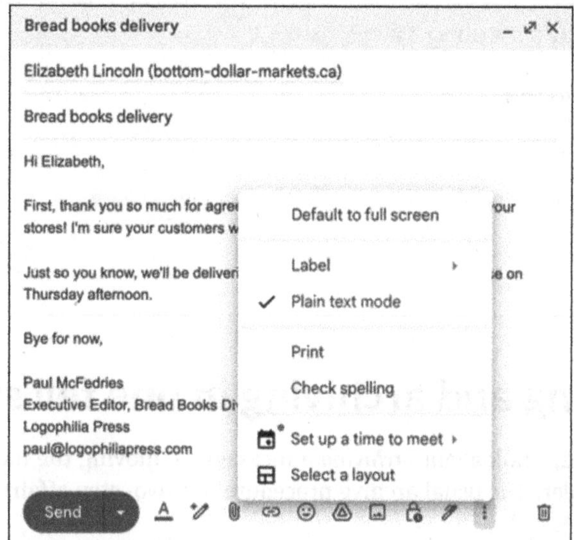

FIGURE 18-1: To send your message with no text formatting, choose the Plain Text Mode option.

Setting the default reply behavior

If you have a message that was sent to multiple people and you want to send your response to everyone, you have two choices:

- Click the more icon and then click Reply to All.
- Scroll to the bottom of the message and then click the Reply All button.

Lots of people find that they use Reply All more often than Reply, so frequently using either of these techniques becomes a bit of a bother. Fortunately, you can ask Gmail to switch things around and make replying to everyone the default. Here's how:

1. **Click the Settings icon and choose See All Settings.**

   Gmail opens the Settings page, with the General tab displayed.

2. **For the Default Reply Behavior setting, select the Reply All radio button.**

   To revert to having Reply as the default, select the Reply radio button instead.

3. **Click the Save Changes button at the bottom of the Settings page.**

   Now, as shown in Figure 18-2, Gmail displays the reply to all icon to the right of a multi-recipient message for one-click access.

Friday's meeting External Inbox ×

Paul McFedries
to me, Paul, Karen
11:31 AM (9 minutes ago)

...is cancelled.

Nah, just kidding! In fact, the meeting is now three hours instead of two!

See you then,

P.

FIGURE 18-2: Gmail now displays the reply to all icon to the right of any message that was sent to multiple people.

Replying and archiving in one fell swoop

In Chapter 2, I talk about *archiving* a message — moving the message to Gmail's All Mail folder. The usual archive procedure is a two-step affair:

1. **Click Reply to send a response to the sender of the message.**
2. **Click Archive to move the received message to the All Mail folder.**

If you find yourself performing these two steps over and over, you can quickly talk Gmail into combining them into a single step:

1. **Click the Settings icon and choose See All Settings.**

   Gmail opens the Settings page, with the General tab displayed.

2. **For the Send and Archive setting, select the Show "Send & Archive" Button in Reply radio button.**

   To revert to the default behavior, select the Hide "Send & Archive" Button in Reply radio button instead.

3. **Click the Save Changes button at the bottom of the Settings page.**

Now when you click Reply or Reply All, the resulting message window, shown in Figure 18-3, includes both a Send button (the one on the right) and a Send & Archive button (the one on the left). If you click Send & Archive, Gmail sends the reply *and* automatically moves the original message to the All Mail folder. Sweet squared!

FIGURE 18-3: Click the Send & Archive button to automatically archive the original message.

Setting the default text style

Earlier in this chapter, I talk about how you can format your message text with a different font, text size, color, and other attributes. If you find that you're continually making the same text formatting adjustments, you can save some wear-and-tear on your fingers by setting those adjustments in the Gmail equivalent of stone. Gmail offers a Default Text Style setting that includes the font, type size, and text color. Here are the steps to follow to change this setting to something that suits your typographical style:

1. **Click the Settings icon and choose See All Settings.**

   Gmail opens the Settings page, with the General tab displayed.

2. **For the Default Text Style setting (check out Figure 18-4), use the Font, Size, and Text Color controls to format the text as preferred.**

   Under these controls, the text *This is what your body text will look like* shows the result of your labor.

   If you make a mess of it, you can start from scratch by clicking the remove formatting icon (pointed out in Figure 18-4).

3. **Click the Save Changes button at the bottom of the Settings page.**

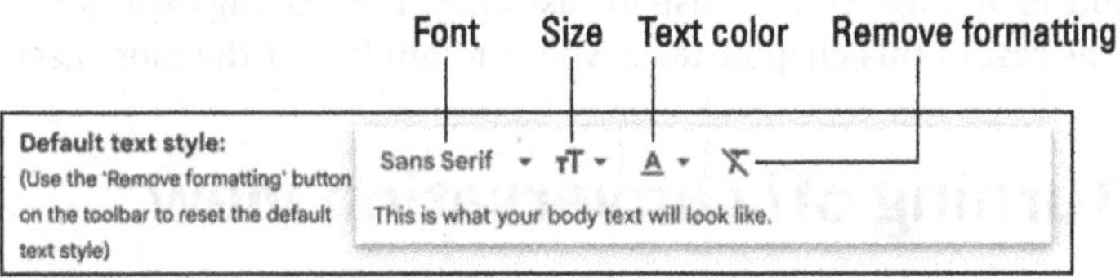

FIGURE 18-4: Use the Default Text Style controls to customize your email text.

Preventing Gmail from creating contacts automatically

One of Gmail's default settings is that when you send a new message to — or reply to a message from — someone not in your Contacts app, Gmail automatically adds that person's email address to the Other Contacts section of the Contacts app.

Why would Gmail do this? Because, that way, the next time you start to enter that person's email address in the To, CC, or BCC field, Gmail displays the address so that you can select it rather than type the whole thing. This is called *auto-completing* the address.

That's a laudable reason, for sure, but it does mean that you'll end up with tons of potentially useless addresses in the Contacts app. Sure, those addresses are tucked away in the Other Contacts section, but if you really don't want all those addresses accumulating, you can turn off address auto-completing by following these steps:

1. **Click the Settings icon and choose See All Settings.**

   Gmail opens the Settings page, with the General tab displayed.

2. **Scroll down to the Create Contacts for Auto-Complete setting and then select the I'll Add Contacts Myself radio button, as shown in Figure 18-5.**

3. **Click the Save Changes button at the bottom of the Settings page.**

Create contacts for auto-complete:	○ When I send a message to a new person, add them to Other Contacts so that I can auto-complete to them next time ◉ I'll add contacts myself

FIGURE 18-5: Select the I'll Add Contacts Myself radio button.

Five Stupendous Read Settings

Reading messages in Gmail seems like another just-this-side-of-trivial task. After all, to read a message, you click it and then peruse the text, in either the message window or the reading pane. Done and done, right? Not so fast. Gmail has lots of settings you can use to customize the reading experience to suit your style. The rest of this chapter takes you through five of the most useful.

Turning off conversation view

By default, Gmail organizes messages by *conversation*, which refers to an original message and all of its replies, replies to replies, and so on. That's a sensible setup because it makes it easy to follow the trend of the conversation and locate a particular reply. Conversations also keep your inbox neat, because the entire conversation resides within a single message in the inbox.

Still, many people don't like organizing messages by conversations *because* all the messages are hidden within the original message. These people prefer to have all their messages out in the open.

If you fall into this camp, you can follow these steps to turn off Gmail's default Conversation view:

1. **Click the Settings icon and choose See All Settings.**

   Gmail opens the Settings page, with the General tab displayed.

2. **Scroll down to the Conversation View setting and then select the Conversation View Off radio button, as shown in Figure 18-6.**
3. **Click the Save Changes button at the bottom of the Settings page.**

Conversation View:
(sets whether emails of the same topic are grouped together)

○ Conversation view on
◉ Conversation view off

FIGURE 18-6: Select the Conversation View Off radio button.

Adding importance markers

Gmail monitors how you use the app and the messages you receive as a way of figuring out which messages are important and which aren't. If Gmail's analysis tells it that a message is important, Gmail automatically adds the Important label to the message, which means that you can view the message outside the noise of your inbox by selecting the Important label on the main menu.

That's mighty handy, but there's a fly in this soup: The only way to know whether Gmail has declared a message to be important is to view the contents of the Important label. That is, Gmail offers no indication in the inbox about which messages are important and which aren't.

If that seems just plain wrong to you, here's how to fix it:

1. **Click the Settings icon and choose See All Settings.**

   Gmail opens the Settings page, with the General tab displayed.
2. **Click the Inbox tab.**
3. **For the Importance Markers settings, select the Show Markers radio button, as shown in Figure 18-7.**

TIP

   If you think it's creepy that Gmail is analyzing your messages for importance, I hear you. Fortunately, you can turn off this snooping behavior. On the Inbox tab, select the Don't Use My Past Actions to Predict Which Message Are Important radio button.
4. **Click the Save Changes button at the bottom of the page.**

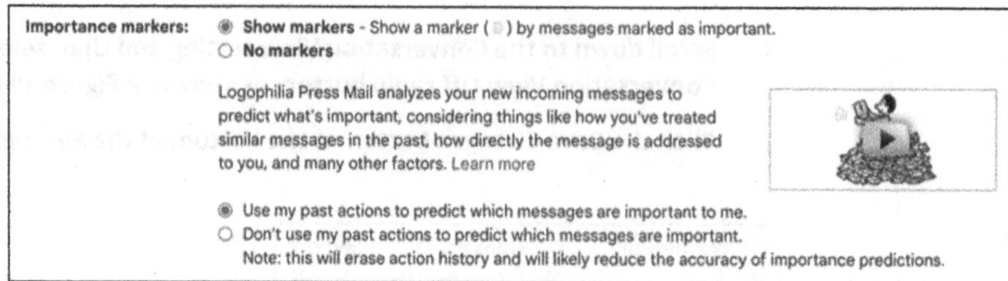

Importance markers:
Show markers - Show a marker ( ) by messages marked as important.
No markers
Logophilia Press Mail analyzes your new incoming messages to predict what's important, considering things like how you've treated similar messages in the past, how directly the message is addressed to you, and many other factors. Learn more
Use my past actions to predict which messages are important to me.
Don't use my past actions to predict which messages are important.
Note: this will erase action history and will likely reduce the accuracy of importance predictions.

FIGURE 18-7: Select Show Markers to know which messages Gmail has marked as important.

Setting the maximum page size

Gmail's labels can end up with a ton of messages in them. Gmail handles long message lists by dividing the list into separate pages, with up to 50 messages (or conversations, if you're still using conversation view) per page. Depending on how you work, 50 will seem like either a ridiculously large number or a ludicrously small number.

Either way, the number isn't set in stone, and you can follow these steps to set a different maximum page size:

1. **Click the Settings icon and choose See All Settings.**

   Gmail opens the Settings page with the General tab displayed.

2. **For the Maximum Page Size setting, select in the Show *X* Conversations Per Page drop-down list how many messages (or conversations) you want per page, as shown in Figure 18-8.**
3. **Click the Save Changes button at the bottom of the Settings page.**

Maximum page size: Show 50 conversations per page

FIGURE 18-8: Select your preferred maximum page size.

Managing notifications

By default, Gmail doesn't display a notification on your computer's desktop when a new message comes in. That's probably just as well because many studies have shown that the notification of a newly received message (and its accompanying ping) is a big distraction and, therefore, a major productivity killer.

That said, you might want to risk the distraction anyway and give Gmail permission to display desktop notifications. It's also possible to configure Gmail to show a notification only for messages labeled as Important, so that might be a compromise worthy of consideration.

Here are the steps to follow to give Gmail permission to display desktop notifications and to configure those notifications:

1. **Click the Settings icon and choose See All Settings.**

   Gmail opens the Settings page, with the General tab displayed.

2. **In the Desktop Notifications setting, select Click Here to Enable Desktop Notifications for *Company* Mail (where *Company* is the name of your business).**

   Your web browser asks if you want to allow `mail.google.com` to show notifications, as shown in Figure 18-9.

3. **Click Allow.**
4. **Select the desktop notification option you prefer:**
   - *New Mail Notifications On:* Select this radio button to get a desktop notification for all incoming messages.
   - *Important Mail Notifications On:* Select this radio button (as shown in Figure 18-10) to get a desktop notification only for incoming messages that Gmail labels as Important.

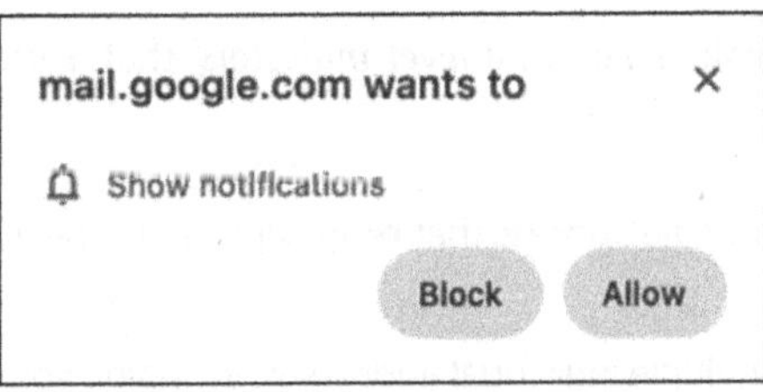

FIGURE 18-9: Your browser wants to know if you'll allow Gmail to show notifications.

Desktop notifications: (allows Logophilia Press Mail to display popup notifications on your desktop when new email messages arrive) Learn more

Click here to enable desktop notifications for Logophilia Press Mail.

- ○ **New mail notifications on** - Notify me when any new message arrives in my inbox or primary tab
- ◉ **Important mail notifications on** - Notify me only when an important message arrives in my inbox
- ○ **Mail notifications off**

Mail notification sounds: Welcome

FIGURE 18-10: Select Important Mail Notifications On to get desktop notifications for only important messages.

5. **In the Mail Notification Sounds list, select the sound that Gmail plays during the notification.**
6. **Click the Save Changes button at the bottom of the Settings page.**

Indicating messages sent to only you

If you receive a ton of mail from mailing lists and similar group messages, it's handy to differentiate between messages you receive via the list or group and messages addressed to you directly. (Differentiating messages in this way has the benefit of improving spam detection, because many junk messages are sent as bulk mailings.)

For the messages you receive, there are three addressing levels to differentiate here:

- Messages sent to a single address that represents a mailing list or group
- Messages sent to multiple individual addresses, including yours
- Messages sent only to your address

It's not universally true, but from your perspective, the preceding list can be treated as an indicator of increasing message relevance. That is, messages sent to a mailing list or group are more likely to be not all that relevant; messages you receive that were sent to multiple people are likely to be more relevant; and messages sent only to you are likely to be the most relevant.

Gmail has a feature called *personal level indicators* that reflects this relevance hierarchy:

- Messages sent to a single address that represents a mailing list or group get no indicator.
- Messages sent to multiple individual addresses, including yours, get an arrow (›) indicator.
- Messages sent only to your address get a double arrow (») indicator.

If this sounds like a sensible arrangement, follow these steps to start using personal level indicators:

1. **Click the Settings icon and choose See All Settings.**

   Gmail opens the Settings page, with the General tab displayed.

2. **Scroll down to the Personal Level Indicators setting and select the Show Indicators radio button, as shown in Figure 18-11.**
3. **Click the Save Changes button at the bottom of the Settings page.**

Personal level indicators: ○ **No indicators**
◉ **Show indicators** - Display an arrow (›) by messages sent to my address (not a mailing list), and a double arrow (») by messages sent only to me.

FIGURE 18-11: Select the Show Indicators radio button.

IN THIS CHAPTER

» Protecting your network and your Google account with a super-duper password

» Taking security to the next level with verification options

» Beefing up Gmail security

» Managing which of your online activities are tracked by Google

» Monitoring your account for suspicious devices

Chapter 19

Ten Ways to Enhance Privacy and Security

Google Workspace is useful because it contains so many great apps for such a wide variety of activities: email, scheduling, contacts, documents, spreadsheets, presentations, meetings, chat, notes, and much more. The downside to this impressive variety of uses is that your Google Workspace apps end up storing an equally impressive variety of work and personal information. And the more you use the Google Workspace apps, the more information about you gets stored online. You can quickly end up with big chunks of your professional and personal lives stored in the cloud, so it pays to take whatever steps are required to keep that data safe and to control who can access it and when.

In this chapter, I help you investigate ten ways to enhance the security and privacy of your Google account and your Google Workspace apps. Yep, it takes a bit of time to implement these measures, but believe me when I tell you that the time you spend will prove to be an excellent investment.

Make Sure Your Wi-Fi Network Is Locked Up Tight

The first step in securing Google Workspace doesn't have anything to do with Google Workspace directly. Instead, this step is all about securing the network that you use to access the internet (and, hence, Google Workspace): your Wi-Fi network. If you access your Google Workspace stuff only through a big-time corporate network, you can merrily skip this section because the nerds over in IT have it covered. However, if you, like most people, do some (or a lot of) Google Workspace tasks at home, you need to take action to batten down your Wi-Fi hatches.

A secure Wi-Fi network is necessary because of a practice called *wardriving*, where a dark-side-of-the-Force hacker drives through various neighborhoods with a notebook PC or another device set up to look for available wireless networks. If the miscreant finds an unsecured network, they use it for free internet access (such a person is called a *piggybacker*) or to cause mischief with shared network resources, including accessing Google Workspace applications running on a network computer.

The problem is that wireless networks are inherently vulnerable because the wireless connection that enables you to access your Google Workspace apps from the kitchen or the living room can also enable an intruder from outside your home to access the network. Fortunately, you can secure your wireless network against these threats with a few tweaks and techniques, as spelled out in the following list.

REMEMBER

Most of what follows here requires access to your Wi-Fi router's administration or setup pages. Refer to your router's documentation to learn how to perform these tasks.

- **Change the router's administrator password.** By far the most important configuration chore for any new Wi-Fi router is to change the default password (and username, if your router requires one). Note that I'm talking here about the administrative password, which is the password you use to log on to the router's setup pages. This password has nothing to do with the password you use to log on to your internet service provider (ISP) or to your wireless network. Changing the default administrative password is crucial because it's fairly easy for a nearby malicious hacker to access your router's login page and because all new routers use common (and, therefore, well-known) default passwords (such as password) and usernames (such as admin).

- **Change the Wi-Fi network password.** Make sure your Wi-Fi network is protected by a robust, hard-to-guess password to avoid unauthorized access. (Refer to the upcoming sidebar "Coming up with a strong password.")
- **Beef up your Wi-Fi router's encryption.** To ensure that no nearby mischief-maker can intercept your network data (using a tool called a *packet sniffer*), you need to encrypt your wireless network. Some older routers either have no encryption turned on or use an outdated (*read:* not secure) encryption called Wired Equivalent Privacy (WEP). The current gold standard for encryption is Wi-Fi Protected Access 3 (WPA3), so make sure your router uses this security type.
- **Check your network name for identifying info.** Make sure the name of your Wi-Fi network — known as its *service set identifier* (SSID) — doesn't include any text that identifies you (for example, Joe Flaherty's Network) or your location (123 Primrose Lane Wi-Fi).
- **Update your router's firmware.** The internal program that runs the Wi-Fi router is called its *firmware.* Reputable router manufacturers release regular firmware updates to not only fix problems and provide new features but also plug security holes. Therefore, it's crucial to always keep your router's firmware up to date.

COMING UP WITH A STRONG PASSWORD

As I show in this chapter, making Google Workspace more secure involves setting passwords on three items: your Wi-Fi network and your Wi-Fi router's administration app, which I talk about in the earlier section "Make Sure Your Wi-Fi Network Is Locked Up Tight," as well as your Google Workspace account, which I discuss later (refer to the section "Secure Your Google Account with a Strong Password"). However, it's not enough to use just any old password that pops into your head. To ensure the strongest security for your Google Workspace account, you need to make each password robust enough that it's impossible to guess and impervious to software programs designed to try different password combinations. Such a password is called a *strong* password. Ideally, you should build a password that provides maximum protection while still being easy to remember.

(continued)

(continued)

Lots of books suggest ridiculously abstruse password schemes (I've written some of those books myself), but you need to know only three things to create strong-like-a-bull passwords:

- **Use passwords that are at least 12 characters long.** Shorter passwords are susceptible to programs that try every letter combination. You can combine the 26 letters of the alphabet into about 12 million 5-letter word combinations, which is no big deal for a fast program. If you use 12-letter passwords — as many experts recommend — the number of combinations goes beyond mind-boggling: 90 quadrillion, or 90,000 trillion!
- **Mix up the character types.** The secret to a strong password is to include characters from the following categories: lowercase letters, uppercase letters, punctuation marks, numbers, and symbols. If you include at least one character from three (or, even better, all five) of these categories, you're well on your way to a strong password.
- **Don't be obvious.** Because forgetting a password is inconvenient, many people use meaningful words or numbers so that their passwords will be easier to remember. Unfortunately, this means that they often use extremely obvious terms, such as their name, the name of a family member or colleague, their birthdate, or their Social Security number. Being this obvious is just asking for trouble. Adding 123 or a punctuation mark (!) to the end of the password doesn't help much, either. Password-cracking programs try those.

Secure Your Google Account with a Strong Password

Your experience with Gmail, Calendar, Drive, and all the other Google Workspace apps is only as secure as your Google account. Therefore, it's vital to ensure that your account is locked down. Fortunately, that task requires just two things: giving your account a strong password (as I describe in this section) and turning on Google's two-step verification feature (which I discuss in the next section).

Your Google account's first line of defense is a strong password. First, refer to the earlier sidebar in this chapter, "Coming up with a strong password." After you have a bulletproof password figured out, follow these steps to change your existing Google password:

1. **Access your Google account settings.**

   Either of these methods is sure to work for you:

   - Sign in to any Google Workspace app, click the Google Account button in the top-right corner, and then click Manage Your Google Account.
   - Surf directly to `https://myaccount.google.com` and sign in to your account.

2. **In the pane on the left side of the page, click Security.**
3. **In the How You Sign in to Google section, click Password.**

   Google, ever cautious, asks you to sign in again.

4. **Enter your password and click Next.**

   Google displays the Password page.

5. **In the New Password text box, type your new, strong password.**

   Before proceeding, make sure the Password Strength indicator reads *Strong*, as shown in Figure 19-1.

6. **Reenter the same password in the Confirm New Password text box.**
7. **Click the Change Password button.**

   Google applies the new password to your account.

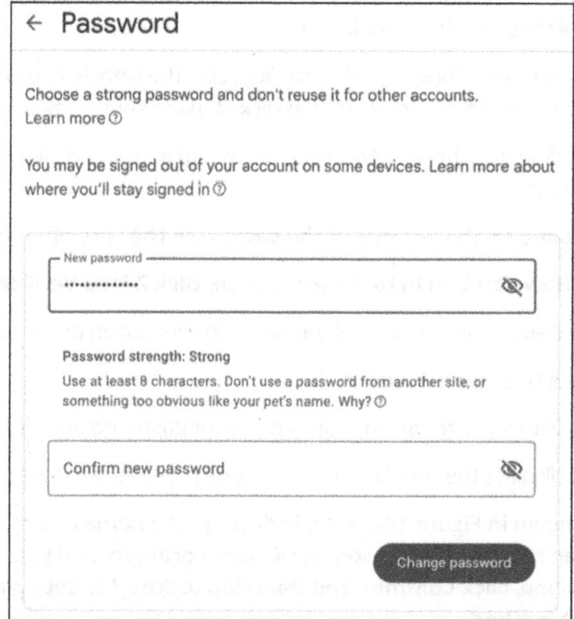

FIGURE 19-1: On the Password page, modify your Google account password.

Enable Google's Two-Step Verification

A password made of steel is a necessary security feature, but, sadly, it's not a sufficient security feature. Malicious users may still worm their way into your account with guile or brute force, so you need a second line of defense. That line is a feature that Google calls *two-step verification* (which is a more comprehensible name than what the rest of the internet most often uses for the same feature: two-factor authentication). The *two-step* part means that getting access to your Google account requires two separate actions:

1. **Sign in using your Google account credentials.**
2. **Verify that you're authorized to access the account either by entering a verification code that Google sends to you or by using a phone or other device to provide the verification.**

You can configure two-step verification to receive a verification code via either a text message or an automated phone call, or you can designate your phone or a security key (a special USB stick that connects to your computer or other device) as the method of verification.

Here are the steps to follow to enable two-step verification, and tell Google how you want to receive your verification codes:

1. **Access your Google account settings.**

   Either of these methods works fine:

   - Sign in to any Google Workspace app, click the Google Account button in the top-right corner, and then click Manage Your Google Account.
   - Surf directly to `https://myaccount.google.com` and sign in to your account.

2. **In the pane on the left side of the page, click the Security tab.**
3. **In the How You Sign In to Google section, click 2-Step Verification.**

   Google displays an overview of the two-step verification process.

4. **Click the Get Started button.**

   If Google asks you to sign in again, enter your password and click Next.

   Google displays the Let's Set Up Your Phone page, shown in Figure 19-2.

5. **If, as shown in Figure 19-2, Google displays the name of a phone you own that can receive the two-step verification prompts and you want to use that phone, click Continue and then skip to Step 7 to set up a phone as a backup method.**

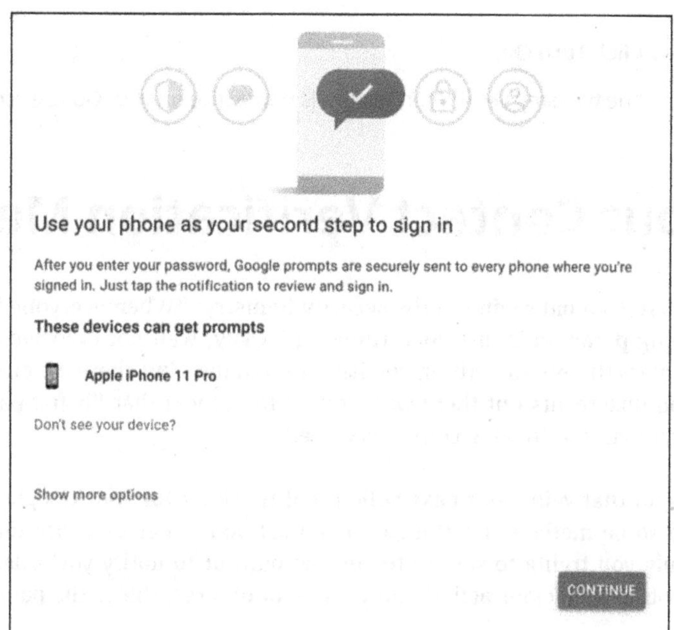
Use your phone as your second step to sign in
After you enter your password, Google prompts are securely sent to every phone where you're signed in. Just tap the notification to review and sign in.
These devices can get prompts
Apple iPhone 11 Pro
Don't see your device?
Show more options
CONTINUE

FIGURE 19-2: On this page, specify how you want to receive your two-step verification codes.

6. **Click Show More Options, and then click one of the following:**
   - *Security Key:* Select this option if you have a security key attached to your device. Follow the prompts that appear to configure your security key to use with Google's two-step verification.
   - *Text Message or Phone Call:* Select this option to receive the two-step verification codes via text or an automated call. The next few steps assume you chose this option.
7. **Enter your phone number.**
8. **Select the Text Message radio button.**

   If, for some reason, you don't want to (or can't) receive your verification code via text, select the Phone Call radio button instead.
9. **Click Next.**

   Google sends you a verification code via text message (or phone call, if you went that route).
10. **In the Enter the Code text box, type the code you received, and then click Next.**

    If the code you get looks something like G-123456, just enter the numbers into the text box.

    Google asks if you want to turn on two-step verification.

11. **Click Turn On.**

    The two-step verification feature is now active on your Google account.

Set Up Your Contact Verification Methods

There's an old saying in the security industry: "When everyone is out to get you, being paranoid is just good thinking." Okay, well not *everyone* is out to get you (unless there's something you haven't told me), but there are enough malefactors and miscreants out there who *are* out to get you that "being paranoid" is just a synonym for "having common sense."

So, in that vein, your next bulletproofing chore for your Google account is to set up some methods for Google to contact you either to verify that it's really and truly you trying to sign in to your account or to notify you when it thinks it has spotted suspicious activity on your account. (Yes, this is the paranoid part.)

Follow these steps to configure your account with a phone number and an email address that Google can use to verify you:

1. **Access your Google account settings.**

   Which of the following methods you use is up to you:

   - Sign in to any Google Workspace app, click the Google Account button in the top-right corner, and then click Manage Your Google Account.
   - Surf directly to `https://myaccount.google.com` and sign in to your account.

2. **In the pane on the left side of the page, click Security.**
3. **In the section named How You Sign In to Google, click Recovery Phone.**

   Google displays the Recovery Phone page.

4. **Click the Add Recovery Phone button.**

   The Add Phone Number dialog appears.

5. **Type your phone number and then click Next.**

   Google lets you know that it will send a verification code to your phone.

6. **Click the Get Code button.**

   Google sends you a verification code via text message.

7. **In the Enter the Code text box, type the code you received, and then click Next.**

   If the code you get appears similar to G-987654, just enter the numbers into the text box.

8. **Click the Verify button.**

   Google adds the recovery phone number to your account.

9. **Click the back icon to return to the Security page.**

10. **In the section named How You Sign In to Google, click Recovery Email.**

    Google displays the Recovery Email page.

11. **Enter the email address you want to use for verification, and then click Next.**

    Be sure to use an address other than your Google Workspace address (such as a personal email address).

    Google sends a verification code to the address you entered and displays the Verify Your Recovery Email dialog.

12. **Open your email, note the verification code, type the code in the Verification Code text box, and then click Verify.**

    Google adds the recovery email to your account.

Hide Images in Gmail Messages

You can make your Google Workspace email address more private and secure by thwarting any external images inserted into email messages you receive. An *external image* is a picture file that resides on an internet server computer instead of being embedded in the email message. A special code in the message tells the server to display the image when you open the message. This code is usually benign, but the same code can also alert the sender of the message that your email address is working. If the sender is a spammer, knowing that your email address works usually results in your receiving even more junk email. You can prevent this by disabling external images.

HOW WEB BUGS WORK

Many spammers include in their messages a type of external image called a *web bug*, which is a small and usually invisible image, the code for which is inserted in the email message. That code specifies a remote address from which to download the web bug when you display the message. However, the code also includes a reference to your email address. The remote server notes that you received the message, which means your address is a working one and is, therefore, a good target for further spam messages. By blocking external images in Gmail, you also block web bugs, which means you undermine this confirmation and so receive less spam.

Here are the steps to follow to configure Gmail to not display external images in the messages you receive:

1. **Click the Settings icon and then choose See All Settings.**

   Gmail opens the Settings page, with the General tab displayed.

2. **For the Images setting, select the Ask Before Displaying External Images radio button, as shown in Figure 19-3.**

   To revert to always showing external images, select the Always Display External Images radio button instead.

3. **Click the Save Changes button at the bottom of the Settings page.**

   Gmail asks you to confirm.

4. **Click Continue.**

FIGURE 19-3: Select the Ask Before Displaying External Images radio button to hide server images in the emails you receive.

Images:	○ **Always display external images** - Learn more ◉ **Ask before displaying external images** - This option also disables dynamic email.

Now, when you display a message that contains external images, the notification shown in Figure 19-4 appears. You have three options:

» *If the message is clearly (or even possibly) spam,* leave the images hidden and thank yourself for being proactive about your security.

» *If you're sure the message is safe,* click Display Images Below to unhide the images.

» *If you know the sender and trust them completely,* click the Always Display Images from *Address* link, where *Address* is the address of the person or entity who sent the message. This tells Gmail to always display images in messages sent from this address.

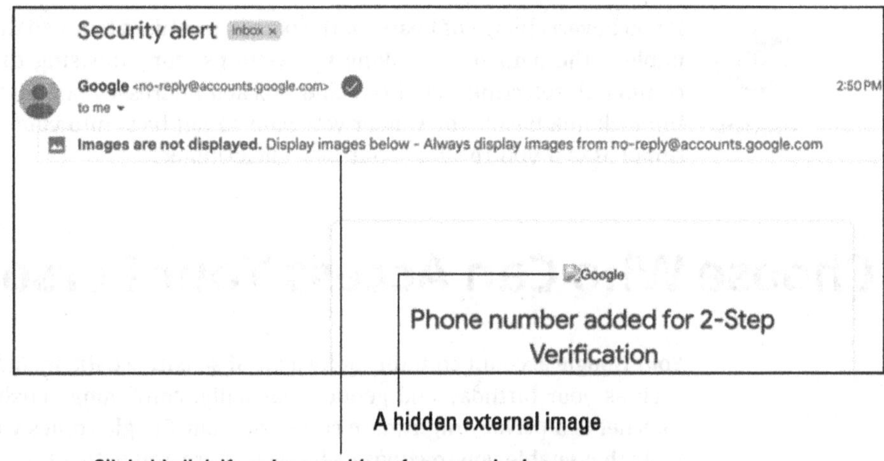

FIGURE 19-4: With external images hidden, this notification appears in any message that comes your way with external images.

Blocking Senders in Gmail

If you've tried out any of the Google Workspace collaboration features that I go on and on about in Part 3, here's hoping you've discovered that your peers and colleagues are a welcoming, supportive bunch. You might already have made quite a few new friends. However, in any group of people, no matter how amiable and helpful that group might be overall, there are always one or two bad seeds. It might be Boring Bill, who goes on and on about nothing, or Insufferable Sue, who boasts about even the most minor accomplishment. Or it might be something more serious, such as someone who sends you vaguely (or even overtly) creepy or menacing messages.

Whatever the reason, life's too short to deal with such nuisances, so you should follow these steps in Gmail to block that person from sending you more messages:

1. **In Gmail, display a message from the person you want to block.**
2. **Click the more icon.**

3. **Click Block *"Name,"* where *Name* is the name of the social pariah you want to shun.**

   Gmail asks you to confirm the block.

4. **Click Block.**

   Gmail adds the person's address to the Blocked Senders list. Future messages from that person will go automatically to Gmail's Spam label.

If you have a change of heart (or the person promises to mend their ways), you can unblock the person by clicking the Settings icon, choosing the See All Settings command, selecting the Filters and Blocked Addresses tab, and then clicking the Unblock link beside the sender you want to put back into your good books. When Gmail asks if you're sure about this, click Unblock.

Choose Who Can Access Your Personal Info

Your Google account contains quite a bit of sensitive data, including personal data such as your birthday and gender. Normally, combining sensitive data with the internet is a privacy nightmare come true, but Google comes with a decent set of tools that enable you to choose what you share and with whom.

For privacy purposes, Google divides your world into three sharing categories:

- **Only You:** The data can be accessed by only you.
- **Your Organization:** The data can be accessed by only you and each person in your Google Workspace organization.
- **Anyone:** The data can be accessed by everyone who cares to look.

Google applies default privacy settings for data such as your birthday (Only You), your profile picture (Your Organization), and your name (Anyone). Use the following steps to customize these and other privacy settings.

1. **Access your Google account settings using one of the following methods:**
   - *Sign in to any Google Workspace app, click the Google Account button in the top-right corner, and then click Manage Your Google Account.*
   - *Surf directly to* `https://myaccount.google.com` *and sign in to your account.*

2. **In the pane on the left side of the page, click Personal Info.**

3. **In the Choose What Others See section, click Go to About Me.**

   Google opens the About Me page. Figure 19-5 shows an example.

4. **Click an item in your personal info.**
5. **Click who can access the info: Only You, Your Organization, or Anyone.**

   Note that these options aren't available for all your personal info.

6. **Click Save.**

   Google saves your new setting.

7. **Click the back icon.**
8. **Repeat Steps 4–7 for the rest of your personal info.**

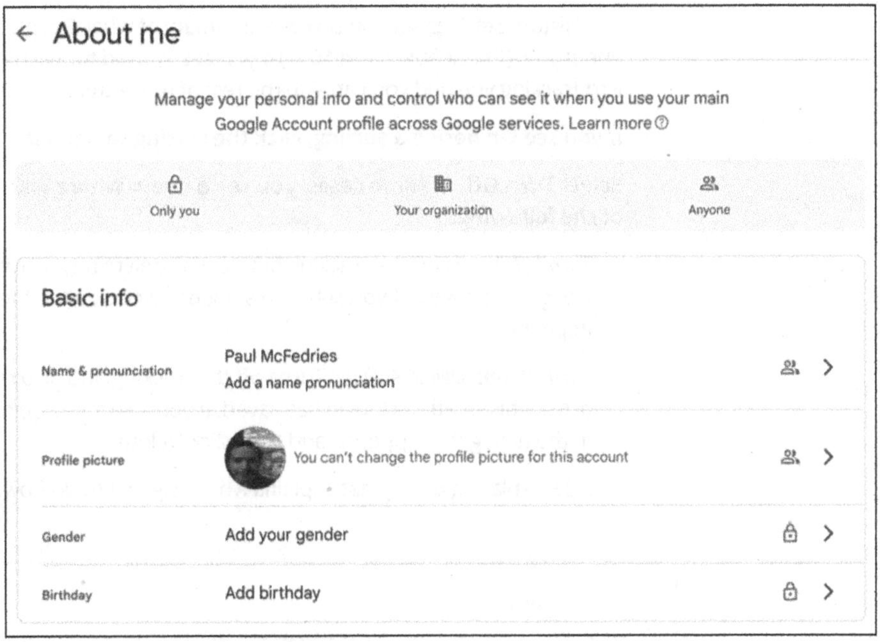

FIGURE 19-5: On the About Me page, specify who can access your info.

Manage Your Activity Controls

Google can keep track of various activities while you're online, including where you go on the web, which Google Workspace apps you use, how you've used Google Maps, and what you watch on YouTube.

If you're not comfortable with Google tracking some or all of these activities, you can use your account's *activity controls* to decide what, if anything, Google saves about you.

Happily, these activity controls should be turned off by default, but it's worth checking. Here's what to do:

1. **Access your Google account settings in one of the following ways:**
   - *Sign in to any Google Workspace app, click the Google Account button in the top-right corner, and then click Manage Your Google Account.*
   - *Surf directly to* `https://myaccount.google.com` *and sign in to your account.*
2. **In the pane on the left side of the page, click Data & Privacy.**

   The History Settings section shows a summary of what Google is tracking about you. (Check out Figure 19-6.) If you see Paused for each setting, Google isn't tracking you and you can skip the rest of these steps.
3. **If you see On beside a setting, click the setting to open it.**
4. **Select Turn Off. In some cases, you see a menu where you must click one of the following:**
   - *Turn Off:* Turns off the tracking but doesn't delete any activity history that Google has saved. If you select this option, click Got It in the dialog that appears.
   - *Turn Off and Delete Activity:* Turns off the tracking and also removes all activity history that Google has saved. If you select this option, click Next in the dialog that appears, and then click Delete.

   Google displays a dialog that explains what it's going to do now.

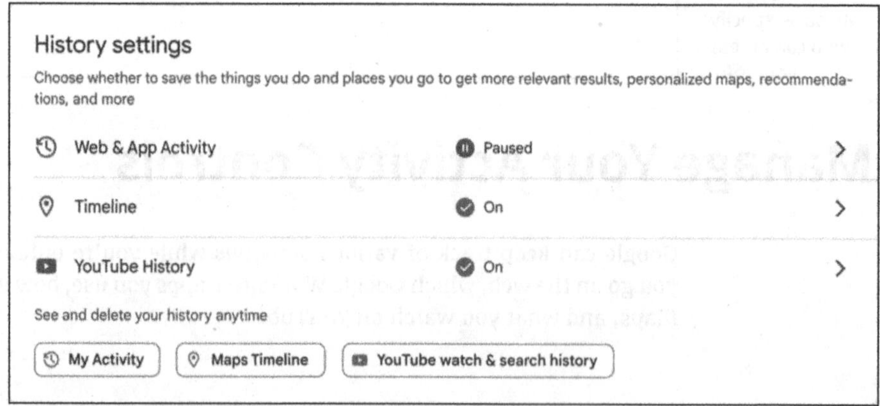

FIGURE 19-6: The History Settings section shows you what Google monitors about you.

5. **Click the back icon.**
6. **Repeat Steps 3-5 for any other activity control that's turned on.**

Manage Your Devices

Even with your Google account locked down behind a strong password, a nefarious user might still gain access to the account. The most common way that someone can gain access is if you use the same login credentials on another website and that site is hacked and its users' login data stolen. That data is then usually sold or posted online, and before long some stranger logs in to your formerly secure Google account.

TIP

If you want to check whether your Google login credentials have been compromised, go to the Have I Been Pwned? site at `https://haveibeenpwned.com` and then enter your Google login email address. (*Pwned* — it's pronounced "owned" — is hackerspeak for having been defeated or controlled by someone else.)

You certainly don't want any unauthorized reprobate to access your account, so you should do three things:

- Use a unique password for your Google account.
- Activate two-step verification, as I describe earlier in this chapter.
- Periodically check your account to determine whether a device you don't recognize has logged in to the account.

For the last of these items, here are the steps to follow to check for unrecognized devices that are logged in to your Google account:

1. **Access your Google account settings by doing one of the following:**
   - *Sign in to any Google Workspace app, click the Google Account button in the top-right corner, and then click Manage Your Google Account.*
   - *Surf directly to* `https://myaccount.google.com` *and sign in to your account.*
2. **In the pane on the left side of the page, click Security.**
3. **In the Your Devices section, click Manage All Devices.**

   Google offers up the Your Devices page.
4. **If you don't recognize a device, click the device name and description and then click the Don't Recognize Something? button.**

Google opens the Let's Secure Your Account dialog, which sensibly tells you to sign out of the device.

5. **Click Sign Out on Device.**

   Google signs out of your account on that device, and then asks if you want to change your password, which is highly recommended at this point.

6. **Click Change Password and then follow the prompts to configure your account with a new password.**

Manage Third-Party Apps

It's fairly common to give non-Google apps and services access to Google Workspace apps such as Docs, Sheets, and Drive. That access is often convenient, but if you stop using a particular third-party app or you change your mind about offering that access, you should revoke the app's access to your Google account for security purposes. Here's how:

1. **Access your Google account settings using one of the following methods:**
   - *Sign in to any Google Workspace app, click the Google Account button in the top-right corner, and then click Manage Your Google Account.*
   - *Surf directly to* `https://myaccount.google.com` *and sign in to your account.*
2. **In the pane on the left side of the page, click the Security tab.**
3. **In the Your Connections to Third-Party Apps & Services section, click See All Connections.**

   Google offers up the Third-Party Apps & Services page.

4. **Click the app that has the access you want to revoke.**
5. **Click Delete All Connection You Have with *App*, where *App* is the name of the app.**

   Google asks if you're sure about this.

6. **Click Confirm.**

   Google revokes the app's access to your account.

Appendix

Glossary of Google Workspace Terms

absolute cell reference: A cell reference where Sheets uses the actual address of the cell.

active cell: The currently selected cell, which Sheets designates by surrounding the cell with a heavy border and by displaying a small square in the bottom-right corner. See also *mixed cell reference* and *relative cell reference*.

AI: See *artificial intelligence*.

animation: See *object animation*.

all-day event: A Calendar *event* that either has no set time or that consumes one or more entire days (such as a birthday or a vacation).

artificial intelligence: An app or device that can perform tasks that appear similar to human capabilities such as learning, summarizing, decision making, and creating content. See also *Gemini*.

attachment: A file sent along with an email message.

auto-complete: To show a list of items — such as names or email addresses — that match what you've entered so far into a text box. You can then select the item you want from the list rather than finishing the text entry.

back channel: An informal communications channel that operates in addition to the main channel of communications in a meeting. In a Google Meet video meeting, participants can use the Chat feature as the back channel.

BCC: See *blind courtesy copy*.

blind courtesy copy: A copy of an email message sent to a recipient without that recipient's name or address appearing to the other message recipients.

bot: Software that can be added to a chat and that has been programmed to respond to specific phrases, questions, or events.

category: In a Sheets chart, a grouping of data values on the horizontal axis.

CC: See *courtesy copy*.

character spacing: The amount of horizontal space taken up by the characters in a *typeface.*

cell address: In a Sheets worksheet, a cell location created by combining the cell's column letter and row number, such as A1 or C25.

cell: The intersection of a row and a column in a sheet or table.

chat room: A special area in Google Chat that enables you to not only exchange messages with your team, but also organize those messages into multiple conversation threads, share files and other resources, add chat bots, include people from outside your organization, and more.

cloud: The online home of the Google Workspace apps and any data you've stored in Google Drive.

collaboration mode: How a user is permitted to work on a shared file. There are four collaboration modes: Viewing, Commenting, Suggesting, and Editing.

Comma Separated Values: See *CSV.*

comment: Text used to annotate part of a document.

conversation: In Gmail, an original message and all of its replies, replies to replies, and so on.

courtesy copy: A copy of an email message sent to a secondary recipient.

CSV: A file format for exchanging data in a row-and-column format where, for each row, the column data is separated by commas.

data marker: In a Sheets chart, a symbol that represents a specific data value (such as a column in a column chart).

data series: In a Sheets chart, a collection of related data values.

data type coercion: A Sheets feature where the data type of a cell is determined by the content of the cell.

delegate: A person who you have authorized to make changes to your Calendar events; to give such access to a person.

encryption: A technique that scrambles data in a way that makes the data unreadable by everyone except the person for whom the data is intended. All Google Workspace data is encrypted.

event: Appointments, vacations, trips, meetings, and anything else that can be scheduled in Calendar.

external image: An image that appears in an email message where the picture file resides on an internet server computer instead of being embedded in the message.

feet: The fine cross strokes that are the hallmark of a *serif typeface.*

filtering: Applying criteria to data so that you only see those records that meet your criteria.

first line indent: Paragraph indentation that shifts only the first line of the paragraph away from the left margin by a specified amount.

font: For type nerds, a specific implementation of a *typeface*, such as 14-point, italic Verdana. For the rest of us, a synonym for typeface.

footer: A section that appears at the bottom of each page between the bottom margin and the last line of text.

footnote: A short note at the bottom of a page that provides extra information about something mentioned in the regular text on that page.

formula: A collection of values and symbols that together produce some kind of result.

fritterware: A software program that offers so many options and settings that you could fritter away hours tweaking and playing with the program.

function: A predefined formula that calculates a result based on one or more arguments, which are the function's input values.

Gemini: A Google Workspace service that gives you access to a generative AI that, based on a prompt, can produce text in Docs, images in Slides, and more.

generative AI: An artificial intelligence agent that can produce content — usually text, an image, or a video — based on the content of a prompt.

GIF: A web graphics format used to create short, simple animations. Pronounced as either "giff," with a hard *g*, or "jiff," with a soft *g* (your call).

hanging indent: Paragraph indentation that shifts all but the first line of the paragraph away from the left margin by a specified amount.

header: A section that appears at the top of each page between the top margin and the first line of text. Any text, graphics, or properties you insert in a header appears at the top of every page in the document. Typical header contents include the document author, the document title, and the date the document was created or modified.

iCalendar: A file format for storing that contains calendar data.

joining info: For a Google Meet video meeting, the data that can be used to join the meeting, particularly the meeting address and the meeting's dial-in phone number and PIN.

killer app: A software application that is so useful, so popular, or so essential to its underlying technology that the app is seen as indispensable to that technology.

label: In Gmail, a category applied to one or more messages that enable you to organize your messages. In Contacts, a name applied to a group of related people.

landscape orientation: Paper orientation in which the text runs across the long side of the page and down the short side.

left-ragged: Having the left ends of each line in a paragraph unaligned because the text is right-justified.

legend: In a Sheets chart, a guide that shows the colors, patterns, and symbols used by the *data markers* for each *data series.*

line spacing: The amount of space between each line in the paragraph.

mail server: An internet-connected computer that your email provider uses to store and send your email messages.

margins: The blank space to the left and right, as well as above and below the document text (including the header and footer).

message body: The main text of an email message.

mixed cell reference: A cell reference that uses both a combination of relative and absolute cell reference formats. See also *absolute cell reference* and *relative cell reference.*

monospaced: A *typeface* that uses the same amount of horizontal space for each character. See also *proportional.*

mute: To stop displaying Gmail messages associated with a specified conversation.

named range: A range of cells to which a name has been applied.

object animation: A visual effect applied to a specific slide element, such as the slide title, bullet text, or an image.

operand: In a Sheets formula, a cell reference, a value, a range, a named range, or a function name.

operator: In a Sheets formula, a symbol, such as the plus sign (+), that combines two of the formula's *operands* in some way.

orphan: The first line of a paragraph where that line appears by itself at the bottom of a page.

out-of-office autoreply: See *vacation responder.*

out of office event: A special type of Calendar event that blocks out a specified chunk of time on one or more days to alert others that you're not available for meetings or other work-related stuff.

page break: The transition from one page in a document to another.

permission level: The *collaboration mode* that a user has been assigned for a shared file. The three permission levels are Editor, Commenter, and Viewer.

personal level indicator: A Gmail feature that tells you how relevant a message is to you based on how you were addressed in the message.

pivot: To move a field from one area of a pivot table to another.

pivot table: A Sheets data analysis tool that condenses a large range of data into a concise tabular summary.

placeholders: Slide objects that you fill in with text, images, charts, and other content.

POP: An internet system for retrieving incoming email messages.

portrait orientation: Paper orientation in which the text runs across the short side of the page, and down the long side.

Post Office Protocol: See *POP*.

prompt: Text that describes the content and style of the output you want a generative AI to produce.

proportional: A *typeface* where the horizontal space allotted to each character varies according to the width of the character. See also *monospaced*.

range: Any group of related cells in a sheet. A range can be as small as a single cell and as large as the entire sheet.

range coordinates: The address of a rectangular range in the form UL:LR, where UL is the address of the cell in the upper-left corner of the range and LR is the address of the cell in the lower-right corner of the range.

range name: A label that has been applied to a *named range*.

relative cell reference: A cell reference given in relation to another cell. See also *absolute cell reference* and *mixed cell reference*.

reminder: A Calendar item that displays a pop-up window to remind you to do something or be somewhere.

right-ragged: Having the right ends of each line in a paragraph unaligned because the text is left-justified.

SaaS: An application that resides in a cloud service and is accessed exclusively online. All Google Workspace apps are SaaS apps.

sans serif: A *typeface* that doesn't contain *feet*.

section break: The transition from one section in a document to another.

Secure Sockets Layer: See *SSL*.

serial number: In Sheets, a number that represents a date or time; a date serial number is the number of days since December 31, 1899; a time serial number is a decimal fraction of the 24-hour day.

serif: A *typeface* that contains fine cross strokes at the extremities of each character. See also *feet.*

sharing: Collaborating on a document, spreadsheet, or presentation by assigning other users a *collaboration mode.*

sheet: A work area in a *spreadsheet* file where you add your data and formulas.

silo: A person or department that can't or won't share information with other people or departments in the company.

slide layout: The arrangement of the *placeholders* on a slide.

slide master: A kind of design center for your presentation where the slide master's typefaces, type sizes, bullet styles, colors, alignment options, line spacing, and more are used on each slide in your presentation, and any object you add to the slide master also appears in the same position on each slide.

slide transition: A special effect that displays during the change from one slide to the next in a presentation.

snooze: To temporarily hide Gmail messages associated with a specified conversation.

software as a service: See *SaaS.*

spreadsheet: A file that contains one or more *sheets.*

SSL: A protocol that creates a secure connection for checking, receiving, and sending email.

style: A predefined collection of formatting options.

subtask: A task performed within a larger task.

suggested edit: In Docs, a temporary change to a document that the document owner (or some other person with Editing access) can later accept or reject.

table: A rectangular arrangement of data organized into rows and columns, where each column represents a field (a specific category of information) and each row represents a record (a single entry in the table).

task: A piece of work that needs to get done, such as a chore, a job, or an errand.

template: A document, spreadsheet, or presentation that comes with predefined text, formatting, and even an image or three to get you off to a good start.

text wrapping: Determines how document text interacts with an image inserted on the page.

transition: See *slide transition.*

two-step verification: A Google security feature that requires two separate actions — such as signing in with your account credentials and entering a verification code sent to a mobile device — before you can access your account.

type size: A measure of the height of a *typeface*, from the highest point of a tall letter such as *f* or *h* to the lowest point of an underhanging letter such as *g* or *y*.

typeface: A related set of letters, numbers, and other symbols that has its own distinctive design.

vacation responder: An automatic reply that is sent to people who email you while you're out of the office.

vCard: A special file format that contains the data from a single contact.

web bug: A small and usually invisible *external image* inserted by spammers into an email message and that contains a code that uniquely identifies the recipient of the message.

widow: The last line of a paragraph where that line appears by itself at the top of a page.

working hours: The days of the week you work and the times on those days that you've set aside for work.

world clock: In Calendar, a clock that shows the current time in a specified time zone.

Index

A

B

C

D

E

F

G

H

I

J

K

L

M

N

O

P

Q

R

S

T

U

V

W

Y

About the Author

Paul McFedries is a technical writer who has written more than 100 books, which have sold more than 4 million copies worldwide. Paul's Wiley titles include *Macs All-in-One For Dummies, HTML, CSS, & JavaScript All-in-One For Dummies, Microsoft Excel Data Analysis For Dummies*, and *iPad and iPad Pro For Dummies*, 2024-2025 Edition. Paul invites everyone to drop by his personal website (`https://paulmcfedries.com`) or follow him on X (Twitter) (`@paulmcf`).

Dedication

To Karen and Chase, who make life fun.

Author's Acknowledgments

If we're ever at the same cocktail party and you overhear me saying something like, "I wrote a book," I hereby give you permission to wag your finger at me and say, "Tsk-tsk." Why the scolding? Because, although I did write this book's text and take its screen shots, that represents only a part of what constitutes a book. The rest of it is brought to you by the dedication and professionalism of Wiley's editorial and production teams, who toiled long and hard to turn my text and images into an actual book.

I offer my sincere gratitude to everyone at Wiley who made this book possible, but I'd like to extend a special "Thanks a bunch!" to the folks I worked with directly: executive editor Steve Hayes, acquisitions editor Hanna Sytsma, managing editor Sofia Malik, project editor Susan Pink, and technical editor Guy Hart-Davis.

Publisher's Acknowledgments

Executive Editor: Steve Hayes
Acquisitions Editor: Hanna Sytsma
Managing Editor: Sofia Malik
Project and Copy Editor: Susan Pink
Technical Editor: Guy Hart-Davis
Proofreader: Debbye Butler

Production Editor: Pradesh Kumar
Cover Image: © davidf/Getty Images

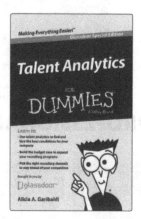

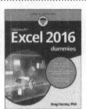

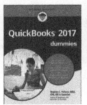

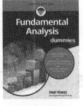

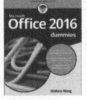

Small books for big imaginations

9781119177173
USA $9.99
CAN $9.99
UK £8.99

9781119177272
USA $9.99
CAN $9.99
UK £8.99

9781119177241
USA $9.99
CAN $9.99
UK £8.99

9781119177210
USA $9.99
CAN $9.99
UK £8.99

9781119262657
USA $9.99
CAN $9.99
UK £6.99

9781119291336
USA $9.99
CAN $9.99
UK £6.99

9781119233527
USA $9.99
CAN $9.99
UK £6.99

9781119291220
USA $9.99
CAN $9.99
UK £6.99

9781119177302
USA $9.99
CAN $9.99
UK £8.99

Unleash Their Creativity

dummies.com

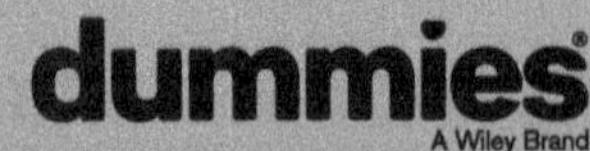